Before
the Parade
Passes By

Before
the Parade
Passes By

GOWER CHAMPION AND THE GLORIOUS
AMERICAN MUSICAL

John Anthony Gilvey

St. Martin's Press

New York

BEFORE THE PARADE PASSES BY. Copyright © 2005 by John Anthony Gilvey.
All rights reserved. Printed in the United States of America. No part of this book
may be used or reproduced in any manner whatsoever without written permission
except in the case of brief quotations embodied in critical articles or reviews.
For information, address St. Martin's Press, 175 Fifth Avenue, New York, N.Y. 10010.

www.stmartins.com

"Before the Parade Passes By," from *Hello, Dolly!* Music and lyric by Jerry Herman.
© 1964 (Renewed) Jerry Herman. All rights controlled by Edwin H. Morris & Company,
a Division of MPL Music Publishing, Inc. All Rights Reserved. Used by permission.

Frontispiece photograph of Gower Champion © H. Montgomery-Drysdale

Book design by Michelle McMillian

Library of Congress Cataloging-in-Publication Data

Gilvey, John Anthony.
    Before the parade passes by : Gower Champion and the glorious American musical / John
Anthony Gilvey.—1st ed.
        p.   cm.
    Includes bibliographical references (p. 349) and index (p. 359).
    ISBN 0-312-33776-0
    EAN 978-0-312-33776-6
    1. Champion, Gower, 1919–1980.   2. Dancers—United States—Biography.
3. Choreographers—United States—Biography.   4. Theatrical producers and directors—
United States—Biography.   I. Title.

GV1785.C463G55   2005
792.8'2'092—dc22
[B]
                                                                    2005049408

First Edition: November 2005

10   9   8   7   6   5   4   3   2   1

In memory of
Lowell S. Swortzell
Pioneer in Educational Theatre
teacher, mentor, friend
and
for my students
Let your limelight shine.

Contents

Before the parade passes by
I'm gonna go and taste Saturday's high life
Before the parade passes by
I'm gonna get some life back into my life
I'm ready to move out in front, I've had enough
    of just passing by life
With the rest of them, with the best of them, I
    can hold my head up high!
For I've got a goal again
I've got a drive again
I'm gonna feel my heart coming alive again
Before the parade passes by!

Look at that crowd up ahead
Listen and hear that brass harmony growing
Look at that crowd up ahead
Pardon me if my old spirit is showing
All of those lights over there
Seem to be telling me where I'm going
When the whistles blow and the cymbals crash
    and the sparklers light the sky
I'm gonna raise the roof
I'm gonna carry on
Give me an old trombone, give me an old baton
Before the parade passes by!

—JERRY HERMAN

Before
the Parade
Passes By

PROLOGUE

Since boyhood, the sandy coast of Southern California with its mazes of rocky crags towering high above the Pacific had been Gower Champion's refuge for reflection. But on this mid-May morning, the customary stroll along his favorite stretch of Malibu Beach brought no solace. The crisis called for decisive action. Resolving it would require the same steady perseverance and clear-eyed skill of the surfers who danced over the mighty crested waves before him. The slightest miscalculation could send him plummeting into disaster like a Santa Monica mountain house in the midst of a mudslide.

Heavy-hearted, he returned home and phoned old friend and librettist Michael Stewart, explaining his decision. Given the state of his health, it would be disastrous to continue. Doctors warned that the stress of staging a major musical could prove fatal, and that conserving his strength was crucial to preserving his life. Regrettably, he had to withdraw from *42nd Street;* his decision was final. Mike understood; no one knew better what a tough choice his friend had made. At length, their conversation ended and Gower hung up the phone retreating to the garden to tend his prized azaleas.[1]

Five months later, he was Broadway-bound with a vengeance.

ONE

The Young Prince

1919–1935

"At ten pounds, two ounces, he's likely to become an All-American fullback," declared the doctor in attendance at the birth of the second son of John Champion and Beatrice Carlisle on June 22, 1919.[1] Almost immediately, however, the appeal of the child and his future prospects were lost on the boy's discontented father. John's work as an advertising executive for clothing manufacturer Munsingwear, though it lacked the thrill of the gridiron, was satisfying and productive enough. His marriage was not. Beatrice, or Betty, as she was called, was as intelligent, conscientious, and competent a wife as one could hope for, but her warmth and affection seemed ever distant. With hope of bridging that distance long gone, he grew wearier of her emotional aloofness each day.

Betty, on the other hand, was equally perturbed with the escalating indifference her husband was displaying toward their three-year-old elder son, John, and herself. Even the details of welcoming their new child to 402 South Fifth Street, the family's home in the prosperous Chicago suburb of Geneva, Illinois, were left to her. When she proposed Alfred Gower Carlisle Champion as the name for the boy and further suggested they call him Gower after her mother, Belle Gower, in whose home they resided, John voiced no objection. Whether preoccupied with the children or in denial over the perilous state of the marriage, Betty underestimated John's passive indignation. One evening about four months after Gower's birth, he brusquely declared that he was divorcing her to marry his secretary. Betty was stunned and became enraged. Apart from the divorce itself, what she resented most was the callous way he had chosen to reveal his decision. Her devotion deserved better, and his utter disregard of that fact would embitter her for life. The divorce followed quickly; Betty retained custody of the boys, and John remarried at once.

Continuing to raise the children in the Chicago area under the specter of this humiliation was not for Betty. Distance was what she needed, and the greater the distance between her and the philandering playboy who had failed to meet her standards, the better. However, a $90 monthly alimony check would not support her and the boys. By the time Gower was two and a half, she had used her skills as a dressmaker to forge a new life. She purchased a car, loaded it with the boys and everything she owned, and then drove across half the continent to Los Angeles, a place where her sister and many of her relatives had already resettled.[2]

Staunch Christian Scientist that she was, Betty had to concede that California did seem to be the new promised land touted by radio evangelist Aimee Semple McPherson. Indeed, the fair Los Angeles climate that greeted the family in January 1922 was a happy contrast to the bleak, icy weather of northern Illinois they had left. A happy reunion with her sister Patricia and her husband Bud March in Hancock Park and the picture of the boys at play on the beach were confirmation enough that here their lives could begin anew.[3] Days later, Betty acquired modest housing in town and began to renew contacts with friends in the area, many of whom were also Christian Scientists.[4] Among them was Edna Gregg, who had moved to Santa Monica sometime before with her husband and two children. Her son, Jess, was Gower's age, and the two boys quickly became friends. Whenever the families gathered for Sunday jaunts, holidays, or birthdays, Jess and Gower, whom Jess dubbed "Gar," were inseparable. When the boys were five, the Greggs moved closer to central Los Angeles; Gar's family eventually did, too, but to a different neighborhood. The families still kept in touch, but Jess and Gar would travel in different circles until young adulthood, when they would renew their old friendship.[5]

Like her circle of friends, Betty Champion held high regard for the studied, sedate, and personal nature of Christian Science, which she preferred to the faddish and common display of Aimee McPherson's fiery Pentecostal Revivalism with its throngs of frenetic believers. Even so, the two faiths had some striking similarities. Both stressed the power of spiritual healing as understood and practiced by their founders, two dynamic female ministers. Christian Science founder Mary Baker Eddy, who in 1879 established the Church of Christ Scientist in Boston, taught that there is only one reality—the spiritual. All else—the physical world with its affliction, dissension and death—is merely a misconception or a distortion of the divine universe made apparent when the healing power of Jesus Christ is manifested. Thus there are many believers who, in time of illness, favor divine revelation over medical or medicinal treatment. In Eddy's unique philosophy with its "things-are-not-as-they-seem" view of the world, Betty Champion found the perfect explanation for what happened in life.

Betty's practice of Christian Science was the austere kind—assiduous, resolute, sober, but joyless. With John's divorce, joy had perished along with the love that had engendered it. Since then, an overweening religiosity to which she steadfastly clung had supplanted the loss. As she confided one afternoon to Edna Gregg, "I could not live my life without this faith. It has given me the only hope I have—the only love I have."[6]

However great the love Betty found in Christian Science, it would never be sufficient to quell the pain of John's infidelity and rejection. She began to coach her sons in her own version of the divorce, making every effort to portray their father as a salacious good-for-nothing. Taking little pleasure in life, she grew increasingly suspicious and sanctimonious—attitudes that not only tested close friends like Edna Gregg, but also made her a rigid overseer of Gower and John, whose every move she strictly monitored.[7]

The divorce had turned Betty into a very private person whose sole form of socializing was the bridge club she hosted weekly in her home. Yet even these occasions failed to temper her austerity. Once when Gower defied her, she lost her composure and slapped him across the face in full view of her guests. Still, physical punishment of this kind was rare, the usual practice simply to consign the offender to a corner of the kitchen where he stood facing the wall until he had learned his lesson.[8]

Although puritanical, Betty's parenting technique was not without love or purpose. The boys had to learn that success in life stemmed from setting high standards, then achieving them through unwavering discipline and care. To this end, and also to compensate for the absence of the family's father, Betty often played father as well as mother. She was determined that John and Gower should become conscientious, respectful, and industrious men of breeding. They were encouraged to take pride in themselves and were given every affordable advantage. With family income barely sufficient to support a middle-class existence, those advantages often came with difficulty, which she resourcefully overcame by taking on a host of small jobs like selling subscriptions to magazines and memberships to the Del Mar Club, the local beach club where John and Gower would take their girlfriends to dance as teens.[9] If her motherly approval had to be withheld from her children to insure they conformed to her quality standards, then so be it. She was not raising a pair of "momma's boys." With time Betty's manner of discipline proved to have the intended effect on her sons—at least externally. Inwardly, however, Gower resented his mother's perfectionism and, in self-defense, began withdrawing from her emotionally.

John, in comparison, took his mother's high-powered expectations more in stride. College-educated at the University of Southern California for a leading place as a businessman in his uncle's oil company, he eventually would opt for a simpler life with a relative modicum of prosperity as the proprietor of a boys' and men's retail clothing store on Ventura Boulevard near Laurel Canyon. From boyhood, his relationship with Gower was a warm one, moderate in its show of affection, but always respectful. Even in college, John, the tall, handsome, and excellent ballroom dancer saw to it that his brother also had his fair share of cavorting at the Del Mar Club. With John at the wheel, together the brothers would go dating with their girlfriends. In later years, when Gower's professional dance career began to flourish, it would amuse John greatly to have a younger brother who was becoming a star. Eventually, however, traveling in different circles and the lack of common meeting ground would take a toll, and they would begin to grow apart.

Young Gower's education began in the local public grammar school until his poor performance there (due to a hearing disorder) prompted his mother to transfer him to Lawlor's School for Professional Children, a private grammar school for child performers, which Judy Garland also attended. A year later, he returned to public school after the nurse at Lawlor's pinpointed the source of his hearing problem—excessive earwax. (Betty would never think of consulting a physician about her son's condition; her strict religious mores forbade it.) Still, his introduction to the arts at Lawlor's, short-lived as it was, impressed him deeply. As a result, he began appearing on local children's radio programs like *Bill, Mack and Jimmy*. When not in school or delivering newspapers, he could be found singing for 50 cents and his dinner at the Pig'n Whistle, a popular family restaurant next door to Grauman's Egyptian Theatre on Hollywood Boulevard.

Performing was far more fun than delivering newspapers, and the money he earned was almost as good. By the fall of 1931, the twelve-year-old joined his brother at the Norma Gould School of Dancing on Larchmont Boulevard near Paramount Film Studios to take dance and piano lessons. His mother, who never had any intention of training either son for the stage, was convinced that social dancing should be a necessary part of their development.[10] By the end of the first term, however, pigeon-toed Gower had displayed such skill that his schoolmates refused to participate in any of the ballroom dancing contests he entered. Their reluctance was quite understandable, for once he began teaming with a beautiful brunette (almost a full head taller than him) by the name of Jeanne Tyler, all competition ceased.[11]

Because Norma Gould's classes were more etiquette lessons than serious dance, Gower and Jeanne decided to leave after two years to seek more advanced training at the Elisa Ryan School of Dancing in Beverly Hills. There, amid the school's white-glove cotillions and child film performers like Jane Withers and Shirley Temple, they studied under Thomas Sheehy, learning rudimentary tap and ballroom dancing, including the waltz, fox-trot, and quickstep. They also participated in the dramatics program headed by Ben Bard. Before long, Gower and Jeanne were testing their skills in numerous dance contests at Los Angeles–area beach clubs, junior high schools, even airports, winning most of the competitions they entered.[12]

Apparently young Champion cut quite a figure at the Ryan Studio, even captivating five-year-old Shirley Temple, who later confessed an "unrequited love" for the "happy and handsome"[13] young man. In the dramas staged by Bard, he frequently played her father and, as a result, quickly became her idol. Some years later, when Temple was a teen, they occasionally dated, but the results were to yield only "a low-tempo flirtation"[14] because of his career ambitions and inability to overcome her father's objections. Mr. Temple, uneasy with the nine-year age disparity between his daughter and the dancer, was further aggravated when his would-be-son-in-law peeled flakes of sunburned skin from his arms and dropped them on the floor of the family's latest Cadillac. Still, Gower continued his pursuit undaunted. As late as the fall of 1945, on the eve of Temple's marriage to Sergeant John Agar (a B-movie actor seven years her senior), he arrived at her residence, begged her to cancel the wedding, danced with her, and then kissed her. She later mused: "For true lovers it would have been a savored moment of regret. In our case, it was more dumb than daring. Had I agreed to jilt Sergeant Jack, Champion would have been lost in the dust of his own departure."[15]

By 1932, Gower, now a good-looking, charming, bright, and perfectly mannered thirteen-year-old with an aristocratic bearing, was attending Bancroft Junior High School. With no father to emulate and a rigid disciplinarian for a mother, he was also developing into an overly deferential and elusive teen. To some, like the girls who admired him, he was "the young prince."[16] To others, put off by his perceived diffidence, he was simply "the prince."[17] He paid them no mind.

In history class at Bancroft, he sat behind Marjorie (Marge) Celeste Belcher, a petite, vivacious blonde later to become his co-performer and first wife. His interest in dance had never surfaced in their conversations and remained virtually unknown to her until he and Jeanne performed a ballroom number in the school's annual ninth-grade talent show. The revelation was especially surprising to Marge. Her father was the renowned silent film choreographer Ernest Belcher, who operated one of the largest and most prestigious dance schools in Los Angeles, where she was both a student and an instructor. While attending the talent show to help with programming and to watch his daughter perform her specialty, a Portuguese hat dance, Belcher became so taken with Gower's talent, charm, and natural stage presence that he offered him a full scholarship to his school at once.[18]

The response of Belcher's new pupil to systematic dance training was remarkably undistinguished: he would fall out of the most elementary pirouettes, then make light of his error by shamefacedly crawling toward the piano and climbing to the top. (His antics, amusing at the time to the class and his good-natured teacher, contrasted remarkably with the fierce discipline he would later exhibit as a choreographer and director.) Ballet classes at Belcher's, often two or three times a week, failed to temper Gower's preference for ballroom work. With Jeanne, he continued to study at Elisa Ryan's studio and win local competitions. Dance was merely a pastime, and secondary to more important things like going to the beach and socializing with his girl. All that was about to change.

TWO

The Dance to Fame

1936–1942

On the evening of February 26, 1936, Gower and Jeanne suddenly found themselves in an elite class: one of ten couples gracing the dance floor of the Ambassador Hotel's Coconut Grove who had been selected as finalists in the "Veloz and Yolanda Dance to Fame." From this annual contest, sponsored by the *Los Angeles Examiner,* the finest amateur ballroom dancers in Southern California were chosen. Only the previous evening, before a crowd of thirty-five hundred assembled in the hotel's auditorium, had these ten been singled out from among five hundred others participating in the "Elimination Ball." Now they waited nervously as the judges determined the best among them.

The judges were a distinguished but intimidating lot: talent scouts from Metro-Goldwyn-Mayer (MGM) Studios, creators of popular dances like the Carioca and Continental, dance instructors from the nation's leading schools, even the president of the Screen Dancers' Guild. Completing the panel were the famed dance team of Veloz and Yolanda, also the honored guests of the proceedings. They stepped forward to announce the winners as the master of ceremonies called the capacity crowd to attention.

Winners Gower and Jeanne, two local sixteen-year-old high school students and the youngest competitors, were elated with the judges' unanimous decision. With the incentive of a $150 cash prize from the *Examiner* and a week's engagement at the Coconut Grove, the pair now had the chance to turn professional—maybe even become as renowned as Veloz and Yolanda, who presented them that evening with the contest's golden trophy. In little more than a year, they would realize both goals.

Their debut at the Coconut Grove on April 24 was so successful that the management extended their appearance five additional weeks. When the Music Corporation of America (MCA), then one of the nation's top talent agencies, offered a contract for nightclub and theatre performances, they readily accepted. A nine-week run at the Mural Room of the Hotel St. Francis in San Francisco was followed by a six-week return engagement at the Coconut Grove.[1] Just as Gower was starting his senior year at Fairfax High School and Jeanne hers at Van Nuys High, MCA announced a booking for the Gold Coast Room of the Drake Hotel in Chicago. With the aid of Belcher and Ryan School instructor Sheehy, Gower immediately began choreographing new material. By October 1936, "America's Youngest Dance Team" was Chicago-bound, with Betty Champion as chaperone.

Gower was deeply troubled by the inevitable reunion with his father, still residing in Chicago with his second wife and two children. John Champion had long disapproved of his son's interest in dance, and even had threatened to cut off alimony payments until Betty reminded him that it was she who had custody of their son and was raising him as she saw fit. Gower's newfound success quickly melted John's objections. Shortly after the Drake opening, the elder Champion could be seen entertaining Munsingwear clients at a table near the dance floor. Only a few weeks later, his son and Jeanne began appearing in the company's advertisements. But John Champion's sudden paternal stirrings—however genuine—were disquieting to his son, who had long since abandoned any expectations of the father who had abandoned him. To Gower, the very idea of establishing a real rapport with his father seemed as ridiculous as the imitation of John Champion he gave for the amusement of his friends. Still, deep within him was the desire to connect, which he could not act on even if he wanted. He was too much a satellite of his mother's world. For the present, at least, son and father would remain civilly estranged.[2]

The Chicago experience had another significant consequence for the good looking, blond, 135-pound, seventeen-year-old, who in the past year had added a full eight inches to his height and by now stood head and shoulders above his five-foot-two partner at six feet. His pastime had become his profession, and his cavalier attitude toward the regimen of dance had to change. In total contrast to his conduct at the Belcher School, he now became disciplined and focused in his Chicago classes. During rehearsals with Jeanne, he applied himself with a diligence and single-mindedness that would soon reveal his true skills as a dancer and choreographer.

At the conclusion of their seventeen-week run at the Drake, MCA scheduled the team for a series of tours with some of the leading dance bands of the day, including the Eddie Duchin, Guy Lombardo, and Wayne King Orchestras. These "road shows," which preceded or followed the showing of a major film, took Gower and Jeanne to Boston, Philadelphia, Baltimore, Washington, Pittsburgh, and Detroit. Essentially a vaudeville entertainment, the road show was built around a popular dance band or singer as headliner, with lesser acts—acrobats, ventriloquists, and dance teams—as stock entries comprising the remainder of the bill. Generally, these appeared prior to a featured act, which, in turn, was second in billing only to the headliner. An unknown but noteworthy act would then follow, increasing the audience's anticipation prior to the appearance of the headliner and the finale.

Gower studied the structure and varied content of the road show, learning to sustain an evening's entertainment by manipulating the audience's attention and expectations. He applied these early lessons in the director's craft to his own act, which soon rose to the coveted next-to-closing spot. As *Variety* explained, "Why they are so situated on the bill becomes apparent before they have danced out half their first routine. To say they are distinctive would be understatement, to mention their refreshing youthfulness, their swell routines, surprise lifts, would only give a sketchy impression of one of the most unique dance duos to come to Boston in many a season."[3] There was a price to pay, however, for the distinction.

Life on the road with the dance bands was rigorous, requiring great discipline and stamina from the youngsters. Because their act went on next to last, they often would not leave the theatre until midnight or 1:00 A.M. By that time, they were famished because they could not eat a full meal before the performance. Following dinner, they retired to their hotel rooms for the night, rising early the next day for a full session of dancing, singing, and dramatics lessons in addition to their regular schoolwork, which Betty guided. Afternoons were devoted to performances— often four or five a day—or rehearsals. On some occasions, they even would appear in an afternoon stage performance at a local movie house, then spend the evening entertaining in a nightclub or musical theatre production. For Gower and Jeanne, all this was simply part of developing and maintaining the reputation they were establishing; they thought nothing of it.[4]

Despite its demands, road show life had lighter moments, often products of Gower's mischievous ways. For example, one feature of Wayne King's show was his nine-member female vocal group known as The King Choristers, who performed in long formal gowns while standing upon a series of bleacherlike open metal steps positioned behind the orchestra. One evening during a performance, Gower armed some men in the company with water pistols and then stealthily led them to the area underneath the steps. At his signal, the battalion commenced fire right up the women's dresses. Another time, a particularly haughty female vocalist received a quick attitude alignment once Gower learned of her fear of mice. After boarding the train that night and waiting until all were asleep, he took a dead mouse he had killed earlier in the afternoon during a ballroom rehearsal with Jeanne and, with a piece of gum, hung it by the tail to the ceiling of the singer's berth while she slept. In the morning, the passengers awoke to a horrific scream that almost brought the train to a dead halt.[5]

With the repeal of Prohibition in December 1933, nightclubs again flourished in major hotels and vied for promising talent to lure patrons. For better acts of a dying vaudeville, two shows an evening in the posh comfort of a prominent hotel was a dream in comparison to the four-or-five-performance-a-day stress of the road show. Gower and Jeanne's swift rise to featured status prompted MCA to groom them for an engagement at one of New York's top clubs. In preparation, they were sent to Montreal, where they opened at the Normandie Roof of the new Mount Royal Hotel on June 17, 1937.

Critical praise was unanimous. They were hailed as "the apotheosis of carefree youth manifestly at home in every form of ballroom routine." Their ability "to introduce a variety of steps and poses that are instinctive with rhythmic grace" caused them to be "vociferously and deservedly applauded and recalled again and again."[6] Others acclaimed them as "the most expert ballroom team seen here for a long while," "glib and assured comedians," and "the real hit of the evening."[7] Weeks later, Gower and Jeanne continued to impress: "They are certainly well worth seeing, not once but many times, for their dancing always seems novel, fresh and expressive of the spirit of youth, and they put so much of their personalities into it that it seems something beyond the usual clever team exhibition."[8]

Still largely unschooled in the ways of show business, the pair was somewhat bewildered by the critical reception and sudden celebrity conferred upon them by reporters, fans, and hotel staff alike. The English as well as the French press provided full-page feature coverage, patrons furnished free passes to local amusement parks, even the hotel's chef prepared special dishes each evening for midnight supper— their main meal of the day. It seemed the entire city of Montreal had adopted them along with fellow performer Vera Fern, a young, talented ballerina whose equally solicitous stage mother had miraculously bonded with Betty Champion. In addition to overseeing the careers of their children and designing and sewing their costumes, the two chaperones had something else in common—a deep loathing for their ex-husbands, which they candidly shared with each other. Typical of their repartee was a comment Vera once overheard Betty impart to her mother concerning John's dissent over Gower's interest in dance. "My ex-husband was so angry with me for sending Gower to dancing school," she remarked, "that he told me I was turning him into a fairy. Now, he's eating his words."[9] Gower's success was Betty's retribution on John; nothing could have pleased her more.

Minus the constant scrutiny of their mothers, the trio of teens was free for once to enjoy themselves. They made many friends, including hotel bellboys and elevator operators who politely refused to take them to their floor unless they named it in French. As a result they soon learned to *parler français*. Vera, whose mischievous streak equaled Gower's, prevailed upon Jeanne to join her in short-sheeting his bed, mismatching his socks, and tying his ties together. Though concerned that the pranks might anger her partner, Jeanne nonetheless acquiesced. Whatever objections Gower might have were of little consequence to Vera, whose relationship with him was a spirited one in which they tried to top each other's wild puns and practical jokes. Their interplay was humorous even to Betty, who often became an accomplice in the impish assaults on her son. Still, it was plain to Vera that a relationship with Gower beyond these limits would be impossible because it was certain to incur the displeasure of his mother.[10]

Jeanne, on the other hand, had genuine feelings for Gower that Betty made every effort to crush. One evening, when her exuberant partner congratulated her with an intimate kiss for an excellent performance, his mother openly accused her of taking advantage of her son. Tearfully, Jeanne protested that he had only kissed her because of the good work she had done, but Betty remained unmoved. She viewed their relationship strictly as brother and sister and insisted that they behave that way toward each other. Knowing Gower's equal affection for Jeanne, she did everything to discourage him from proposing to her. "I was convinced that such a marriage would be a mistake," she later stated. "Not that Jeanne Tyler wasn't a lovely girl; she is, but I knew that Gower should first have the opportunity of going out with other girls. After all, you can't judge how lovely one girl is unless you've been out with others."[11]

Propriety demanded that Gower have his own quarters, so for three years Jeanne roomed with Betty until the conflict between them forced her to live with friends in New York once the act became established there. Meanwhile, his mother's incessant meddling would create difficulty not only for Gower, but more so for Jeanne, who had been raised far more independently. Once when playing Miami, for instance, Jeanne went for a walk and met with a major interrogation upon her return. When she refused to report her whereabouts, Betty retorted that she must have been doing something shameful. Incidents like this placed Gower at the center of an inescapable struggle. To free himself, he reluctantly began to date other women. While still in Chicago, he saw a good deal of a young beauty named Dolly Thon, and for a time his mother thought he might marry her. Years later, when she pressed him as to why he did not propose to Dolly, he retorted, "I guess you took care of that, too, Mother."[12]

The team's repertory now consisted of fourteen different routines, all choreographed by Gower, who also arranged the music for each. These works included "Smoke Gets in Your Eyes," a romantic dance; "Calamity Jane," a sprightly, carefree number; "Tango Argentine," a thrilling South American piece; "Japanese Sandman," which conveyed the lure of the Orient; "Darktown Strutters Ball," a crowd-pleaser with the pair stepping out in real cakewalk style; "Waltz, My Darling," "Waltz Together," and "Twilight Time," three capricious numbers accenting grace and rhythm; and "Dardenella," "Yesterdays," and "Feets," three inventive routines.

The remainder consisted of "The Veolanda," a specialty they had learned from Veloz and Yolanda after winning the "Dance to Fame"; "Strut Parade"; and "The Merry-Go-Round Broke Down."[13]

"Strut Parade" and "The Merry-Go-Round Broke Down" merit special mention as examples of a dance form unprecedented in the work of the era's dance teams and distinctly characteristic of Gower's work with Jeanne and later with Marge Champion. These were "story dances"—narratives told through dance and pantomime. In "Strut Parade," a military step that changed into an old-time Southern strut and back again to the tune of "Dixie," the dancers appeared as two youngsters with no place to go. Hearing a parade in the distance, they responded to the urge of the throbbing music as it moved closer and closer. When the parade rolled around the corner, they joined with it in a full-fledged cakewalk—a real Dixie strut with sensational trimmings. "The Merry-Go-Round Broke Down," inspired by a popular song which soon became the Looney Tunes theme, told the story of a young couple at a carnival who board a carousel and get caught up in its whirling excitement. Surprised when the machine breaks down at the height of the fun, they abandon it, departing in disappointment.

Gower's interpolation not only liberated a narrative form of dance previously found only in ballet, but also challenged the expectations of audiences accustomed to more conventional fare from dance teams. Audience approval of this adaptation is evidenced by the fact that both "Strut Parade" and "Merry-Go-Round" remained in the team's repertory as much as a year later and inspired similar works, including "Tintypes," the story of an old photograph come to life; "Vaudeville 1910," which related the exploits of two entertainers in the early part of the century; and "The Missionary and the Maiden," the tale of a cleric's surrender to the spell of a South Seas girl.

In the late 1940s and 1950s, similar story dances would become the trademark of Gower's nightclub and television performances with Marge Champion. They also prefigured the ballets he would in time choreograph for the musical theatre. In little more than a year, he had succeeded in creating an original act that was both polished and free of clichés. Most ballroom teams of the era mimicked the slick Latin style of Veloz and Yolanda or the airy sophistication of Fred Astaire and Ginger Rogers, but Gower and Jeanne transcended this norm by combining skill, youth, and personality with "an inexhaustible stock of new and unusual features and routines."[14]

The novice performer/choreographer was also becoming a director, applying to the act what he had learned on the road. Out of a sizable repertory, he could assemble a different group of routines for each engagement. In essence, he created a series of miniature revues that mixed dance and music with drama and ballroom spectacle. Some of that spectacle was the result of the extraordinary elevation he could achieve as a dancer, making him seem to soar above the stage with ease. By contrast, the five-foot-two Jeanne was so light and facile that he could lift, dip, or spin her as if weightless. Also, their "drawn-up" or erect torsos gave a distinct bearing to the way they carried themselves onstage. These were early signs of a Champion style, which, when fully realized, would be as discernible as the tight turned-in angularity of Bob Fosse or the long-limbed, head-flung-back style of Michael Bennett.

Gower and Jeanne were held over at the Normandie Roof for eighteen weeks—an astonishing record considering that, at the time, most acts usually played only for two or three. "I think it was our lack of sophistication and our youth," Jeanne recalls. "Youth has a lot going for it. We were both good-looking kids and had lots of personality—just bubbling with it. Also, Veloz and Yolanda had taught us that one of the keys to success is making the audience feel you're madly in love. Whether you are or you aren't, you've got to play that to each other."[15] It was a lesson the youngsters mastered with ease because by now they were very much in love—with their chaperone still fighting it every inch of the way.

On October 30, Gower and Jeanne were honored by the management of the Normandie Roof with a farewell party and invited to return a year later for the nightclub's first anniversary (which they later did for an additional sixteen weeks). Before then, however, performances at the Boston and Cleveland Statler Hotels with the Sammy Kaye Orchestra were the final steps to a triumphant New York debut at the Waldorf-Astoria's Empire Room on New Year's Eve 1938. Their popularity is evidenced by the fact that within a week of opening, the management moved them to the hotel's more prestigious Sert Room. Soon they would be the only dance team of their day to play all three top nightclubs in New York: the Sert Room at the Waldorf, the Persian Room at the Plaza Hotel, and the Rainbow Room atop NBC Studios in Rockefeller Center.[16]

Offstage, Champ and Tyler, as they called each other, found separate interests to pursue. Jeanne enjoyed sewing and collecting hand-crafted figurines as well as unique bracelet charms representing the cities they played. Gower, an avid collector of phonograph records with an impressive library of classical discs, was also becoming adept at photography, and toted a camera everywhere. A fourth member of the troupe, Max, their pet cat, added a touch of home on the road.

Broadway choreographer Robert Alton had seen the team perform while in Montreal. His dances for *Anything Goes* (1934), *The Ziegfeld Follies* (1934, 1936), and *Leave It to Me* (1938) had established him as one of the theatre's premier choreographers. By tailoring specific routines to the skills of solo performers and breaking the traditional chorus line into small groups to fill the stage with a variety of movement, he had revolutionized stage dancing. In this way, he gave old-fashioned hoofing a choreographic integrity equal to ballet.[17] Similar traits would later define Gower's own choreography. When he and Jeanne were invited by Alton to incorporate their act into a Broadway revue opening in the summer of 1939, they readily accepted. Following an engagement with Orrin Tucker's Orchestra at the Palmer House in Chicago and a tour with Wayne King, they joined the cast of *Streets of Paris.*

The last important revue of the period between 1920 and 1940, *Streets of Paris* was produced by comedians Ole Olsen and Chic Johnson in conjunction with the Shubert Brothers and starred comedians Bobby Clark, Bud Abbott and Lou Costello, and Luella Gear. Featured together with Gower and Jeanne were French crooner Jean Sablon and the harmonizing Hylton Sisters. But the evening's chief attraction was the American debut of Lee Shubert discovery Carmen Miranda. Bedecked with her trademark fruited headdress, six-inch heels, and multicolored beads, the "Brazilian Bombshell" generated quite a sensation as she extolled the torrid delights down "South American Way."

Equally memorable was the dance Alton created mocking British Prime Minister Neville Chamberlain's recent sellout of Czechoslovakia to Nazi Germany. Presented as the newest dance craze, "Doin' the Chamberlain" was sung by instructor Luella Gear while a chorus of Chamberlain lookalikes, led by Gower and Jeanne as the Duke and Duchess of Windsor, strutted about the stage waving black umbrellas. This "English goose-step" by songwriters Jimmy McHugh and Al Dubin invited participants to shed caution and "Squirm like a worm," "Be a wise side-stepper," "Then appease just to please" in imitation of the dance's namesake.[18]

Behind the scenes, equally hilarious play was provided, compliments of Gower's devilish sense of humor. *Chanteur* Sablon, with whom he shared a dressing room, was persnickety, and his constant fault-finding made him unpopular with the company. One evening he got his comeuppance when Gower opened a can of pepper-pot soup and dumped it into the sink, pretending to be nauseous. When Sablon arrived to wash, the scene so nauseated him he almost missed his cue.

About the same time Gower and Jeanne were appearing in *Streets of Paris,* Vera Fern was performing in Rodgers and Hart's *Too Many Girls.* Once more, the three attended dancing, singing, and acting classes together and frequently met when the theatres were dark on Sundays. On one of those occasions, Gower took Vera to see Walt Disney's first full-length animated feature, *Snow White and the Seven Dwarfs,* to acquaint her with the work of his schoolmate Marge Belcher, the model for the film's heroine. Although they had only dated sporadically back in California, he still held a deep regard for the lithesome ballerina. Consequently, he was less than happy with the news of her recent marriage to the Disney artist who had illustrated her movement for the popular film only now at the end of its initial release. Upon exiting the theatre that evening, he was visibly agitated and told Vera, "C'mon, we're going to the telegraph office."[19] When they arrived, he dashed off a wire to Marge with one word—"Stinker!"—signed it, and dispatched it. Unprepared for marriage as he was, he nonetheless expected that the future Mrs. Champion—Marge, Jeanne, or whoever—would carry the torch for him until he was ready to commit. Disturbing as Marge's marriage was, he quickly learned that life stops for no one.

Grief over Marge and continued devotion to Jeanne did not cause him to marvel any less at the impact he was having on others. With his good looks, refinement, and personable intensity, he won the attention of others effortlessly. One evening, Jess Gregg, now his best friend, introduced him to a young lady whom he was dating, but not particularly serious about. "Gower gave her 'the look,'" he recalls, "and she was truly knocked out by it. I was furious. It was galvanizing."[20]

People drawn to him struck a chord deep within. But the Champion charisma had its down side, too. Once, when he was in New Haven for the tryout of a show, a score of adolescent girls squealed affectionately at Gower as he and Jess strolled by. Though his celebrity could not compare to Frank Sinatra's, he was ill at ease with the kind of adoration teenage girls were heaping on the crooner and wanted nothing like it from his fans. "Women would come up to him and want to paw him, to 'feel' him. He always hated it," recollects Jess.[21] Gower made a powerful impression on people; his presence was mesmerizing.

Streets of Paris, which opened on June 19, 1939, concluded an eight-month run at the Broadhurst Theatre in February 1940, and then toured Philadelphia, Washington, Pittsburgh, and Chicago, where it closed on May 8, 1940. Just prior to the closing, Gower and Jeanne left the company to commence engagements at the Strand Theatre in New York and the Earle in Washington. By the middle of June, they were back in New York as featured performers in the stage spectacular at Radio City Music Hall. When the couple opened at the Rainbow Room on June 24, 1940, Gower had just celebrated his twenty-first birthday.

The frequency of the team's New York bookings led Betty to acquire an apartment there that would finally give them a home base. Vera Fern's mother had done the same, and when the two families were both in town, they would often invite each other to their homes for Sunday dinner. One afternoon the Ferns arrived at the Champions to find a frightful sight. Earlier that day while in the shower, Gower had hit his right eye on the shower head. So terrible was the resulting hemorrhage that the pupil could not even be seen. With less than twenty-four hours to his next performance, the Ferns wondered how he would be able to go on. As he insisted he would, Betty promptly interjected that the situation was well in hand, thanks to the intervention of her Christian Scientist practitioner in California, with whom she had spoken earlier by phone. This only increased the alarm of the dinner guests, who could see that the condition of the eye was serious and required immediate medical care. True to his word, Gower performed the following evening with the pupil still partially obscured, but two days later when the Ferns again encountered him, the hemorrhage was gone and the eye was completely clear. Impressive as the speed of the healing was, it made Vera and her mother very uncomfortable because of the gratuitous risk Betty had taken with her son's health.[22]

When not in New York, the team resumed road show tours with more name bands of the day—Xavier Cugat, Shep Fields, Hal Kemp—making it a practice to collect the signatures of their maestros as a keepsake. In an age of dance crazes like the jitterbug, bandleaders respected Gower's resolve not to cater to common expectations by exploiting what was popular. Only once did he bend this rule by devising a routine to Rachmaninoff's "Prelude in C Sharp Minor," which he introduced in Chicago during a second road tour with the Eddie Duchin Orchestra. With Duchin's piano virtuosity driving the accompaniment forward, the dance gradually grew in tempo until it gyrated with swing music and jitterbug. Gower further enriched the repertory with "Campaign Can-Do," a satire on an aspiring politician's bid for public office; "Country Garden," a tale of incipient romance; "I Dream of Jeannie with the Light-Brown Hair," a soaring *pas de deux;* "London Again," a trio of dances capturing different moods of life in the British city; and "Dress Rehearsal," inspired by personal incidents from their travels. Among these was a performance they once gave at a benefit. When the orchestra accompanying them continued playing chorus after chorus nonstop, the pair improvised for twenty minutes until finally reeling off the floor exhausted.

The team returned to Broadway in *The Lady Comes Across,* a revision of producer Dennis King's *She Had to Say Yes,* which had folded out of town the previous season. The musical was not only to have starred Ray Bolger, who was replaced by comedian Joe E. Lewis, but also to have marked the return to the stage of Jessie Matthews, queen of the British film musical, who by now was nearing the end of her reign. With the onset of World War II, Matthews risked her life crossing the Atlantic at a time when British ships were easy prey for German submarines. Though she arrived safely in New York, news of the torpedoing and sinking of the ship bearing her luggage exacerbated the stress of being separated from her husband and daughter at the height of the London blitzkrieg. These things, plus the anxiety of not having danced on stage for almost ten years, began to affect her deeply.

One afternoon during a rehearsal, Matthews, who was particularly fond of Jeanne, asked her to bring some tea. When the tray was set before her, she unwittingly poured the tea into the saucer instead of the cup. As soon as she realized what she had done, she bolted from her chair into the long hallway, running at top speed toward the large window at the end. Jeanne, in pursuit, called to Gower for help. Fortunately, his swift intervention saved Matthews, but the star was clearly in no condition to perform; Evelyn Wyckoff, Gertrude Lawrence's secretary in *Lady in the Dark,* assumed her role.[23]

The musical, which opened January 9, 1942, and closed after three performances, did give Gower and Jeanne the opportunity to work with choreographer George Balanchine. One of the acknowledged leaders in classical ballet, Balanchine was also one of Broadway's most innovative choreographers, who had successfully adapted ballet to the musical stage in Rodgers and Hart's *On Your Toes* (1936), *Babes in Arms* (1937), *I Married an Angel* (1938), and *The Boys from Syracuse* (1938). Like Alton, his initial impression of the team's work was so favorable that he permitted Gower to create their sequences for *The Lady Comes Across.* Having now won the esteem of two of the most reputable choreographers of the day—Alton and Balanchine—any question the young performer may have entertained concerning the merit of his work must surely have seemed groundless.

Gower and Jeanne resumed club appearances, playing the fashionable Brook Club in Miami in March and, in May, the Empire Room of the Palmer House in Chicago. Anxious about retaining the reputation he had earlier established in his birthplace, the young choreographer was especially delighted when critics noted the maturity and uniqueness of his work, particularly the serious but charming story dance "The Missionary and the Maiden." "This amusing little pantomime," wrote one, "is admirable dancing technique. It is witty; it has exquisite touches of philosophy and an understanding of human nature—all without being anything more imposing than a thoroughly enjoyable encore number."[24]

Adding to the exuberance of the occasion was a reunion with Vera Fern, who had just opened at the Chicago Theatre. She invited Gower to attend the get-together for the younger members of her company that her mother was giving Saturday evening after the show. Following his performance that evening, Gower arrived—without his mother's permission—about midnight at the apartment in the theatrical hotel where the Ferns were staying. It was a high-spirited reunion. Vera's mother made scrambled eggs for the crowd, and there was plenty of the wild card games and cutting up the two dancers loved. When the gathering finally broke up around four in the morning, Gower took his leave, telling the Ferns how much he had enjoyed the evening and looked forward to joining them later that Sunday for dinner at his home.

When Vera and her mother arrived that afternoon, they could hardly ignore the edge in Betty's greeting. Her soon-to-be twenty-three-year old's attendance at the party without her consent so incensed her that she forced him to stand in a corner of the room for the entire duration of the Ferns' visit—which he did without protest. "I have never seen a more perfect example of self-control than I saw from Gower that dreadful evening," recalled Fern. "It must have been extremely hard for him to stand there in that corner. I didn't know what to do, but I think he wanted me to admire him. I thought that he showed great self-control. But Mother and I couldn't wait to get out of there."[25]

No wonder. Betty's denial of the maturity of her son—the family's breadwinner now for over five years—was as shocking and sad as Gower's collusion in it. Nevertheless, his only protection was to maintain composure and self-control; as long as he did that, Betty could not prevail. This unruffled but measured behavior—part self-defense, part internalization of his mother's "things-are-as-not-as-they-seem" credo—would remain throughout adulthood. Rarely was he given to displays of temper, which he considered to be boorish and crass. However great the turbulence within, composure was to be upheld regardless of cost—even when it resulted in bleeding ulcers that came and went throughout life. Self-possession was the key; anything less showed vulnerability or weakness. It was the lesson he internalized from his mother's discipline.

A musical satire-fantasy, *Count Me In,* was to mark Gower and Jeanne's final appearance together. First presented by the Reverend Gilbert V. Hartke at the Catholic University of America in Washington, D.C., it was produced for Broadway by Olsen and Johnson, who, with the Shuberts, aimed to duplicate their *Streets of Paris* success. Robert Alton, fresh from *Panama Hattie* (1940) and *Pal Joey* (1940), was again the choreographer. Extraneous variety acts completely overwhelmed the plot, which concerned the attempts of a father, Charles Butterworth, to rival the war efforts of his wife, Luella Gear, and children. Opening at the Barrymore Theatre on October 8, 1942, *Count Me In* received unfavorable notices, and closed after a brief run of six weeks.

With his brother, John, now in the service, Gower's awareness of the war intensified, and with it, a growing unease with the draft deferment he had been granted as his mother's sole source of support. Night after night as he and Jeanne continued performing in the country's top clubs, he could no longer ignore the remarks of patrons who asked why he was not in the service. He wanted to enlist, yet was troubled by the hardship it would bring to Jeanne and their relationship, now a serious romance. She urged him to do what he felt was best; he joined the Coast Guard, heedless of his mother's appeals.

The evening before his departure was the closing night of *Count Me In* and the last performance the team would give. In the audience Walter Winchell noted a special poignancy in their portrayals of the duty-bound young man headed for the Navy and the anxious young nurse fearful for his life. While they danced, Gower once again asked, as he had every night of the show's run, "Will you wait for me?" But this time, when she answered yes, the irony was more than Jeanne could bear, and she broke into tears.[26]

THREE

Story-Dancing Champions

1943–1947

Seaman First Class Champion spent his initial year of duty as a platoon leader on Catalina Island off the Southern California coast. In his second year, he was recruited as a dancer for the Coast Guard musical *Tars and Spars,* a regulation military revue akin to Irving Berlin's better-known *This Is the Army* and also notable for bringing to prominence a young comedian by the name of Sid Caesar. After touring a year with the show, the sailor's repeated requests for more active duty were finally granted. Following a brief engagement of *Tars and Spars* at New York's Plymouth Theatre in 1943, he spent his third and final year as a public relations worker aboard a troop transport in the Atlantic and Pacific and even found time to keep in theatrical trim by producing four shows on ship.[1]

As for Jeanne, MCA urged her to find another partner, but she refused out of devotion to her former teammate, still high in her affections. She remained in New York working for Saks Fifth Avenue as a personal shopper for celebrities and powerful figures like Madame Chiang Kai-shek. One day while on leave, Gower paid a call to renew their romance and discuss what they might do after the war. To her surprise, his plans did not include marriage. When the topic finally surfaced, he made it clear that as much as he loved her, he was apprehensive about marriage and children. What security could he provide for a family in his present state without job or income? He proposed that they simply go on seeing each other indefinitely—an idea totally unacceptable to Jeanne, who was unwilling to put off her hope of marriage and family any longer. The two parted as friends. Not long thereafter, Jeanne returned to California and married physician Ned Estridge.

Discharged in the fall of 1945, Gower resumed civilian life in Los Angeles. Since reviving his ballroom career was out of the question now that Jeanne was married, he decided to establish himself as a solo dancer: "I hated it, but it was the only thing

I knew how to do. I could make good money dancing, and it was better than working in chop suey joints or grousing around looking for a job."[2] He did obtain a screen test from 20th Century-Fox, but it failed to net him an offer. One day, while making the rounds of other studios, he met his former dancing teacher and mentor Ernest Belcher, whose affinity for the struggling dancer prompted an invitation to resume studies at his school. Gower could not refuse the one man who had come closest to being a father to him. His uncle, Bud March, the husband of his mother's sister, had been quite generous with material things, including the use of a car, and was clearly proud of his achievements on stage and in the service. But "Mr. B" cared for him the way a father cares for a son, loving him as one of his own children.

Naturally, Gower inquired about Marge, and was told that she was performing professionally in New York under the name of Marjorie Bell and appearing in the Broadway production *Dark of the Moon*. He also learned that her recent marriage had ended in divorce. Belcher could easily see that the young man was still taken with his daughter and, immediately after the meeting, wrote her the happy news, "Boy is back in town!" Back home in the music halls of his native England, he, too, had started out as part of a ballroom dance team called *The Celestes* (hence the middle name he gave his daughter). To see Marge and "Boy," as he fondly referred to Gower, team up together was his greatest wish—a wish he also hoped would make his daughter's life more blissful than it had been.

The marriage of Ernest Belcher and Gladys Baskette had been anything but blissful, even after Marge's arrival on September 2, 1919, for Gladys Baskette Belcher was one of those imperious types who storm through life demanding to see the manager. She had a devastatingly beautiful daughter by her first marriage, a gifted child named Lina Baskette (later Lena Basquette), and she was determined to help her achieve screen stardom whatever the cost. (A featured child ballerina at the 1915 San Francisco World's Fair and namesake of Universal's *Lena Baskette Featurettes*, Lena later became the *première danseuse* of the 1923 *Ziegfeld Follies* before marrying movie mogul Sam Warner, the shrewdest and most resourceful of the three Warner brothers, at age eighteen. Returning to Hollywood in 1927, she quickly achieved screen celebrity as the lead in Cecil B. De Mille's *The Godless Girl* [1929]. But her career began to sag with Warner's untimely death and ensuing court battles between herself and his brothers over his vast estate and their daughter. After a string of minor films and several suicide attempts, she eventually was reduced to bit roles before retiring in the late thirties.[3])

Marge was three and a half years old and her brother, Richard, six months, when their mother and half-sister left Los Angeles in 1923 for New York. They were expendable; Lena was not. For the time, their care was relinquished to their father, an amiable man who taught them how to play, dance, and enjoy life. Gladys finally returned in 1927, a virtual stranger to Ernest and the children. For the next ten years, tensions between the spouses escalated until Belcher finally separated from his wife shortly after Marge's first marriage.

His career, in comparison, was remarkably successful. An accomplished and refined professional, he was the most sought-after Hollywood choreographer of his day. His intelligent grasp of the camera's capabilities enabled him to produce quality film footage in record time, making him the first choice of directors like D. W. Griffith and Cecil B. De Mille for filming major dance sequences. He also established and conducted the largest and most distinguished dance school in Los Angeles—the University of the Dance, at 607 South Western Avenue—where Vilma Banky, Loretta Young, Betty Grable, Gwen Verdon, and Rod La Rocque all studied ballet or ballroom under his direction. With such credits, it was indeed appropriate that the press dubbed him "The Ballet Master to Movieland."[4]

From age eight, Marge spent nearly all of her afternoons at her father's school learning ballet, tap, Spanish dancing, and acrobatics. Soon she was conducting evening classes for working women and appearing as a dancer in the Los Angeles Civic Opera productions of *Blossom Time* and *The Student Prince*. This led to her first break on the legitimate stage, performing opposite her handsome partner, Louis Hightower, in *Tonight at 8:30*. One evening a talent scout saw the five-foot-two, 102-pound thirteen-year-old and was taken with her flawless performance, piquant quality, and lovely face. His endorsement led Walt Disney to sign her and Louis as the models for Snow White and Prince Charming in his first full-length animated film, *Snow White and the Seven Dwarfs* (1937). In 1939, she made her major motion picture debut in *The Story of Vernon and Irene Castle,* starring Fred Astaire and Ginger Rogers, and later joined Disney again as the model for the Blue Fairy in *Pinocchio* (1940) and the prancing hippopotami of *Fantasia* (1940).

Marge had known Gower since junior high school and had often seen him at her father's studio, but after only a few dates she reluctantly lost him to the road and Jeanne Tyler. Still, in the diary where she normally recorded only the names of beaus and the places they had taken her, an evening spent with her schoolmate at the Del Mar Club in Santa Monica had merited her one and only comment: "Dancing with Gower. Happy Time." The boy was only a memory when several years later, at age seventeen, she eloped to Santa Barbara with top Disney animator Art Babbitt. Shortly thereafter, she went to New York, where, under the name of Marjorie Bell, she was booked with the Three Stooges and billed as the original Snow White, performing a toe dance similar to the one she created for her animated counterpart.

But as her career blossomed, the marriage began to fail, eventually ending in divorce. Then an appearance in a short-lived show, *The Little Dog Laughed* (1940), resulted in a broken toe—a misfortune that kept her from dancing for two years. Undefeated, Marge used her convalescence to develop her vocal and acting skills, and as a result soon landed a straight dramatic role in *Portrait of a Lady* (1941), playing the soubrette to leading lady Ruth Gordon.

She returned to dancing for the Broadway musical *What's Up?* (1943)—a short-lived first effort by songwriting novices Alan Jay Lerner and Frederick Loewe. In rehearsal the trouble with her toe resurfaced. The show's choreographer, George Balanchine, sent her to his own doctor to make certain that it would properly mend. Though *What's Up?* ran only sixty-three performances, the experience helped Marge to land the title role in a revival of the musical *Sally* at the prestigious Paper Mill Playhouse in Millburn, New Jersey. In attendance one evening was composer Richard Rodgers, who saw in her the makings of a top star and sent her to distinguished vocal coach Clytie Mundy to help ensure it. In 1947, he fulfilled this prediction by offering her a leading role in his new musical, *Allegro*.

After her mother's death in 1944, Marge opened in Broadway's *Dark of the Moon* on March 14, 1945, as the Fair Witch—a role she played for the next eight months. At her father's prompting, she invited Gower to come to New York to search for work and take in the theatre scene in early December 1945. After a series of fruitless auditions for the film studios, he welcomed her offer and headed for New York. There was no question as to which hit he would see first. The evening he attended *Dark of the Moon,* Marge betrayed her nervousness by falling out of a tree in one scene and forgetting her lines in another.[5]

Gower's auditions for *Call Me Mister* and *Annie Get Your Gun* failed to win him a job, but his relationship with Marge quickly turned into an ardent romance—one he insisted remain noncommittal. After a month of steady dating, things came to a sudden halt when news of a film contract with MGM forced him to rush back to Hollywood early in 1946. Thanks to his cunning agent, Irving "Swifty" Lazar, who had advanced his cause via the screen test for Fox, he was now part of Metro's leading-man pool. But the excitement of the moment did not deter his pursuit of Marge, with whom he corresponded almost daily. Though letter-writing was a challenge for her, for him it was a pleasant custom that would remain with him throughout life. A profusion of letters traversed the miles between them until Marge's arrival in Los Angeles that summer to visit her father.

Happily reunited, they were soon spending almost every afternoon together. Then, without warning, Gower's visits ceased. Once more, misgivings about marriage and children plagued him. With his life still unsettled, marriage and its responsibilities were equally unsettling. To take on the duties of family life, he first had to have a firmly grounded career, and there was no guarantee when or if that would happen. A bewildered Marge returned to New York, saddened that the months of letters and weeks of visits had amounted to nothing. As for Gower, his contract with MGM would prove to be a profound disappointment, yielding only "one rotten picture—*Till the Clouds Roll By*—in which I danced across the screen in strawberry pink hair with Cyd Charisse."[6] This indignity was precisely what marred "Smoke Gets in Your Eyes," the ballroom number with Charisse that marked his screen debut.

The film, a largely fictitious rendering of the life of composer Jerome Kern, was created by the same team Gower and Marge would later join for *Show Boat* (1951): producer Arthur Freed, director George Sidney, and choreographer Robert Alton. Gower's previous association with Alton on Broadway likely influenced his being cast in the film, but just who was responsible for his anomalous hair color is unknown. What is certain is that during the film's preview in Glendale, California, the audience hooted and derided the performer as he waltzed across the screen sporting the bizarre hair. Immediately, Gower rose from his seat and walked out of the theatre. The next day he went to MGM president Louis B. Mayer and bought out his contract. Fortunately, the equally embarrassed producers decided to cut the number to a barely noticeable thirty seconds prior to the film's release.

The damage to his career had been contained, but that brought little consolation. After bouncing from coast to coast experiencing rejection after rejection, this recent humiliation served only to erode his self-confidence further. Upon returning to New York in January 1947, he confided to Jess, now also living in New York, that the fiasco had been the most devastating of his life, forcing him to spend all he had to buy back his contract. Nevertheless, to remain at MGM after such disgrace was to court certain death.

Jess applauded the gutsy decision, but was alarmed by the despondency evident in his friend's physical condition. In his room at the Hotel Windsor, the pallid and gaunt twenty-seven-year-old lay flat on his back with stomach ulcers—the consequence of consuming a year's worth of disappointment. As a rule, he never discussed his health, and Jess, a practicing Christian Scientist, never raised the subject, since he knew Gar had no interest in the religion of his mother or, for that matter, any religion. Though he exhorted his friend to discuss what he was going through, it was useless. Triumphs Gar could easily share, but defeats he buried deep within himself. Maybe the anguish or shame often associated with failure prevented him from expressing his disappointment. Whatever the cause of his reluctance, throughout most of his life he would allow himself no external means to share frustrations or to purge the effects of adverse experiences. No matter how troublesome the hardship, he felt no need for a trusted confidant with whom he could freely voice his feelings. Personal difficulties were private matters to be treated and resolved privately.

Though taciturn about his personal trials, Gower was rather loquacious with Jess on the subject of Marge, whom he recently had resumed seeing. Near the end of his convalescence at the hotel, he introduced her to his best friend and delighted in the way they took to each other. As his spirits lifted, he began an objective assessment of his career. Indeed, a fresh start was necessary. For a whole year now, he had auditioned for others, executing their choreography and following their directions with no success. His work with Jeanne, on the other hand, had consistently flourished because of his artistic control of the act. To avert future disasters, his complete autonomy had to be assured; otherwise he would be forever subject to every director's aesthetic caprices. With no work in the offing, he reluctantly began to consider forming another dance act. Marge was now appearing in Duke Ellington's *Beggar's Holiday,* dancing with Paul Godkin, a young man who had studied with her father and whom the management of the Waldorf-Astoria had approached to start a dance duo. Godkin was sure he and Marge would make a terrific team. When she cannily relayed this news to Gower, the reply was swift: "If you dance with anyone, you dance with me!"[7]

South of Houston Street in Greenwich Village, Gower found an abandoned church, eerie but affordable. He saw it as a combination living area and rehearsal space that could be subleased to various groups at different times as a means of generating income for himself. Despite reservations about the subleasing notion, Marge and Jess joined him in the preparations, investing whole afternoons handsanding the floor. To their amazement, Gower's idea prospered with clients who quickly filled available rental times.

Not long after the opening of *Beggar's Holiday* in late December 1946, Marge left the show to begin daily rehearsals with Gower. Each day, Jess watched with fascination as the intimate bond between the couple, now so apparent off the dance floor, carried over into their work. For Marge and Gower, dance had become a visible expression of their love. Still, despite this evidence of their happiness, Jess was concerned. Much as he loved them both, when Marge confided to him her desire to marry Gower, he could barely restrain the impulse to say, "Don't!" What troubled him specifically was Gower's abrupt and bewildering mood shifts from amicable companion to aloof stranger.

He had first observed the changes a year and a half before when vacationing back in California. He was spending the summer at Laguna Beach and had invited Gar and a friend to join him for the weekend. From the moment of their arrival, Gower was his wildly antic self, plotting good-natured mischief at every turn.

Then, suddenly, he became withdrawn and inaccessible. Not knowing what to make of this, Jess turned to the friend for an explanation. "Well, he's always been like that," was the reply. "He doesn't share his bad times with anyone." Accustomed as he was to the behavior, the friend did not deem it a matter for concern, but Jess had found the sudden changes in temperament jarring, though he never confided so to Marge. Clearly, she and Gar had found contentment in each other; there was no sense in undermining that.[8]

In rehearsal, the dancers were preparing a nightclub act emphasizing the story dances previously introduced with Jeanne that, in time, would become the hallmark of their own work. Gower later explained what was to distinguish their act from the standard fare of the day: "Rather than merely show pretty patterns, we always based every dance on a story—comic, romantic or serious. We eliminated the familiar whirls and twirls, and in their place, fixed within a limited range, we substituted two- and three-dimensional choreographic movements."[9] "Marseilles," the first story dance the choreographer created for the new act, is an example of three-dimensional movement executed within fixed bounds.

"It was about an American sailor," recalls Marge, "who was on a transport during World War II which stopped over in a French port. We always imagined that he was out on leave for a night and wound up alone on a promontory overlooking the sea. He was thinking about his girl back home. I was a French girl thinking about my lover who was also at sea."[10]

To establish the situation, Gower composed monologues, which functioned in the manner of soliloquies, expressing the inner thoughts of the characters Marge and he portrayed. Each monologue was spoken from upstage center at a microphone placed in front of the orchestra on the bandstand. Only the speaker's face was illuminated. The music, a bergerette,[11] conveyed a pensive Gallic atmosphere. The story unfolded first through the sailor's reminiscences of his girl back home. In the midst of his reflection, a spotlight picked up the French girl as she entered downstage, deep in contemplation of her own lover. Small movements—a walk, a turn, an occasional swoop—conveyed not only her longing, but also that of the sailor as he spoke. Perhaps she was a vision of the girl he described, a possibility that strengthened as the two exchanged places and she told of her lover. As she did so, the sailor danced, still lost in his reverie, his movement likewise becoming a physical expression of her words. When the girl ended her reflection, the music grew more intense as she and the sailor danced separately—still unaware of and unrelated to each other. Movement was diagonal, each occasionally encircling the other in the manner of a do-si-do. The climax brought them face to face, where for an instant each saw the long-desired lover in the eyes of the other. They were mistaken. Sadly, they parted and walked to opposite sides of the stage as the music faded. The three-dimensional movement—walks, turns, swoops, and diagonal do-si-dos—was all fixed within the limited range of the characters' self-absorption or failure to "see" each other.

His two-dimensional work within limits is seen in a later number, "By-Play for Drums," from the Broadway revue *3 for Tonight* (1955). As subjects in a scientific experiment measuring the effect of music on the nervous system, he and Marge sat on two stools rapidly extending and contracting their arms and legs to the wild beat of "Kitten on the Keys." The movement conveyed the dimensionality of a cartoon—length and breadth without depth. This, of course, contributed to the number's comic effect. *Bye Bye Birdie*'s (1960) "Shriners' Ballet," with the limbs and faces of Chita Rivera and her companions appearing and disappearing from the top of a long buffet table; *Carnival*'s (1961) "Always, Always You" with James Mitchell thrusting sword upon sword into a basket concealing all but the head of Kaye Ballard; and *Hello, Dolly!*'s (1964) "It Takes a Woman" with Vandergelder's employees popping in and out of the scene from different levels of his Hay and Feed Store would be later examples.

By confining the stage movement only to what was essential, Gower found that simple action, full of dramatic substance and depth, served his choreographic and directorial objectives best. In terms of his act with Marge, he expressed it this way: "We don't go in for strong-arm stuff—holding a girl over your head with one arm. In fact, we only do a couple of lifts a show."[12] But each move contained a telling simplicity: free and unadorned, yet meaningful and expressive.

The rest of the act was comprised of "Margie," a romantic piece that drew upon their relationship; "Three Blind Mice," a dance round in which they initiated the same steps on different bars of music; and "Showing the Town," a series of parodies spoofing the dance styles of Agnes de Mille and Paul Draper. These were combined with "Vaudeville 1910" and "The Missionary and the Maiden," which Gower had previously performed with Jeanne.

He planned to introduce the new act in Montreal atop the Mount Royal Hotel's Normandie Roof where he and Jeanne had enjoyed earlier acclaim. Work on the act was completed just as news reached them of a booking there to begin on April 25, 1947. The new team of Christopher Gower and Marjorie Bell—Gower and Bell for short—was set to debut, but there was one problem. They were broke! Before they could leave New York, there were costume bills and rent to settle, and though the thought of skipping town on their creditors was entirely out of the question, even if they had wanted to, it would not have been possible, for they lacked even the $40 train fare to Montreal. A day or so later, however, a long envelope addressed to Gower arrived via post from MGM—severance pay for the unfulfilled months of his contract. Money from the lion's mouth! Though enough to put them in the black, they still lacked train fare. With a $40 loan from Jess, six routines, and three costumes, they set out for Montreal.

"Smash!" wired Gar to Jess in New York. In less than forty-eight hours, they had won the acclaim of every critic in town. Other bookings quickly followed: the Bradford Roof in Boston, the Municipal Opera in St. Louis, the Palmer House in Chicago. By autumn, they would be ready for their New York debut at the renowned Persian Room of the Plaza Hotel.

Back in New York, Marge received word from choreographer Agnes de Mille that Rodgers and Hammerstein wanted her to do a final audition for a leading role in their new musical, *Allegro*. That evening, Gower met her for dinner at Schrafft's on 52nd Street, listening intently as she explained the dilemma of having to choose between a promising nightclub act and a possible major role in a Broadway musical. He advised her to audition, and even offered to find a substitute for the upcoming Chicago booking upon completion of their St. Louis commitment. If she received the role, he assured her that they could still be married after the closing performance. Marge was hysterical. In all their time together, the subject of marriage had been *verboten,* yet proposing in this manner was so like him. She immediately accepted, declining the callback to remain with him and the act.

Arriving in Chicago, they quickly began formulating plans for a wedding to take place between the conclusion of their current engagement at the Palmer House and their New York opening at the Persian Room as featured act to Liberace. On Sunday, October 5, 1947, they planned to fly to Los Angeles for an afternoon wedding in the garden adjoining the home of Gower's Aunt Patricia and Uncle Bud. In preparation, Betty Champion traveled to Chicago to fit her soon-to-be daughter-in-law for the same dress that she and her sister had worn at their weddings and also to provide some new gowns that Marge needed for the act.

Not since junior high school had Marge been in the company of Betty, who had frequently sewn the ribbons to her dancing shoes in gratitude for the dance scholarship her father had awarded Gower. It was Betty who also had made sure that she enjoyed an occasional evening of dancing at the Del Mar Club under the escort of her son, whom she frequently had to coax into offering an invitation. Such memories would forge a happy rapport between them based on equality and mutual esteem. After all, Marge was not a teenager new to show business needing to be shielded from its corruption, but a twenty-seven-year-old wise to its ways; and Betty, for her part, was mellower and less restrictive now that she had retired from chaperoning. The result was that Betty provided a mother's care and support to Marge, and Marge a daughter's affection that included a deep admiration for the selfless effort it had taken to raise the Champion boys. Betty even found a new identity, thanks to Marge, who affectionately nicknamed her "Buzzy" because of her constant buzzing about. The name soon caught on with family and the many friends she had acquired during retirement. Every now and then, when the very proper Buzzy would let her decorum slip a little to express a playful side not unlike her younger son's, it could be devastatingly funny—like the time she visited Marge and Gower in Chicago shortly before their wedding.[13]

Returning to the Palmer House after rehearsal one afternoon, Marge entered the room she was sharing with Betty on the hotel's eleventh floor and stood there aghast. Leaning from the window, her future mother-in-law was taking careful aim and naughty delight in dropping tomatoes to the street below. When Marge asked what she was doing, she remained undaunted in her mission, replying with her usual propriety: "Well (*Plop!*), it's sort of fun (*Plop!*), don't you think (*Plop!*)?" Gower missed the scene completely because hotel rules separated unmarried men from unmarried women, consigning them to separate sections of the building. It was safer by far for him to be housed on other side of the hotel, next door to Liberace.

Whatever the wedding ceremony of Marjorie Celeste Belcher and Alfred Gower Carlisle Champion lacked in solemnity, it more than made up for in sheer hilarity. During the exchange of vows, Marge looked down for a moment and became so distracted by the big dents in the minister's shoes made by the bunions on his feet that she almost forgot to say, "I do." Minutes later, a minor struggle ensued during the exchange of rings when, to her embarrassment, the bride found that the ring she had purchased was too small for the groom's finger. That did not stop her from trying to make it fit! When her efforts failed, the minister tried, then the best man, Gower's brother, John. They failed. Finally, the groom decided to wear the ring just below the nail of this finger rather than risk injury due to everyone's well-intentioned efforts.

The gold ring with three slim bands that Gower then placed on Marge's finger had the phrase "More than happy time" engraved inside. It expressed his wish for a future even more joyous than the happy time Marge had recorded in her diary the night they first danced together. In a lighter moment during the reception, the groom confided to the bride how fortunate they were to have had a swift wedding, for he doubted that either of them could have withstood the fallout from nuptial announcements bearing the names "Belcher–Champion." Names and jokes about names would always be sources of amusement for the two of them.

A honeymoon was out of the question. On the heels of their Sunday wedding came their television debut on *The Milton Berle Show* on Tuesday, October 7, then their New York debut at the Persian Room where on Wednesday, October 8, they opened as the featured act once more for Liberace. Their new designation as "Marge and Gower Champion" gave Marge top billing yet kept Gower's first and family names together so that they would remain in the public consciousness after he ceased dancing to pursue a directing career. Soon the Champions were headliners themselves, performing with the most popular orchestras of the day at Washington, D.C.'s Mayflower Hotel in November and, later, the Boston and Detroit Statler Hotels in January and February 1948.

It was around this time that Gower created another story dance, one that in time would become the signature piece of the act. He called it "County Fair." In it, he and Marge portrayed two youngsters who arrive at a fair to find it closed for the season. To ease the disappointment of the girl, the boy creates an imaginary fair of his own. Picking up a discarded pennant, he becomes a drum major with baton, then a carnival barker with a cane pointing out the attractions of a make-believe midway. The girl now joins him in the game, inviting him to test his strength by taking mallet in hand and striking a blow at the base of a tower to ring the bell at the top. Despite great effort, he fails. To his amazement, she succeeds with no effort at all. They take in other amusements—a bowling match that he loses and she wins and a nickelodeon where she seduces him away from a "girlie picture" by employing her own wiles. Eventually, they themselves become the major attraction of the fair, performing a series of steps, lifts, and leaps that bring the number to a dazzling finale. The motif here, which he first used in "The Merry-Go-Round Broke Down" with Jeanne, would continue to figure prominently in his work until it emerged as a full-blown musical for the stage—*Carnival.*

Each club date presented different problems in dancing space, music, and lighting. Gower designed each number to evoke a distinct mood, which Marge and he worked diligently to achieve. Facial expressions had to convey the correct emotion, body positions the exact meaning, music and lighting the proper atmosphere for every number in the act. No detail escaped his eye. He spent as much time rehearsing music and lighting cues as he did for the performance. Fade-outs, fade-ins, no shadows, long shadows, or vaudeville glare—everything had to fit the mood. As one critic expressed it, "Marge and Gower Champion's is one of the most carefully planned acts in show business."[14]

Their program, a mixture of youthful charm and elegant movement, was long for a dancing act—a half-hour—but singing, clowning, and dialogue filled in the gaps between numbers, and helped to keep the perspiration down and their breathing and voices under control. Huffing and puffing from one number to the next would have detracted from their performance, so they learned to control breathing by keeping the diaphragm still. It worked well until the perspiration started popping out all over. By that time, they were grateful for those breaks between numbers, especially when giving midsummer performances in stifling and humid clubs.

Soon they hired their own accompanist and musical director, Richard Pribor

(Priborsky), who took charge of the various orchestras in each of the clubs they played. Since his earliest performances with Jeanne, Gower had never forgotten what it was like to be at the mercy of a different conductor for each engagement. One time when performing with bandleader Eddie Duchin, the musicians were following the dance team's special arrangement of Rachmaninoff's Prelude in C-Sharp Minor, while the conductor, who played only by ear, was directing what he thought he was hearing. Duchin would skip entire bars of music unwittingly, leaving Gower and Jeanne to improvise until they could find their musical bearings.[15]

Pribor's direction, by comparison, was as precise as Gower's choreography, insuring a quality musical performance faithful to the team's orchestrations and tempo. Pribor also composed the scores for new routines Gower would choreograph after several intensive work sessions with him and editorial reviews by Marge. "When I get an idea," he explained, "I get so excited it gets hold of me and runs away with me. After Dick Pribor and I work on it a couple of days, I do it for Marge. By then I'm too close to it, but Marge comes in with a whole fresh point of view and I'm anxious for her reactions. If she says, 'This doesn't feel right here,' or 'This I don't like,' then I will readily agree with her. If I am strong enough to argue her down, then I'll believe I'm right."[16]

No matter who was right, both agreed on the need to constantly maintain focus in an atmosphere where falling trays, mad laughs, or table talk could compromise that special lift or trick they had worked months to perfect. "It's something you have to learn to live with if you don't want to make a psychiatrist rich," observed Gower. "Even so, I wouldn't mind it so much if I could just find a busboy who'd drop his tray in tempo."[17]

FOUR

Broadway, Televisionland, Hollywood

1948–1950

With the act successfully launched, Gower now focused on a longtime goal: becoming a Broadway choreographer. The opportunity came rather unexpectedly in early January 1948 when producer George Nichols III and librettist-director Bert Shevelove offered him a revue called *Small Wonder*. He accepted the position pending completion of his Midwest tour with Marge. The tour proceeded as planned until the Champions returned to Chicago's Palmer House that March. By then, pain in Marge's right knee had become so severe that she retired directly to bed following the final performance. Remaining engagements had to be canceled because of a cyst on her kneecap that required immediate surgery. The newlyweds were without savings or residence, so Gower's father invited them to stay at his own home, where Marge went to recover after the operation.

During his service in the Coast Guard, Gower had started to foster a relationship with John that was warmly received. As a result, he soon realized that his father was not the person his mother had spoken of so disparagingly. The bond that was forming between them was strengthened by the father's pride in the son, who delighted in his father's recognition.

Leaving Chicago, Gower drove Marge to Los Angeles, where they spent the remainder of her convalescence in his mother's care. Betty's unsolicited advice, a constant source of irritation to him, was the price he paid for assuming control of his world and consigning her to a tiny part of it. Betty deeply resented the restriction. Apart from creating Marge's gowns for the act, she no longer had any real role in Gower's life, professional or otherwise. After years of struggling to produce opportunities for him, she now felt he no longer valued her. Attempts to gain his recognition by volunteering advice on the management of his professional and personal affairs only alienated him more. Gower, who had dutifully surrendered to Betty's utterly engulfing control throughout his youth, now made certain that he was in control of his adulthood. To achieve this, he distanced himself from her as much as possible—right up to the day of her death.[1]

With Marge unable to perform and *Small Wonder* rehearsals not due to start until late July, Gower grew more and more restive until music director George Bauer, a *Tars and Spars* alumnus, invited him to act as consultant for a revue scheduled to open at the Las Palmas Theatre in mid-June. Bauer's "consultant" began attending rehearsals, soon advanced to choreographer, and by opening night was responsible for most of the actual direction of *Lend an Ear*.

Billed as an "intimate revue" with sketches, music, and lyrics by Charles Gaynor, it had originally been commissioned by Frederick Burleigh, director of the Pittsburgh Playhouse, where it premiered in April 1941. Plans for a Broadway production were abandoned when the author was drafted into the military. Following the war, Gaynor and actor William Eythe staged a successful revival at a summer theatre in Cohasset, Massachusetts. When Eythe later offered to produce it on the West Coast, Gaynor accepted, and by May 1948 a Los Angeles production was in rehearsal.[2]

In addition to Eythe, the twenty-one-member cast included dancer Gene Nelson and a lanky, wide-eyed blonde with a vocal range from deep foghorn to squeaky hinge: Carol Channing. Marge, who assisted Gower with the show, had instantly recognized Channing's comic flair and urged him to audition her. Gower found a whole host of roles for Channing, including a publicity-driven socialite desperately striving to live up to tabloid gossip and a Lily Pons-like diva reduced to "Words Without Song" when her bankrupt opera company is forced to perform sans orchestra.

Gower's choreography showed remarkable versatility: a gunfire-filled comic ballet entitled "Santo Domingo"; the wistful "Friday Dancing Class," in which boys and girls struggled with the awkwardness of their first attempted romance; and "I'm Not in Love," a conventional love ballad with a Freudian twist. Here, employer William Eythe serenaded secretary Linda Ware as manifestations of his alter ego (dancers Gene Nelson and Bob Scheerer) bounded about the stage expressing his inner feelings. But the evening's *tour de force* was the first act finale, "The Gladiola Girl," a burlesque of 1920s musical comedies in the tradition of *Good News, Oh, Kay!*, and *No, No, Nanette*.

Gaynor's "mini-musical" exploited every known convention of the genre: flappers, lounge lizards, Long Island estates, bootlegging, and mistaken identity. Gower's staging added to the frivolity with parodies of the "Varsity Drag" ("Doin' the Old Yahoo Step") and "Tea for Two" ("In Our Teeny Little Weeny Nest"). With the enthusiastic response of the Los Angeles critics encouraging the producers to launch a Broadway run, Gower flew to New York on July 26, 1948, to prepare *Small Wonder* for its opening at the Coronet Theatre.

His entry into the Broadway choreographers' circle would be inauspicious because *Small Wonder* director Bert Shevelove firmly controlled the proceedings, leaving him little opportunity to develop the creative staging that had distinguished *Lend an Ear.* As the weeks progressed, the director continued to edit the dances, and the more he did, the more the choreographer chafed under his direction. The few instances when Gower actually won Shevelove's approval came only after a long and arduous battle.[3] Though *Small Wonder* received tepid notices upon opening on September 15, 1948, and ran for only 134 performances, its choreographer earned some favorable comments. One reporter declared the dance numbers "a credit to Gower Champion,"[4] while another found them "pretty, sophisticated, and restrained."[5] After the opening of *Small Wonder,* the Champions played a return engagement at the Persian Room. By the end of their run, plans for the Broadway production of *Lend an Ear* had solidified, and at once, Gower prepared for its December 16 bow at the National Theatre.

So greatly did the choreography of *Lend an Ear* contrast with that of *Small Wonder* that one critic asked, "Was Gower Champion saving his best stuff . . . for this show or was *Small Wonder* just a second thought which he cared too little about?"[6] With *Lend an Ear,* Gower emerged a more generally versatile choreographer than critics had imagined, displaying greater skill with group direction. Furthermore, the dances had more substance with dynamics and phrasing of movements that were better focused than in *Small Wonder.* While remaining completely in character with the revue's themes, he had created patterns that were fresh, novel, and often complex.[7]

Lend an Ear was the direct result of lessons learned from his nightclub work, especially the story dances. Like his acts with Marge and Jeanne, it relied on youth, verve, abundant humor, impeccable taste, and imagination for its effects, rather than on the customary opulence of most revues. His exquisite marriage of innovative staging with the material also distinguished the show from run-of-the-mill counterparts. Virtually everything in it was dependent on choreography that was staged with brilliance and extraordinary vitality. Gower had made the show dance, and for it, he was honored with the Tony, Donaldson, and *Dance Magazine* awards as the Best Choreographer of the 1948–49 season.

In late fall of 1948, television producer Max Liebman, another *Tars and Spars* associate, offered the Champions a contract for weekly appearances on a live ninety-minute broadcast sponsored by the Admiral Television Company. *The Admiral Broadway Revue,* later called *Your Show of Shows,* was television's first variety show and starred comedians Sid Caesar and Imogene Coca. The Champions made their debut on January 28, 1949, with two numbers: "The Night Has a Thousand Eyes" and "Dance with Me," the opening number to their nightclub act.

The Revue's "new-to-television" variety format generated extensive press coverage. Even *Life* magazine sent a crew of photographers and reporters to cover rehearsals. In April, when the Champions performed for the White House Correspondents' Dinner in Washington, D.C., President Truman singled out their performance, and hailed them as the personification of American youth and spirit. The endorsement prompted *Life* publisher Henry Luce in attendance to feature the dance team on the magazine's cover. The resulting publicity brought the Champions national attention.

With *The Admiral Broadway Revue,* Gower learned to adapt his work to a new medium—one still very much in its infancy. As one reviewer commented, "The team of Marge and Gower Champion is without question one of the most refreshing, imaginative and crisp duos to grace the dance floor in many a day and, when it is assisted by better camera work, should show to even better advantage."[8]

To exhibit dance effectively, television would require staging techniques distinct from the intimacy of the nightclub or the spectacle of the Broadway stage. Working with *Revue* choreographer James Starbuck, Gower quickly learned that large groups of dancers were best displayed while moving in unison, and that more intricate ensemble work was most effective when limited to smaller groups of four, five, or six dancers. Likewise, dance duets in which partners were distanced more than five feet from each other were ineffective because of the extreme long shot the camera had to make. Reducing the distance between the dancers made for a stronger picture. Finally, use of a close-up could capture subtleties of movement and expression often lost on the stage.[9]

Gower studied these and other techniques and, in the coming decade on programs such as the *Ed Sullivan, Perry Como, Jack Benny,* and *Dinah Shore* shows, employed them to advantage in his performances with Marge. Eventually, the major networks would seek his directing and staging expertise for their musicals, dramas, and special presentations. These experiences would likewise influence his staging for the musical theatre. In *Carnival,* he introduced the small all-dancer corps of four in "Sword, Rose, and Cape," and for the title number in *Hello, Dolly!,* he used both the position of the male chorus and a dramatic shift in lighting to bring the audience in for a close-up on Carol Channing during the verse of the song.[10]

The allure of television, however, soon turned to delusion for the team as the manic pace of *The Revue* caught up with them. They were losing weight, working seven days a week, and scrambling to come up with new ideas or each performance. After creating thirty-two routines—two a week for sixteen weeks—they left. "It was the same grind, week after week," said Gower. "At the end of the show,

I'd say to Marge, 'What'll we do next week?' and we'd start all over again trying to devise something new and smart, going into our grueling practice routine once again."[11] There were no regrets. Besides, Gower had just been invited to choreograph a major Broadway musical.

Producer Herman Levin had seen *Lend an Ear* and was truly impressed with the choreographer's 1920s musical parody, "The Gladiola Girl," and its leading lady, Carol Channing. With Channing already slated to play the gold-digging flapper in the new musical he was co-producing with scenic designer Oliver Smith, Levin was certain that Champion would bring the proper spirit to the dances and invited him to stage *Gentleman Prefer Blondes* (1949). Gower was ecstatic, for it all but guaranteed the continued momentum of his career as a Broadway choreographer. Still, the backers needed to be sold on the idea, so Levin and composer Jule Styne brought them to see the team's performance at Bill Miller's Riviera in Fort Lee, New Jersey, on June 14, 1949.

The backers' enthusiasm convinced Levin to immediately draw up the contract; meanwhile, Gower and Marge freed their schedule of club bookings for the next six months to do the musical's rehearsals and pre-Broadway tour. Just as Gower was about to sign, co-producer Smith, who had been out of town, arrived and announced that he had already promised the position to Agnes de Mille. Because Smith was a longtime friend of Marge's and an admirer of Gower's work, he himself undertook the unhappy task of breaking the news to the couple. It was a bitter disappointment to them, especially after having just moved into a new apartment. Gower's response was icy: he never wanted to speak to Smith again. With no other choice, he and Marge resumed performances at the Riviera, and then flew to Los Angeles to headline at the Mocambo on August 14.[12]

"You danced whenever you could get a job," Gower later recalled, "and you went wherever the job happened to be. We finally worked our way west into the Mocambo, a tiny place about the size of a four-room apartment, full of posts and pillars—it was awful, but we needed the money. Like a B movie, we were an immediate smash and it was New Year's Eve every night."[13] If the Champions had any apprehension about how the act would play on their home turf, they need not have feared. Both *Lend an Ear* and broadcasts of *The Admiral Broadway Revue* had been seen by many in their home town, including Clark Gable, Dan Dailey, Joan Crawford, June Haver, Milton Berle, Veloz and Yolanda, Tony Martin, Cyd Charisse, and Michael Todd—all of whom were in attendance opening night to cheer them on.

The Champions really gave them something to cheer about. "Rarely has a dance duo so moved a Hollywood nightclub audience as did Marge and Gower Champion on their opening night," wrote Lee Zhito of *Billboard*. "Under their spell, dance takes on a third dimensional quality and becomes a living, vibrant entity glowing with laughter and love."[14] *Variety* hailed them as "the most accomplished dance team playing the nitery circuit these days," highlighting the "prodigious skill" binding together "a sheaf of humorous, exciting and colorful moods."

The praise of the Los Angeles critics brought the team numerous offers, one of which was a film for Paramount Studios, *Mr. Music* (1950), in which they would appear with Bing Crosby. Gower was also to choreograph and direct the dance sequences. But it was MGM president Louis B. Mayer himself, a frequent patron, who made the offer of their dreams. "We signed with MGM because they gave us a two-picture-a-year deal, and that had to do with Mr. Mayer as well," recalls Marge. "Arthur Freed wanted us very much, and I already knew a lot of people at MGM. It was the ideal studio for us. We were allowed to do everything that we could fit in between the two pictures—Vegas, New York shows, anything at all. Except for television—absolutely no television."[15] Following the completion of *Mr. Music,* the Champions signed with MGM. The irony of the occasion was not lost on Gower, who secretly delighted in being courted by the same studio from which he had re-signed only two years before.

Mr. Music, an adaptation of Samson Raphaelson's play *Accent on Youth,* was an agreeable but thin vehicle for Bing Crosby that did not exactly stretch his artistic range. Directed by Richard Haydn with songs by Johnny Burke and Jimmy Van Heusen, it told of a songwriter (Crosby) whose golfing interests prevail over his composition of a new score until a coed from his alma mater (Nancy Olson), hired as his secretary by his producer (Charles Coburn), succeeds in curing his writer's block. Performers Peggy Lee, Groucho Marx, and Dorothy Kirsten also appeared but, like the Champions, were unrelated to the plot.

Gower, who had been told to prepare three extended dances—two duets and a large-scale production number—staged the team's dance sequences, which were filmed late in 1949. In the end, only one—"Life Is So Peculiar," which comes in the middle of the film at a party given by Crosby to celebrate his completion of a new score—made it into the movie. The two others were consigned to the cutting room floor and have not been seen since: a ballroom piece for a nightclub sequence (the end of which is used as a segue into that scene) and a production number for the film's finale. This was to take place in the theatre of Crosby's alma mater, where Olson was to present a number from the new score she had inspired him to write. Though the actual film footage has long been lost, surviving still photographs indicate that this was a story dance about a wedding in which the bride and groom exit boarding a train. Trains, one of Gower's favorite motifs, would figure prominently in works ahead. At a time when automobiles and airplanes were rapidly becoming the country's chief means of transportation, trains evoked simpler times, when Gower traveled from city to city during the road days of his youth. No longer titans of the American landscape, railroads would be used as a point of reference in his musicals, glorifying the excitement they once stirred.

The one number that remained in the film, "Life Is So Peculiar," takes place at a party in the living room of the songwriter's penthouse and is introduced by Crosby and Peggy Lee, accompanied by Gower at the piano. A dance then follows in which he and Marge use various furnishings in the room to develop the playful mood established by the singers—dancing atop the piano, leaping over or bouncing off an overstuffed chair, pursuing each other around a card table, then swinging from the awning poles of a terrace roof garden. The angular pole-swinging was to become a Champion choreographic signature used again and again—even in his final work, *42nd Street,* for the "Dames" number, in which chorines frolicked on a huge Art Deco jungle gym.

Upon completion of *Mr. Music,* the Champions awaited notification from MGM concerning the first picture under their new contract, but since the studio did not as yet have a suitable vehicle, it released them for other work. In the interim, they hosted the finals of the Harvest Moon Ball in New York and Chicago, and then accepted a four-week engagement at the Peacock Court of the Mark Hopkins Hotel in San Francisco, where they opened on February 5, 1950. Then an extraordinary opportunity came via the president of RKO Pictures, billionaire Howard Hughes, who asked them to coach and choreograph star Janet Leigh in her musical film debut. By now, MGM had the dancers slated for *Show Boat,* but with the rest of the casting not finalized, they were allowed to accept. On loan to RKO for nearly a year, the Champions worked eight hours a day with Leigh on a sound stage Hughes had rented at Goldwyn Studios. He never set foot on his own RKO lot out of fear it would bring him bad luck.

For Gower especially, this was a chance not only to make a fine musical performer of a talented actress, but also to develop his choreographic skills. To date, all of his dances—whether for nightclub acts, revues, or films—had been created under pressure; his work during the summer of 1950, by contrast, was leisurely and without deadline.

One morning, after three weeks and the completion of about half a number, the film's director, James V. Kern, informed him that Mr. Hughes wanted to see how Miss Leigh was progressing. Champion, usually intolerant of having his work viewed "in progress," on this occasion welcomed having the big boss as an audience. The next morning Hughes dropped in for a few minutes, said "fine," and left.

The Champions continued at Goldwyn for months, at a cost to Hughes of $1,000 a week in rental alone. Though he visited twice more, the script remained unfinished and the leading man remained unsigned, as well as the three female dancers who were to support Leigh. Shortly after MGM recalled them for the filming of *Show Boat,* the Champions went to Hughes for a parting conference that caused quite a stir.

"What are you so upset about?" Hughes inquired with a shrug. "Why are you so interested in that picture? Why, you two could work for me forever."

"Yeah," retorted Gower, "work forever and nothing is produced. That job meant so much to us professionally and to go through it all for nothing."[16] Within weeks of their departure, RKO announced Tony Martin as Leigh's leading man, Ann Miller, Gloria De Haven, and Barbara Lawrence as her three supporting dancers, and Sid Silvers and Hal Kanter as writers for what became *Two Tickets to Broadway* (1951).

The Champions' encounter with the eccentric Hughes had taught them an important lesson. "Hollywood is a place where you can get fed up to the Adam's apple or just laugh," commented Marge. "It's best to just laugh it off."[17] The pair laughed all the way to the bank. With the proceeds from the Hughes affair, they purchased a house on Woodrow Wilson Drive in Los Angeles, which Gower suitably dubbed "the house that Howard Hughes built," and for once, there was no traveling, no hotel rooms, and no more worries about money now that they had steady income from MGM.

FIVE

MGM

Now with time and a home in which to entertain, the Champions could gather their extended family for holiday celebrations—festive times with the occasional controversies common to all families, like tensions between in-laws or dismay over Marge's exchange of a suckling pig for the traditional Christmas turkey. Few relatives, however, were ever entirely comfortable with their show business talk. After almost five years, it became clear that their attempts at family unification were going nowhere; by then it was time to start a family of their own.[1] Their relationship with MGM would endure for about the same time. First featured in *Show Boat* (1951) and *Lovely to Look At* (1952), they would soon rise to starring roles in *Everything I Have Is Yours* (1952) and *Give a Girl a Break* (1953) before concluding with *Jupiter's Darling* (1955).

The studio's Technicolor treatment of Jerome Kern and Oscar Hammerstein II's 1927 classic, *Show Boat,* was the third time the musical had been adapted for the screen. Universal had produced a bowdlerized silent film version in 1929, and in 1936, a "talkie" more faithful to Hammerstein's libretto in which many members of the original Broadway cast reprised their roles. Initially, the MGM version was to have included Frank Morgan as Captain Andy Hawks, Ethel Barrymore as Parthy Hawks, and Judy Garland as Julie Laverne, in addition to Howard Keel as Gaylord Ravenal, Kathryn Grayson as Magnolia Hawks, William Warfield as Joe, and the Champions as Ellie May Chipley and Frank Schultz.[2] By the time the film was ready to go into production, however, Morgan had died and was replaced by Joe E. Brown, Agnes Moorehead was substituted for Barrymore, and Ava Gardner was cast in place of the ailing Garland.

Producer Arthur Freed compressed the time span of Hammerstein's plot, which traced the lives of three generations of performers working on board the *Cotton Blossom*. He also altered some of the characterization. Hammerstein had portrayed the dance team of Ellie May Chipley and Frank Schultz as a pair of second-string hoofers. Freed disagreed. He and director George Sidney preferred a first-rate pair and found exactly that in Marge and Gower, whose two big dances, "I Might Fall Back on You" and "Life Upon the Wicked Stage," were both winners—the result of a happy collaboration with *Streets of Paris* choreographer Robert Alton.

"I Might Fall Back on You" is presented as a performance on the *Cotton Blossom*'s stage. Ellie and Frank sing the number to each other while sitting back-to-back on a small garden love seat, which pivots as their feet push against the floor. The revolving seat is literally the axis expressing the relationship between the wary maiden and would-be suitor they portray, as well as their own offstage romance. Gower later used similar means to express relationships between characters in his stage musicals. In *Bye Bye Birdie,* Dick Van Dyke pushed Chita Rivera around on a luggage cart as he sang "Rosie," and in *I Do! I Do!,* Robert Preston spun Mary Martin around on a revolving bed for "I Love My Wife."

While Frank moves the seat clockwise, Ellie sings of her objections to his advances; then she pushes the seat counterclockwise, as he sings back his defense. The movement emphasizes the friendly battle of wits between the two conveyed in the lyrics of the song. At the conclusion of the vocal, the love seat slides into the stage right wings as the dance commences. Frank merrily teases Ellie, stealing her parasol and tossing it into the air far from her reach. He returns the parasol, doffs his hat, hurls it into the wings stage right, then turns and catches a cane thrown to him from the wings stage left. As the music climaxes, Ellie finally relents and joins Frank in a cakewalk, which culminates in a series of fifty-seven hitch kicks.

The dance firmly establishes several points essential to Freed's version. Early in the film, Captain Andy comments that Frank "is stuck on Ellie." The number reveals that the feeling is mutual. The quality of the performance also suggests that Ellie and Frank are destined for more sophisticated establishments. "I Might Fall Back on You," therefore, prepares us for their later appearance as a married couple and their New Year's Eve performance in one of Chicago's high-class nightclubs, the Trocadero, where they present their second piece, "Life upon the Wicked Stage."

When Ellie enters the Trocadero's stage as a disenchanted actress and sings "Life upon the wicked stage ain't ever what a girl supposes," she is actually commenting on the film's previous scene in which show boat actress Magnolia Ravenal has been deserted by her co-actor husband, Gaylord. As Ellie continues, the source of her discontent (and Magnolia's) becomes apparent—rejection by the male "types" who frequent the stage world. Stage door johnnies, roués, gift-bearing rich old men, and melodramatic heroes (all comically played by Frank) fail to take notice of her. Summoning her determination, she plays the coquette, dropping her handkerchief to catch the attention of passers-by. Though she fails on the first attempt, she later succeeds when a reluctant young man, again played by Frank, retrieves the handkerchief with his right foot. Astounded, Ellie drops it again. The gentleman gives his own to her. She swoons, and then quickly rallies to work her charms on him once more. This time, the charm works. As they dance, he gradually drops his defenses until completely won over by her. To her delight, Ellie finds life upon the wicked stage not so disheartening after all.

When *Show Boat* opened at Radio City Music Hall on July 19, 1951, there was abundant praise for the Champions as well as for the film. They were described as dazzling, wonderfully accomplished dancers whose numbers were fresh, original, and artistically executed. Critics found no lack of the elements that go into a superlative film. Beauty, warmth, and artistry served to make this new version of *Show Boat* everything a fan's heart could desire.[3] Both performers were thrilled with the critical response, but Gower was especially delighted with the handsome way in which Freed, Sidney, and Alton had framed the dancing. Ironically, the dancers almost did not appear together.

Mayer, impressed early on with the efforts of his new dance team, called them to his office one day after rehearsal. "He spent a few minutes telling Gower how he must keep me simple and pure," explains Marge. "I was thirty years old but didn't look it. He was raving on and kept saying, 'She's as light as the breeze,' and kept blowing his cheeks out to indicate the breeze."[4]

Warm-up over, L.B. made his pitch: he wanted Marge to play the lead opposite Gene Kelly in *An American in Paris*. "At this point, I didn't know the man," says Marge. "He was so funny and absolutely charming, and he was trying to talk me into doing something he hadn't even discussed with Gene Kelly."[5] She and Gower were a team, and no one, not even L. B. Mayer, could have one without the other. "It was Gene Kelly's musical and there was nothing in it for Gower, so I said I didn't want to do the film. So that's what we told our agent."[6]

From *Show Boat* director George Sidney, Gower learned that the staging of each number in a musical must not only develop characters and plot, but also be consistent with the film as a whole. Sidney firmly believed in subordinating the various elements of production to the story. In his earlier works, notably *The Harvey Girls* (1946) and *Annie Get Your Gun* (1950), the staging of the musical numbers had been equally integral to the plot. Gower had employed a similar technique in his story dances and revue work, as yet had found no opportunity to do so with the book musical. MGM gave him that chance. His work with Sidney and Alton on *Show Boat* and director Mervyn LeRoy and choreographer Hermes Pan on *Lovely to Look At* validated his thoughts on musical staging and prepared him for the plot-allied numbers he would later create for film and stage. He emerged from these experiences convinced that "a dance number in a musical should advance, or at least enhance, the plot. No matter how cleverly conceived, it should never go off by itself and drift away from the mainstream of the show."[7]

Following the filming of *Show Boat,* Gower returned to New York in January 1951 as choreographer for *Make a Wish.* Harry Rigby and Jule Styne produced the show in association with Alexander H. Cohen. All three would later figure prominently in Gower's musicals of the early 1970s: Rigby as producer of *Irene,* Styne as composer of *Prettybelle* and *Sugar,* and Cohen as producer of *Prettybelle. Make a Wish* was based on Ferenc Molnar's comedy *The Good Fairy,* and featured songs by Hugh Martin and a book by Preston Sturges. Nanette Fabray starred as a lovely but mischievous young orphan named Janette who breaks from her guardians to enjoy the bustling, glittering life of bohemian Paris. Romanced by middle-aged Marius Frigo (Melville Cooper), one of the wealthiest men of the city, Janette ultimately falls in love with Paul Dumont (Stephen Douglas), a struggling young law student. Companions Ricky (Harold Lang) and Poupette (Helen Gallagher), who aid and abet Janette's exploits, received a good portion of Gower's choreography.

Various locales of the city—the Café Victor, the Folies Labiche (which opened with a partially raised curtain to reveal dancing feet, an idea the choreographer would later use on a grander scale in *42nd Street*), a Students' Ball, and the Galerie Napoleon Department Store—provided settings for a remarkable array of dances. But dances alone, no matter how well conceived, do not guarantee success, a fact that the press underscored after the disastrous Philadelphia opening. Immediately, *Guys and Dolls* librettist Abe Burrows was brought in to rescue a musical that suffered from John C. Wilson's lack of direction and Sturges's humorless book. As he combined forces with Burrows, Gower also turned to Jess, whose solid story sense proved so helpful that he would often consult him as an unofficial "devil's advocate" on future productions. "Gar's" work on *Make a Wish* had greatly impressed Jess, by now making his own mark in the theatre as assistant to directors Elia Kazan and Joshua Logan, while launching a career as playwright and novelist.

With the combined effort of the three the first act of *Make a Wish* improved remarkably in no time, but the rewrite of Act II never happened because Burrows suddenly disappeared, hauled off to Washington by federal agents to testify before the House Committee on Un-American Activities. With no recourse, the show went to New York, where it opened at the Winter Garden Theatre on April 18, 1951, and folded after 103 performances.

Happily, Gower's choreography was received most enthusiastically. Though the first act ballet, "Students Ball," was lauded as one of the truly exciting interludes of the season, it was "The Sale," with its pack of voracious bargain hunters wreaking mayhem in the Galerie Napoleon Department Store, that alone was worth the price of admission. Frenetic searches for bargains, edgy attempts to try on hats, greedy rummaging through merchandise, and the unctuous skill of shoplifting were among the wry details that the choreographer sketched in with acrid mimicry. The cartoon had a whirling low-comedy finish in which the store's pompous manager received his due when customers suspended him from a revolving ceiling fan. "The Sale" was compared with the best of Jerome Robbins's ballets: as hilarious as the "Keystone Kops" number in *High Button Shoes* and imaginative as the "Uncle Tom's Cabin" episode in *The King and I*.[8]

Given the phenomenal response to the choreography, it is indeed lamentable that Gower would not attempt another full-scale musical until 1960 with *Bye Bye Birdie*. Nevertheless, *Make a Wish* was a significant step in his evolution as choreographer and director. In it, he conquered the choreographic demands of the book musical with expanded and more animated versions of his story dances tailored to character and plot. Finding the humor within narrative situations like the department store sale, he exploited it with staging that energized the production. Comic story dances like "The Sale" would soon inspire others: the "Shriners' Ballet" in *Bye Bye Birdie,* the "Waiters' Gallop" in *Hello, Dolly!,* and the "School Yard Ballet" in *The Happy Time*.

Returning to Hollywood in the fall of 1951, he continued to develop this method in his films with Marge. Working with Fred Astaire's choreographer, Hermes Pan, on *Lovely to Look At* (1952), a remake of Jerome Kern and Otto Harbach's *Roberta* with Howard Keel, Kathryn Grayson, Red Skelton, and Ann Miller, he developed one number that bears special mention for the unique way it expresses the relationship between characters. "I Won't Dance" takes place in a couturière's workroom where Gower, as American tourist Jerry Ralby, playfully utilizes tools of the trade—dress forms, tape measures, stools, and racks of clothing—to conquer the suspicions of proprietress Clarisse, portrayed by Marge. The use of properties to define or clarify relationships would become another key feature of Gower's staging. In *I Do! I Do!,* he would fill the stage with children's clothes, toys, and games during "Love Isn't Everything" to signal the approaching parenthood of characters Agnes and Michael.

Also distinctive of "I Won't Dance" is the smooth and facile manner with which the dancers employ the props—the result of hours upon hours of practice not possible in other entertainment venues. "Quite often we're not allowed sufficient time to perfect a routine if it's for a TV show, a theatre engagement or a special performance," Gower once explained. "Oh, the number may look swell to the audience, but it doesn't satisfy Marge or myself. In motion pictures we are given the chance to work out every detail until the production is thoroughly polished. The result is worth every hour spent—to us and to the audience."[9]

The detailed and thoroughly polished nature of his work with Marge at MGM carried over into his stage work, planning and rehearsing performers' use of props, whether part of a dance or not. Frequently, this would require that he practice with the prop himself until skilled in its use. Only then could he understand firsthand not just the challenge but particularly the danger to which the performer might be subjected, be it swords thrust through a box containing the comedienne (*Carnival*), gigantic butterfly wings for a comic free-for-all (*Hello, Dolly!*), or multicolored corkscrew slides for bathing beauties (*Mack and Mabel*).

Two other sequences in *Lovely to Look At* accent the art of the Champions. "Smoke Gets in Your Eyes," a stunning ballroom piece performed amid a star-studded Milky Way, perfectly expresses the romance of the characters they portray. This contrasts greatly with the fiery sensuality they project in "The Fashion Show," the lavish spectacle that concludes the film. Here, Gower, attired all in black with red gloves, is a sinister figure with designs on a diamond bracelet worn by Marge, a fashion model adorned in a red gown, who shrewdly spurns his advances.

With co-starring roles in three films to their credit and plans for their own starring vehicle now under way, Gower and Marge were becoming more and more a part of Hollywood society. When the Academy of Motion Picture Arts and Sciences invited them to present the Oscar for Best Art Direction on March 20, 1952, at its annual awards ceremony, it was a sign that they truly had arrived.

Everything I Have Is Yours (1952), originally announced as a Technicolor musical to star Red Skelton and Vera-Ellen,[10] eventually became the first film to star the Champions, who played Chuck and Pamela Hubbard, a husband-and-wife dance team similar to themselves. Following the Hubbards' sensational Broadway debut, Pamela learns that she is pregnant and must retire from dancing for the next nine months. In the meantime, Chuck finds a new partner, Sybil Meriden (Monica Lewis), and continues performing. Throughout her pregnancy, whatever pain Pamela feels, Chuck also experiences symbiotically—hence the title of the film. Conflict ensues as a result of Pamela's desire to return to the stage and Chuck's insistence that she remain home to care for their daughter. Though the marriage comes critically close to divorce, the reconciliation of the pair provides a cheerful finale.

Whatever the screenplay by producer George Wells lacked in inspiration was offset by the performances of the Champions and the numbers that Gower created with co-choreographer Nick Castle—numbers he wanted to be integral to the story, such as it was. While reading the script, he noticed that no number had been conceived as part of the plot; rather, each took place in the context of a performance given either in a theatre or at a private party. He suggested to Castle a dance duet to take place early in the picture as the couple walked home from the theatre after rehearsing into the early morning hours. With the approval of Wells and director Robert Z. Leonard, songwriters Johnny Green, Rex Newman, and Douglas Furber composed a number befitting the scene. Gower and Castle then went to work on the staging for "Like Monday Follows Sunday."

In the search for an incident to trigger the sequence, the two explored a multitude of ideas: the Hubbards being chased by a squad car, lifted by a freight elevator, even squirted by a janitor hosing down a sidewalk. The final solution was the least complex: a casual walk down a street. Following the rehearsal, it would begin with the pair exiting the stage door of the theatre, going through an alley, then out onto a street. Along their path would be various levels and properties around which choreography could be shaped for Chuck to ease Pamela's opening-night jitters by vowing to follow her "Like Monday Follows Sunday." A section of the back lot was prepared and shooting scheduled over a number of days because of the complicated nature of the choreography. In order to control the lighting and create the illusion of night, an immense black-velour tent was draped over the entire set.

The result exemplifies Gower's ability not only to use narrative situations and actions as a basis for choreography, but also to build a number imperceptibly. As the couple walks down the alley, an anxious Pamela maintains a brisk pace, while Chuck attempts to raise her spirits by doing comic turns as a derelict, bellhop, and acrobat and playing with lanterns and broken umbrellas. The walking becomes small jetés, and the jetés, turns and lifts. Once Chuck leaps onto a loading dock, the number has grown from walking into a full-fledged dance in which the pair mimic mannequins in store windows, accidentally trip a burglar alarm, and cavort over subway gratings. When they arrive at their apartment, the dance ends as it began, with the two going quietly off together.

The number serves to establish the identities of the characters as well as their relationship, thus achieving Gower's goal to advance the narrative by means of the choreography. Furthermore, so imperceptibly does the dance rise out of the narrative situation that its appearance is subtle, not obvious as in most musicals of the day. Many of his numbers for Broadway musicals would begin in this fashion, likewise building gradually to rousing climaxes. "When Mabel Comes in the Room" from *Mack and Mabel* (1974) would grow from two people intimately sharing coffee and doughnuts in a deserted movie studio to a full production number that gradually included the entire cast. "Grand Impérial Cirque de Paris" from *Carnival* and "Before the Parade Passes By" from *Hello, Dolly!* are other examples. "Like Monday Follows Sunday" is the antecedent to all of these.

Early in the rehearsal period, Gower had an appendicitis attack and required emergency surgery. Rehearsals were canceled for the duration of his recovery. Upon his return, he and Castle resumed work on his solo dance number, "Serenade for a New Baby," to be performed before a little girl in a playpen. When the choreography, involving a large assortment of toys, was finished, the collaborators went to the sound studio the following morning, where an unusually large orchestra under the direction of David Rose recorded the accompaniment. The recording finished, the choreographers returned to the studio that afternoon to film the sequence. To their dismay, they discovered that they had failed to take into account all the intricate moves involving the props. Despite the dancing Gower had done with the orchestra during the recording session, the tempo was entirely too fast. Sheepishly, they went to Johnny Green, the imperious head of the music department, returned to Rose, and explained that the take was unusable. Green could have insisted that they adjust the dance to the recording, but instead placed an emergency call to Rose and the musicians and had them return for a second take that same day.

Such cooperation insured a production worthy of the studio's motto: "Do it big, do it right, and give it class." This was the Golden Age of the Hollywood musical, and MGM had a most distinguished reputation—one to be maintained whatever the cost. For fiscal year 1951–52, almost half of the studio's forty projected films would be musicals, absorbing a hefty portion of its $64,000,000 budget.[11] But in the wake of television's popularity, within two years musicals would stir little interest, leaving the studio at a loss to replace the vast source of income they once generated.

Another highlight of *Everything I Have Is Yours* is "Casbah," a ballet featuring Marge as a shy, bespectacled young tourist who wanders from her guide and companions into a Casablancan den of corruption where she meets an assortment of underworld figures. Gower, leader of this dark commune, gradually wins her over to its licentious atmosphere. Marge herself gives a winning turn in Johnny Green and Johnny Mercer's "Derry Down Dilly," a solo dance in which she employs several clever tricks with hats to woo her husband away from his new dancing partner. The film's final number, a haunting dream sequence all in red with the dancers clad in white, begins with Marge pursuing a screen full of Gower and Monica Lewis dancing couples and concludes with a magnificent duet by the Champions.

In the film, Marge displays genuine ease in her acting, whereas Gower seems less comfortable. A letter to his wife written during her convalescence from knee surgery in 1948 confirms this observation: "When I pre-think a speech or a simple series of words," he wrote, "then come to the moment of saying those words, they become a speech. A memorized 'part.' They are not immediate, nor do they seem anymore to be honest. I say them aloud and I watch to see how they sound not only to you, *but to me,* watching my own reactions, my own words and finding myself in the horrible position of player and audience at the same time."[12] Perhaps his objectivity as a choreographer prohibited him from becoming subjectively immersed in a role as an actor.

Though the critics found the plot fragile, "even for plots of its kind," they enjoyed this "flashy showcase" of a film with its "lively dance routines."[13] Regarding the performances, Gower gave "a very pleasing account of himself," and Marge continued "to show promise as an ingénue who could get by without a dance or song."[14] The dancing, of course, garnered the greatest praise, especially "the well-staged Casablanca," and "the dazzling charm and humor" of Marge's "Derry Down Dilly," with Gower's "Serenade to a Baby" and their "Like Monday Follows Sunday" the "most impressive of the delightful routines."[15]

Successful as they were at Metro, the Champions began to realize that, like their colleagues, their contract had been firmly designed to prevent them from performing in other media—particularly television. Studio brass were utterly paranoid about losing performers to their new competitor and therefore made it impossible for them to accept television appearances. This was especially frustrating for the couple, whose nightclub, theatre, and television work had brought them national acclaim long before MGM took notice. What public appearances the studio did allow were usually for state occasions such as the "Inaugural Festival" of newly elected President Dwight D. Eisenhower, in which they performed with Allan Jones, Tony Martin, Adolphe Menjou, Walter Pidgeon, and George Murphy. (Upon landing in Washington, a severe case of ptomaine poisoning promptly put Gower in the hospital and almost caused him to miss the event.) Daily workouts to remain in top dancing condition could never compare with nightly opportunities to refine their craft before a live audience. *That* was the best way to stay in shape.

Frustration with this policy of forced indolence was giving the Champions second thoughts about remaining in film. Finally, in June 1952, the studio offered them leading roles in a property originally intended for Gene Kelly, Vera-Ellen, Debbie Reynolds, and Carleton Carpenter entitled *Give a Girl a Break*.[16] Reynolds, fresh from co-starring opposite Kelly in *Singin' in the Rain*, would share top billing with Marge and Gower. Featured players would include Carleton Carpenter, who had been paired previously with Reynolds in two of the studio's musicals, character actor Kurt Kasznar, and newcomer Helen Wood.[17] Jack Cummings would produce, and *Singin' in the Rain*'s Stanley Donen direct. Donen and Gower planned to share the choreography credits.

Gower's work consisted of three numbers: one with Debbie Reynolds—"Applause, Applause," the film's finale—and two with Marge—"It Happens Every Time," a dreamy *pas de deux*, and "Challenge Dance," a jazzy duet amid the rooftops of Manhattan. This number expresses another attribute of his choreography—using dance to resolve conflict. Here, Gower is a stage director trying to pressure his ex-wife, played by Marge, into auditioning for the leading role in his new musical. When he unexpectedly appears at her apartment demanding to know why she has not auditioned, she explains that she has been too nervous. As she retreats to the terrace, he follows and challenges her to dance, but she shuns him. He confronts her again, and she avoids him once more. Gradually, this stepping-to-confront and turning-to-escape pattern gives rise to a thrilling duet that reunites them as they cavort over the rooftops of the city.[18]

Gower would resolve conflict in a similar manner when staging Broadway musicals. In *Hello, Dolly!*, shopkeepers Mrs. Molloy and Minnie Fay are about to summon the police to arrest hapless intruders Cornelius and Barnaby when Dolly intervenes by teaching them to dance. In "Dancing," the conflict gradually diminishes as the couples become more confident dancers and more aware of their mutual attraction. By the conclusion, Mrs. Molloy and Cornelius and Minnie Fay and Barnaby are not only reconciled, but also clearly in love. The tap ballet sequence of the title number in *42nd Street* is a similar case. Following the murder of her lover, the heroine expresses her loss by joining the chorus for the remainder of the dance, thereby resolving her grief by dancing. Both "Dancing" and the "42nd Street Tap Ballet" are rooted in "Challenge Dance."

"It Happens Every Time" is a stunning example of Gower's lyrical style and also of his predilection for choreography built around poles. His character, the show's director, envisions a longed-for reconciliation with his ex-wife, which will solve his personal as well as theatrical problems. His dream unfolds against a canvas of light blue, yellow, and pink swirls with endless rows of black poles occasionally broken by white paper lanterns of various shapes. The song Gower sings to Marge (via dubbing) leads to a *pas de deux* in which the two swing from pole to pole in opposition to each other. Just as they begin to intertwine, Marge suddenly disappears into darkness, and Gower finds himself alone within a spotlight atop a lofty plane. One by one, each of the three women vying for the lead in his show appear, Marge being the last. Just as he discovers her, she is lost in a chorus of women who sweep about him. In desperation, he leaps from the platform onto a pole, which he slowly descends to a lower plane where Marge awaits him. There the dance ends where it began—among the poles—as the two finally come face-to-face, questioning, rather than touching, each other. It is a pose that perfectly expresses the uncertainty of the relationship between their characters.

The finale, "Applause, Applause," encapsulates three staging techniques he later would use to streamline the Broadway musical: scenic minimalism, use of levels, and choreographed transitions. As a choreographer and later as a director, his primary focus was on the performer. To accomplish this, he would use minimal scenery and position the chorus at various heights in relation to the featured player. The scene here is that of a carnival, but a carnival in the abstract, a carnival suggested by the exuberance of Gower as a dancing emcee in white pinstriped suit, hot pink shirt, and straw hat who is accompanied by several pairs of hand-clapping arms from upstage. These belong to a chorus of roustabouts attired in black turtlenecks and hot pink-striped pants who stand on landings of different heights leading to a stage in the upper left area. As the emcee dances from level to level and the chorus moves in opposition, Reynolds as the star appears on the carnival stage in white pinstriped ballet dress to sing "Applause, Applause." She leaps and struts with the emcee and chorus until a puppet booth arrives via treadmill (which allows for a smooth transition from one section of the number to the other). There, the two performers employ a series of props to comically portray various personae from the theatre. The booth glides off left as various carnival performers—clowns, jugglers, acrobats, fire-eaters, even two dancers in a horse costume—appear one by one, then gradually fill the stage as the emcee and star lead them to the climax.

Ironically, "Applause, Applause" is a foreshadowing not only of Gower's staging technique, but also of some of his better-known musicals. Apart from its obvious relationship to *Carnival,* there is the treadmill later used to animate the furniture in *I Do! I Do!,* the isolated human appendages that would open *42nd Street* (dancing feet in that instance, as opposed to clapping hands here) and, of course, the dancing horse of *Hello, Dolly!* Finally, there is Debbie Reynolds, whom he later would direct in *Irene* and *Annie Get Your Gun.*

Once more, Gower created wonderful dances for a flimsy plot—a hackneyed treatment of stage-door romance even more meager than *Everything I Have Is Yours.* When the star of a Broadway musical quits just three weeks before the opening, three women compete for the role, each encouraged by a different male member of the production staff. In the end, two of the women have conflicts that force them to withdraw, leaving Reynolds's character the winner. Needless to say, no one was thrilled with the story, least of all director Donen, who felt he deserved better after giving the studio one of its biggest hits with *Singin' in the Rain.* He was further irritated by the producer's open admission of poor judgment in thoughtlessly pursuing the weak yarn's film rights from the start. Like it or not, Donen was saddled with Cummings's mistake. It was senseless to protest; Cummings was the nephew of president emeritus Louis B. Mayer, who still wielded considerable influence.

In addition to the performers, there were other factors with potential for a quality production. Husband-and-wife screenwriters Albert Hackett and Frances Goodrich (*The Thin Man, It's a Wonderful Life, Father of the Bride*) would pen the screenplay, which was based on a story by crime novelist Vera Caspary (*Laura, A Letter to Three Wives*). Two songwriting experts, composer Burton Lane and lyricist Ira Gershwin (whose recent success with the studio's *An American in Paris* had emboldened him to resume writing for new musicals), would craft the score. Saul Chaplin and André Previn would share the musical direction—another plus.[19] To all this Donen would add a special element he himself had discovered—one sure to invigorate the mediocre plot, give the film a certain distinction, and supply him with the incentive necessary to direct it.

Shortly before rehearsals commenced in September 1952, the director received the screen test of a gifted young dancer he had first seen in *Talent 52*, an annual Broadway event that showcased the work of young professionals for an audience drawn from the radio, television and film industries. The test—two scenes from William Saroyan's *The Time of Your Life*, in which the performer played the tap-dancing character of Harry—was so amazing that Donen immediately made a change in the casting. Carleton Carpenter was replaced with Bob Fosse.[20]

Fosse had a number of things in common with Gower. He was born in Chicago on June 23, 1927, precisely eight years and one day after Gower's birth, June 22, 1919. Even more curious were the parallels between Gower's career and his. Among the dance teams replacing the Champions after they left *The Admiral Broadway Revue* were Bob Fosse and his wife at the time, Mary Ann Niles (later to appear in *Carnival*). When Gower was headlining nightclubs with Marge, Fosse did likewise with Niles, going so far as to introduce their act with the pun, "You've heard of the Champions? We're the runners-up."[21] Fosse's self-deprecation deflected his rivalry with Gower—a rivalry Gower thought little of until the day Donen's *wunderkind* arrived on the set of *Give a Girl a Break*, sights aimed at becoming the next Gene Kelly, or at least Donald O'Connor. For Fosse, nothing seemed impossible; after all, here he was running neck-and-neck with Gower Champion, who was performing and doing choreography for Metro's musicals. Starting with *Give a Girl a Break*, he would be doing that as well, thanks to his alliance with Donen, one that generated friction from the outset.[22]

"Marge, Gower and I got along famously," explains Debbie Reynolds. "And Bobby Fosse and Stanley Donen—*they* got along famously. So it was kind of like two camps. Bobby and Stanley had aligned themselves, and they just thought we were really corny. They were Mr. Show Biz, and we were no talent. We were okay, but we weren't as great as they. They were far greater. So they got along very, very well, and we didn't seem to work out to get along with them. I don't think it was competitive. I think it was absolutely one-sided."[23]

Neither Reynolds nor the Champions had any idea just how one-sided it would get.

As rehearsals commenced, strange things began to happen. There were major changes in the picture, unscheduled changes—changes in script, changes in roles, changes in the choice of scenes to be shot. Soon it was obvious that *Give a Girl a Break* was really *Give a Hoofer a Break*, and the stars were exceedingly unhappy about it. Reynolds was being used as a throwaway, and the Champions had been all but written out of a picture that was being shot and reshot daily.[24]

In its initial preview, the film was about Bob Fosse, and when L. B. Mayer saw it, he exploded at Donen: "Why are you giving me this movie about this guy I never heard of before? He's not good-looking. All he does is dance. What happened to the script that I approved? What happened to the picture I authorized?" He forced Donen and the company back into production to reshoot until the film was closer to what had been approved. Though the Champions and Reynolds had their starring roles restored, the final product, with the exception of the dance sequences, was lackluster, indicative of Donen's attitude toward the project from the start.[25]

To ease their humiliation, studio executives premiered the film in Brooklyn, rather than Manhattan, but critics soon uncovered what they had tried to hide. "Stanley Donen's direction is uninspired, the tempo dragging, with the entire production having a certain listlessness,"[26] proclaimed one.

Songwriters Lane and Gershwin, whose score fared no better, could not distance themselves far enough from the film. Lane gibed that it should be renamed *Give a Song a Break* and even attempted to have his name and Gershwin's expunged from the credits. At the end of the premiere, Leonore Gershwin asked her husband if he held stock in MGM. "Yes," he confessed. "Sell it!" she snapped (which he promptly did—at a sizable loss).[27]

As for Fosse, his chicanery earned him such a reputation for being an operator that no star was willing to work with him. What success he would enjoy as a film performer would be moderate at best—far from Kelly's or O'Connor's—because the reign of the Hollywood musical was over. By comparison, the Champions had fared better, but that success was not worth the angst of their recent fiasco with Fosse and Donen. Plainly, it was time to give their contract a break.[28]

SIX

Performer and Choreographer

1953–1955

On April 30, 1953, Marge and Gower danced out of the grasp of MGM, turning down an exclusive one-picture-a-year contract that would have put them in a higher income bracket, but also would have denied them the right to make television and nightclub appearances as well as films with other studios.[1] Dancers want to dance, not sit around waiting until some studio executive decides to devise a vehicle for them. Even so, the team considered another offer from Howard Hughes, first proposed three years before, to remake the RKO musicals that had starred Fred Astaire and Ginger Rogers. After viewing all of the films, the Champions agreed to begin with *Follow the Fleet*, but discussions with the studio never advanced beyond a few tentative decisions concerning the order in which the new films should be made. Concerned that the memory of Astaire and Rogers might yet be too fresh in the public mind, Gower thought it best to drop the project. From youth, he had idolized Astaire, and he would not compete with his idol. However, he did accept an offer to choreograph a film for the studio at a future date.[2]

The very same week the Champions terminated their contract with Metro, they also launched a new act—a prelude to an international tour, beginning with the London Palladium at the time of Queen Elizabeth's coronation, then Monte Carlo, Cannes, Deauville, and Biarritz. The months of rehearsal paid off splendidly the evening of May 3, when they opened at the Flamingo Hotel in Las Vegas to critical raves. "One of the best all around shows this spa has had in a long time," declared *Variety*, ". . . each choreo enacted is a lovely swirl of momentum aided by a premise as the pair unfold their ideas."[3] *The Hollywood Reporter* added, "Marge and Gower Champion are wowing them at the Hotel Flamingo currently . . . Capacity business assured with top-heavy advance reservations. Material is fresh and appealing as their terps unfold in story-like fashion."[4]

That freshness was especially evident in the alterations Gower had made to the act, including the addition of a quintet of three men and two women called "The

Cheerleaders," whose vocal and dance support now enabled him to stage more expansive and sophisticated material. Opening with the sprightly "Let's Dance," in which he and Marge explained the basic tenets of the act through song and dance, they whirled into the lyrical "Underneath the Clock." Inspired by an incident from their own marriage, this confrontation and reconciliation of husband and wife via dance took place beneath the grand, constantly ticking clock of a railroad station. Running from her husband, the upset wife, suitcase in hand, arrives at the station just minutes before the departure of the next train. Her equally perturbed husband soon overtakes her, snatching away her suitcase, which she, in turn, intercepts and places firmly before her. They begin to pace in opposition to each other with husband stepping-to-confront wife and wife turning-to-avoid husband. But before long, his contrite manner moves her, touching off a dramatic reconciliation to the tune of Vincent Youmans's "Time on My Hands." At the climax, the two are just about to reunite when the conductor sounds his "All Aboard." The wife has second thoughts. She picks up her suitcase, walks toward the train, but then turns and slowly walks toward her husband. He takes her suitcase, she rests her head on his shoulder, and together they leave the station.

Reprised from previous appearances was their signature "County Fair," followed by the delightful "Margie," during which they alternated resting on a chair while still maintaining continuous action. This again provided a respite before the more demanding footwork required for "Revival," the finale. Here, Gower portrayed a charismatic preacher whose impassioned call for reform not only stirs his congregation, The Cheerleaders, but also a little country girl played by Marge. Invited by preacher and assembly to enter into the rejoicing, the girl slowly takes up the swinging rhythm of the spiritual they sing—Vincent Youmans, Billy Rose, and Edward Eliscu's "Great Day." Once she catches the spirit of the gathering, the number reaches fever pitch with her leading the congregation in joyful praise.

In late May, during a return engagement at Bill Miller's Riviera, the Champions were approached by television personality Ed Sullivan to perform on his popular Sunday evening variety series, *Toast of the Town* (later *The Ed Sullivan Show*). An admirer of Gower and Jeanne in his early days as a syndicated newspaper columnist, Sullivan was similarly taken with the work of the Champions when he later turned television host. Though delighted to have their first television appearance in over two years, Gower and Marge were completely astonished by the one stipulation Sullivan insisted upon: the entire program was to be exclusively devoted to them. Previously, only three other artists had been similarly honored: playwright Robert E. Sherwood, composer Richard Rodgers, and director Joshua Logan. Though Gower protested that their career as a team had not been long enough to merit such distinction, Sullivan remained firm. On June 14, he hosted "The Marge and Gower Champion Story," during which the couple performed three numbers from their act ("County Fair," "Underneath the Clock," and "Revival") and "Smoke Gets in Your Eyes" from *Lovely to Look At*. Segments from their films ("Life upon the Wicked Stage" from *Show Boat* and "I Won't Dance" from *Lovely to Look At*) completed the hourlong tribute.[5]

Sullivan's national broadcast of their story resulted in a flood of nightclub, television, film, and theatre offers they were now at liberty to accept unhampered by contract restraints. Overnight, managers of the most prestigious nightclubs in the country were vying for their return; representatives of *Lux Video Theatre* were offering them the first dramatic musical written for television; executives at Columbia Pictures were proposing a film with Betty Grable; producers Paul Gregory and Charles Laughton were asking them to star in a Broadway revue; and even their former employers at MGM were trying to lure them back for a film with Esther Williams. However, before considering any of these opportunities, they first had to cancel their European tour. The quest for international fame would have to be postponed till a later time.

In the late summer of 1953, following appearances at San Francisco's Fairmont Hotel, Los Angeles's Coconut Grove, and New York's Persian Room, the couple went to work on "A Bouquet for Millie," a half-hour program for *Lux Video Theatre*. Billed as the first dramatic musical written for television, it had a story by Joseph Cochran about a young couple, Millie and Tim O'Connor, who, although much in love, almost allow a petty quarrel over flowers to ruin their marriage. Millie, especially fond of bouquets, wishes that Tim would use them as a means of expressing the romantic side he carefully keeps in check. But walking through the neighborhood with flowers in hand is something Tim's machismo will not allow for fear of being derided by his cronies at the local bar. The couple's argument turns violent, and Millie drags Tim into court for striking her. The judge offers him the choice of spending thirty days in jail or sending Millie a bouquet for ten consecutive nights. Grudgingly, he accepts the deal. On the eleventh day, after taking a ribbing at the pub, he comes home without the flowers. Just as she is about to pack her bags, a friendly florist arrives with a dozen roses—Tim's romantic side spontaneously expressed at last.

Broadcast live by CBS on the evening of December 17, "A Bouquet for Millie" marked the Champions' dramatic debut, which the critics recognized as a "memorable, if not distinguished" effort with acting that was "fresh and diverting."[6] The choreography, staged by Gower, came at the end: an abstract piece amid a flowery effect, which encompassed the performance space. Some critics found it too meager a dose of the team's forte. They wanted more footwork and less lip service to the script; but for the Champions, "A Bouquet for Millie" was the first in a series of efforts to stretch their abilities and diversify their work in preparation for the day when they would cease dancing.

After completing their remaining nightclub engagements and again presenting the Oscar for Art Direction at the annual Academy Awards,[7] the team started rehearsals for Columbia's *Three for the Show* (1955), originally *The Pleasure Is All Mine*, which occupied most of the spring of 1954 for Gower and Marge. Based on a play by Somerset Maugham, this remake in Cinemascope and Technicolor of the studio's *Too Many Husbands* (1940) was written by Edward Hope and Leonard Stern and starred Betty Grable as a showgirl, who to her alarm discovers that she has acquired two husbands. Just as she is about to embark on a honeymoon with present spouse Gower, former husband Jack Lemmon, a Korean War pilot, reportedly killed in action three years before, suddenly reappears. Marge, as the wife's best friend, plays a dancer happy to accept whomever Grable finally decides to yield. Produced by Jonie Taps and directed by H. C. Potter, its cast also included Myron McCormick, Paul Harvey, Robert Bice, and Hal K. Dawson. With the exception of Gower's duet for Marge and himself, the renowned Jack Cole did the choreography.

Having started as a dancer with the Denishawn Company, Cole later formed his own troupe, specializing in Asian dances. Once he turned Broadway choreographer, he created a jazz-influenced style full of intricate hand gestures, wide stances, and knee drops—different types of movement that dancers call "into the floor." Gwen Verdon and Carol Haney were among those he trained in this method, which he used to great effect in stage works like *Kismet* (1953), *A Funny Thing Happened on the Way to the Forum* (1962), and *Man of La Mancha* (1965). For Gower, whose uplifted, lyrical style was the antithesis of Cole's, working with the choreographer was sheer torture. Nevertheless, both he and Marge adapted admirably to Cole's style, as their work in the unusual *commedia dell'arte* sequence that opens the film proves. Here, Gower plays a libidinous Punch pursuing showgirl Grable to the consternation of Marge's Judy, who attempts to bridle his passion.

Cole, an extremely exacting and assiduous person, preferred stage work to film because it not only gave him greater artistic control, but also distanced him from those studio moguls whose aesthetic sense he deemed coarse. One morning, he had the misfortune of encountering Columbia Pictures president Harry Cohn after his first ballet, a production of *Swan Lake*. Cohn, completely transfixed by the performance, was still clearly in a state of childlike wonder. Ebullience unrestrained, he declared to Cole, "That music was sensational! You've just got to use it in the new Grable film!" The horrified choreographer tried to convince him that separating Tchaikovsky's music from the ballet for which it was intended would show extremely poor taste. But there was no reasoning with Cohn, who stubbornly insisted that the music be used. Cole, meanwhile, bided his time, plotting revenge.

By now, dream ballet sequences, introduced by choreographer Agnes de Mille in *Oklahoma!* (1943), had become conventional fare in Broadway and Hollywood musicals (as films like the Champions' *Everything I Have Is Yours* and *Give a Girl a Break* showed). Cole, who loathed them, had been contracted to choreograph not one but two for *Three for the Show*. The first, "Down, Boys," he had already conceived as a tongue-in-cheek parody of the genre in which Grable would imagine herself as a voluptuous sultana taking stock of her male harem—Gower and Jack Lemmon included. However, up until this time, he could find no inspiration for the second dream ballet that was to succeed Marge's reflective rendition of George and Ira Gershwin's "Someone to Watch over Me." Now he had a solution. He would use the *Swan Lake* music Cohn demanded and also teach the mogul a lesson in aesthetics he would not soon forget. For this ballet, the choreographer would draw inspiration from two bizarre sources: a popular perfume advertisement in which a formally attired couple waltzed among a group of candelabra-bearing footmen, and a picture that hung in his study of a pair of corseted swashbuckling women in a sword duel. The result would be the dream ballet to end all dream ballets—an outrageous lampoon with pistol-waving *femmes fatales* angrily fending off suitors, candelabra-bearing footmen darting in and out, Champion duets full of outlandish lifts, wild spins, and plaintive glances, and Marge's escape aboard a huge revolving chandelier. Cole's hilarious send-up was made all the more comical by the presence of the Champions themselves, who at times seemed to be parodying their own dream ballets for MGM.

In addition to "Someone to Watch Over Me," the high-spirited duet with Marge, which concludes the film, Gower did make one other noteworthy contribution to *Three for the Show*. This was a farcical sequence in which he and Lemmon come "home" to the same apartment, preparing it for an evening of romance with wife Grable, each going about his business—chilling champagne, arranging flowers, fluffing pillows, preening, and so forth—unaware of the other's presence. Like his comic dances, scenes such as this profited from a form of staging in which he blended choreography with *shtick*. A Yiddishism that has become part of the theatrical lexicon, *shtick* is synonymous with what is more properly known as "business": inventive bits of nonverbal acting encompassing everything from chewing a piece of gum to more sophisticated movement like a fistfight. Gower's "coming home" sequence in *Three for the Show* is the earliest example of his choreographed shtick and full of the split-second timing and genial slapstick that would later mark his direction of shows like *Hello, Dolly!* and *Mack and Mabel*.

In the spring of 1954, the team took starring roles alongside Esther Williams and Howard Keel for MGM's Cinemascope and Eastmancolor musical epic, *Jupiter's*

Darling. Produced by George Wells and directed by George Sidney, it was based on the play *The Road to Rome* by Robert E. Sherwood. The screenplay by Dorothy Kingsley dealt with the romantic liaison between Roman aristocrat Amytis (Williams) and Carthaginian invader Hannibal (Keel) and the promise he gives her to desist from sacking Rome. Marge and Gower played an improbable but engaging pair of slaves called Meta and Varius, who distinguished the undistinguished narrative with "If This Be Slav'ry" and "The Life of an Elephant." (A third number—an engaging *pas de deux* in which Meta frees Varius from his bonds—was cut before the film's release, but was later found and added to the laser disc release.) For these numbers, Gower would again be sharing the staging tasks with choreographer Hermes Pan.

In the first, Varius, the caretaker of Hannibal's famous elephants, is a slave purchased by Amytis for her maidservant, Meta, who is smitten by his brawny charm. (To acquire the proper Hollywood "look" of a slave, Gower undertook a daily regimen of weightlifting. So impressive were the results that one critic was prompted to remark, "The studio should have put Gower in a short tunic long ago and let us see his muscles as he dances his unparalleled routines."[8]) Once Meta unfastens his chains, Varius whirls her about the market's stalls of watermelons, oranges, and chickens as a prelude to a duet in which they use a series of staccatolike, arrested moves to mime the poses of figures like those painted on ancient vases. At the climax, they climb to a pulley system high above a stall, which carries them down its cables right into a display full of pottery. As they regain their bearings, an angry Meta searches for Varius amid a disarray of broken merchandise. Slowly, he rises with his head stuck inside a terra cotta pot, which she promptly shatters over his head.

The Champions' second number boasted one of the most unusual chorus lines ever assembled: eleven elephants weighing eighty thousand pounds combined and ranging in age from twenty-five to eighty. With the exception of two babies discovered in a Hollywood nightclub, Gower and Hermes Pan recruited most of their pachyderm performers from the Cole Brothers Circus. By and large, the dance directors found them an exceptionally amiable and light-footed lot, each able to perform some special step, be it a front foot dance, a hind leg stand, a three-legged hop, a waltz, a merry-go-round, or a shimmy. The number was built around these special skills of "the girls," as Gower called them, who stood an average eight feet tall and weighed about eight thousand pounds apiece. Because the screenplay described Gower's character of Varius as caretaker of the elephants who, according to legend, transported Hannibal's armies across the Alps, songwriters Burton Lane and Harold Adamson used that premise to compose "The Life of an Elephant." This became a vehicle for Varius to explain to Meta the benefits of an elephant's existence—a life they likewise could be happy leading.

Rather than impose a preconceived routine upon the girls, which they would have to learn from scratch, Gower and Pan began by auditioning them to determine the talents of each. This, in turn, helped them create a general picture of how the number should progress and look—a dance duet with elephant accompaniment. No chorine was ever more carefully scrutinized. The choreographers lined them up, viewed them from all angles, and watched the steps each could perform. "Tessie could twirl," Gower remarked, "so we made a mental note and passed on to Wilma, who waltzed. After finding that Sharon could shimmy, Marge and I adapted our actions to theirs. When we found that Burma could do a three-legged hop, we inserted a step in which the three of us would hop to music. The same with Jean's cakewalk."[9]

Once rehearsals were under way, Gower soon discovered that the girls were highly intelligent and adaptable, with a remarkable ability to pick up new sections of the dance quickly. He ascribed this to their affinity for music, adding that "by rehearsing them over and over and repeating the steps we had in mind for them to do, they picked up the rhythm and learned what each count and beat of the music stood for."[10] This is apparent from the start of the number.

As Varius sings to Meta about the tricks his elephants can do, the animals stand on their hind legs, do front-leg dances, and shimmy to illustrate his point. Meta, unimpressed, quickly changes her tune as she is suddenly lifted by one elephant, which perches her in the crook of its trunk and starts spinning around. Varius demonstrates more tricks: three elephants lift their right legs and plant them on the backs of each other, then do the same with their trunks. In the meantime, Meta rides out from behind them seated upon a black baby elephant that joins the two dancers in one-legged hopping, rocking, and spinning. While the couple move on to another step, the baby elephant continues to spin until they go back to retrieve it. The three then dance ahead to a big elephant with a harness holding a large peach-colored silk scarf. They take the scarf and tie it around the head of the baby elephant, which proceeds to join them in another series of hops. As the slaves continue hopping forward, the elephant scampers off and issues a distress call, whereupon they rush to its aid only to find it sitting on its hind legs, too tired to dance. It collapses to the ground sprawled on its side and goes to sleep as Varius and Meta gingerly dance off with the remaining elephants so as not to disturb it. For a moment, Meta disappears, but as three other elephants—sizes large, medium, and small—enter tail-joined-to-trunk, she emerges as the fourth and smallest of the lot. She rejoins Varius, and together they lead a parade of prancing elephants in a cakewalk until the finale, when one lifts them into the crook of its front legs while doing a hind leg stand.

The number succeeds because the Champions make it seem a spontaneous celebration of elephants and their ability to surprise, charm, impress, and amuse. Furthermore, by using the elephants' specialties as the overall movement pattern and having the dancers adapt accordingly, a natural interplay between dancers and animals is achieved, allowing both to be completely at ease with each other. Thus, in terms of Gower's evolution as a choreographer, "The Life of an Elephant" plays a significant role, for it marks the first instance of his preference for more general staging over strict choreography. In other words, he was now beginning to develop an interest in the overall movement pattern and impact of a number, rather than in the individual steps themselves. By the end of his career, this would become his distinct method of working.

The Champions' work in *Jupiter's Darling*, their final film for MGM, received enthusiastic notices. But successful as their work with the elephants had been, it still was intimidating: next time they were asked to dance with animals they would choose dogs.

Jupiter's Darling was also the last film in which the Champions performed together. "Suddenly we were famous," Gower later mused, "but movie musicals were over. We finished off Betty Grable in her last film, then we finished off Esther Williams in *her* last film, and it was back to the closet for the old act again. We didn't care, because we never thought of ourselves as movie stars, anyway."[11] Even so, the films of the Champions remain inestimable records of their craft.

In the autumn of 1954, Gower would do far more than just pull the old act out of the closet; he would re-create it for a new medium—one in which both he and Marge had performed separately as youths, but had never taken on together. The Champions accepted a proposal from MCA's high-flying producer Paul Gregory and his partner, actor Charles Laughton, to star in a stage production that would take them on a rigorous three-month tour of fifty-seven cities and culminate in their one and only Broadway appearance together. The producers also invited Gower to direct and choreograph their "diversion in song and dance" called *Something to Rave About*, which he soon renamed *3 for Tonight*. It was the first time he would be billed as director, for even though he had staged and choreographed the musical numbers for *Lend an Ear*, he was not credited with the direction. Hal Gerson, who directed the sketches, had received the title. But because of the revue's overall reliance on song and dance, the producers had printed "Production Staged by GOWER CHAMPION" at the end of the credits in recognition of his contribution. Now *3 for Tonight* would give him the chance to merit full distinction as both director and choreographer.

A hybrid entertainment combining elements of concert and revue, *3 for Tonight* was so named because of its three principal components: the dancing of the Champions, the singing of Harry Belafonte, and the harmonizing of a vocal ensemble known as The Voices of Walter Schumann. Gregory and Laughton planned to stage the divertissement in the manner of their earlier series of successful dramas: *Don Juan in Hell* (1951), *John Brown's Body* (1953), and *The Caine Mutiny Court-Martial* (1954). Convinced that spectacle impeded the actor's work by pulling audience attention toward visual effects and away from the performance, the producers substituted drapes and stools for conventional stage scenery and made minimal use of properties and costuming. In this way, they underscored the actor's craft.

Gower, whose early works like "Strut Parade," "The Merry-Go-Round Broke Down," and "Marseilles" had developed out of a similar economy imposed by the limitations of the nightclub stage, not only was capable of working within such bounds, but also of exploiting them to full advantage. Hence, he was instinctively drawn to this novel form of entertainment, which shunned the common spectacle and comic sketches of revues in favor of an unadorned reliance upon pure song and dance. Still, a coherent and integrated presentation would have to be forged out of *3 for Tonight's* diverse trio of talents without compromising the artistic integrity of each.

Within each performer's repertoire, he found a cache of musical narratives, which evoked various moods. For each of these stories, whether sung or danced, he created a specific setting, incorporating Schumann's vocal ensemble into the action whenever appropriate. For "Sylvie," a folk ballad expressing a prisoner's longing for his lover, singer Harry Belafonte was seated on a stool with his head and shoulders bathed in light and a guitarist silhouetted behind him. Like the singer's approach to the song, the staging was simple and direct. Belafonte's "Noah," recounting the biblical tale of Noah and the Ark, was a revival meeting with the singer a fiery preacher and the chorale his equally spirited congregation. The comically dolorous calypso "Matilda" told of a West Indies man jilted by a faithless woman who stole his money and absconded to Venezuela. The chorus became a Caribbean rhythm band joining Belafonte in the song's refrain.

The Champions likewise contributed their share of narrative to the proceedings. In addition to "Underneath the Clock" and the high-stepping "Harvest Moon," Gower created a production number, "Summer in Fairview Falls," which transferred the Cinderella tale to a small town in America's heartland where a beleaguered housemaid (Marge) abandons her chores to attend the town's annual picnic, befriends a local misfit (Gower), and, in so doing, conquers the disapproval of her small-minded neighbors (Schumann's Voices). His "By-Play for Drums," in which he and Marge appeared as subjects in a laboratory experiment measuring the effects of certain musical phrases and tones on the involuntary nervous system, was yet another contribution.

Imagination, the theme relating the various musical vignettes, was illustrated in the opening sequence by raconteur-master of ceremonies Hiram Sherman (replacing Don Beddoe just before the Broadway opening) through a simple bit of shtick Gower devised. Sherman fished a pencil out of his pocket, held it up under a strong light, and blithely announced that it was a lilac twig. The audience was perfectly willing to call it a lilac twig because the game seemed worth their cooperation. When a pretty chorus girl strolled past the storyteller and demurely accepted the dubious posy as a small gift, even the sense of a game disappeared: from then on it was a lilac twig and nothing else.[12]

Rather than restrict Sherman solely to commentary, Gower integrated him into the proceedings as a character. For "Summer in Fairview Falls," he intervened in a fight between townsmen and misfit and also portrayed a scientist for the laboratory experiment with the Champions in "By-Play for Drums." Like the role of the Stage Manager in Thornton Wilder's *Our Town* (likewise dependent upon minimal staging), Sherman facilitated the imaginative exchange between performers and audience not only by establishing the setting, but also by participating in the action of the narratives themselves.

Glowing critical recognition greeted the performers upon their arrival at New York's Plymouth Theatre on April 6, 1955. Belafonte was recognized at once as a brilliant performer with incandescent singleness of purpose shown in the way he altered the shape, color, and entire character of the stage with nothing more than a song.[13]

The Champions' knowing work demonstrated both humor and buoyancy as Gower opened the show by leading Schumann's impeccably trained "voices" through some amusingly cartooned calisthenics. Marge's last feeble flicker of life, as Gower attempted to put a stop to the nonsense, was a wonderfully engaging improvisation.[14] With their rhythmic magic, the dancers convincingly transformed the simple draped setting into railroad stations, picnic grounds, or whatever else the occasion demanded. "Not since Fred and Adele Astaire skimmed the boards," remarked George Oppenheimer, "has there been so beguiling a dance team," adding, "They have never, in the time they have been working for motion pictures, exhibited one-quarter the humor, the charm and the warmth that they bring to the stage. All of which adds up to a dubious tribute to the power of glorious Technicolor, lavish sets and bad stories."[15]

There were also accolades for the newly arrived director, whose invention and impeccable artistry had not only made gala parades of the chorus exits and entrances, but also created a disciplined production that effectively supported the talents of the cast.[16] "It is not a book show," commented one reviewer, "yet the integral divertissements are so adroitly pieced together and so deftly narrated by the 'story-teller,' Hiram Sherman, that the show has more unity and cohesion than most musicals."[17]

For all its merits, Gower's work played a bit too coyly for some, particularly *New York Times* critic Brooks Atkinson, who was disturbed by performers' "clever mannerisms" that drew more attention to them than to the material, thereby defeating the candor of the bare stage. The choral deportment of Schumann's Voices with their "self-conscious entrances [and] mawkish smiles [which] sweetly condescend to the audience" was one instance; the use of properties, like the stools, which "the direction treats as if cute props instead of pieces of utilitarian furniture,"[18] was another.

However valid Atkinson's objections, no such posturing was apparent the evening of June 22, 1955, when *3 for Tonight* was broadcast live on NBC.[19] Though an abbreviated version of the original stage performance, it nonetheless captured the unique work of both its performers and choreographer-director. As such, it reflected not only the approval of the majority of newspaper columnists, but also that of television critic Jack Gould, who reported in the *New York Times,* "Wednesday night was not an hour of TV; it was an hour of theatre brought to TV. In each number, there was a sublime crispness, competence and sureness of movement that can come only from painstaking rehearsal and an extended run. Each number was a gem; a viewer could take his pick."[20]

3 for Tonight seemed to have everything going for it—big-name talent, clever staging, and excellent notices. Even so, it lasted only four months on Broadway before moving to the Greek Theatre in Los Angeles, where it finally closed after a week's engagement. "It was a hit," Gower later explained, "but unfortunately Belafonte's management was more interested in having him go back to Las Vegas where he made $11,000 a week, than in continuing the show. That was the kind of show we could have taken all over the world."[21] However great his disappointment, it was eased by the fact that *3 for Tonight* was not merely an artistic success, but also a financial one from which he and Marge justly profited as a result of the extensive tour. This newly acquired wealth now gave them the opportunity to become self-employed by establishing their own production company through which all of their nightclub, television, film, and personal appearances and special projects would be booked.

In the lives of the Champions, the number five had played a recurring role: they were married on October 5, Gower first saw the light of day on Fifth Street in Geneva, Illinois, and some of their biggest successes had come on the fifth day of the month. So when they, George Mercador, Al Melnick, and Bernard Silbert chartered their new company in Sacramento on August 27, 1955, as directors, it seemed only logical to call it "Champion Five, Inc." Although a film titled *Chicago Blues*, based on an original screenplay by Blake Edwards, was to have been the company's first effort, it never went before the cameras. Still, a significant role was in store for Champion Five, Inc. as Gower prepared to stage musicals for Broadway.[22]

The aftermath of *3 for Tonight* found Gower at the crossroads of his professional life. At age thirty-six, he was becoming less and less enchanted with juggling the combined duties of performer, choreographer, and now, finally, director. On one occasion, producer Paul Gregory told him he was trying to be "a whore and a madam at the same time. I decided I'd rather be a madam. I turned down the choreographer's job on *My Fair Lady* (1956) to become a director."[23] This decision was the first step toward realizing a longtime ambition: "All during the years that my wife and I danced as 'Marge and Gower Champion,' I was more interested in staging our acts and setting up the routines we used than in their eventual execution."[24]

Yet even with a distinguished reputation as a performer and choreographer, directing opportunities did not come easy. Any offer that would advance his goal, he took—even an industrial film for Bell Telephone, which he landed by using his performing ability as bargaining and trading bait.[25] Meanwhile, he would take the staging of his act with Marge to greater heights and, in so doing, gain the experience that would plant him permanently in the director's chair, but only after recuperating from another bout with stomach ulcers.

The perfect antidote was a summer vacation in France including a week in Paris with Jess as guest. "Compound interest on that forty-dollar loan," Gar said, referring to the money Jess had provided for the team's Montreal debut eight years before. Since then, the three of them had been inseparable, and the holiday brought them even closer. They had a splendid time for which Jess was especially grateful. Back in New York, while they were rustling up their luggage, he turned to Gar and said, "Thanks." The response, recalls Jess, "was such a warm look as if to say, 'I know. I had a good time, too.' And yet the three of us had dinner together that same night—a marvelous place—and it was almost like Marge and I were perfect strangers to him."[26] All at once Gower had turned as remote and impassive as he had been genial and expressive—the same pattern Jess had first noticed ten years before at Laguna Beach and had observed several times since, as baffling as it was erratic. "So I never knew with Gower," he muses. "I never knew."[27]

SEVEN

Director

1956–1959

In 1956, the Champions were in demand more than ever, continuing to appear at the country's most prestigious supper clubs. "The answer to their success," as one reporter remarked upon their opening at the Hotel New Frontier in Las Vegas, "must be found in originality and personality, for other teams are also able to go through flawless and intricate dance routines without ever achieving the status of stars."[1] That originality and personality were what made the Champions "the only dance team in existence that Las Vegas show-bookers would dare to headline."[2] It also accounted for the fabulous response they received at the Coconut Grove in January 1956, where they attracted the biggest New Year's Eve crowd in the club's history and the largest in ten years on New Year's Day.[3]

The new edition of their act, titled "Dancing on Air," now included four song and dance men—Brad Thomas, Jimmy Harris, Bob Dixon, and Pat Rocco—who set up the various themes of the numbers. For "We Forgot to Mention Dance," the opening sequence, Gower used them as a means of focusing the attention of the audience before he and Marge entered to give an amusing enumeration of every conceivable dance known to humanity. To Dixon's vocal of "Where or When," the Champions twirled into a bittersweet climax of the standard, which the quartet then followed with a witty exposition to "Aphrodite and the Thief." In this number, Gower, as the artful Duke McGee, attempted to steal a precious vase from the hands of a statue of Aphrodite, played by Marge, which suddenly springs to life to keep the treasure from the thief's grasp. Once more, "Margie" served as an interim breather for the couple, making way for the quartet's setup for the "Happy Clown" finale. The last story dance Gower created for the act, it began with the pair seated at makeup tables as two unhappily complaining clowns donning their outfits in preparation for a circus performance. The ringmaster's whistle sounds, and they run into the ring with a boisterous big-top routine full of deft slapstick maneuvers and pantomime. The story concluded with a reaffirmation of their love for each other as well as for the circus, which they expressed in Jeff Bailey and Jack Latimer's "When You're a Clown." The critics hailed the piece as "a fitting finale to a superb offering"[4] with movements that "contained the nobility of fine dance theatre."[5]

In March, news that Marge was pregnant and due to deliver their first child sometime in late November delighted the expectant parents, who were further delighted by Gower's newly acquired membership in the Screen Directors' Guild. This was a most fortuitous event, considering that it would be months before Marge could resume performing. Gower's admission to the Guild, which also included television directors, came through the endorsement of two of his longtime mentors: *Show Boat* director George Sidney and the eminent screen and stage director Rouben Mamoulian.

Master of the integrated musical in which all the elements of a production work together to advance the plot, Mamoulian was able to visualize an entire work in musical terms and give it unity of style. To achieve this, he demanded artistic control over all the elements. His film musicals *Love Me Tonight* (1932) and *High, Wide, and Handsome* (1937), and his musicals for the stage, *Porgy and Bess* (1935), *Oklahoma!* (1943), and *Carousel* (1945), were all precedent-setting works that brought substance, order, and artistic balance to the genre. Even though he never worked professionally with Mamoulian, Gower deeply admired the director's work and quickly became a trusted protégé. When he finally turned to directing for the musical stage, Gower would likewise insist upon the same artistic control to insure the unity of style he had so admired in Mamoulian's works. Apparently Mamoulian thought highly of the aspirant's work, too; his unqualified recommendation— together with Sidney's—helped him not only to gain entry into the guild, but also to win his first directing assignment.

Sidney, now the impetus behind a weekly half-hour television series called *Screen Directors' Playhouse,* was eager to find competent directors for a medium still considered second-rate by most film directors. When he invited Gower to stage an expanded version of the "Happy Clown" number from the act to star Marge and himself, the new screen director immediately went to work on Jean Holloway's teleplay for *What Day Is This?* It recounted the story of the two feisty clowns through three numbers—George M. Cohan's "Yankee Doodle Dandy" and "Mary's a Grand Old Name," and "When You're a Clown" from the act. After the segment aired on June 5, 1956, a full-page advertisement appeared the following day in the *Hollywood Reporter* featuring a silhouetted figure in a director's chair with the words *What Day Is This?* set in medium type above it and "DIRECTED BY GOWER CHAMPION" below. Gower relished his moment of arrival and was not about to let it pass by unheralded.

Soon he had an impressive collection of television directing credits that included *Mischief at Bandyleg* (1957), an Irish fantasy in which he starred with Marge; *The Dachet Diamonds* (1959), a mystery drama with Rex Harrison; *Cindy's Fella* (1959), a romantic comedy with Jimmy Stewart; and *Accent on Love* (1959), a musical revue with Louis Jourdan, Jaye P. Morgan, Ginger Rogers, Mike Nichols, Elaine May, Marge, and himself.[6] "For the most part," he later professed, "much of that phase of my career went unnoticed—and that probably was a blessing! Nobody was really watching what I was doing—and if anyone did see it, he didn't know I'd done it—so I worked experimentally, finding a personal style I liked. In the back of my mind was an idea about taking on a New York musical."[7]

Between directing assignments and club engagements, he and Marge continued to make frequent television appearances not only as a dance team on variety programs, but also as actors in dramas in order to diversify their reputation. One such effort was the *General Electric Theater* presentation of "The Rider on the Pale Horse," a light but poignant fantasy of the American West by Helen Eustes, which aired on CBS on November 4, 1956. In it Gower portrayed a strange and legendary figure known as Mr. Death, who, as the Rider on the Pale Horse, comes to claim the life of Billy Be-dog-gone-bank-tree (Richard Creen), a ne'er-do-well mortally wounded in a poker game fracas. Marge, as Billy's girl, Maude Applegate, follows Mr. Death to his cabin in the clouds to plead for the life of her lover. There she has a change of heart and stays to fall in love with the fateful rider of the pale horse.[8]

Beyond the desire to stretch their abilities, the team had more fundamental reasons for accepting straight dramatic roles in teleplays such as this. Dancing superstars, like Fred Astaire and Gene Kelly, were beginning to disappear from the scene; likewise, dance teams were now largely a thing of the past, with the Champions themselves the only one to have reached the top in the previous twenty years. Given the decline in the production of film musicals, the closing of numerous nightclubs with floor shows that once had opened with dance acts, and the arrival of television, with its many variety shows using dancers but denying them star billing, the dearth of dancing stars was not surprising. To survive, dancers would have to cultivate a host of skills, including comic and dramatic acting as well as singing. No matter how talented, those who ignored the need to diversify did so at their own risk, for as Gower acknowledged, "It's unfortunate, but it looks as if the day of dance stars has gone into eclipse."[9]

With opportunities declining for dancers, the decision to turn to theatre and television had proven a wise one for the Champions, giving them steady employment and the financial means to leave their home on Woodrow Wilson Drive for a more spacious one originally built by Ronald Reagan for Jane Wyman on Cordell Drive in the Hollywood Hills. The timing could not have been better. On November 20, 1956, Marge gave birth to their first child, Gregg Ernest Champion, named after Jess Gregg and her father, Ernest Belcher.

Through the summer and most of the fall of that year, Gower fulfilled his contract with RKO to choreograph a musical entitled *The Girl Most Likely* (1958). The last film the studio was to produce, this musical remake of *Tom, Dick and Harry* (RKO, 1940) would be released almost two years after its completion, much to its choreographer's displeasure. It recounted the story of a rather flighty young woman, played by Jane Powell, who is engaged to three men—real estate salesman Tommy Noonan, boat mechanic Cliff Robertson, and millionaire Keith Andes—and her quandary as to which one she should marry. Singer Kaye Ballard (replacing original choice Carol Channing), dancer Kelly Brown, Judy Nugent, Una Merkel, and Frank Cady guide Powell in choosing the man she really loves: the mechanic. Hugh Martin and Ralph Blaine crafted the tuneful score, which was effectively blended with Nelson Riddle's arrangements and Gower's choreography.

Director Mitch Leisen and producer Stanley Rubin gave Gower a free hand in creating and shooting the musical numbers, which, in comparison to the rest of the film, have a style completely their own. Champion's last work in the genre of the film musical, they are of two distinct types: those that form part of or advance the story and those that stand apart from or comment on it. The first type is represented by a "travelogue" number in which the cast of attractive young singers and dancers actually kick and splash in the water as part of the dance routine. "Balboa," filmed on a quayside during the offseason at the southern California resort of the same name, grows out of a simple meeting between Powell and Robertson at a beachside snack bar. Gradually it becomes a full-blown production number celebrating young love—a pedestrian subject, which in Champion's hands becomes what James Powers of the *Hollywood Reporter* described as "one of the most exciting ensemble performances ever seen in a film musical."[10]

The number succeeds because Gower choreographed the camera movement along with that of the large chorus containing only a minimum of trained dancers. That way he set the entire beach in motion through an eclectic series of natural movement patterns—splashing, kicking, swimming—which appear spontaneous but, in fact, were carefully orchestrated and rehearsed over a six-week period. The combination of this with the constantly changing photography makes every corner of the screen burst with lucid, congruous, and exhilarating movement. To get the camera to dance along with the energetic ensemble, Gower coordinated the efforts of forty divers, swimmers, and dancers, together with those of cinematographer Robert Planck, to whom he assigned the problem of filming the number in about eighteen inches of water. The choreographer wanted to shoot from different angles beyond the beach out in the ocean. Planck's solution was to install an air hose with

130 pounds of pressure immediately below the camera to blow away any mist or drops of water that would collect on the lens during filming.[11] "Balboa" is also an early example of Gower's ability to organize a large number of dancers and non-dancers into patterns that produce a unified statement—a skill that would soon become characteristic of his work as a Broadway director-choreographer.

Even when the dancing took place within a contained space, as it did on the two soundstages converted into a Mexican market for "All the Colors of the Rainbow," he found ways of animating the photography. Here, while using dancer Kelly Brown to emphasize and expand the movements of nondancers Powell, Andes, and Ballard, he also had the camera follow the four as they cavorted through stalls, played hide-and-seek, and disguised themselves beneath huge sombreros. The result is an entire scene shot through with movement thanks to Champion's rare ability to see with the eye of the camera.

The film's second type of musical sequence concerns those numbers that stand apart from the story as commentaries on its theme: marriage and money. The best example is "Keeping Up with the Joneses" because it fittingly captures the price married couples pay when they compete with their neighbors. Set against a background of primary colors, it is presented in the abstract by means of a seemingly infinite space extending vertically and horizontally into oblivion. Within this setting are ladders rising seventy-five feet into the air upon which Champion perched six actors who ascended or descended according to how well or poorly they managed to "keep up" with their competitors. The seemingly boundless set literally freed the choreography so it could evolve unhampered by space or gravity. His sequences in previous films, such as "Like Monday Follows Sunday" in *Everything I Have Is Yours* or "Applause, Applause" in *Give a Girl a Break,* could just as well have been performed on the stage to similar effect. In those instances, the camera was used merely to change locale or as a recording device. By comparison, the numbers in *The Girl Most Likely* show what a phenomenal evolution Gower's work had undergone since *Mr. Music*—so phenomenal that it is indeed lamentable he never made another film musical. By the time RKO offered him another assignment, he and Marge were already committed to something else.

Deciding to put their nondancing skills to a more rigorous test, the Champions accepted the invitation of comedian Jack Benny and his television production company, J and M Enterprises, to star in a weekly situation comedy replacing Ann Southern's long-running series, *Private Secretary*. In January 1957, they agreed to do *The Marge and Gower Champion Show,* a series of six programs—two live and four filmed—to alternate with Benny's show on a biweekly basis. At once, Gower began painstaking plans for the series, even adding a studio and, later, an office to the family's new home where he and Marge could both work and also be with their son. But the new addition soon became his inner sanctum—a place where he removed himself from family and the world beyond to pursue his muse unrestrained. Once sequestered there, nothing—phone calls, meals, not even Marge's entreaties—could rouse him from this self-imposed exile, which he relished greatly. Creation required concentration, and concentration, the imposition of an absolute silence necessitated by his unusually keen sense of hearing. (On one occasion, he had given Marge the gift of an expensive watch with a cloisonné case, which had to be opened in order to read the face. Each night before retiring, she had to bury it in the thick carpet beneath the bed to mute what little sound it made; otherwise the noise would keep him awake all night.)

So seriously did Gower take his work that his drive and rigid standards seemed at times to border on the obsessive. Yet for all his perfectionism, he was quite modest about his achievement. While he was touring with *3 for Tonight* at the University of North Carolina at Chapel Hill, a professor in the dance department asked him what the source of his psychokinetic impulse was. "I just go for the hand," he replied. Simply put, applause was the end for which he created, and to achieve it he would give his all, often at the expense of other priorities.[12] At the end of the day, when he finally emerged from his cloister to resume contact with the outside world, he was as affable and attentive as could be, at least until that instant when, once again, his charm would shut down, making him seem remote to those in his company—even his own family.

The producers planned to film the first episode of the Champions' television show to give the stars ample time to prepare for the two live broadcasts, which were to follow. Featured also on the initial program would be Gower's "Ballet of the Expectant Father," which he intended to choreograph and perform in celebration of Gregg's birth; the dance, however, was not to take place. The morning of March 13, when filming for the first episode was to commence, Marge left the house for an early makeup call at the studio where Gower was later to join her. On the way, he lost control of the car while winding through Laurel Canyon, and crashed at the intersection of Hollywood Boulevard and Laurel Avenue. Paul Harrison, the show's producer, who was only a few minutes behind, suddenly came upon his star sitting on the ground outside an overturned car, holding his bloody face in his hands. Harrison rushed him to Hollywood Receiving Hospital, where after a series of X-rays he was treated for a lacerated lip, bruised jaw, and several loose teeth, including one that was dislodged. The producer telephoned Marge, who directly left the studio in full makeup to join her husband and accompany him to Mount Sinai Hospital, where he was further treated and finally released. Gower was badly shaken by this brush with death, and so was Marge. Since Gregg's birth, they had agreed to travel separately so that in the event of an accident, there still would be one of them to care for him. It was their hope that this prudent policy would never have to be put to the test, yet there it was only weeks after its implementation. It was fortunate that Gower's injuries were not more serious than they had been.[13]

The first episode was now two weeks away from its March 31 airdate—time enough for Gower to heal sufficiently for an appearance on a live broadcast, but not for the filming, which had to be done immediately. The producers decided to do a live presentation with a new story about Gower sustaining a broken toe that confined him to a wheelchair. Though the accident had not compromised his dancing skill, his facial injuries precluded any possibility of close-ups (which somehow he had managed to avoid when presenting the Oscar for Art Direction with Marge at the Academy Awards on March 27), so Marge teamed up with Jack Whiting, who played her father, and special guest Dan Dailey for the dancing. Between Gower's limited participation and the technical pitfalls of live broadcasting, the show had an undistinguished premiere, which other directors and writers attempted to undo in subsequent episodes. Recognizing his talent as a congenial television host, the writers, at the advice of Jack Benny, gave Gower a monologue at the beginning of each segment. Marge had a sharp comic sense, so her character was given a bubbleheaded quality in the manner of Lucille Ball and Gracie Allen. The general consensus of the critics was that the Champions performed superbly, but that their writers kept digging up tired old situations and lines.

In the quest to find the right combination for a long-running show, various writers and directors were employed, with no success. Finally, one Saturday morning, as the Champions were breakfasting on the patio of their home, a letter arrived by special delivery. It was from the sponsor of the program informing them that he was withdrawing his support of the show. Although at the time Gower told the press that he and Marge "felt completely relieved" and "weren't sore at anybody,"[14] the fact of the matter was that they had been embroiled in a real power struggle. They had wanted to do a musical program emphasizing dance; the sponsor and MCA, their agency, wanted a situation comedy; and producer Jack Benny wanted a comic revue. As a result, the program had what Gower called "an unresolved directional focus—meaning it didn't quite come off."[15] With everyone pulling in a different direction and the changes in directors and writers, the show was a major disappointment to its stars. "The experience embittered me," Gower later recalled, "It left scars."[16] By the beginning of June, *The Marge and Gower Champion Show* had expired.

Just before the demise of the show, negotiations commenced for them to appear in the London production of *Bells Are Ringing*, but the musical had no substantial dancing in it, and composer Jule Styne did not care to do the kind of revision necessary to star a dance team. However, that disappointment was somewhat mitigated by an invitation from Secretary of State John Foster Dulles to entertain Great Britain's Queen Elizabeth II at a state dinner to be given in her honor on October 19, 1957, in Washington, D.C. That evening, as the team whirled through their "County Fair" number before the royal visitor, one of the straps of Marge's white sequined gown broke. Then, as she and Gower danced on, the other strap gave way. Although the dress stayed in place, the dancing halted abruptly as she clutched her hand to the front of it and bowed gracefully. An apologetic Gower addressed the Queen and the white tie, long-dress assembly, saying, "So happy were we to appear before this distinguished gathering that, as you see, we rushed out and bought Marge a new dress. Unhappily, it has parted company. We had planned two more numbers, but instead we regretfully must part company, too."[17]

The audience laughed politely, and then broke into spontaneous applause—the loudest coming from the Queen herself—as the disheartened couple exited gracefully into the wings. The incident, distressing enough in itself, was compounded by the fact that this was to have been the fulfillment of a dream deferred when plans for their London premiere at the time of the Queen's coronation were canceled. The following morning, just as they were about to board the plane for their flight home to Hollywood, a courier arrived with a note and gift for Marge. Opening the note, she read, "The Queen and I enjoyed your dancing very much last night. This is just to express our sympathy for the unfortunate mishap to your dress!" It was signed, "Philip." She opened the gift and, to her delight, discovered two green orchids—one from the Queen and one from her husband, Prince Philip.[18]

Following the release of *The Girl Most Likely* early in 1958, the team announced the establishment of their new dance school, the Marge and Gower Champion Workshop. Located at 331 North LaCienega Boulevard in Beverly Hills, it was to be the first laboratory where not only dancers, but also singers and actors, could work together with renowned professionals in their field to create and refine their art. Through the years, Marge's father, Ernest Belcher, who had long been one of the most respected dancing teachers in Hollywood, had lost touch with his students as his administrative load increased and forced him to retire from teaching. Now, his daughter and son-in-law wanted to give him an opportunity to practice once again alongside other dance professionals of renown like Charles Wideman, Irina Kosmovska, Lewis DePron, Dolores Blacker, and Marie Bryant. Thomas Sheehy, with whom Gower had studied as a boy at the Elisa Ryan School of Dancing, was appointed director of the workshop, which was to offer classes from preschool through professional in all styles of dancing, including ballet. It was a wonderful idea, but a task requiring a vast amount of time, attention, and effort—all of which the Champions had little of now that they were raising a family as well as pursuing a career. It never got off the ground.[19]

While continuing to make television and nightclub appearances with Marge and direct for television, Gower began to search for a stage play to direct. His best offer came by way of William Tregoe, operator of the Avondale Playhouse-in-the-Meadows, a tent theatre in Indianapolis, who had sent him a play by William Mercer titled *Hemingway and All Those People* in the spring of 1958. Champion Five, Inc. could acquire Broadway production rights, Marge could play the lead, and he could direct—a perfect combination.

Less than perfect, however, was the manner in which he took charge of the proceedings, directing with too firm a hand. Not only did he fail to give the actors sufficient latitude to improvise and explore their characters, he also neglected to take into account the configuration of the Avondale Playhouse—a tent theatre with an arena stage and a formidable challenge for a director who had only worked the proscenium stages of conventional theatres. Tensions developed as his exacting staging technique clashed with the less rigorous style of the actors. Ultimately, the evening of his debut as a director of drama on July 29, 1958, was far from a triumph. "Like all of his colleagues, Champion worked hard to make a play," explained one critic. "The material isn't there."[20] In the wake of unfavorable notices, plans for a New York debut were scuttled. For Gower, the failure was not in directing the actors as if they were dancers, but in not having full control over the whole production—theatre and script included. Thereafter, to insure success he insisted on having absolute authority over every aspect of the works he staged. It was the only way to avoid another *Hemingway*.

Now approaching age forty, the Champions were more discerning than ever about the nature of projects they undertook in an effort to maintain the hard-earned reputation they had built over the years. Despite the fresh and varied manner of their nightclub and television performances, their agent, Al Melnick, would often submit screenplays or television dramas with prosaic, or worse, ludicrous plots. One was a script for a film called *International Wedding* in which Gower would play a high jumper from the United States who meets Marge, a swimmer from Czechoslovakia, at the Melbourne Olympics, where their romance unfolds once they discover their mutual love of dance. The mere mention of such a film was so preposterous that it was turned down flat.

On February 28, 1959, CBS aired a musical revue with the Champions, Jaye P. Morgan, Louis Jourdan, Ginger Rogers, Mike Nichols, and Elaine May called *Accent on Love*, which Gower also directed. Because the *Hemingway* experience had so completely exhausted his flair for complex staging, this presentation would be comparatively elementary, consisting of stools and chairs for props and very straightforward camera angles. The unusual construction of the show was not lost on the reporters, one of whom noted that its "most significant aspect was the unusual manner in which the assembled talent was utilized. Each of the principals was given the spotlight but all were used to complement one another's big moment, with no vocal or dance ensembles to clutter the stage."[21] As the program opened with each of the principals seated on stools, Jourdan began the narration, which described different kinds of love calls, including a car horn blast, a champagne cork pop, a telephone ring, and the plaintive voice of Elaine May whining, "Walter, Walter." Then Jourdan led the ensemble as the conductor of the series of sounds. Thus, the concept and the juxtaposition of sounds were emphasized, rather than the staging. Champion was coming of age as a conceptual director.

This revue, together with two earlier specials—*No Man Can Tame Me,* a musical with John Raitt, Gisele MacKensie, and Eddie Foy Jr., and an adaptation of George M. Cohan's 1906 musical *Forty-Five Minutes from Broadway* (1959) by Walter Kerr and William H. Graham, starring Tammy Grimes and Larry Blyden— moved NBC to offer Gower six specials to produce and direct for the 1959–1960 television season. Tempting as the offer was, television was not the venue in which he wanted to continue plying his craft. His greatest success thus far was as a director-choreographer for the dance acts and revues he had staged. He was aiming for a Broadway musical and was even considering what he might do with the hodgepodge of a script for one he had recently received.

Meanwhile, he would bide his time, for there was plenty to keep him busy between his burgeoning directing career and his performances with Marge, not the least of which was the dance they performed to the Oscar-nominated song, "A Certain Smile," sung by John Raitt during the Academy Awards ceremony on April 6, 1959.[22] The response that evening from peers gathered from around the world made the Champions long more than ever for the chance to go international with the act. Important as that was, there were other issues stirring a growing restlessness in "Gar" that Jess Gregg keenly sensed as the two lay sunning themselves on a high terrace in Miami one afternoon. "I want to quit dancing. I'm pushing forty," Gar confided, "and after that it's all downhill for a dancer."

"What'll you do instead?" asked Jess. "Direct?"

He nodded. "And not just the dances. I want to stage the whole bloody show."

"What about Marge?" His glance was wry.

"Do you even have to ask? This is what she's been waiting for—the chance to start a family."[23]

With the advent of the recently negotiated Cultural Exchange Program between the United States and the Soviet Union in 1959, Ed Sullivan decided to take his Sunday evening variety series to Moscow that August to tape a ninety-minute special for broadcast on September 27. When the news reached the Champions, Marge called Sullivan to propose the team for the tour and immediately received his unqualified approval. Both she and Gower felt that "Let's Dance" and "Underneath the Clock" were best for the occasion, but because the former required a narration at certain intervals, Gower attended Berlitz classes to learn how to speak it phonetically in Russian. Eventually, his pronunciation became so good that once the tour commenced, the Russians themselves assumed he spoke their language fluently and often started conversations with him.

The day-to-day escalation of the Cold War had brought diplomatic relations between the two nations almost to a standstill, so the tour was "restricted" to the cities of Moscow and Leningrad for a total of fourteen performances. Yet in recognition of the need to diffuse tensions and promote dialogue, both governments fully endorsed this extraordinary venture, pledging their full support to the television host. Such cooperation would be crucial if Sullivan were to realize his vision of Marge and Gower dancing in the celebrated marble subway of the Soviet capital, mezzo-soprano Risë Stevens singing in Red Square, and other performers entertaining before a fabulous backdrop of ancient onion-domed churches. In the end, he would get most of what his "Invitation to Moscow Variety Show" required, but not without first getting his Irish up over the arrogant nonchalance of the Soviet Ministry of Culture, the agency in charge of hosting the event.

Follow spots for performers, colored gelatins for lights, and a stage from which to hang the elaborate sets brought from the United States were just a few of the many essentials originally promised, then intentionally denied by the Russian cultural bureaucracy. After two full weeks of this, Sullivan reached his limit and fired off a wire to Soviet Premier Nikita Khrushchev in protest. Within thirty minutes, the boorish martinets who had thwarted the project suddenly became congenial ambassadors of national goodwill, obstacles miraculously vanished, and Sullivan, his cast, and crew could have anything they wanted. They even could tape the show in Red Square, on a riverboat, in the Russian Circus, and in the Puppet Theatre. Though Marge and Gower never did get the opportunity to dance in the marble subway, the overwhelming approval they received from the people of Moscow and Leningrad was something they would not soon forget, for it brought them international fame at long last.

The evening they opened at the Green Theatre in Gorki Park was a particularly unsettling one for them. Twelve thousand people had packed the outdoor amphitheater, the largest audience the couple had ever played before, and their response at the conclusion of the first number jolted the dancers. Instantly, the entire throng roared what sounded like a tremendous "boo" along with cries, which grew in intensity as all began clapping in unison. Marge was almost in tears when she left the stage, but everybody in the wings was grinning broadly. The interpreter quickly explained that the cries were not "boos," but "moos"—the Russian equivalent of "more." The Champions had earned the highest accolade the audience could bestow. It meant that the clapping would not cease until there was an encore, which the elated couple promptly gave.[24]

The team's appearances in Leningrad and Moscow in the summer of 1959 would be their final ones together. Prior to the tour, they announced the dissolution of the act.[25] Marge would devote herself more to domestic responsibilities now that Gower had accepted a script from producer Edward Padula for a rock 'n' roll musical about teenagers called *Let's Go Steady*. Though less then enthralled with the subject matter, he agreed to direct and choreograph what in time would become his first Broadway musical, *Bye Bye Birdie* (1960).

EIGHT

A Revusical: Sardonic, Yet Stylish

Bye Bye Birdie

1960

By the time Padula brought *Let's Go Steady* to Gower in the summer of 1958, both Fred Astaire and Morton DaCosta (*The Music Man*) had already declined offers to direct.[1] One look at the libretto by Warren Miller and Raphael Millian, and Gower did the same. To win him over, Padula fired the writers, hired and fired a succession of others (including Mike Nichols and Elaine May), then finally heeded the advice of the musical's songwriters Charles Strouse and Lee Adams to engage Michael Stewart.[2] The writer, who had collaborated with the team on revues for Green Mansions, a summer resort in the Adirondacks, joined them in December 1958.[3]

From the beginning, Padula viewed *Let's Go Steady* as a "happy teenage musical with a difference"[4]—the "difference" being an affectionate and whimsical portrait of teens as opposed to the violent one promoted in the somber *West Side Story* the previous season. The idea apparently impressed Texas millionaire-industrialist L. Slade Brown, who acquired the means to finance the show.

A year later, on June 25, 1959, Padula forwarded Stewart's revision of *Let's Go Steady*—now entitled *Love and Kisses*—to Gower, who remained unimpressed.[5] "The book was nowhere," he later stated. "It was a straight satire on a rock 'n' roll singer. I'd seen enough of those on TV. I wanted social commentary, with the emphasis not on the singer, but on how and why masses of people reacted to him."[6]

Although an improvement over the work of his predecessors, Stewart's first draft of *Love and Kisses* was largely an effort to salvage the score of *Let's Go Steady* while rewriting its tired plot about a couple on the brink of divorce whose children persuade them to reconcile. Yet even as the social commentary filtered into Stewart's later revisions and the project became more attractive, Gower still hesitated, with good reason: the producer wanted him not only to direct and choreograph, but also to play the lead opposite Marge.[7] At age thirty-nine, undertaking the triple duties of director, choreographer, and performer, as he had done on *3 for Tonight*

five years before, was out of the question. "I wouldn't dream of directing and performing in the same show. It's sheer egocentric madness. There comes a point when
you've got to be out front. Who can be two places at once? I told Padula I'd enjoy
directing much more than starring. And Marge wanted to stay home with our
son."[8] Padula capitulated. On August 8, 1959, the press reported that Gower Champion would direct and choreograph *The Day They Took Birdie Away.*[9] In coming
months, the musical would be rechristened *Going Steady,* and still later, *Goodbye
Birdie Goodbye* before receiving its final name.[10]

A show about a rock 'n' roll singer was an odd choice for Gower, whose disdain
for the new music was considerable. (He regarded rock 'n' roll as a fad, like swing
and jitterbug before it, and therefore had refused to use it in the dance act.[11])
Though the prospect of swarms of teenage girls swooning over a pop idol was an
idea certainly ripe for exploitation (and something he himself had had a brush
with in his youth), it was the family-oriented nature of the piece that appealed to
him. "It came at a time in his life when we had been married a long time," explains
Marge. "I think the first nine years of our lives when we didn't have children, he
wouldn't have been drawn to the material. But beginning with *Everything I Have Is
Yours,* anything to do with family kept creeping into our work. Even 'Nursery
Rhymes,' our final television special for *The Bell Telephone Hour,* was about family.
So he couldn't have been sucked into *Bye Bye Birdie* unless we had already had a
child. All of that had become less scary to him."[12]

Gower's preference for family-oriented material was also something Jess noted
upon his return from Europe in the fall of 1959. "When he told me that he was going into rehearsal with *Birdie,* I stayed at their apartment a few days before I went
back to my own, and we went through the script together. I remember thinking I
wish he didn't like this family-type stuff quite so well; there were more exciting
things I thought he could do."[13] The explanation may have been rooted in his upbringing. "Gower had not had a great deal of family life himself," adds Jess, "and I
think it was something that, in his mind, he yearned for. He didn't know how to
handle it except in the theatre. His biggest successes were with family value things,
and I thought they were a little sweet on self. But for a while, he made a great thing
of it."[14] Indeed he did. *Carnival* (1961), *Hello, Dolly!* (1964), and *I Do! I Do!* (1966)
were all major success, but with the failure of *The Happy Time* (1968), his penchant
for family fare would fade.

Because the creators of *Bye Bye Birdie* were novices to the book musical, pundits
underestimated this satire on the rock 'n' roll phenomenon then captivating teens
and panicking parents. Gower's sole stage directing credits were revues. Padula, a
former director (Lerner and Loewe's *The Day Before Spring*) and production man-

ager (*No Time for Sergeants, Seventh Heaven,* and *Saratoga*), was undertaking his first professional venture as a producer.[15] Stewart, Strouse, and Adams had previously written only for nightclub and off-Broadway revues.[16] Even the major performers—Chita Rivera, Dick Van Dyke, Kay Medford, and Paul Lynde—were not exactly household names. (Rivera, a sensation in *West Side Story,* took the part of Rose Grant after Carol Haney [illness] and Eydie Gormé [pregnant] turned it down. Consequently, the character's surname became "Alvarez" and the jokes about her "Polish" lineage, "Spanish." As for Medford and Lynde, their roles were virtually nonexistent at the time of their signing. Gower won them over with the understanding that he would build the parts around their unique talents, which he did.[17]) In the end, however, these "drawbacks" would emerge as the chief strengths of the production.

Under the director's steady hand, *Birdie* gradually became a hilarious but tasteful satire, combining Robert Randolph's cartoonlike sets, Miles White's colorful costumes, and Peggy Clark's attractive lighting with songs, dances, and dialogue that poked fun at American pop culture and its impact on the public. But all this did not spring fully realized from Gower's imagination. It was a painstaking process assembled bit by bit, which his script, notes, and schedule for the production clearly show. From inception to Broadway opening, Gower worked ceaselessly with his collaborators to fuse *Birdie* into a cohesive whole. To do this, he first applied the practice of the day, using the musical numbers to advance the story. But the show's double plot (Rose and Albert's on-again/off-again romance, and small-town America's reaction to a visit from a rock superstar) defied conventional organization. Moreover, the sketchlike comic scenes, humorous characters (many of them rooted in vaudeville "types"), and satiric nature of the work made it seem more like a fanciful revue on the order of *Lend an Ear* or *Streets of Paris,* rather than a traditional book show. Gower let his theatrical instinct prevail; he restructured the show like a revue using the score as key. Building number upon number, he generated a variety of moods calculated to entertain. In this way, *Birdie*'s numbers and the feelings they evoked determined the course of its plot, unlike most musicals of the day whose plots dictated the score.

Skilled as they were in the art of revue, Stewart, Strouse, and Adams immediately connected with this approach and worked tirelessly with Gower through fall 1959 and into the six-week preproduction period, December 21 to January 30, 1960, to better the book and score. Stewart's *Love and Kisses,* with its new emphasis on rock idol "Ellsworth" (later Conrad) Birdie and the music industry magnates who plot his every move for adoring fans, lost half of its first act after Gower's initial review. Cliché scenes like a local Sweet Shop complete with soda-sipping teens quickly vanished along with characters such as beatniks (by then passé) and a seedy theatrical agent named Stanley Wezelle (whom Stewart would later resurrect for *One of the Girls* [1970], an original libretto suggested by the film *Some Like It Hot* [1959]).[18] The writer quickly responded with improved scenes, stronger characters, and trimmer dialogue with funnier "zingers" (as Gower called his comic lines).

While the libretto was being redrafted, Strouse and Adams revised the score. Act I was shaping up nicely. Rose's frustration with mother-fixated beau Albert was captured in "An English Teacher"; the teens had a bouncy rock cantata, "The Telephone Hour"; Birdie's "Honestly Sincere" and "One Last Kiss" burlesqued the pulsating style of rock icon Elvis Presley; "How Lovely to Be a Woman" and "One Boy" were apt summations of ingénue Kim MacAfee's joy in achieving physical maturity and romance; and the Cohanesque "Normal American Boy" gave Albert and Rose a patriotic guise to conceal Conrad's indiscretions from fans made suspicious by a probing New York press. "All Woman," a romantic duet for Rose and Albert, was eliminated, and "Togetherness," a march in which Albert and Rose tried to mollify the MacAfees after they expressed reservations about taking in Ellsworth as a houseguest, was replaced with a parental paean to TV host Ed Sullivan, "Hymn for a Sunday Evening."[19]

Act II required more substantial work. A reprise of the teens' "The Telephone Hour," with a spider web of phone lines stretching into infinity, had been planned as the opener, but this later gave way to a duet for Rose and Kim, "What Did I Ever See in Him?" Gone was "Don't Be the One to Let Show Business Down," in which Mae and Albert bolstered Ellsworth's spirits following his humiliation on national television. (Too similar to Irving Berlin's "There's No Business Like Show Business," thought Gower.) Also cut were "Thief of Love," Kim's boyfriend's debut as a rock singer, and "Nothingness," the beatniks' summation of their philosophy of life. The choral rouser, "A Lot of Livin' to Do," and Albert's ballad, "Baby, Talk to Me," were substituted. "The Shriners' (originally "Kiwanis") Ballet" was added, along with a comic lament airing the parents' vexation with "Kids," which supplanted their former "The Younger Generation." Rose's "Older but Wiser" with Kim yielded to her eleven-o'clocker, "Spanish Rose," which paved way for the finale, "Rosie."[20]

After plotting the score for the dances with arranger John Morris, Gower spent the remainder of the preproduction period at the Winter Garden Theatre constructing the dances with associate choreographer Gene Bayliss, and then rehearsing them with the principals and conductor Elliot Lawrence, with whom he would later reteam for *Sugar* (1972).

Rehearsals with the full company began on February 1 and continued through March 11 on the Lower East Side at the Phyllis Anderson, an old Yiddish theatre on Third Avenue. Each day the director would promptly arrive, leather-bound script in tow and Marge at his side, who would give a discreet whisper in his ear whenever his inspiration slowed.[21] "She was responsible for many of the best ideas," explains Strouse. "I never got close to Gower. I found him to be a very cold man, very controlling and very controlled. Each day he ate the same lunch: a bacon, lettuce, and tomato sandwich and a glass of milk. He was immaculate, exceedingly neat. His rehearsal outfits, with everything just so in cashmere pastels, made us feel like we were homeless."[22] The pastels quickly gave way to black T-shirt and slacks and white tennis shoes—his trademark rehearsal attire in every show thereafter. Gradually, the contour of the "revusical" became more discernable as Gower pulled songs, story, and staging together.

Stewart was making great strides with the libretto, exploiting the humor in the tale of the riotous farewell American teens give to rock idol Conrad Birdie (Dick Gautier) upon his induction into the Army. This now folded in effectively with the story of Conrad's manager, Albert Peterson (Dick Van Dyke), who is shattered by the prospect of losing his star performer, but heartened when Rose Alvarez (Chita Rivera), his intrepid secretary and long-suffering fiancée of eight years, proposes that he write a farewell song for the singer to perform on national television to a fan chosen to receive his final civilian kiss. Albert agrees, and Rose selects fifteen-year-old Kim MacAfee (Susan Watson) of Sweet Apple, Ohio, as the honoree.

One hysterical complication piles upon another as Birdie brings the town to a collective swoon and shatters the tranquility of the MacAfee household. Albert's overbearing mother, Mae (Kay Medford), arrives from New York to undermine his romance; Kim's father (Paul Lynde), mother (Marijane Maricle), and brother (Johnny Borden) mug their way onto *The Ed Sullivan Show* for Kim's big moment with Conrad, which is destroyed by her jealous boyfriend Hugo Peabody (Michael J. Pollard), and Rose, miffed by Albert's failure to confront Mae. She escapes to a local roadhouse to join a group of Shriners in a wild frolic while Conrad departs for the town's icehouse with Kim, whose father rallies neighbors in a frantic search to rescue her and her friends from his spell. Calm is finally restored when the parents retrieve their errant offspring, Hugo reconciles with Kim, and Albert dispatches both Conrad and Mae aboard the next train out of town. As it departs, Rose returns. Impressed with his take-charge attitude and decision to forsake the music business for a position as an English professor in a small college town, she agrees to become his wife.

With Stewart's rollicking libretto now fusing with Strouse and Adams's lively songs, Gower's stage mystique increased momentum. A filmed prologue accompanying the overture contrasted frames of Birdie disporting his pelvis with expressions of disapproval from President Eisenhower, Russian Premier Khrushchev, and the previous generation's teen icon—Frank Sinatra.[23] For "The Telephone Hour," the adolescent population of Sweet Apple was shown monopolizing local phone lines via Randolph's multilevel jungle gym honeycombed with primary-hued cubicles. Each cubicle housed a singing teen—telephone receiver in hand—in a distinctive acrobatic pose. The arrangement was theatrical and practical, establishing physical separation without losing the shoulder-to-shoulder volume and group presence of a chorus.[24] The prosperity of AT&T had never been so clearly or charmingly explained.[25] "The Telephone Hour" was also the first of many production numbers in which Gower used levels as a means of conveying unique and impressive stage pictures.

"How Lovely to Be a Woman" was infused with tongue-in-cheek humor. As Susan Watson sang of the pleasure of wearing the mascara, lipstick, heels, and beautiful clothes of womanhood, she dressed herself in the dowdy trappings of regulation teenage attire—shapeless sweater, blue jeans, baseball cap, argyle socks, and scuffy, pink-furred slippers. The idea was piquant, the execution funny, and the result devastating.[26]

The appeal of "Put on a Happy Face" stemmed from Albert's attempt to cheer two glum girls disturbed by Conrad's induction. One (Sharon Lerit) made an especially splendid foil for Van Dyke, whose singing, nimble dancing, and comical attempts to get her to smile made the song a standout.[27] Even so, this was not how the choreographer had initially envisioned the number.

Strouse recalls that Gower's original staging of "Put on a Happy Face" centered on Albert's attempt to cheer Rose (dispirited by Mae's intrusion). Audience response to the number during the show's Philadelphia tryout was "brilliant," with Van Dyke getting "a fantastic hand" and Rivera "an instant success."[28] However, Marge felt that it would be more effective as a dance duet for Van Dyke and the girls. With pressure mounting from *Birdie*'s backers to replace Van Dyke with a bigger name, Gower tried the number her way. "And the minute it started," relates Strouse, "everybody just ate it up. . . . They stopped the show every time. Today that seems typical, but it was very inventive in 1960."[29] It was also a unique showcase for Van Dyke's musical talents, making it clear that he was a song and dance man of considerable ability.

"Honestly Sincere," *Birdie*'s adenoidal aria, saw a gyrating Dick Gautier, clad in skintight gold lamé jumpsuit, sideburns, and pomaded black mane, generate a street-corner delirium that drove townsfolk into a state of mass collapse. For the director, the number was a nightmare: "I had a horrible time with the fainting scene. At first, I tried to stage it with formal dance patterns. I was about halfway through when I realized it was all wrong—formal choreography stifled the fun of it. The scene needed a wild, improvisational quality and I think I finally achieved it with twisting, falling bodies fixed in position. The only person who moves around a lot is Birdie."[30]

Only a few choice gestures were needed to carry "Hymn for a Sunday Evening," as father, mother, daughter, son, and a gathering swarm of suddenly exalted neighbors turned to the footlights, composed their faces, clasped their hands, and elevated their souls to chant the praises of "Ed . . . Ed Sullivan"—the television host whose variety show was a Sunday-evening ritual in homes across the nation.[31]

The choreographer also created four distinct dances for Rivera. The first was "One Boy," a solo in which she danced with various-sized suitcases. "How to Kill a Man" was a *danse macabre* in which Rivera envisioned her callous fiancé meeting his demise by means ranging from the guillotine—as she knitted à la Madame Defarge—to the underworld with her as a black-veiled mafiosa trailing behind his coffin.[32] In "Spanish Rose," she burlesqued Hispanophila in all its aspects, from *cante hondo* to "La Cucaracha," but scored her biggest triumph seducing a pack of befezzed males in Champion's supreme contribution of the evening—the "Shriners' Ballet."[33] It was a hilarious dance that took place mainly under a long table when Rivera, bent on forgetting Van Dyke, invaded a Shriners' meeting. Approaching the startled clubmen, the lithe and attractive dancer bumped, thumped, and teased until the meeting became a wild demented orgy left to the audience's imagination as arms, legs, heads, and flowerpot hats frantically appeared from under the table, then vanished without trace.[34]

"Rosie" brought the musical to an unconventional end: a duet for Van Dyke and Rivera sung with her seated upon a luggage cart that he steered gracefully about the stage. By closing the evening this way, rather than with an elaborate chorus number, Gower demonstrated rare intelligence and taste.[35]

On Friday afternoon, March 11, before departing for a three-and-a-half-week tryout at Philadelphia's Shubert Theatre, the cast gave a dress rehearsal for an invited audience. This "gypsy runthrough," a common practice of the day, was so-called because the audience consisted mostly of dancers or "gypsies" who, like the cast, traveled from show to show. The response of *Birdie*'s gypsy audience was ecstatic—certification that the Philly-bound cast had a hit on their hands.

The momentary elation failed to sway Jess, whose stillness Gar noted with agitation as their taxi wound uptown following the runthrough. "The part of Rose was too tough, and Albert was unpleasant," he recalls. "They were funny in a way, but not likeable. None of the characters particularly mattered to me. Why? Because there was no particular conflict that appealed to me. I just didn't find anything to *like* about that."[36]

True friends will speak the truth, whether pleasant or not, and Jess finally told

Gar exactly what he thought. Marge blanched at the fierce expression on her husband's face as he exploded, "*Your* trouble is you want everybody to be Mary Pickford!" "I don't want everybody to be Mary Pickford," answered Jess, "but I want to *like* somebody a little bit." The taxi arrived at Jess's door, and as he quietly exited, Gar glanced away crossly. Only Marge said good night before the taxi sped off.

Two days later, a still touchy Gar phoned Jess demanding him to repeat his critique, and then promptly hung up upon hearing it again. In seconds, he phoned back, spouting, "This is a show about kids; you're too old to understand!" Now Jess hung up. Back and forth they battled for over an hour until finally agreeing to meet over breakfast the next morning to explore ideas that might enhance the characters. Although Jess gave no specific advice out of respect for Stewart's work, the brainstorming session was so productive that Gar had him travel with the show (and later ones) as his unofficial devil's advocate.[37]

On March 16, just as the curtain was to go up on the first tryout performance, the show was halted until a $75,000 bond could be posted to cover production costs; Padula phoned everyone to try and raise the money, finally reaching Goddard Lieberson of Columbia Records, who agreed to guarantee the bond in exchange for album rights to the musical.[38] "If Goddard hadn't agreed or wasn't reachable," Gower later explained, "there never would have been a *Bye Bye Birdie.*"[39]

When the show finally opened to the critical raves of the Philadelphia press, the cast realized just how far the director had taken them. "When I first read the script," comments Susan Watson, "I thought this was one of the most stupid things I'd ever read. But Gower had all these marvelous ideas. When we went to Philadelphia, he made a lot of really radical changes. Songs were shifted from the first to the second act, and he would have everyone up in his hotel room working on the show. But Gower always knew where he was going with it, and what he wanted."[40]

Among his wants, disciplined performance was a priority. When the cast, now riding high on the raves of gypsies and critics alike, took liberties with the show the second night out of town, he quickly curbed their overconfidence. The following day he summoned them one by one into a dressing room where he read them the riot act.[41] Composure restored, he swiftly filtered out their "improvements."

Gower's intense discipline was not surprising given the exacting nature of his upbringing and the dance profession out of which he came. Yet integral as it was to his craft, it was not especially unique. Contemporaries like Jerome Robbins and Bob Fosse were no less methodical and rigorous. But Gower differed from them greatly. "He was lighthearted," explains Chita Rivera. "His work was very comedic, and very light, very colorful, very smooth—the Hollywood approach. He had done the whole framework of the 'Shriners' Ballet' without me—and when he showed it to me, I looked at it and said, 'You don't even need me.' It was so wonderfully conceived. But Gower was a taskmaster. If he said he was going to rehearse something at 12:03, it was 12:03."[42]

In the last days of the Philly tryout, Gower continued to introduce changes. Consistent with his view of *Birdie* as a "family show" was the trimming of burlesquelike character Gloria Rasputin, played by Norma Richardson. "Mike Stewart had written some very sleazy comedy," Jess explains, "mostly around a character named Gloria Rasputin, and Gower told Mike, 'I don't want it in here. I don't want anything that kids can't come and see.' And out it went, and the show was improved by it."[43]

When *Bye Bye Birdie* hit the boards of New York's Martin Beck Theatre on the evening of April 14, 1960, skepticism swiftly turned to acclaim. The show was hailed as the funniest, most captivating, and most expert musical comedy in several seasons by the critics, who also agreed that one of the best things about it was that practically no one of renown was connected with it.[44] Among those catapulted to superstardom that night, Chita Rivera, in her first leading role, confirmed the promise she showed in *West Side Story* with a singing, dancing, and comic virtuosity that proved she belonged in the front rank of her profession.[45] Dick Van Dyke, in what would be a Tony Award–winning performance, sputtered fretfully in the scenes with his mother, mugged amusingly in the comedy bits, and danced with the carefree grace of a Fred Astaire.[46] As his mother, Kay Medford was a scream as a grandly glum mink-drapped *yenta* from the Bronx prepared at once to hurl herself under train wheels to stop her thirty-three-year-old baby from dashing into marriage.[47] Paul Lynde's comically edgy *paterfamilias* found a perfect foil to his lunacy in Marijane Maricle's bewildered Mrs. MacAfee, and Dick Gautier brilliantly captured the best and the worst of Conrad Birdie, the hip-swinging, beer-swigging lout with a nasty disdain for his worshipers and a sense that this world is crazy, man, crazy.[48] Susan Watson, in the role of small-town girl Kim MacAfee, virtually ran away with the evening for sheer young attractiveness, and Michael J. Pollard, as her sweatered swain Hugo Peabody, added boyish charm.[49]

Nor was the appeal of *Birdie*'s confident kids overlooked. Reviewers noted how the teens really looked like teens and were taken with their attractive movement and behavior.[50] The observation must surely have pleased the director considering the problems he initially encountered in casting: "I had to find twevle dancers, six girls and six boys, but they had to be between the ages of fourteen and seventeen. They had to sing nicely, speak lines as well as dance, be well trained and attractive. They had to have the innocent, scrubbed look of the Midwest, not the sophisticated attitude of 'Showbiz.'"[51] Gower searched a full month before finally assembling a dozen teens drawn not from the ranks of experienced New York theatre dancers, but from newcomers across the country making their first Broadway appearance.[52]

The uniformly broad and hilarious performances drawn from the cast were just some of the many contributions of the real hero of the evening, whose work was generally regarded as the production's mainstay—one that deftly entwined his own silken style with a counterforce of comic factors and illustrated expert teamwork resourcefully commanded.[53] To a book that actually consisted of two stories, Gower had brought a sense of unity while providing plentiful stage magic with an endless array of inventive touches, as well as dances and chorus numbers that exploded with brilliant comic imagination.[54] But he had done one other thing of enormous importance. To a story treating the potentially insipid matter of the silly swooning over an idiotic singer, he had brought, in the words of the *Post*'s Richard Watts Jr., "not only perfect taste but also the appeal of warmheartedness."[55] In this way, *Birdie* defined the features of Champion's stagecraft in the twenty years to come—brilliant imagination fused with endless inventive touches, then tempered with perfect taste and warmheartedness to unify production.

Fast action, broad humor, and rarely flagging pace helped to make *Birdie* a prime example of the unsophisticated but vigorous, brawny style of musical comedy popular at the onset of the 1960s.[56] At the conclusion of the 1960–61 season, it won the Tony for best musical and Gower was doubly honored for best direction and choreography.[57] Yet for all his inventive and award-winning staging, he had essentially kept to the custom of directing the book scenes as if they were part of a straight play, only turning his work musical for the songs and dances.[58] In the end, the search for a more effective approach—one that would minimize dialogue scenes to better integrate them with songs and dances—would require streamlining the conventions of the book musical itself. In *Carnival, Hello, Dolly!,* and subsequent productions, he would apply to book scenes the same ingenuity that characterized his musical numbers by intensifying action through choreographed movement and fashioning seamless transitions from dialogue into song. He would also substitute standard changes of scenery with the continuous staging he had started to explore in *Birdie.*

In 1960, scene changes were still largely made by conventional "blackouts"—brief intervals when the stage is completely dark that mark the end of one scene and the start of another. When time is required to set the subsequent scene, the orchestra plays music to cover the change. Once the new setting is in place, lights come up, cover music ceases, and performance resumes. These transitions, brief as they might be, are static and break the audience's focus by disrupting the flow of action.

Today's continuous staging, on the other hand, is dynamic and propels action forward by dissolving one scene into another in full view of the audience. According to scenic designer Oliver Smith, it was Joshua Logan who began directing continuously staged musicals as early as 1938 with *I Married an Angel*, and retained the practice throughout his career.[59] Though effective, Logan's transitions were dramatic rather than musical. He was not a choreographer and therefore unable to create transitions through dance or stylized movement.

Gower learned continuous staging from his club work, which he and Marge performed on an unlocalized stage, never exiting once the act began. Number followed upon number with transitions part of performance. His adaptation of this practice to the musical stage added one significant factor: choreography. While performers moved or danced, lighting shifted, music played, and scenery changed all in one huge choreographed movement that advanced action without pause.

In the twenty years following *Birdie*, Gower consistently applied this technique to every scenic transition in every musical he directed. As a result, continuously choreographed staging became *de rigueur* in the theatre. Yet inasmuch as he popularized continuously choreographed staging, he cannot be credited with its invention. Jerome Robbins first used it in *West Side Story* during the transition from "Bridal Shop" to "Dance in the Gym." Maria began to whirl in her new dress, the shop slid off, and a flood of brightly colored streamers poured down. Then as she turned and turned, going offstage, Shark girls, dressed for the dance, whirled on, followed by Jet girls and boys from both gangs. With that we were in the gym.[60]

Gower's application of the technique—what he called a "brownout"—was all the more amazing because it took place essentially with the full cast remaining onstage and in place while the scenery changed around them. The transition from *Birdie*'s "Penn Station" to "Sweet Apple" illustrates the point.

During the applause following "Normal American Boy," lighting dimmed slightly while billows of steam from the departing train filled the stage. Members of the crowd standing downstage then turned their backs to the audience to strip off topcoats (collected by passersby) concealing their Sweet Apple costumes. In the midst of this, Penn Station was flown out and Sweet Apple Depot flown in as the mayor, his wife, and additional townsfolk maneuvered through the crowd and into place as the train came back on. Finally, full lighting was restored, revealing a totally transformed scenic picture—a picture that had never vanished, but had faded into another.[61] Though the remainder of *Birdie*'s scenic transitions was as conventional as those of *West Side Story*, the brownout laid the foundation for future works, which would be continuously choreographed throughout. By streamlining the way productions were mounted, Gower would soon bring the staging of conventional musicals to its highest peak and pave the way for the concept musicals to come.[62]

With the critical and popular success of *Birdie*, Gower Champion joined the elite line of director-choreographers initiated by Agnes de Mille with *Allegro* in

1947. More important, he could now completely devote himself to his new profession confident that the performer's life of which he had grown tired was finally at an end. Still, that life had played a significant role in his directing career—one that he readily acknowledged: "Since Marge and I have hung up our professional dancing shoes as a team, I see just how important and vital were the years we spent on the nightclub circuit now that I'm concentrating on directing."[63]

On the morning following the opening of *Bye Bye Birdie,* Michael Shurtleff, casting director for one of Broadway's major producers, steered his employer's attention to the musical's enthusiastic notices. The gloating Shurtleff, who for some time had pressed for the hiring of the new director-choreographer, was quickly chastened by David Merrick's pragmatic reply: "Yes, I see. We let other people take the chance. *Then* we take them."[64] Now that Padula had taken the chance producing the first Champion musical, Merrick would take it from there. Days later, Gower received the script for a musical adaptation of the MGM film *Lili.* From it, he would fashion *Carnival,* his second success.

NINE

Gentle Blockbuster

Carnival

1961

A stage adaptation of a film musical? Was Broadway now paying back Hollywood for years of exploitation? Maybe not, but the very idea of bringing MGM's *Lili* to the stage raised more than a few eyebrows when David Merrick first proposed it after the film's phenomenal success. The screenplay had been based on a short story inspired by a popular children's television program, *Kukla, Fran & Ollie,* which premiered in 1948 on NBC. Both young and old were drawn to its charming hostess, Fran Allison, and her daily interplay with Burr Tillstrom's puppets—especially the bulb-nosed boy, Kukla, and the shy but endearing dragon, Ollie. What distinguished the program was the astonishing fact that each live broadcast was done completely without a script. The resulting spontaneity owed much to Allison's uncanny way of relating to her co-stars: it was truly as if they were intimate friends. Indeed, many adult viewers felt that the hostess herself became a young girl in the course of her half-hour chats with Tillstrom's creatures.

Three years later, in "The Man Who Hated People," writer Paul Gallico drew upon this novel rapport for his story of Millie Maynard, a children's TV show hostess who befriends a menagerie of puppets manipulated by a talented but mordant puppeteer, Crake Villerage, whose face bears scars of the mishap that cut short his career as an ice hockey pro. Gallico's story, published in the October 28, 1950, edition of the *Saturday Evening Post,* immediately caught the attention of MGM executives.[1] They commissioned screenwriter Helen Deutsch to pen a version that shrewdly replaced the story's setting of TV (then Hollywood's chief competition) with a modern-day European carnival. Retained was Gallico's idea of a guileless heroine embraced by a group of puppets that speak the love their wounded master cannot express. The result was *Lili,* the unexpected hit of 1953, starring Leslie Caron as a wide-eyed French waif who joins a traveling circus where she meets Paul Berthalet (Mel Ferrer), the sardonic lame puppeteer she learns to love, Jacquot (Kurt Kasznar), his amiable co-worker, Marcus the Magician (Jean-Pierre

Aumont), who dazzles her for a time, and Rosalie, his sophisticated assistant (Zsa Zsa Gabor).

Convinced of the film's potential as a stage musical, Merrick secured the rights in December 1958, commissioning Deutsch to draft a plot outline based on her screenplay and French composer Gerard Calvi, recently of the hit revue *La Plume de Ma Tante* (1958), to pen the score. A year later, when Calvi's inability to write sensitive English lyrics forced him to withdraw, Merrick engaged Harold Rome, who had written the scores for his productions of *Fanny* (1954) and *Destry Rides Again* (1959).[2] Unhappy with the choice, Deutsch proposed Bob Merrill, a young songwriter whom she had recently introduced to MGM. After early song successes like "How Much Is That Doggie in the Window," "Mambo Italiano," and "If I knew You Were Coming, I'd Have Baked a Cake," Merrill turned to Broadway with full scores for *New Girl in Town* (1957) and *Take Me Along* (1959). Since the latter was a Merrick production in which Merrill had demonstrated skill as both composer and lyricist, the producer readily acceded to Deutsch's request.

From the outset, he wanted only one person to direct and choreograph, but in the spring of 1960, Gower was bent on following up his award-winning *Bye Bye Birdie* with a nonmusical play. Though the prospect of making a stage musical of a popular film was not the least bit enticing, he agreed to hear the score. "Bob Merrill inveigled me into listening to the music he had composed. That did it. Once I heard his songs, I was hooked. They immediately suggested to me just how I would like the movements and scenes of the show to take shape."[3]

His vision called for an uninterrupted flow in the presentation, a flow requiring exclusion of conventional scene changes. "Why not, I thought as I lay awake that night, do away with the curtains altogether? I have always hated curtains. They shut everything off and put a period on things."[4] Imperceptibly, this unadorned empty space would undergo a magical transformation as a ragtag troupe of players creates a world of enchantment—and trickery—that mesmerizes Lili and audience alike. This idea of a tawdry circus unfolding Lili's story within its huge tent raised during the prologue and lowered at the finale was revolutionary. It would transform the entire production by organizing its elements and defining its locale. It would also allow the director to retain the basic story while altering the terms of its telling. Although the term had not yet been coined, this would be a "concept musical," in which one supreme idea pervades and unites every element of the production—music, lyrics, dialogue, choreography, design, and direction.[5]

The show's title change reflected its emerging identity. Merrick's *Carrot Top*, named for the redheaded puppet that helps Lili, became Champion's *Carnival* on July 27, 1960, when he signed on just three and a half months after *Birdie*'s opening.[6] In the weeks ahead, an elusive exclamation point following the title would appear—as it does in Deutsch's initial draft of the book—then disappear for the Washington premiere, then reappear in Philadelphia. Sometime during the Broadway run, it would be permanently dropped, possibly because Gower felt that it gave the wrong impression. "It *isn't* a blockbuster," he insisted, "it's a gentle show."[7] Whether gentle or blockbusting, his second musical would also be the first in a series of seven he would direct for Merrick. Successive works would include *Hello, Dolly!* (1964), *I Do! I Do!* (1966), *The Happy Time* (1968), *Sugar* (1972), *Mack and Mabel* (1974), and *42nd Street* (1980)—a remarkable record indeed considering the tumultuous nature of their relationship.

After weeks, sometimes months, of searching for the right leading players, Gower would submit his final choices only to have Merrick jeopardize them by demanding that they accept salaries only slightly better than those of chorus members. Though in the end the producer would capitulate and provide more equitable pay, it was at *his* discretion, without concern for the director pressured to begin rehearsals on schedule. Already heated moments during out-of-town tryouts were raised more than a few degrees when Merrick unexpectedly appeared, railed about the condition of the production, and then threatened to close it. Aware of the problems and well into solving them, Gower learned to counter these tactics by simply vanishing from the scene, confiding his whereabouts only to a trusted few. Before departing he would also urge the company to stand firm until his return, diffusing whatever dissension Merrick might wreak in his absence.[8] Invariably, everyone remained loyal to the director, who promptly resumed work upon the impresario's departure. In Merrill's words, "Gower was the only one Merrick couldn't eat up or spit out; he could out-Machiavelli David."[9]

However jarring, Merrick's behavior was not entirely unjustified. As Merrill also noted, Gower became "imperious—absolutely steel"[10] at the onset of rehearsals, barring everyone—even script and songwriters—from the theatre. "His *mother* couldn't come into the rehearsal hall," adds Marge, "if he could have eliminated me (his special assistant), he would have been happy."[11] Only within a tightly controlled environment, one virtually free from outside interference, did he feel secure enough to devote himself completely to the challenges at hand. Like fellow director-choreographers de Mille, Robbins, Fosse, and Bennett, he viewed rehearsal as the most delicate stage in a musical's formation, a time of experimentation when performers (and director) needed to be shielded from unpredictable, disruptive, or demoralizing forces. Merrick had that potential, Gower reasoned, so he kept him at a distance.

Like Gower, Merrick hailed from the Midwest, the product of a fractured marriage. Born David Lee Margulois (pronounced "MAR-gew-lis") to Russian-Jewish immigrants in St. Louis, Missouri, on November 27, 1911, he was the youngest of five children. Amateur theatricals initiated the boy into the world of theatre—a world where he could flee a miserable childhood and Jewish roots he loathed for a life of success like that of his idol, legendary producer Florenz Ziegfeld. Armed with a law degree, a lucrative marriage, and a new name, he came to New York in 1940 as an office assistant to producer Herman Shumlin. In the years that followed, he worked a variety of positions—from backstage to box office—that schooled him in the ways of the theatre.[12]

In 1949, after his production of the British comedy *Clutterbuck* opened to tepid notices, he staged an unconventional but clever advertising campaign that soon earned it a profitable run. When the Harold Rome musical *Fanny* (1954) similarly floundered, he countered with an array of promotional gimmicks, including the placement of a scantily clad papier-mâché likeness of belly dancer Nejla Ates in a prominent area of Central Park. The result was a staggering 888 performances. By the time of his association with Gower, Merrick was indeed a latter-day Ziegfeld with a prolific record of hit dramas (*Look Back in Anger, A Taste of Honey, Becket*), comedies (*The Matchmaker, Romanoff and Juliet, The World of Suzie Wong*), and musicals (*Jamacia, Gypsy, Irma La Douce*) the great showman himself would have envied. Five feet eleven, large-boned and fleshy, with swarthy features, a black mustache, and pomaded hair, he wore pinstriped suits that conveyed a propriety his trademark Homburg hat mocked. On Broadway, his instinct for worthwhile theatrical projects was as legendary as the chicanery and ruthlessness he used to promote them.[13]

By contrast, at the time of their first meeting Gower's fair complexion, clean-shaven face, wavy brown hair, and winning smile projected all the vitality, charm, and confidence of an accomplished performer. Six feet tall, he was small-boned, with broad shoulders and a narrow torso. His well-bred bearing conveyed both virility and dominance, particularly evident in the way he used his hands, wrists, and arms. Frequently, performers—Dick Van Dyke, Jerry Orbach, and Robert Goulet among them—would study his deportment to acquire the physicality of the characters they portrayed. Gower was an artist with meticulous and systematic work habits tempered by a fairly constant civility; Merrick, an entrepreneur, furtive and opportunistic in business, eccentric in behavior.

"He had to be controversial and confrontational all the time," recalls Merrick associate producer Samuel (Biff) Liff. "With David, people were to be *used* and used at what they did best. He was a pragmatist who also forced them to do their best work. He wanted quality, but he always wanted to best somebody, meaning that he wanted to make sure he had the best deal of anybody. He was a tough negotiator, so was Gower. They had a business relationship. So there was a very strong relationship from that respect; they each knew what they wanted."[14] Indeed they did, and it was this common obduracy, rather than their differences, that caused frequent feuds.

Beyond the obvious similarities—their Midwestern birthplaces, chaotic childhoods, and passion for the theatre—both were workaholics driven by insecure, suspicious, and headstrong natures to succeed through means of control. Both operated on the premise that in order for one to prosper, the other had to be held in check—a thought at once intriguing and alarming, which may explain why they loved and loathed working together. Given this dynamic, neither could afford to relinquish his defense or underestimate the power of the other. Yet, in the end, that is precisely what Gower would do—a fatal mistake.

In the fall of 1960, however, it was not sparring with Merrick but articulating his vision for *Carnival* that occupied him. To effectively apply his concept at every level of the production, he undertook a period of intense research. "He looked at the movie *Lili* quite a lot," Marge remembers, "and knew he wanted to avoid some of the sentimentality of it. He looked at movies like Fellini's *La Strada,* that had to do with that genre of the little carnival, the wandering circus. He really immersed himself in that. If anything, the production would be a celebration of that kind of entertainment."[15] This concern was apparently the subject of his earliest discussions with Deutsch regarding the musical's scenic structure, for as the preface to the libretto, which she submitted to him on September 15, states, "there are no bridging scenes-in-one for set changes, no blacking-out for set changes, no house curtain, no show curtain."[16] Scenic transitions "read like movie dissolves . . . because the scenic plan involves the changing of sets before the eyes of the audience (by the Roustabouts) . . . The basic background of the entire show remains constant. Set pieces are brought in to suggest various areas."[17]

The carnival described here is the impoverished one conceptualized by the director, not the lavish spectacle of *Lili*. It is "weather-beaten and worn (with a) faded, seedy quality in the equipment, the costumes, and even the people, (giving it) a beauty all its own."[18] A prologue also replaces the overture. "I hate overtures," the director complained. "All audiences do during them is wave to each other and gab, if they're close enough."[19] Clearly, they were just another one of those conventions that impeded flow. But unlike the filmed prologue to *Birdie,* this one would be choreographed, opening simply with a performer who ambles onto the vacant stage, leans against the proscenium arch, and then fingers a tune on his concertina. House lights dim and stage lights brighten. Gradually an empty meadow on the outskirts of a town becomes a bustling panoply of carnival life as roustabouts construct the giant show tent, booths, and amusements, and show folk perform their various specialties. The libretto also ends as it begins, with the carnival gradually dismantled until the area is completely deserted once more.

Yet even with the action generally confined to the carnival site and certain changes in characterization (a singing Lili rather than a dancing one, a tougher Rosalie, a walrus substitute for the strong man puppet, etc.), the libretto was still too reminiscent of the screenplay. No surprise then that Gower, who knew how he wanted the story to be told, would quickly find this hybrid of the film and his vision of the stage production unacceptable.[20]

The theatricality and improvisational nature of the hit off-Broadway musical *The Fantasticks* so impressed him that he asked its librettist-lyricist, Tom Jones, to co-author *Carnival* with Deutsch in the fall of 1960. When Jones declined out of concern that his work with collaborator-composer Harvey Schmidt might be compromised, Gower turned to Michael Stewart, who accepted.[21] Stewart completed the first draft with Deutsch, who then withdrew from the project. In acknowledgment of her efforts, the phrase "Based on material by Helen Deutsch" appeared just below Stewart's credit as librettist. Now it was up to him to make the story of Lili conform to the director's vision. Henceforth, the carnival's "big top" became the meeting place where the starry-eyed waif thrilled to the talents of its dwellers, especially debonair magician Marco and the puppets of embittered cripple Paul Berthalet and assistant Jacquot. It was also the arena in which she confronted the disenchantment born from the advances of souvenir salesman Grobert, the failure of her first job, and Marco's liaison with Rosalie, which bring her to the brink of suicide. Ironically, in that same world with its shattered illusions, Lili would also find genuine treasure. The puppets, whom she treats as real creatures, lead her to triumph on the midway and ultimately to the understanding that it is not they she adores, but Paul, who has used them to express his love for her.

No sooner had Stewart commenced the second draft as sole author than Merrick suddenly and inexplicably fired him. Hired at a time when the book was sorely in need of revision and a librettist willing to cooperate with the director, he had managed to work certain advantages into his contract that Merrick ordinarily would not have granted. Equally perplexing to the writer was Merrick's rehiring of him only thirty-six hours later. Perhaps it was the producer's way of reminding him (and the director) just who wielded the power.[22] Ultimately, Stewart would overcome these difficulties to fulfill Gower's wish to have the musical tell the story on its own terms—terms wholly dependent upon the concept of the third-rate circus that entrances the heroine.

As with *Birdie,* Gower's vision of the production would gradually materialize over the course of countless sessions with production staff and numerous additions, deletions, and revisions of scenes and songs. Today, musicals are generally developed in workshops conducted months—sometimes years—before they reach Broadway. But in the 1960s, musicals like *Birdie* and *Carnival* were shaped under the rigors and time constraints of rehearsals conducted prior to a pre-Broadway tour—the true test of a director's mettle, during which substantial revisions were made. Thanks to Gower's forethought and planning, *Carnival* was spared such last-minute labor, debuting in Washington, D.C., as a fully realized production.

For Stewart, though, this meant penning a series of three drafts before a final version that incorporated all the unique touches that he and Gower had in mind. Any improvements in the libretto also affected Merrill, who was called upon to rewrite some numbers or compose new ones as needed. This was a delicate matter for the songwriter who, from the beginning, had carefully striven to avoid comparison with the film's popular "Hi-Lili, Hi-Lo." His number for Lili and the puppets was "Pompom," which, like the remainder of his score, had stressed French rather than Tin Pan Alley influences. Each time director and librettist arrived at Merrill's home to listen to new or revised songs, they left disappointed that he had not yet produced "the hit song." One day, in the heat of frustration, Merrill angrily improvised a tune. To his dismay, Gower exclaimed, "That's it!" and *Carnival* received the theme that was soon to become its hit—"Love Makes the World Go Round."[23]

Of the twenty-four songs described in Deutsch's original libretto, Merrill would replace four more in addition to "Pompom." Paul's protest against carnival life, "I Won't Ride," originally sung before a revolving carousel, became "I've Got to Find a Reason" once Gower decided against the carousel (probably because it evoked the Rodgers and Hammerstein musical of the same name). A production number for Marco, "I Never Met a Girl I Didn't Like," and a duet for Marco and Lili, "Of Course I Do," in which he insinuated an affair while she unwittingly agreed, merged into "Sword, Rose, and Cape." "Magic, Magic" replaced "Little Fishes" as the theme for Marco's act, and Jacquot's ballad, "The Melody Is Far Away," became his rousing ode to circus life, "Grand Impérial Cirque de Paris." The Roustabouts' "The Outskirts of Nowhere" disappeared along with an additional song for Lili and the puppets, "The Colonel and the Lady," and one Jacquot was to have sung while collecting contributions from spectators, "Feed the Puppets."[24] In addition to Merrill's songs, dance music arranger and rehearsal pianist Peter Howard would supply additional music to accompany the staging and dances Gower would devise for the "Prologue," "Sword, Rose, and Cape," and "Carnival Ballet."

Gower's concept similarly affected the technical areas. Scenic designer Will Steven Armstrong created imaginative sets and impressive lighting that transformed the bare stage into a whirling carnival before the eyes of the audience. New scenes would be brought about by lowering decorative banners from starlit skies, moving on circus wagons and midway booths, and darkening the backdrop to make silhouettes of the inhabitants (an effect Gower would later revisit with equally stunning effect in his "There's No Business Like Show Business" ballet for

Annie Get Your Gun and "Shadow Waltz" for *42nd Street*). All was calculated for beauty and pace and, above all, a mood of childhood regained.

For costume designer Freddy Wittop, the director's view of the production coincided perfectly with his own: "My concept of the costuming was contrary to the glamorous and overdressed Hollywood production of the movie *Lili*. I saw it as a rather pathetic French provincial circus, a traveling tent show, and Gower completely agreed with my views."[25] Thus began a ten-year association with the director terminated only by the designer's retirement in 1971.

To reflect the broken-down, dowdy nature of the carnival, Wittop found an effective way of giving a threadbare look to brand-new costumes. "I sprayed them, dipped them in gray, washed them and even painted perspiration stains on them. Of course the lines of dowdiness had to be drawn somewhere! During our Washington tryout, Gower caught the performers sitting on the stairs to the dressing rooms in their stage costumes during a break. He laughed and called out, 'Don't sit there; you are dirty enough already!' "[26]

In the end, Gower was quite pleased with the response of his colleagues to his vision and their plans for its execution. "All of us concerned with *Carnival*—Will (Steven Armstrong), Michael Stewart, Freddy Wittop, Bob Merrill and I—saw eye-to-eye about the illusions we wanted to evoke and sustain."[27] Confident that book, music, scenery, and costumes would reflect the desired atmosphere, he now turned to the puppets and how best to present them.

They, too, had to be integrated into the flashy carny. He insisted that they not only be "big enough to be easily seen in a large theatre," but also demonstrate "a provincial simplicity, a style so unfamiliar that it could be described as an 'exclusive' for *Carnival*."[28] This is precisely what Tom Tichenor exhibited when auditioning for him, Deutsch, and casting director Michael Shurtleff in September 1960. The director's friendly greeting and request to dispense with a formal presentation immediately put the Tennessee television puppeteer at ease. "Gower said, 'Just let us see what kind of puppets you have and what you do with them.' This was a great relief. My puppets could speak for themselves. The interview—it was more than an audition—ended with the usual, 'You'll hear from us.' "[29] Two months later, Tichenor did hear, and by December 19 was back in New York attending a two-hour conference with the director and new librettist Stewart to discuss the physical characteristics of the puppets.

A few weeks later, Tichenor presented walrus Horrible Henry to the director, winning instant approval. "Gower let out a whoop of joy. 'Don't change a hair on him. He's perfect!' "[30] But initial versions of Marguerite—an offbeat Marlene Dietrich—boy Carrot Top, and fox Renardo would require further effort. Soon, the "Dietrich" puppet developed into a worldly fifty-year-old ingénue. While designing her wig, Tichenor pinned a yellow feather boa on her head to keep her from looking bald. The effect added such an unexpected flourish to her appearance that it stayed. Next came Renardo the fox, a slick character with a sharp, pointed look. His eyes with sneaking lids and subtle slyness looked wonderful close up, but had to grow until they carried to the last row. "This was not television with close-ups," admitted the puppeteer. "This was the theatre, where every member of the audience deserved to see every detail. I was learning."[31]

With the production now only days away from the first rehearsal, Carrot Top's identity continued unresolved until Gower suggested a return to the "little-boy clown" idea of earlier discussions. Shortly thereafter, Tichenor added the final and principal member of the quartet. Still, his work was not quite finished. Each of the four had to be duplicated, some as many as four times, to facilitate rapid changes of costume. The puppeteer would also be asked to design two colorless puppets— Mother Goose and Jackie Horner—for the "Fairyland" number in which Schlegel criticizes Paul for their lack of charm. "The puppets in *Carnival*," summed up Tichenor, "are not brought on as a specialty act. They are characters in the plot, and audiences accept them as such."[32] This explains why Gower selected them with the same precision and care he demonstrated in casting the human performers.

At the time of Tichenor's audition in September 1960, the director also viewed several specialty acts—acrobats, jugglers, and performing dogs, like those of a traveling circus. From these, he selected aerialist and stilt-walker Dean Crane, the Argentine juggling team of the Martin Brothers, and the Canines of Paul Sydell, a favorite of nightclubs and television variety shows.[33]

By the beginning of October, his quest for major performers was under way. To find a Lili who could "sing and dance beautifully, have a continental charm, the gamin quality of an Audrey Hepburn and be an absolute waif,"[34] the director would comb nightclubs and theatres in New York, Philadelphia, London, Paris, and Rome. Though Merrick had tried to get Leslie Caron and Dean Jones to play Lili and Paul as early as March 1960, he abandoned these efforts after failing to persuade Caron to reprise her role for the stage. Under Gower, one of the first to audition was twenty-four-year-old Italian-born coloratura soprano Anna Maria Alberghetti. Finding her "a little unbending, lacking warmth and charm needed for the part,"[35] he flew to Europe to continue his search, only to return in mid-October empty-handed.

With auditions about to begin, Alberghetti's theatrical agent prevailed upon him to reconsider her by attending a Philadelphia nightclub appearance. When she turned from sophisticated material to dance a Charleston in a funny hat, the director observed the "quality of a little girl dressed up in her mother's clothes,"[36] and invited her to join those he was considering for the role. Following a close competition with Carol Lawrence during final callbacks, Alberghetti was announced as Lili on November 16, 1960. "I always thought of Anna as too sophisticated with that upsweep hairdo," Gower later commented, "but she has the perfect quality— and the voice—for this role."[37]

One way of blunting some of the story's sentimentality would be to secure actors who could lend an edgy aggressiveness to some of the characters. The role of pup-peteer Paul Berthalet, seen by the director as a rough and angry figure with an un-relieved antipathy toward the world, was one example. Many auditioned, but in the end, Champion offered the role to Jerry Orbach, whose portrayal of El Gallo, the narrator of *The Fantasticks,* completely won him over. "Strangely enough," Orbach recalled, "Gower and David Merrick both saw me in *The Fantasticks,* and just gave me the part of Paul (without an audition). In *The Fantasticks,* I did a lot of singing and they knew I could handle that, but they had no idea if I could do the puppet work or have the kind of bitter, world-weary, disenchanted qualities that Paul is supposed to have. I was thrilled, naturally."[38] In coming months, Champion's ver-bal assurance would be all Orbach could count on until he signed a contract upon attending his first rehearsal at the Phyllis Anderson Theatre on January 21, 1961. "I guess they knew I wouldn't turn it down,"[39] quipped the young actor.

If a dancer-actor capable of combining a fiery disposition with an overweening narcissism could be found for Marco, sentiment might be further minimized. Again, the casting notes indicate that several major dancer-actors competed for the role, including Gene Nelson and George Chakiris, but the final choice was James Mitchell, a principal dancer in many shows best known for his malcontented Harry Beaton of *Brigadoon* (1947). He joined the cast on January 16, 1961. Marge de-scribes his selection as a "most brilliant piece of casting. He was wildly good-looking, but what made him so interesting above all those other dancer-actors was this caldron inside of him. Agnes (de Mille) recognized it, and so did Gower."[40] Mitchell himself further clarifies why the director wanted a dancer in the part: "A magician by trade is very flashy. Some of them move wonderfully. Almost dance. So I imagine that was in Gower's head—to use those qualities of the magician."[41]

Making Rosalie comically brash and earthy, rather than glamorously sophisti-cated, was also calculated to avoid the mawkish. The role went to Kaye Ballard, who had previously worked with Gower on the film *The Girl Most Likely.*[42] On January 5, 1961, Ballard declined the leading role of Mama Rose in the national tour of *Gypsy* to play The Incomparable Rosalie. Pierre Olaf, the diminutive French clown of *La Plume de Ma Tante,* emerged as Paul's co-puppeteer and loyal friend Jacquot.[43] Initially, he had reservations about the role. "When they asked me to sign for the show, I kept stalling because I didn't have anything to do but pat the hero on the head. Not very interesting."[44] In time, though, Gower would supply him with the show-stopping "Grand Impérial Cirque de Paris." Harry Lascoe, interestingly, was selected over Zero Mostel for carnival proprietor Schlegel (Schissle in the director's cast list). With Will Lee as souvenir hawker Grobert, George Marcy as roustabout leader Miguelito, and Igors Gavon as Dr. Wilhelm Glass, the casting of roles was complete.

In early January 1961, the director focused on "the score of boys and girls who would meet the audience constantly throughout the show" who "had to be free of that common 'No Business Like Show Business' tired look."[45] Conventional Broadway choruses were composed of two separate and distinct groups: dancers and singers. *Carnival*'s, by contrast, would be an integrated one with versatile performers who not only could dance and sing, but also act. Thus, a variety of other carnival entertainers and personnel—roustabouts, cyclists, harem girls, musicians, clowns, and a quartet of German female dancers, the Bluebird Girls from Dusseldorf—rounded out the chorus.

Gower's thorough search for multitalented performers is reflected in his casting requirements for the female chorus. "I was dealing with a French circus. I wanted the girls to look sexy, of course, but looks were one of my last considerations. They had to be well grounded in ballet and jazz. Not only that, but I wanted to hear them sing, and, in most cases I had them speak lines. You can't put a girl with a Georgia drawl into a musical about France, not even a show about the south of France."[46]

Many of the three hundred young women who auditioned were baffled by his request to perform period dances, like the Charleston, Black Bottom, and Big Apple, in addition to regulation jazz and ballet steps. Though such dances were clearly atypical for a circus musical, they nevertheless gave him an idea of what kind of energy the performers could project across the footlights. These dances were also a means of reducing the competition for the nine openings in the women's chorus. He later explained the rationale behind the exhaustive casting techniques: "Forty per cent of directing is really casting. When you cast your people, you should know what you're going to get out of them. If you don't, you work harder or try to get someone else."[47] Unlike the casts in his succeeding musicals, the ensemble of *Carnival* would see no replacements following initial casting.

One casting matter was still unresolved: which one of two auditioning burros would pull Ballard's cart for her entrance in the prologue? Favoring Amos over Elmer, he quipped, "I hope to be remembered as the director who made an actor out of an ass, instead of one who made an ass out of an actor."[48]

Asinine was exactly what he thought of the meager three-hundred-dollar-per-week salary Merrick wanted to pay Ballard and Mitchell during rehearsals. When he learned from them that this was only a hundred dollars more than what chorus members were paid and would hardly cover their agent and accompanists' fees, he told Merrick to hire the performers at a proper wage immediately or find a new director. With everything now set and ready for daily rehearsals, the delay angered him. At the eleventh hour, the producer capitulated and Gower got his cast.[49]

His production schedule for *Carnival* covered the eight-week period from January 9 to March 5, 1961. During the first four weeks, many other things besides auditions concerned him. Sessions with Stewart and Merrill to polish libretto and songs are listed, as are ones with music arranger Philip J. Lang and designers Armstrong and Wittop. Not a single detail was spared his scrutiny. "We went over the script," Wittop recalled, "and, of course, I made a lot of sketches first, and then we discussed them. Sometimes Gower asked me to redo a certain thing because he saw it differently. But not a stripe of a costume or a design could pass his acceptance before he put his initials on it. If the initials were on it, that was the way it was going to be executed, completely."[50]

That "GC" had to be on the dances, too. Mornings were almost exclusively devoted to plotting the choreography for "Sword, Rose, and Cape," the "Carnival Ballet," and "Beautiful Candy" with dance music arranger Peter Howard and, later, associate choreographer Gene Bayliss. ("Grand Impérial Cirque de Paris" would be added in the sixth week, followed by the "Prologue" in the seventh.) "Sword, Rose, and Cape," a parody of the Spanish flamenco dancing popularized by José Greco, was the first number to develop. Though complex, it required only a small corps of male dancers, rather than a full chorus, which made it a good place to start. Howard's prior experience as accompanist for a flamenco team proved a real asset, for it had given him a facility with all kinds of Spanish rhythms. "I decided to use all those 5/4 rhythms as the leitmotif of the whole thing," Howard explains. "Umpapa, umpapa, umpa, umpa, umpapa—that became the basis for the whole number."[51] The 5/4 rhythms also complemented Merrill's music for the song, as well as the nature of his lyrics that characterized Marco as a contemporary Don Juan with predatory designs on Lili.

In the final verse of the song, the roustabouts suggest that Marco "perpetrate a rape" in imitation of notorious lovers past. He feigns dismay. How dare they even conceive the thought! Yet the subsequent dance clearly establishes that this is precisely what he has in mind. Though Lili may think that the five men are showing off solely for her amusement, their playfulness is actually a subtle form of seduction calculated to obtain her favors in the sporting tradition of a medieval joust or duel. This also tempers the sentimental plot—exactly what the choreographer intended.

His notes call for Miguelito and the three other roustabouts to do solo improvisations that bring them ever closer to Lili, who is seated on a stool downstage right. Marco soon intervenes, tossing them away from her before eliminating each in "pantomimed swashbuckling swordplay."[52] Snatching a piece of drapery and using it as a bullfighter's *muleta,* he attracts his last foe, sending the man into a dive that propels him facefirst across the carnival's platform stage, through its curtained opening, and out of sight. The number now peaks as Marco, makeshift cape on shoulder, dances upon the platform stage, then leaps to the ground and continues with cape waving, footbeats, and hand claps. One by one, the men join him, building the intensity until all are beating, clapping, dropping, shouting, and turning, closer and closer to Lili, still rooted to her spot. The dance ends as the men lift her into the air, then toss her into the arms of Marco, revealing to the audience the dark side of this world, as yet unseen by Lili.

To give the piece authentic flamenco style, the choreographer sought the advice of Wittop, who, under the stage name of Federico Rey, had been a Spanish dancer of some repute and onetime partner of the celebrated Argentinita. The result perfectly suited the characters, combining the kind of joshing natural to carnival folk with dance steps they surely would have seen while touring Spain, performing on European stages, or watching a Hollywood musical.

As with *Birdie,* the dances in *Carnival* were calculated to advance plot—a lesson Gower learned while at MGM. "You use the bodies of the dancers as instruments, like the keys on a typewriter, to tell a story," he explained. "I hate dancing for the sake of dancing in a show. It should be used to aid the story line. In one scene in *Carnival,* dancers are used to suggest a kaleidoscopic view of a carnival through the eyes of a disillusioned girl."[53] The "Carnival Ballet," the climax of the first act, was developed in sections over the four-week period prior to rehearsals with the full cast on February 6, 1961.

After ruining the carnival's main attraction—Marco's magic act—Lili is fired by Schlegel, who rescues the show and signals the ballet by introducing the four Bluebird Girls from Dusseldorf. With their long, braided, flaxen hair decked with cornflowers and deceptively virginal "Tanz mit Mir" polka, they mollify the clientele while roustabouts clear the remains of the magic act and Schlegel coaxes a stunned Lili into the wings. From the audience, drunken townsmen pour onto the stage while the interior of the main tent dissolves into the carnival midway, with Grobert's souvenir wagon, the puppet booth, Olga's snake charmer's booth, and the platform stage (used earlier in "Sword, Rose, and Cape") all part of the scene.

Evening unfolds with Schlegel mounting his barker's podium to draw the crowd's attention to various attractions: the aerialist ascending the "Leap for Life" ladder that rises high above, Olga on the platform stage beckoning with an erotic dance, dogs performing tricks, Siamese twins taking a bow, and jugglers tossing clubs. As the locals force the Bluebirds to dance with them, the mirthful play grows tense. The antics of the dogs appease some, but others prefer the voluptuous Olga, whom they seize from the stage and lift high into the air, leaving her place to one of their band struggling to dance with a Bluebird. Gradually, all are caught up in a fractious revel that swiftly dissolves into a drunken slow motion as they stagger past Lili, who has exchanged carnival stage costume for street clothes, suitcase, and purse. A townsman lunges at her and Schlegel ushers her away. While people lean against or lie on each other, Lili notices the leap ladder as the aerialist, suspended from a wire by one foot, slowly falls and spins.

The madness now diminishes as the people walk or stagger off, leaving behind them the dead end of a carnival night. Schlegel descends the podium, orders a roustabout to turn off a string of electric lights, and then turns off another himself. Spying Lili at downstage left, he looks at her at length with disgust before turning off another string and ordering two roustabouts to push off Grobert's wagon. As they do, Grobert emerges and, at the sight of Lili, contemptuously flips his money clip before departing. Schlegel turns off the last string of lights, and exits through his office door. Alone now before the "Leap for Life" ladder, Lili prepares to ascend its rungs to her death.[54]

This surrealistic bacchanal with its aura of moral desolation was a master's stroke, the capstone to Lili's increasing disenchantment with carnival life. Gower achieved this by intermingling a synthesis of what would actually occur in life with an eclectic use of technical dance. Sequences featuring vaudeville and social dance steps merged with marching, acrobatics, and a range of circus routines in a deceptively simple narrative with an almost imperceptible complexity. Every movement was tailored exactly to each character, a skillful mélange similar to what Fokine fashioned for *Petrouchka*.[55]

In the ballet and throughout the production, Gower injected elements of environmental staging into the proscenium-framed format by occasionally using the aisles for entrances and exits, as in the scene near the end of Act II in which Lili parts company with Marco. Here, Alberghetti, poised on a stage extension built over the orchestra, spoke with Mitchell, who stood beneath her in the aisle. This was just one of the ways the director reduced the barrier between audience and actor without compromising theatricality. Though he respected the need to maintain the illusion of reality, he nonetheless felt that the removal or breaking-down of certain conventions could heighten theatrical effect. "Beautiful Candy," presented early in the second act by Lili, the puppets, and the ensemble, is a prime example.

The number centers on Lili's proposal to the puppets that they spend, rather than save, their first earnings. After all their hard work, are they not entitled to "a perfectly good waste of time?"[56] The astonished puppets quickly bend to her point of view. Out of this simple pretext, however, comes an integral turning point in the action as the audience watches lovers Lili and Paul (via his puppets) turn completely spontaneous and at ease with each other for the first time. To underscore the moment, Gower staged Merrill's carefree waltz with puppet refrains and calliope vamp as a captivating festivity that flowed out from the puppet booth onto the midway and beyond. Little by little, the chorus filled the stage, joining the swaying puppets and spirited Lili while, in the audience, hawkers, novelties and candy in hand, punctuated the tempo with their cries as they ambled along the aisles. In essence, "Beautiful Candy" served a dual purpose: staging that captured a girl's elation over making it big as a midway attraction, and storytelling that, basically, related her first date with her beau. As impresario and raconteur, Gower was in top form.[57]

Once more Jess was on hand as Gar's dramaturge. "After the tremendous success of *Bye Bye Birdie,*" he recalls, "everyone began yessing Gower. He was always pretty sure of his ideas, but needed to talk them out, that's part of the creative thing. So he said to me, 'Do you think we could just put our friendship on the line and talk things out and, if you don't agree with me, tell me you don't, and why?' We had, as a result, some wonderful talks, usually about book structure where I felt the climax was wrong or the show got slow."[58]

Jess's acuity was exactly what Gower needed. On one occasion just three weeks before the Washington premiere, the pair met to discuss a means of energizing the middle of the second act. As he remembers, "Gower looked at the show this time and said, 'What does it need?' I said, 'I wonder if people are going to think it's too artistic or too full of mood?' He replied, 'What I need is a showstopper! It takes guts to be corny, but I've got that kind of guts.' "[59] The result was "Grand Impérial Cirque de Paris," which climaxed with the entire cast in a "Rockette" kickline.

The inspiration could not have come at a more opportune time. Only days before, while dining at a local Chinese restaurant with the company, Pierre Olaf had planted a fake message inside a fortune cookie and slipped it to Gower, who opened it to discover that he would soon be providing a major dance number for the actor's character of Jacquot. This seemed quite impossible since the one remaining dance spot in the second act had been promised to Mitchell. "One day Gower just put his arm around me," recalls Mitchell, "and said, 'The second act number is Pierre Olaf.' I could easily see why [from] where it was placed and what kind of number it was—the elevation and pitch."[60]

Sneaking onto the empty stage and peering from his old-fashioned eyeglasses, Olaf reminisced about the glory days when Schlegel's troupe was the pinnacle of the Parisian circus world. He then clasped his hands, bit his tongue, and began to shuffle in a strange little circle of bliss. Soon he was joined by carnival dancing girls who tried to learn the step while keeping pace with him. From there, the dance built into an exciting, vigorous, almost abandoned romp as one member of the troupe after another joined the line, taking up the special conventions of the can-can guaranteed to leave the audience breathless with delight.[61]

The antithesis of the nightmarish "Carnival Ballet," this number was the performers' daydream of a happier time when they would all play the show of shows. In the end, Gower's gutsy corniness would pay off when "Grand Impérial Cirque de Paris" won *Dance Observer* magazine's recognition as one of the best dance numbers of the 1960–61 season.[62]

Ironically, the very number that had triggered the show's concept was the last to be staged. In the "Prologue," Gower not only overturned convention by eliminating curtains and overture, but also introduced the unit set to the Broadway musical via the environment he foresaw. The tone of the evening was established as Jacquot rambled onto the empty stage—a deserted meadow near a southern European town in the early dawn—and began to squeeze a plaintive waltz from his concertina. While the orchestra picked up the strains of "Love Makes the World Go Round," proprietor B. F. Schlegel arrived to survey the area, joined gradually by members of his gaudy troupe, whom he supervised in erecting booths, hanging banners, stringing lights, unfurling posters, and raising the main tent. *Voilà! Le Grand Impérial Cirque de Paris*—complete with harem girl, performing dog, stilt walker, even a dwarf with a bugle! Schlegel, now the center of an eye-popping midway, exhorted the troupe to parade into town, trumpeting their own brilliance with the rousing "Direct from Vienna," led by Rosalie and the chorus.[63]

Gower wanted Lili to watch transfixed as the carnival sprang to life before her. "By opening the show in this way," he later explained, "I felt that the action would flow, that everyone out front would unconsciously become immersed in the scene and look at the small traveling circus through Lili's enchanted and naïve eyes."[64] From prologue to finale, the action *did* flow, especially in the way the show folk trouped back and forth, establishing a unifying rhythm not so much through real dance, but in carefully measured movement subtly employed to immense effect. Big numbers were not jammed in, not planted obviously; they were part of the action. Everything was attractively set within the show's symmetry. It was Gower's own sense of the inevitability of life that made this continuous flow possible. This flow was also "an essential part of his contribution to musical theatre," stated stage manager Lucia Victor. "*Carnival* is a superb example of that. There is not one activity that is not inevitable for those characters in that particular situation. One thing simply leads to another [as the "Ballet" does to the suicide], and sort of dissolves and overlaps. You never have to wait to get interested again. The audience is caught while they are still on tip-toe."[65]

The director's sense of pacing, the ability to know when to increase or decrease momentum and change mood, also aided flow. This was evident in the way the numbers were placed in the show. Each number had a designated purpose, which strategically linked it to the rest. This interdependence was such that the elimination of one number could compromise the effect of the next. The correlation between "A Very Nice Man" and "Mira" illustrates the point. Alberghetti's first song of the evening was "A Very Nice Man," a number centered on Champion's fondness for props that almost seemed a throwaway.

"Mira," which followed it, drew a warm and winning response from the audience. "Subconsciously," explains Alberghetti, "I really wanted that first song not to remain in the show. So one night in Washington, we deleted it, and made "Mira" my first song. And as incredible a reaction as 'Mira' used to get, when we took the first song out, it just didn't work. And I learned one of my many lessons on what pacing was all about. Gower understood that so well."[66]

The second four weeks of rehearsal—February 6 to March 5—consisted of staging the remaining numbers and book scenes. Among the numbers created during this period was the mock love duet for Mitchell and Ballard, "Always, Always You." While the two serenaded each other with pledges of deathless yet capricious devotion, Mitchell plunged several well-aimed swords into a box housing Ballard, who made the most of having only her head protrude by assuming a different comic expression in response to each thrust.

Gower knew the trick existed and may actually have seen it performed by a magician during his road show or nightclub days. After learning the details of its execution (probably from Roy Benson, the professional magician he hired to coach Mitchell), he had the box constructed to the required dimensions and placed on rollers so each of its four sides could be revealed to the audience. Only after mastering the trick himself and determining the most effective angles for the penetration of the swords did he invite Mitchell to learn the routine. Then *he* assumed Ballard's place in the box prior to rehearsals with her. It was one of his cardinal rules to acquire a firsthand working knowledge of risky or unusual props before rehearsing performers with them.[67] During *Hello, Dolly!*, he worked with butterfly wings required for the "Come and Be My Butterfly" sequence long before he introduced them to the women dancers, and he did the same with the multicolored corkscrew slide used by the bathing beauties in *Mack and Mabel*. Such precautions helped insure the safety and comfort of cast members.

Work with actors on book scenes would eventually require him to adopt an approach distinctive from his customary one with dancers. "The choreographer is more dictatorial than the director," Gower observed. "The very nature of his work requires him to tell dancers exactly what to do. Yes, you *tell* the dancer. As a director, you *point* the actor in a direction and let him carry it from there, and if it doesn't work, you start again or revise or adapt."[68]

At the time of *Carnival*, limitations with the actor's vocabulary forced him to adhere to the choreographer's mode of expression—a factor that occasionally complicated rehearsals. One such instance occurred while Orbach was working with Alberghetti on the scene in Act Two in which Paul cruelly rehearses Lili beyond limit. Orbach explained: "Gower asked me if I would do the scene walking around Anna Maria in a circle, making the circle smaller and smaller until I would end up face to face with her. I said, 'Do you mean you want the scene to get more and more intense and that I should get more and more angry?' He said, 'Yes, *that's* what I mean.' At that point (in his career), all of his communication was in the visual sense."[69]

Gower himself admitted using this approach: "It's very simple really. I'll have a visual conception of how I want a scene to look, and I may very well tell an actor to do something that, to him, seems completely arbitrary. But for a good actor, this presents no problem. I couldn't care less what he does to come up with it and make it work. Whether he uses the Method or a vaudeville style or whatever. Just as long as he gives me what I want."[70] To get what he wanted, he created a flexible working environment for the actor. Mitchell comments that with Gower it was simply a matter of "there's the stage, you have the script, you are here, and you're going to do this. He didn't say, 'Read that line a little more . . .' nor 'Now if you do this, we'll be able to . . .' He just left you alone, and you developed it yourself. Then he would choose from what he wanted. It wasn't improvising, but there was a freedom about it, and he was delighted with anything you were doing."[71]

Alberghetti recalls a similar experience. "Gower never tried to carve a performance out of you. You brought in your performance. But he would go out into the audience every show and say, 'On a scale of ten, you have it at a nine now—bring it to a ten,' or 'bring it to an eleven.' He had a wonderful way of knowing when to push you, even though he himself was not the kind of director who would sit down with you and talk about the character."[72]

Creating a proper atmosphere for actors also included helping them acquire skills specific to their character. To make Mitchell an able conjurer, professional magician Roy Benson was brought in to teach him how to perform various feats of legerdemain—pulling cigarettes from girls' ears, blue carnations from lighted matches, bowls of goldfish from ladies' hats, shirts off men's backs, and strings of sausages from women's handbags. The director also had Tom Tichenor tutor Orbach in the required puppetry. As part of his training, the actor spent months wearing a puppet on his hand while around the house. By the time of the first performance, he was not only manipulating all four puppets on his own, but also providing a distinctive voice for each. So effective was his puppetry that most thought it the work of Tichenor or some other professional.[73] This included numerous critics who raved about the performance of the puppets but failed to realize that Orbach was the source. Some years later when performing a revival of the show, the actor arranged to have the front of the booth attached with Velcro to emphasize his puppet work. In the final scene of the first act, when he exited the booth after Lili's departure with Jacquot and began disassembling the entire front, the audience realized that there had been no one else inside, and gave him a three-minute standing ovation.[74]

Precision, an inherent part of Gower's work with dancers, naturally carried over into his work with actors. Mitchell recalls one scene with Ballard that they literally played face to face. Time and again in rehearsal Gower would specify the exact distance he wanted between them. "It would drive me crazy!" Mitchell recalls. "I think it drove *him* crazy, too. But he was very precise! I always listened to him because I was a dancer and you are precise. You work on choreography. Actors are not terribly precise; they don't have to be."[75] But in a Champion show they were. Once he determined the specifics of characterization from what the actor brought him, those very same details were to be duplicated without variation every time. No deviation was tolerated.

His organizational sense also contributed to the working atmosphere. At the outset of each rehearsal, performers knew just what he intended to accomplish. If they were uncomfortable with a particular entrance, exit, or moment in a scene, he would never ask them what was wrong with it. Rather, he acknowledged their difficulty and promised to resolve it, which he did in due course. He always seemed to know exactly where actors were uncomfortable and how to correct it.

An ability to tailor musical numbers to performers' specific talents was yet another characteristic of his direction. "Grand Impérial Cirque de Paris" was developed for Olaf on the basis of his high-kicking ability. "Sword, Rose, and Cape" was designed to showcase Mitchell's ballet skills.[76] Into the fabric of numbers like the "Prologue" and the "Ballet," he wove the routines of professional circus artists. In effect, the entire musical was developed around the individual talents of those who originated the roles (which may explain why the show has always been difficult to revive).

There were times, of course, when the working atmosphere was fraught with tension, as on the day when Orbach reported for his first rehearsal. By the time he had joined the company, "Gower had already been working with the dancers for a week. I came up to the stage manager in the wings and said, 'Hi, I'm Jerry.' He replied, 'Shhh. Mr. Champion is thinking.' Gower was standing at the center of the stage, thinking over something. The entire theatre was frozen. Everybody was so afraid."[77] Such moments were formidable ones for cast members. To the performer who dared disturb his silent reflection, the director shot a defiant look (later termed the "Gower glower" by Carol Channing) sure to intimidate. He could also abruptly halt any noisy din with a "tsk" sound made by clicking his tongue against the front portion of the roof of his mouth. Hearing this, the entire company would immediately fall silent and spring to attention.

Staff members were treated much the same. Rather than face the director, Stewart often would slip lines of dialogue to cast members. "Mike would write a joke line or something," related Orbach, "and instead of walking up to Gower with it, he would tell me, 'Here, try this line here with the puppets, and if Gower likes it, we can tell him that it was actually written. That you didn't ad lib it.' He was so afraid to talk to Gower about anything."[78] Under mounting pressure, Gower became less benign and more tyrannical—a bona fide "Presbyterian Hitler," according to Stewart.[79] Dealing with these bouts of despotism was equally exasperating for rehearsal pianist Howard. "I worshipped him and loved him dearly, but he was a creative artist, and as such, had his moments of tantrum and temperament. I remember once in a terrible state of wrath, I wrote down a whole list of rules to be observed when working with Gower. I think it ended with 'Do nothing, say nothing, and offer no advice!' "[80]

Anita Gillette, chorus member and understudy for Alberghetti, describes an episode that occurred during the pre-Broadway run at Washington's National Theatre. Gower had decided that she was too American-looking to play Lili and broke the news to her while staging a scene with Ballard and Mitchell. Gillette entered the theatre and took the seat next to him. "As he was directing the scene, he said, 'Anita, we've decided you're too . . . No, Kaye, I want you to cross on that line. Okay, Jimmy, go on . . . We've decided that you're just not right . . . No, Jimmy, not that line. I want you to cross there . . . We've decided that you're just not right for the role. Of course, you can stay in the chorus if you like.' It was one of the cruelest things that ever happened to me. I've never forgotten it."[81] Gillette decided to remain with the chorus. Auditions produced no suitable understudy for Alberghetti, and *Carnival* opened in New York without one. When Alberghetti became hospitalized not long after the opening, Merrick called Gillette to substitute, which she did to rave notices. He also billed her for the name changes on the marquee after learning of her plans to leave *Carnival* for *The Gay Life*.[82]

After being cheered to the rafters of the Phyllis Anderson Theatre for the gypsy run-through on Sunday, March 5, the thirty-one-member cast departed by special train the next day for Washington, where they opened at the National Theatre on Thursday, March 9. *Carnival* garnered instant favor with the press, who hailed its spirited, imaginative, colorful, and dazzling high style, and fidelity to the spirit of the film *Lili*.[83] One critic even touted it as a pleasant antidote to poisonous confections that gave sentiment a bad name such as *The Sound of Music*.[84] Gower had directed the production with a brilliance that made it enticing even to sophisticates who had never seen a genuine carnival in their lives.[85]

But that brilliance had a price, costing Gower's relationship with Jess dearly because of the troubleshooting role he had asked his friend to assume. "It is possible that he came to regret this invitation," Jess states. "Perhaps we both did. I kept picking at what I felt were weaknesses in the new production—lines that didn't pay off or story points that weren't clear. Occasionally, he made use of the alternatives I suggested, but more often, in struggling to explain to me why my proposals were sheer nonsense, he would force the right solution out of himself. It was what I was being paid to do, but it put a terrible strain on our relationship."[86]

Other strains were showing. As *Carnival*'s tryout tour began, Marge, restaging *Bye Bye Birdie* for the road, remained in New York to look after son Gregg, and minus her presence, Gower became infatuated with Alberghetti. "Sweet-voiced and wide-eyed," explains Jess, "she had an air of great vulnerability, perfect for the role she was playing. I never discussed the matter with Gower. And how much of the gossip reached home Marge never indicated."[87] For the moment, the effect of the rumor on the Champions' marriage was muted by the showman's irrepressible brilliance.

Washington's reception of *Carnival* was unparalleled, surpassing even *West Side Story*'s welcome at the same theatre only four years before. Though the musical was a total sellout for the run (standing room included), Gower kept the fine-tuning going. The sensation the puppets had generated required expansion of their lines, Mitchell's "Sword, Rose, and Cape" lost a verse, and Alberghetti's "A Very Nice Man" was restaged.[88] As *Carnival* moved to Philadelphia's Forrest Theatre, he wondered if a perfect musical could be made from what already seemed a surefire hit: "There are spots in the show that bug me. But I am afraid to fool with them very much. I mustn't disturb the balance of the delicate mechanism, which somehow works in its present form. Yet there are changes I would like to make."[89]

Raves from Philadelphia critics and capacity crowds failed to deter further tinkering in the interest of perfection. A new opening song for Paul, "Before the Wind Blows Out," replaced "I've Got to Find a Reason," possibly because one Washington critic had found it too "didactic."[90] One day just as Gower was on the verge of inserting a second-act ballet with giant versions of the puppets, Merrick charged down the aisle and stopped him flat, announcing that he would tolerate no more changes. *Carnival* had been a tremendous sensation in Washington and if he did not cease his fiddling and restore it at once, the show would be closed. Despite the director's objections, the producer prevailed. The show was frozen, the second-act ballet abandoned, and "I've Got to Find a Reason" restored.[91] *Carnival* would be a success, but not the perfect musical for which Gower had hoped. He returned to New York fifteen pounds lighter than when he left—the cost of shepherding the show through four weeks of tryouts.[92] Heedless of the sign, he donned his customary lucky red blazer for opening at the Imperial Theatre on April 13.

"*Carnival* bursts with the vitality of Broadway know-how," proclaimed *Times* critic Howard Taubman, "and yet is hardly ever vulgar. And in its central story of the young Lili, it has an innocence that is not overwhelmed by the tinsel and flamboyance that surround her."[93] The *Journal-American*'s John McClain hailed it as "a monumental musical . . . quite unostentatious . . . very tasteful and enormously endearing."[94] The *Post*'s Richard Watts Jr. declared it "captures the quality of magic, . . . is frankly sentimental, at times perilously so, but always some stroke of imaginative brilliance in Gower Champion's staging lifts it beyond any danger of potential sloppiness, and its charm, warmth and humor . . . make it a wonderfully winning and thoroughly enchanting entertainment."[95]

Gower's calculated changes in mood, evidenced in the contrast between the indomitable bouncy charm of dreamy numbers ("Prologue," "Grand Impérial Cirque de Paris," and "Beautiful Candy") and the cynical exuberance of nightmarish ones ("Humming," "Sword, Rose, and Cape," and "Carnival Ballet") greatly impressed.[96] Critics richly praised his ringmaster's eye for detail and balance and prestidigitator's command of color and movement. His new-to-Broadway alternative to standard musical theatre staging was also welcomed for its highly inventive style and precise transitions.[97] Henceforth, continuously choreographed staging would become common practice, and musicals would dance from start to finish.

Merill drew compliments for a delightfully tuneful score, admirably suited to the story situations of Stewart's tasteful, affecting libretto with its raffish gusto.[98] Armstrong's setting aptly conjured festive and dark moods, and Wittop's costumes were suitably gaudy for a bedraggled carny.[99] Critics were equally enthusiastic about the performers. Alberghetti, as affecting as the heroine in the film *La Strada*, infused Lili with childlike simplicity, skillful singing, and a friendly rapport with the puppets reminiscent of Fran Allison's.[100] Orbach, in his Broadway debut, was welcomed as a new leading man with the voice, command, and confidence of an actor ordained for stardom.[101] Mitchell brought style, grace, and a genuine authenticity to Marco's phoniness that perfectly complemented Ballard's gem of comic singing and acting as Rosalie.[102] Finally, in the bittersweet role of Jacquot, Olaf proved himself a Chaplinesque clown, short on stature and long on stage expertise.[103]

Not all were completely captivated by *Carnival*'s appeal. Some, the *Herald Tribune*'s Walter Kerr among them, found devices like Lili's pale face and Paul's limp too taxing on audience sympathy, and the magic, promised in the "Prologue" to increase as the characters became better known, to remain basically the same throughout because of a stress on staging over characterization. *Carnival*'s milieu and impeccable mounting were simply more interesting than its people, who, in the end, remained only shadows. Others cited a conspicuous gap between the lyrical staging and prosaic libretto, as well as a bit of redundancy in offering all sides of a subject essentially without a center.[104] Whatever its shortcomings, however, *Carnival,* with its European ambiance and allure, was an extraordinary shift from the sprightly, collegiate playfulness of *Birdie,* and proof positive that Gower Champion was no one-shot Charlie.

Following their seventeen curtain calls, Gower congratulated the cast, and then escorted Marge to the opening night party, where photographers, relishing a confrontation between her and his leading lady, had to content themselves with flashes of the two smiling at each other.[105] Afterward, he promptly headed for La Guardia Airport and boarded a plane for San Francisco, where he was to open the national company of *Birdie* that Marge already had in rehearsal. With two musicals now running simultaneously on Broadway and his native California about to experience his much-acclaimed work, he was at the peak of his form. Ahead was a London production of *Birdie,* as well as a film version for Columbia Pictures.

Nine days later during rehearsal in San Francisco, he collapsed and was taken to Cedars of Lebanon Hospital in Los Angeles for treatment of that recurring stomach ulcer. During his convalescence, Lucia Victor was dispatched to London to assume his duties there, and George Sidney took over the direction of the film. Ordered by his doctors to rest, Gower complied for the sake of Gregg, Marge, and the second child she was now carrying. Blake Gower Champion, namesake of film director and family friend Blake Edwards, would make the family a foursome on February 14, 1962.[106]

By mid-July, *Carnival* had not only paid off its modest $226,624 production cost, but also had received the New York Critics Circle Award as best musical of the season. Merrill was also honored as best composer, Stewart as best librettist, and Gower as best director of a musical. At the Tony Awards in April 1962, Armstrong was recognized as outstanding scenic designer, and Alberghetti tied with Diahann Carroll of *No Strings* for best actress in a musical. Although *Carnival* was nominated for best musical and Gower for best director, the winners were *How to Succeed in Business Without Really Trying* and its director, Abe Burrows. Still, *Carnival* made an impressive showing, remaining on Broadway for two seasons to total 719 performances.

With two Broadway hits now to look after, Gower was soon back in New York, where he was stopped on the street one day by a reporter who congratulated him on Merrick's offer of a lifetime contract. "Whose life?" he joked as he went his way.[107]

TEN

Down the Stairs, 'Round the Orchestra, Affirming Life

Hello, Dolly!

1962–1964

The day after the opening of *Carnival,* Merrick went right to work on reuniting Champion, Merrill, and Stewart for his next big project. That morning over breakfast with Stewart in the Oak Room of the Plaza Hotel, he explained how he had recently acquired the rights for an adaptation of Thornton Wilder's farce *The Matchmaker,* and then invited the librettist to write the book for the new show.[1] Stewart accepted at once and began a first draft.

Merrick's idea was ingenious to be sure. Unlike the sources commonly chosen for musicals, *The Matchmaker* is a stylized work having a heightened reality, perfectly suited to song and dance, and a plot set in late-nineteenth-century New York, a time and place with musical connotations. Even the story's playful romantic comedy and whimsical mood speak dance.[2] Many of these qualities can be traced to *The Matchmaker*'s earliest literary antecedent, *A Day Well Spent in Three Adventures,* a long-forgotten one-act farce composed by British playwright John Oxenford in 1836.[3] It recounts the zany exploits of Bolt, a mischievous foreman, and his naïve apprentice, Mizzle, who, in the absence of their employer, Mr. Cotton, abandon their suburban hosiery shop routine (Adventure 1: "The Set Up") for a day's romp in the city of London (Adventure 2: "The Visit"), returning in time to thwart a burglary and apprehend the perpetrator seconds before the entrance of their employer (Adventure 3: "The Return").

Six years later, in 1842, Austrian playwright and comic actor Johann Nestroy tailored the comedy to Viennese tastes in his four-act adaptation, *Einen Jux Will Er Sich Machen* (He Wants to Have a Lark).[4] Though the two clerks (Weinberl and Christopher) remained the pivotal characters, Nestroy made them more sympathetic by portraying their employer (Zangler the grocer) as a miserly and peevish overlord.[5]

Nearly a hundred years later, Thornton Wilder, acting on a suggestion from

Austrian director Max Reinhardt,[6] wrote *The Merchant of Yonkers,* an American adaptation of Nestroy's play set in early 1880s New York. As the title indicates, the four-act farce concentrated on employer Horace Vandergelder rather than on clerks Cornelius Hackl and Barnaby Tucker. But Wilder's most notable contribution was the addition of an original character, Mrs. Dolly Gallagher Levi, a widowed matchmaker whose cagey but magnanimous nature charmingly disarms her opponents.[7] Produced by Herman Shumlin and directed by Reinhardt, *The Merchant of Yonkers* made its Broadway debut at the Guild Theatre (later the ANTA) on December 28, 1938, with a cast that included Percy Waram as Vandergelder, Tom Ewell as Cornelius, John Call as Barnaby, and Jane Cowl as Mrs. Levi.[8] It closed after 39 performances.[9]

The failure did not deter Wilder from revising the play to accent the one character that had intrigued audiences most. The result was *The Matchmaker,* first performed on August 23, 1954, at the Royal Lyceum Theatre as part of the city of Edinburgh's International Festival of Music and Drama.[10] Under Tyrone Guthrie's rapid-fire direction, Ruth Gordon played the indomitable Dolly Levi; Sam Levene, the cantankerous Vandergelder; Arthur Hill and Alec McCowen, city neophytes Cornelius and Barnaby; Eileen Herlie, hat shopkeeper Irene Molloy; Rosamund Greenwood, Molloy's assistant, Minnie Fay; and Patrick McAlinney, Vandergelder's lackey, Malachi Stack.[11] The play's favorable reception quickly led to a London opening at the Theatre Royal, Haymarket, on November 4, 1954, where it ran a full season before Merrick and the Theatre Guild co-produced it for the American stage.[12]

The Matchmaker made its Broadway debut on December 5, 1955, with Gordon and most of the Edinburgh cast repeating their original roles, save Loring Smith as Vandergelder and Robert Morse as Barnaby.[13] With critical acclaim equaling that of London, the farce accumulated 486 performances before undertaking an extensive national tour.[14]

With Stewart now at work on the musical adaptation of the play, Merrick turned to composer Merrill, who promptly rejected the offer upon learning that Gower would be invited to direct.[15] Vexed over being barred from rehearsals until a time the director deemed appropriate, Merrill refused to work with him again. Although Merrill would later provide lyrics to Jule Styne's music for Champion's productions of *Prettybelle* (1971) and *Sugar* (1972), at this point he was intractable. Merrick would have to find someone else to write the score.[16]

He went in search of the one person he deemed key to the production. Gower was in Hollywood at Paramount Studios preparing to shoot his first feature film, *My Six Loves* (1963), with Debbie Reynolds, Cliff Robertson, Jim Backus, Hans Conried, Eileen Heckart, and David Janssen. This light comedy, about a Broadway star returning home for a much-needed rest and finding six orphaned waifs encamped on her country estate, had the required family appeal that made it an ideal choice for launching his screen directing career. But Gower was also seeking other ways to diversify his craft to avoid being identified solely with Broadway musicals.

He had recently accepted an offer from Lillian Hellman to direct her new play, *My Mother, My Father, and Me.* Following its Broadway opening and his debut as a director of drama, he planned to return to musicals with either Jerry Bock and Sheldon Harnick's version of Miklos Laszlo's play *The Shop Around the Corner* or Richard Rodgers and Alan Jay Lerner's work on extrasensory perception, *I Picked a Daisy.*[17] (The Bock-Harnick piece was *She Loves Me,* eventually produced and directed by Harold Prince and choreographed by Carol Haney in 1963; *I Picked a Daisy* later became the Burton Lane–Alan Jay Lerner musical *On a Clear Day You Can See Forever,* directed by Robert Lewis and choreographed by Herbert Ross in 1965.) In the end, he opted for the Rodgers-Lerner show, leaving Bock and Harnick, as well as Merrick, to look elsewhere.[18]

The producer's project had just about reached a standstill when Jerry Herman, on the advice of Stewart, called upon him with a request to write the score. Even though the recent *Milk and Honey* (1961) had established Herman as a songwriter of note, Merrick questioned whether the composer of an operetta about middle-aged Jewish-Americans on holiday in Israel could capture the Americana of *The Matchmaker.*[19] "He thought I was too *ethnic* for the piece," Herman later recalled. "Mike Stewart told me this, and I was hysterical. I laughed for twenty minutes. After all, *Milk and Honey* had been a stretch for me—my thing wasn't to write middle-aged operetta! But when I met with David, he said, 'I think you're very talented, but I don't really know if you can do Americana.' I asked him to let me try, to prove I could."[20]

Herman procured a copy of Stewart's draft, returned to his apartment, and for the next three days studied the script and composed four songs—"Hello, Dolly!," "Put on Your Sunday Clothes," "I Put My Hand In" (with its lead-in, "Call on Dolly"), and "I Still Love the Love That I Loved," a predecessor to "Ribbons Down My Back."[21] He then arranged a fifteen-minute audition with Merrick.[22] Rarely do established songwriters audition their work for producers, but Herman was determined to make *The Matchmaker* his own whatever the cost.

By the end of the audition, Merrick was thoroughly impressed. "David couldn't believe I'd written those songs in three days. He obviously liked them, because he stood up at the end and said, 'Kid, the show is yours.' "[23] During this same meeting, Merrick advised him to arrange the songs for Ethel Merman, whom he intended for the leading role. "So from the beginning, from the inception of the songs, I wrote everything with her voice in mind. In fact, I wrote the songs in keys that she would be comfortable in."[24]

Once Stewart and Herman submitted a full score and libretto in September 1961, the producer immediately offered the role to Merman, then in San Francisco performing with his national touring company of *Gypsy* (1959). To his surprise, the star declined, explaining that she no longer had the stamina for lengthy commitments and was planning a partial retirement.[25]

With his star search now temporarily sidetracked, the impresario went in search of a director once more. In autumn 1962, after failing to interest Jerome Robbins, Joshua Logan, and Joe Layton, he contacted Harold Prince, whose recently acclaimed staging of *The Matchmaker* for the Phoenix Repertory Theatre made him an ideal choice for *Dolly! A Damned Exasperating Woman*.[26] "I turned it down," Prince explained. "Among other reasons, I didn't care for the score, particularly the song, 'Hello, Dolly!' I couldn't for the life of me see why those waiters were singing how glad they were to have her back where she belonged, when she'd never been there in the first place."[27] With the position of director still in question, Merrick again attempted to secure a leading lady.

For a time, he courted comedienne Nancy Walker; then he saw Carol Channing in the touring production of the Broadway revue *Show Girl*, and was so taken with her that he promised to star her in a musical.[28] Her last one, *The Vamp* (1955), had quickly perished because of inferior direction, all the more reason to have the "benevolent despot" of *Lend an Ear* at the helm whenever the next materialized.[29]

Gower, for his part, had been busy heralding "The Comeback of Sweetness and Light" (as he described it in a November 20, 1962, editorial for *The Hollywood Reporter*). Citing *Carnival* and *My Six Loves* as his stage and screen contributions to a growing movement that included *The Music Man, The Sound of Music, Oliver!, Mr. Hobbs Takes a Vacation,* and *The Wonderful World of the Brothers Grimm,* he observed, "It may well be that the public has just about had it for the angry young men who have spewed their narcissistic nonsense, defeatist philosophy, four-letter word vocabularies and sick idioms from Broadway to Hollywood." Even so, the camps of Edward Albee, Jean Genet, John Osborne, and Tennessee Williams remained unscathed by his assertion that "theatregoers have been surfeited with the look-Ma-I'm-sick school of dramaturgy and their sophomoric, overlabored and trashy output."[30]

By January 1963, though, the comeback of sweetness and light seemed fleeting for Gower. The critical response to *My Six Loves* was poor and his enthusiasm for Hellman's play, despite the excellence of Ruth Gordon, Walter Matthau, and the other members of the cast, was rapidly disintegrating under the author's incessant scrutiny of his work. But the worst humiliation came only a week before the March 21 opening, when Hellman replaced him with Arthur Penn.[31] He later remarked: "It was obvious from the second week of rehearsal I had no autonomy. I wanted to withdraw, but to be frank, I didn't have the guts. It was my first drama and I didn't have the security or position I have now. If it happened now, I'd leave in a minute. I still bear the scars."[32] Indeed, the lesson would remain with him for life. "It taught me one thing. I'll never take a play without being in full control. I had definite ideas about *Mother*—I wanted to make it really far-out farce—but Lillian didn't see it that way.[33]

On the heels of this fiasco came news of the cancellation of the film version of *Carnival* he was to have directed for MGM,[34] a disappointment further compounded by pressure from Lerner to immediately launch production for *I Picked a Daisy*. Even though Gower had worked almost a year without remuneration and was now in need of a two-week break, the lyricist insisted he push forward without delay.[35] Rather than jeopardize his health once more, he resigned. His timing could not have been better. Nearly four months later, on July 10, both lyricist and composer suddenly decided to abandon the project "because an insufficient amount of Mr. Lerner's lyrics blocked Mr. Rodgers from finishing the score."[36] Fifteen days later, on July 25, the songwriters dissolved their partnership.[37] By July 29, Merrick had his director.[38]

The rift with Lerner did not solely determine Gower's decision to stage *Dolly! A Damned Exasperating Woman*. Weeks before signing the contract, he had discovered a concept for creating the continuously choreographed staging he required— a ramp extending from the stage and encircling the orchestra pit. Marge recalls its impact. "It was an architectural or scenic design concept [rather than a thematic concept as in *Carnival*] that really hooked him. The idea engaged him so tremendously that he immediately started with that whole sequence on the ramp [the "Waiters' Gallop" and the title number]—one of the few things that stayed in the show after we went out of town for tryouts."[39]

In coming months, he would strategically orchestrate the use of the ramp in Act I so as not to diminish its effect on the rousing second act title number, the first to be staged. In Act I, it would be confined to Dolly's monologues, certain scenic transitions, and brief moments in some production numbers ("Put on Your Sunday Clothes" and "Before the Parade Passes By"). With the ramp to aid the flow of the production, he turned to casting.

Nanette Fabray was his initial choice for the role of Dolly Levi.[40] Herman remembers, "She was a big favorite of ours. We thought she had spirit. If you watch her in the film *The Band Wagon* (1953), you see why she would have been a good choice."[41] However, it was essential to be sure that Fabray possessed the right qualities, so in August 1963, Gower asked her to undertake some exploratory sessions with him for that purpose. She was astounded by the request. After their work together on *Make a Wish*, he should have been familiar with her abilities. She declined, forcing him to look for someone else.[42]

Reportedly, Ruth Gordon, after working with Gower on the Hellman play, expected to be approached to reprise the role for the musical, and even took singing lessons to prepare for it. Champion never asked her to audition. Her payback was to arrive at the St. James Theatre one evening shortly after the show's opening, dressed in a black gown with long white gloves similar to Dolly's red Harmonia Gardens costume. From first row center, she glared at the stage in cold protest throughout the performance, never applauding once.[43]

Reluctantly, Gower agreed to accompany Merrick to Mineola, Long Island, where Channing was performing in George Bernard Shaw's *The Millionairess*.[44] So firmly had she been associated with the character of Lorelei Lee, Anita Loos's gold-digging flapper of *Gentlemen Prefer Blondes*, that he doubted she could break away from it sufficiently to become Dolly Levi. Following her performance that evening, he and Merrick agreed that she would be totally wrong for the role. "Normally, I'd probably have said nothing and forgotten about it," Champion later reflected, "but Carol and I are old friends. So I went to her apartment that midnight and for half an hour I told her 'no' and why. But she wouldn't accept this. She said, 'Just let me read for you.' So she read. We worked until 3 or 4 o'clock in the morning on Dolly Levi and I began to see something happening. I called David, and told him to meet us at the Imperial Theatre the next day. She read for him and that was it."[45]

Ultimately, it was Channing's unconventional but well-conceived interpretation of the character that convinced the director of her suitability. "I told him about the character," she recalls, "and said, 'She's *funny*, Gower. She's not a heavy thing. She's a *funny woman*. She's so aggravating, we have to laugh.' He watched, and then I did the 'manure speech' for him. [Afterward] I told him, 'She's the biggest wheeler-dealer from the Battery to the Bronx. She yells because she's born under the Second Avenue El.' "[46]

Channing further explained how the essence of Dolly was to be found in her relationship with late husband, Ephraim Levi. "Because she was in love with her husband, she took on all his ways, as we *do* in marriage. You become each other's ancestors, each other's forebears. She became his mother, his grandmother. She was the biggest Hadassah leader. She came out of traditional Jewish mythology because of Ephraim. She's Dolly *Gallagher*, but she married Ephraim *Levi*, and she adored him."[47]

"I'll buy that," Gower responded.[48] On August 5, 1963, *The New York Times* announced: "Carol Channing, the blonde that gentlemen preferred, will return to the musical stage in *Dolly: A Damned Exasperating Woman*."[49]

Beneath Channing's persuasive characterization was something the director had first recognized in *Lend an Ear*—an uncommon form of spontaneity, which, if properly managed, could help set the tone of the production. Gordon Connell, who played the Judge, describes the effect. "Carol is someone who works off a strange combination of preparation and the present moment. She is truly a visitor from another planet whose feet are very cannily rooted in the here and now. It's true [her performance] is calculated, certainly. She's learned it; she's practiced it. She does it so much that she's never at a loss. She is never really caught totally unaware. But that sense of spontaneity—like of danger! She has a danger in her—in her presence and her approach to things that makes us ask, 'What is she going to do next?' So ultimately Gower was very shrewd in casting her."[50]

In mid-September 1963, the director began assembling a cast to match the dangerous spontaneity of his leading lady.[51] His casting notes list the names of forty actors whom he considered for the role of Horace Vandergelder, including Jim Backus, Art Carney, Pat O'Brien, Bert Lahr, and David Burns.[52] He chose David (Davy) Burns, the grand old man of supporting actors, whose Tony Award–winning portrayals of the bungling Mayor Shinn in *The Music Man* (1957) and the feeble lecher, Senex, in *A Funny Thing Happened on the Way to the Forum* (1963) brought prominence late in his career.[53]

Again, Connell, also Burns's understudy, relates what intrigued Champion about the performer. "Davy was possessed—demonically possessed—and one of the funniest human beings that ever was self-invented. And D-A-N-G-E-R-O-U-S!!! He would go off and do this kind of *thing* to conventions, rules and propriety. 'I must behave in a certain way? No!' He was always thinking in those outrageous Marx Brothers ways. He was clearly a match for Carol. Gower was not only fascinated by, but trusting of people [like Davy and Carol] who had made a career of this danger."[54]

In Burns, Gower found a performer who possessed the kind of curmudgeonly foil needed to balance Channing's high-spirited Dolly. There was just one proviso: he wanted the first act finale, a very important moment. Though not a superstar like Channing, he was nevertheless a star whose stature deserved recognition of this nature. Gower assigned him the first act finale, "Penny in My Pocket."[55]

By choosing comedians to play Cornelius Hackl and Irene Molloy, the director broke with the straight portrayal of romantic figures conventional in farce and musicals. This interpretation would also influence the way the roles would be sung. As Herman recalls, "Gower didn't want to go for a typical baritone and lovely soprano."[56] By pairing the comic talents of Charles Nelson Reilly with those of Eileen Brennan, he could avoid romantic stereotypes and infuse ordinarily innocuous roles with that dangerous spontaneity he so admired in performers.[57] "Like any good director," explains Eileen Brennan, "Gower would never limit himself by saying, 'Oh, she's a comedian; she can't handle this.' Good actors will do whatever the script calls for. Certainly, in my career I've run into people who, for the most part, try to 'typecast' you. But good directors don't. They know that an actor is rounded, and that really fine comic actors usually can do drama or any kind of farce. That's what Gower knew. He didn't limit himself by type casting."[58]

Brennan rose to prominence in the title role of Rick Besoyan's spoof of operetta, *Little Mary Sunshine* (1959), which earned her an Obie and the Newspaper Guild's Page One Award.[59] She was also an equally skilled dramatic actress who played Annie Sullivan in the national company of *The Miracle Worker.*[60]

Charles Nelson Reilly was an established character actor with twenty-two off-Broadway credits, including Jerry Herman's *Nightcap* and *Parade* and a revival of *Lend an Ear,* which earned him a "walk-on" in *Bye Bye Birdie* and the opportunity to understudy Dick Van Dyke and Paul Lynde. This led to a featured role as Bud Frump, the malevolent nephew of the boss, in *How to Succeed in Business Without Really Trying,* for which he won the Tony and Variety Poll of New York's Critics Awards.[61]

The role of Cornelius Hackl called for a tall, thirty-three-year-old comic actor who could sing and dance. Though Reilly possessed all these qualities, it was further necessary to learn whether he could handle a ballad, since he would be required to sing "It Only Takes a Moment." At the audition, "I sang this odd choice, a hymn from the movie, *Come to the Stable,* called 'Through a Long and Sleepless Night.' Midway through the song, Gower yelled back to Jerry, who was sitting in the rear of the Imperial Theatre, 'Have you heard enough?' And Jerry screamed, 'Y-E-S!!!' But I got the job anyway."[62]

With Reilly and Brennan as the lovers, it was possible that the action might become too frenetic (as some critics would later maintain).[63] Still, Champion was content to have farceurs who would complement the leading players rather than the colorless lovers common to farce.

The work of petite Sondra Lee, a Jerome Robbins discovery from *High Button Shoes* (1947) who later scored as Tiger Lily in his production of *Peter Pan* (1954), had so impressed the director that he contacted her in Rome to offer her the part of shopkeeper's assistant Minnie Fay.[64] "Gower said he had a role for me," she recalls, "and I was overwhelmed and delighted not to have to audition. That was the most flattering thing he could have offered me especially because I did not know him personally. At the time, he was not a pal or someone I had even met."[65]

With Lee's appealing quirkiness and individuality, the director would have yet another performer whose work would complement that of the other cast members. Despite the sketchy nature of the character at the time and Gower's unusual request to learn to play the accordion for a bit of stage business he intended for the character (and later dropped, to Lee's relief), the performer embraced the role. "If you have a director who is so firm about what his vision is," she explains, "you can hook into that vision. We completely gave him our utmost attention because he knew what he had to do and we just did it." Lee brought a sense of wickedness to the character, as well as a swift, positive sense of humor that never veered off course.[66]

Three different performers would fill the role of Barnaby Tucker before the director settled on one who satisfied him. The first was tap dancer James Dybas, who was replaced during rehearsals by Glenn Walken, brother of actor Christopher Walken. A fine actor, Walken proved ill-suited to the musical's style of movement as a dancer.[67] At Stewart's suggestion, Gower auditioned *Bye Bye Birdie* alumnus Jerry Dodge. Despite concerns that he might be too old for the role, the director was delighted to find that the performer could not only handle the stylized movement, but also convincingly play a seventeen-year-old.[68]

By coupling Dodge with Lee and Reilly with Brennan, Champion created two pairs of eccentric lovers whose antics were certain to enliven the atmosphere of the show. "There was something odd about the four of us," Brennan recalls. "Physically, we were all sort of 'off-center.' For example, I was not an ingénue, and Charles was not a leading man. That might have been what Gower was looking for." Connell puts it another way: "They were all from the same loony bin, down in room number three, with Carol and Davy."[69]

Alice Playten portrayed Vandergelder's wailing niece Ermengarde, and Igors Gavon, Ambrose Kemper, her penniless artist-beau. The role of Ernestina Money, first assigned to former burlesque performer Gloria Leroy, was later altered to suit the talents of Mary Jo Catlett, who played Vandergelder's corpulent "blind date" in the Harmonia Gardens sequence. Other performers included David Hartman (later the host of *Good Morning America*) as Rudolph, the Prussian majordomo of the Harmonia Gardens Restaurant; Amelia Haas as Dolly's former neighbor, Mrs. Rose; Gordon Connell as the Judge, and Ken Ayers as the Court Clerk.

Apart from auditions, meetings concerning scenic, costume, and lighting design, book, songs, and orchestrations also occupied the director during the three-week preproduction period from Monday, September 16, to Saturday, October 6, 1963.[70]

Having made peace over the *Gentlemen Prefer Blondes* debacle during their days at MGM, Gower and Oliver Smith joined forces on *Dolly!* One of the finest, most visually gifted, and prolific scenic designers of the era, Smith had created Tony Award–winning sets for *My Fair Lady, West Side Story, The Sound of Music,* and *Camelot* that exhibited an effortless sense of technique and fulfilled each musical's design specifications with elegance and beauty.[71] Designed to shift swiftly and quietly, his scenery allowed the show to progress while the set changed from the interior of a small bridal shop to a vast school gym as in *West Side Story.*[72] His artistry and Champion's continuously choreographed staging were, therefore, well matched.

Smith's partnership with the director was an amicable and productive one. "We would discuss the needs of the show and how Gower wanted to approach it. He knew it had to move seamlessly and with grace, and the changes had to be attractive. It couldn't be clunky and heavy. If you were working with Gower, that was just *a requirement.* You couldn't think of designing anything else. Then I would simply go out and draw up a scheme and bring it in to show him, and except for minor changes, that was usually what it was."[73]

These minor changes frequently concerned ways of animating the set to make it seem alive, like the ladders Champion asked to have added to Vandergelder's Hay and Feed Store so he could perch members of the men's chorus in various poses on its posts and beams for "It Takes a Woman." The steam train that appeared at the climax of "Put on Your Sunday Clothes" was a similar case. "Gower wanted it so that a man could ride up on the top [of the passenger car]. He thought that all up; all I had to do was provide a ladder as a means for someone to get there. And it had a certain Currier and Ives look, which we were all aware of. He liked the Bentwood portals and the whole look of it very much."[74]

The opening sequence of the Hat Shop Scene (Act I, Scene vii) contained yet another animated effect. When Mrs. Molloy and Minnie Fay pushed the door outside the shop to enter, its exterior revolved into the interior. As they crossed the threshold, the side walls slid in from the left and right wings. Later, during "Dancing," the shop again revolved and its walls receded into the wings as the momentum carried the characters out into the street, where they continued their celebration. Smith summarized the effect: "It was graceful and all done with the dance movement, and so therefore it was like a continuation of the dance. And Gower knew how to use it. Sometimes you make things like that and they're never used at all. That, of course, kills you."[75]

Following Champion's approval, the designs would be executed exactly as planned with the exception of the red color of the Harmonia Gardens exterior scrim, which Smith changed to provide a needed contrast to its red interior in the next scene. "Without saying a word to Gower, I decided to make it a bilious green. When he first saw it in the theatre, he was horrified. He said, 'But Oliver, what happened? It's supposed to be in red?' I said, 'Well, we can't go from a red outdoor set into a red interior, so I changed it.' He said, 'You never asked me.' I said, 'No.' There was an enormous silence because that's just unheard of [in the theatre].

Then he laughed and said, 'Well, you're right. It looks wonderful.' And, of course, it always got a hand going into the Harmonia Gardens. So that was the end of that."[76]

The uniqueness of Smith's artistry was especially evident in the lithographic or rotogravure-like drops he designed for the production, like the blowup of J. J. Fogerty's lithograph of Broadway hopelessly laced with telephone and telegraph wires used in the first scene. Sepia or gray-lavender in color, they bore the influence of French painters like Toulouse-Lautrec, Rousseau, and Bonnard.[77] "They were European-inspired," the designer explained, "although they looked American. Their simplicity made the costumes sparkle in front of them, and gave Freddy Wittop a chance to show off. And that's what design is about in the theatre. You just don't go out and do something. I felt that there was a lot of color in certain sets and I wanted the audience to have a rest, so that they could look at these wonderful people. Freddy did a marvelous job."[78]

Despite the success of *Carnival* and the positive comments accorded his work, few offers had come the costumer's way, so he decided to embark on a world tour beginning in Asia. He had just arrived in India when he received a telegram from Merrick asking, "When the hell are you coming back? Gower may want you on *Dolly!*" Wittop immediately cut short his travel plans and returned to New York, delighted to renew his collaboration with the director.[79]

He studied the script and Smith's scenic designs before completing a series of sketches, which he then brought to Champion. These included designs for a "Sunday parade ["Put on Your Sunday Clothes"] with turn-of-the-century costumes that were very pastel-looking. When Gower saw my sketches, he said no. He wanted them very brassy, in oranges, reds and greens. I started over, and he was right. He knew what it should look like."[80]

In designing the costumes for Dolly Levi, Wittop tried to reflect her character and social status. "Dolly is an *entremetteuse,* a meddler about everything, even about marriage. A marriage broker," he explained. "She has no money, of course, and tries to get in the good favor of Vandergelder because that would give her an income. She, therefore, should look simple, not too rich."[81]

Gower knew it was essential to establish the heroine's "impoverished elegance" (as Wilder termed it) immediately upon her first entrance, so he wanted to give the impression that she had outfitted herself in the salvageable remains of two old dresses.[82] From the waist down, the dress "was on plain (red) material," said Wittop, "and on top of it I had some kind of plaid effect, in another wool, that was pressed over, (to look as if) she could have put it together from two different dresses."[83]

The sequined red dress, which Vandergelder procured for Dolly at the conclusion of the first act and in which she later descended the stairs of the Harmonia Gardens Restaurant for the title number in the second act, was a necessary exception to the impoverished elegance rule. "I just designed it this way because Dolly had to stand out from all the rest. The waiters with whom she does the big number were in a deep green and she had to be in something that completely stood out from that look. White would have been too luxurious and too neat. This red dress just struck me as right. And, on top of that, Mr. Merrick always had to have one red dress in his shows. It was his favorite color. If there were no red dress in the show, he wasn't happy."[84]

For the finale, Wittop designed a striking white dress and hat for Dolly to wear at her wedding to Vandergelder. Though Champion had initially approved the design, he had second thoughts upon its completion. "Carol Channing and I loved it," recalled the designer. "However, Gower looked at it and said, 'Well, Freddy, it's very beautiful, I must confess, but it's not Dolly Levi.' He said, 'This woman, for the moment, is not married yet. She has no money, and this is too luxurious looking.' "[85] Channing confided to the designer that she would contrive some way to wear the dress. One evening during the musical's Washington tryout just as the rest of the cast was completing their bows, Channing entered to take hers in the white ensemble. "It was a surprise to everyone including Gower," recalls Wittop. "But, of course, it was perfect. It was a marvelous climax."[86]

An innovator in the field of lighting design, Jean Rosenthal introduced many techniques that have since become standard practice. Her proficiency, knowledge, and discipline were instrumental in raising the status of lighting design from the stepchild of scenic designers to a full-blown theatrical art with its own artists. Among her credits were *West Side Story, Becket, A Taste of Honey, The Sound of Music, A Funny Thing Happened on the Way to the Forum,* and *Night of the Iguana,* as well as numerous productions for dance companies such as Martha Graham, New York City Ballet, and American Ballet Theatre.[87]

Concerning the challenges of this particular production, she wrote: "It was both simple and complex. We three designers [Smith, Wittop, Rosenthal] had the advantage of many prior collaborations. You can visualize the problems: drops which fly in at various depths, big units which come on and go away again [the Hay and Feed Store, Hat Shop and Harmonia Gardens], the train that moves, the staircase which Dolly descends for the title number of the show, open sets [the Parade scene] and small areas [Dolly's monologues on the runway]."[88]

Using Smith's quarter-inch scale elevation drawings and ground plans, as well as Wittop's costume sketches and swatches of the material from which they would be made, Rosenthal began to create a design that would not only complement those of her colleagues, but also include certain effects requested by the director—like the one he termed "the closeup," used during Dolly's solo in the title number's verse section (beginning with "I went away from the lights of Fourteenth Street").[89]

In order to build the number to a rousing climax, Champion deliberately slowed the pace about halfway through—the point at which Dolly crossed from the stage to the center of the runway to sing the verse. He wanted a lighting effect that would not only correspond to the diminished intensity of the music, but also emphasize Dolly as she sang the verse. By reducing the intensity of the general stage lighting and spotlighting Dolly's face as she stood on the runway, Rosenthal focused the audience's attention on the heroine in a manner similar to a motion picture closeup.[90]

The lighting for the number "It Only Takes a Moment," in the Docket Scene (Act II, Scene v) was a similar case. Champion had placed Mrs. Molloy and Cornelius Hackl at opposite ends of the prisoner's docket in which members of the chorus stood. Again, he wanted general stage lighting eliminated so as to emphasize the faces of the two lovers only.[91]

Lucia Victor, assistant to the director on this and subsequent productions, characterized the relationship between Champion and Rosenthal this way: "What a director does with a lighting artist is to talk about the quality he wants. If the lighting artist is good, and this one happened to be the best that ever was, she knows so many things that the director doesn't, and gives so much more than the director asks for, that all he can do is say, 'Oh, that's wonderful, that's marvelous.' Or occasionally, 'That doesn't seem to be quite bright enough' or 'Can't we heighten that effect there?' "[92] Victor further observed that "to talk about a director's use of lighting is, most of the time, not correct because it is the lighting designer who does all that brilliant work."[93] The admiration, respect, and trust Champion and Rosenthal had for each other would continue through succeeding productions (*I Do! I Do!* and *The Happy Time*) until the designer's untimely death in 1969.

Through the stages of preproduction, rehearsal, and pre-Broadway tour, Gower met almost daily on revisions with Stewart and Herman, who abandoned old scenes and songs and crafted new ones—often overnight—as needed. The scope of these, as well as the evolution of the musical itself, is apparent when the three surviving versions of the director's scripts are compared. Appended to the script for *Dolly! A Damned Exasperating Woman,* the first of the three, is a note from Gower himself, inviting just such a comparison. It reads, "The work done on *Dolly* on the road (Detroit, Washington) is best shown by the difference in these three scripts—before and after."[94]

The three versions are distinguished as follows:

Book One—*Dolly! A Damned Exasperating Woman,* used during the New York rehearsals and Detroit debut performance;

Book Two—*Hello, Dolly!,* the interim script used throughout the remainder of the Detroit and Washington tryouts; and

Book Three—*Hello, Dolly!,* the final version of the script as it appears today.

Though the story of how *Hello, Dolly!* became a blockbuster hit is essentially that of the major changes woven into the show in the weeks following its Detroit opening, the seeds were there from the start in the staging, songs, and book.

Generally, Stewart's libretto for *Hello, Dolly!* differs from Wilder's play in several respects. In *The Matchmaker,* the persona of Mrs. Levi is frequently eclipsed by an array of charming yet extraneous characters used by the author for comic effect. These include Vandergelder's tactless housekeeper, Gertrude; his frustrated barber, Joe Scanlon; and his parasitic clerk, Malachi Stack. Others are Stack's crony, the Cabman; the absentminded spinster, Flora Van Huysen; and her foil, the Cook. Stewart's elimination of these characters and omission of all their soliloquies except those spoken by Dolly gave the heroine greater prominence. He also stressed Wilder's central plot—the anti-romance between a conniver and an object of ridicule—which in musical theatre is as atypical as romance can get.[95]

Other changes included the elimination of the sequence in which Cornelius and Barnaby disguise themselves as women to escape their irate employer (though it appears initially in *Dolly! A Damned Exasperating Woman*) and the addition of would-be heiress Ernestina Money—the corpulent "blind date" Dolly arranges for Vandergelder. In *The Matchmaker,* Dolly refers to a similar character, Ernestina Simple, who never appears. Yet with all these modifications, Stewart never compromised the essence of Wilder's comedy.

Discussing the director's initial response to the musical score, Herman remembers that "Gower wanted to go with the farcical quality of Thornton Wilder's work; therefore, he was delighted, and told me so, that my work was simple, melodic and easy to retain. He said that would make his job so much easier, because they were flat-out musical comedy numbers. There's no apologizing for them, and that's what he wanted the show to be. We became instant friends because we *saw* the same show. Sometimes you get a great director and you don't see the same show. That was not the case with Gower. So we had a pretty easy time of it."[96]

At the time of preproduction in September 1963, the score consisted of fourteen songs. Before the show reached New York, Herman would replace over half of it with new ones, sometimes writing several versions of a particular number before finding one that worked. Concerning this, Champion himself later reflected, "I never remember lyrics, but the songs I cut out of that show are the ones that haunt me in bed at night. Almost everything was rewritten before we opened in New York."[97]

Among the numbers to remain was one that in time would become the musical's signature piece. Upon first hearing it, Gower remarked to Marge, "If I can't make a showstopper out of 'Hello, Dolly!' then I better get out of show business."[98] Just before rehearsals began, the song's appeal would be confirmed for the Champions as they entertained a group of close friends in their enormous apartment overlooking Central Park. That evening Herman played the score for the gathering, saving "Hello, Dolly!" for last. In one hearing, it instantly connected with everyone. "I was crazy about it," Jess recalls. "Jerry played it over and over again, first singing it himself, then with Gower, with Gower and Marge, with their son Gregg, and finally, with everybody in the room. By then, B.G.—as we called Marge and Gower's second son, Blake—knew all the words and sang it right along with Jerry. We all felt that if a two-year-old could sing it, it was a sure sign of a hit."[99]

As preproduction continued, the director asked the composer to recommend an orchestrator, and Herman suggested Philip J. Lang, with whom he had wanted to work. "Phil did the *Annie Get Your Gun*'s and all 'the meat and potatoes musicals' [*Can-Can, My Fair Lady, Take Me Along*], as I call them. I told Gower that I felt Phil would go right for the heart and give us a period sound."[100] That was fine with Gower; he and Lang had developed a great rapport on *Carnival.*

Lang discovered that Champion could readily communicate the kinds of effects he wanted in the orchestrations because he understood the language of music. At rehearsal one day in the Mark Hellinger Theatre, as he and Gower were discussing some specific point in "I Put My Hand In," the opening number of the show, Gordon Connell watched and listened with amazement. "They were looking over the music, the orchestral score," he recalls. "Gower said, 'Now I want the oboe to do this on this beat because I've got Carol doing this with her hand.' I was stunned. My background includes a lot of music. I'm a graduated musician, so I was listening. I thought, 'Here's this dancer person who has come up through the ranks and who surely has developed, but do you mean to say he *reads* music and *knows* what instruments should be heard at certain times?' But that was part of his total concept, his vision. He had an *aural* vision, as well as an *optical* vision, and his aural vision was asking him to be that specific about things."[101]

Working once more with dance music arranger Peter Howard, Gower began to fashion a dance vocabulary distinctive from *Carnival* or *Birdie*—a rare high style designed to evoke turn-of-the-century New York.[102] Marge remembers that this style "was almost arrested movement, like snapshots. The idea was to 'hold,' then have movement in between, then 'hold' again. Gower *was* a camera person: he always had a still camera. I have a feeling that his desire to do snapshot movement really began with the story dance, 'Tintypes,' which he had performed earlier in his career with Jeanne. He wanted to make an opening number that would not only introduce Dolly and her meddling, but also give the feeling of New York at that period, and what better way to do it than in snapshots."[103]

Champion's choreography evolved gradually over a period of months, beginning first in sessions prior to preproduction, then through the preproduction period itself and finally into the rehearsal period with the performers.[104] The number "Dancing" illustrates this process.

In the interest of aiding Cornelius and Barnaby in their first romantic adventure, Dolly teaches them to dance. Once they have mastered the basic steps, the boys become so enthralled that they sing, "Now that we're dancing who cares if we ever stop!" Dolly then pairs them with Mrs. Molloy and Minnie Fay, and lets nature take its course.

Like the song's lyrics, the choreography expressed the characters' desire to dance unceasingly. "It was a whole thing of never stopping," explains Marge. "Of never stopping even for the little bits of dialogue. It starts with Dolly teaching Cornelius to dance, which goes back to *Lend an Ear* and Gower's choreography for 'Friday Dancing Class.' Different characters, but it's still 'Put your right hand here, and put your left hand here, and start.' "[105]

Champion asked Howard to interpolate a leitmotif into the number's dance music for which he could develop a corresponding dance step. This step would then be repeated at certain intervals to express the elation of the characters. "I remember that 'Dancing' was a nice pretty waltz," says Howard. "Very easy. Gower and I were in the studio alone, trying to get an idea for the number—a 'hook,' you might call it. I remember very vividly that I had written a song called 'Make Love to Me' which was like a jazz waltz. It went, 'Make-love to-me, make-love to-me, set-my-heart on fire.' Gower said, 'Play that again.' He got so excited, like a little boy, leaping all over the room, and doing what was to become the basic step for 'Dancing.' "[106]

Structured in the manner of a classic ballet, with various movements or sections used to show the adventures of each character, "Dancing" began in Mrs. Molloy's Hat Shop, where Dolly instructed the clerks and milliners in the basics of the waltz as a group of dancers circled casually outside the window. Gradually the simple lesson grew into a mood of pure jubilation as the walls of the shop gave way to the street, where dancers sauntered by in pairs, trios, and small groups, each in pursuit of an adventure that unfolded not in an abrupt episodic manner, but in flowing movements using tap, bits of soft shoe, and exuberant kicks. Then, just as casually, the dancers vanished, leaving Dolly alone on stage with petite Minnie Fay, circling her like a merry sprite before vanishing, too.[107]

About a week before preproduction, dance captains Lowell Purvis and Nicole Barth joined Gower in the painstaking task of creating specific steps. "There's a step," Lucia Victor observed, "my favorite step in 'Dancing,' which we called the trio step. And that was Lowell Purvis's. Gower said, 'Well, play around with this strain of music here. I want something that turns and does this.' So Lowell played around and Gower said. 'That's it! Now go back, and let's get that.' He would take things that others would do, then work it out, adjust, adapt, and change it."[108]

During preproduction, Champion frequently met with Howard and four or five of the dancers to complete the intricate fitting together of music and steps. By the time of rehearsal, however, a large section of the number still remained that he could only finish with the entire corps of dancers. In this final phase, Victor noted that the choreographer used the dancers much like a painter uses colors on a canvas. "He would take one color [dancer] and put it there, while the rest of the paint [chorus] stood around and waited. They might get to talking too loudly and then he would click his tongue against the roof of his mouth and go, 'Tsk, tsk, tsk.' The whole room would fall quiet; then he would pick another color and apply that. It was fascinating to watch because he put it together bit by bit. If it took him all day to set the first three movements that was fine—everybody else just bloody well waited!"[109]

The first two weeks of the five-week rehearsal period covering October 6 to November 10, 1963, were devoted to "The Waiters' Gallop" and "Hello, Dolly!"—two major second act production numbers that together would form the foundation of the show.[110] This musical diptych would be created and connected by means of the principle of the topper, "the climax no one believes can be surpassed ('The Waiters' Gallop') until the next wonder—the next topper ('Hello, Dolly!')—leaves the audience cheering and the performers gasping for breath."[111]

A comic dance in the tradition of *Birdie*'s "The Shriners' Ballet" and *Make a Wish*'s "The Sale," "The Waiters' Gallop" took place in Act II, Scene iii, when Harmonia Gardens headwaiter Rudolph (David Hartman) announced to the staff the imminent return of beloved former patron Dolly Levi. In celebration of the occasion, he directed the waiters to make the restaurant's famed lightning service "twice as lightning as ever." Then, blowing a whistle, he initiated a breakneck culinary ballet in which each waiter dispatched a host of acrobatic moves with great alacrity. While scurrying from dining area to kitchen and back again, the waiters balanced trays of food, instantly set and cleared tables, and even skewered roasted chickens in midair. The action gradually intensified until the entire covey of them united to perform a score of leaps (skewers or trays in hand), which grew faster and faster as the music concluded.

The dance was divided into nine segments, with brief intervals of dialogue spoken between each by patrons located in two curtained private dining rooms at upstage left and right.[112] With the completion of the initial dance segment to the lively music of "Please, Sir, Mrs. Levi Sent Me," a dialogue segment, using the lilting "Dancing" as underscoring, followed in the right dining room with Cornelius, Barnaby, Mrs. Molloy, and Minnie Fay.[113] Then the dance resumed until overtaken by a second dialogue segment between Vandergelder and Ernestina in the left dining room. This interplay of dance with dialogue continued as headwaiter Rudolph worked the two rooms and Vandergelder lost his purse that miraculously landed in the hands of the clerks just as their bill was due. With that, the dance overtook the dialogue for the waiters' leaping finale.

By alternating the segments of dance with dialogue, Champion created not only a larger, more interesting and cohesive section of the Harmonia Gardens sequence, but also a frenzied atmosphere perfect for the topper, which was to follow. "Waiters" began to take shape on October 2, a few days before the first rehearsal with the full company. David Hartman comments on the step-by-step development of the number and the collaborative nature of its composition.

"In a sense, 'The Waiters' Gallop' was as much the creation of the dancers as it was Gower's. Certainly, the whole concept was Gower's, and a lot of the motion and movement was typical Gower. But to John Mineo, he'd say, 'John, do me something.' Or Joel Craig. Peter Howard would play the piano and they would start to move. Gower would say, 'Great! Hold it! That! Do that again!' It would be a little movement which might become three beats—a spin, a turn, a hand going up with a tray or something. So it evolved count by count by count. That's why it took so long."[114] The title number developed the same way.

On the afternoon of Sunday, October 6, at the Mark Hellinger Theatre, the full cast assembled for the first rehearsal.[115] Champion began by explaining how he intended to use dance as a means of determining the magnitude and characterization of the musical. According to Channing, "He *leveled with* the company, and said, 'Now look. I find my characters and my level of the show through dance. If I were Josh Logan, we'd all be on the script and the dialogue, and in two weeks, we'd drop our scripts, we'd know it, and we'd start. Then we would go on to the music. But I'm not Josh Logan; I am who I am.' I felt the same way he did. If you can find how a character sings and dances, rather than walks and talks, you've got the *soul* of the character. You've got her out of the material world and into the spiritual. That's what Gower knew. Therefore, he said, 'I will have to spend the first two weeks on the 'Hello, Dolly!' number.' He never touched the dialogue."[116]

Though it was planned as a production number from the start, Champion had no idea just how expansive "Hello, Dolly!" would become in the course of its gestation. The ramp encircling the orchestra pit—which permitted the action to be pulled out of the proscenium arch and into the house—so radically altered the conventional stage space as to necessitate creating setting and movement that would be "larger than life."[117] After all, this was Dolly's adventure, experienced not just vicariously through the lives of others as in *The Matchmaker,* but personally in an exuberant reunion with old friends—indeed with life itself—that would spill out over the runway and into the house.

From a central staircase flanked by waiters poised at attention at the base, Channing was to descend to stage level, and then stop at downstage center for a solo performance of the song directed to the waiters. As yet, no music had been composed to cover her entrance, so Gower asked rehearsal pianist Howard to improvise an interim piece. His racy burlesque-like improvisation was so effective that it was immediately incorporated into the score.[118] At the close of her solo, Channing crossed from stage right to left to greet the waiters, who reprised the song to her as they lined up in right profile paralleling the stage.

Since the verse beginning with "I went away from the lights of Fourteenth Street," was more pensive in tone, she was directed to the center of the runway to sing it while the waiters, standing in various reflective poses on stage behind her, hummed the choral accompaniment. The song was then reprised once more, this time with Channing alternating the singing with the chorus, who joined her on the ramp. With the approach of the dance section, Channing and company left the ramp for the downstage area, where they performed a succession of walks, waddles, kicks, and struts that built in intensity one after the other.

Gower had reached the climax of the number. He directed Channing to cross to the stage right side of the ramp, raise the train of her gown, and pass gracefully around, but was at a loss regarding the waiters' movement. For days, he would run the number to this point in search of a solution. Finally, it occurred to him that by having the waiters leap over the orchestra from stage to ramp, he could undercut the side-to-side nature of the movement by taking it directly toward the audience. With this move, the waiters would then be in a position to rejoin Channing for a high-kicking finale.[119]

Channing recalls the number's evolution and its impact on the director's approach to the rest of the show. "Imagine the savvy of the man, that he could go to the back of the theatre—and he did it again and again—and say, 'No, only two steps, not four. That's too many. You're not big enough. You all have to be *bigger* and you have to make it a *higher* movement and a *longer* one.' He did it! Finally, he said, 'Now I've got the level of the show,' and then went on to the rest."[120]

The fusion of "The Waiters' Gallop" and "Hello, Dolly!" had a considerable impact on the cast, bonding them and the director at a crucial stage of the rehearsal process. Hartman remembers what the performers experienced the first time the two numbers were joined in rehearsal.

"Gower said, 'Let's run it!' and sat down. Then we ran the two numbers, and the theatre was electric! I mean it was emotional and everybody knew it. Everybody knew what had happened, that we had a hit. It was exciting! And though everybody was in their crummy rehearsal clothes and sweating, it might as well have been full orchestra, lights and everything else. When we finished, Gower walked down and in his quiet way just looked up at everybody with this kind of pleasant, almost wry smile and said, 'I think maybe we have something.' It was the understatement of all time!"[121]

The process of staging "Waiters" and "Dolly!" had secured the cornerstone of the production, but it also had consumed more than two-fifths of the rehearsal period.[122] As a result, Gower now had only three weeks to mount the remainder of the show and raise it to the level of the second act centerpiece in time for the Detroit debut. He remained remarkably calm in the face of this pressure, with work habits that were both methodical and productive. Applying the topper principle once more, he stabilized the first act by anchoring it to two production numbers—"Put on Your Sunday Clothes" and the aforementioned "Dancing."[123]

Because "Sunday Clothes" celebrates the adventure that affirms and renews life, it is a lyrical expression of the musical's theme. Cornelius voices this sentiment when he exhorts Barnaby to join him in casting off Vandergelder's tyrannous rule by forsaking the dull routine of the Hay and Feed Store for a day well spent in the big city.

References to the pleasures of the day—dime cigars, horse-drawn open cars, shows at Delmonico's restaurant—combine with the lure of romance itself to make this number a compelling invitation to shed inhibition and partake of adventure. Persuaded by this appeal, Barnaby willingly aids Cornelius in orchestrating an explosion of several foul-smelling tomato cans: their pretext for closing the shop. The action then moves to a room above the store where Dolly imparts a similar message to the timid Ambrose and Ermengarde.

For Champion, the finery of parasols, feathers, and patent leather shoes described in Herman's lyrics evoked the image of a "fashion parade on wheels."[124] To achieve this effect, he had Dolly, Ermengarde, and Ambrose descend to stage level at the conclusion of their verse to join Cornelius and Barnaby. He then shifted the scene from the Feed Store to the Yonkers Railroad Station, where a chorus of fashionably dressed couples on a Sunday stroll reprised the song together with the five characters. For the climax, the ensemble, attired in costumes that generated a "fantastic rainbow of color" and sported "every pink, green and yellow ostrich feather known to man,"[125] boarded a steam train bound for New York. More than a visual expression of the theme, Champion's fashion parade on wheels was a scenic transition, which he incorporated right into the plot to advance the action from Yonkers to New York City.[126]

From the start, he viewed color coordination as a salient feature of "Sunday Clothes," equal to the stylized movement of its choreography. In rehearsal, he pinned every member of the chorus with a piece of fabric bearing a particular gradation of the vivid colors selected.[127] Blending warm colors with cool, he arranged each performer according to hue to generate a striking spectrum of color as the cast promenaded along the oval runway out front and a railroad car pulled by an engine spitting smoke and ashes arrived to whisk them off to New York.[128]

Like "Waiters" and "Dolly!" in Act II, "Sunday Clothes" and its topper, "Dancing," gave the director a firm foundation upon which to build the remainder of the first act. Hereafter, rehearsals would focus more on the leading players and their songs, dialogue scenes, and characterization. Concerning this work, Champion made a distinction worth noting. "The choreographer," he stated, "requires that his dancers be expressive in dance terms while the director, in working with actors, tries to elicit the inner feelings of a character through both speech and gesture. The middle ground—not the dividing line—between choreography and direction is what I call staging. This is what links dancing and acting and I think that the choreographer, in the role of the director, can bring something special to the business of staging."[129]

Specifically, musical staging encompasses everything from subdued moments of solitary reflection to the thrill of an entire company belting a song full-tilt. It is where the choreographer becomes stage director, shaping intimate and spectacular moments within the framework of a song's music and lyrics. Unlike choreography, which relies solely on music and story, musical staging gives priority to the words being sung.[130]

One example of Champion's staging of an intimate musical number was the wistful "Ribbons Down My Back," which expressed the young widow Molloy's desire to cease mourning and quit her hat shop routine to embrace romantic adventure anew. Herman explains how his lyrics, based on a line in Wilder's play, inspired Gower to fashion staging that was perfect for the mood of the piece. "Thornton Wilder was so filled with lyric ideas for me. One day while reading the original play I came across [Mrs. Molloy's line], 'This summer we'll be wearing ribbons down our backs'—to catch a beau, I supposed. This was a more charming way of going with her—flirtatious and nicer than my initial effort."[131]

Prior to rehearsals, Herman and Stewart had flown to Los Angeles to meet with Gower. When they arrived at his home, the songwriter said, " 'I have a surprise for you,' and I played him the song. He went, 'That's it! It's so visual! I see a big mirror—one of those wonderful Victorian mirrors on a frame.' So we were in business."[132]

In rehearsal, Gower decided against using a real mirror. Instead, he seated Eileen Brennan on a revolving stool before the audience and had her peer into an imaginary mirror to model a simple, beribboned straw boater.[133] "The mirror was his whole 'kickoff' for the number," Brennan explains. "Then he directed me to get the hat to fall a certain way, to spin it and put it on backwards at the end. All of that was Gower. He had a great feel for grace. He really choreographed that number and was very specific. It was sensational!"[134] This balanced approach reinforced the fetching and coquettish nature of the lyrics without detracting from Brennan's presentation of the song.

Gower certainly had an aptitude for the exaggeration and physical humor of farce, as dances like "The Sale" and "Shriners' Ballet" proved. But with *Dolly!* this ability would be challenged anew as he assembled an entire evening's worth of antics through dialogue scenes, too. These scenes, like his comic ballets, profited from a blend of choreography with shtick.

When Gower spoke about shtick (e.g., "we need some shtick in that scene to liven things up"), it was not simply about concocting a few deft maneuvers and acrobatics to convey the proper mood he was seeking in a certain scene.[135] He was actually referring to a joint effort between the performer and himself involving far more.

Because he had chosen his leading players for their comic expertise, Champion could entrust them with the task of creating the business or shtick for dialogue scenes. He would then take what they had given him and improve upon it in rehearsal. A case in point was the eating sequence between Dolly and Vandergelder in the fourth scene of the second act. According to Carol Channing, "Gower told us, 'You and Davy take this eating scene. I don't do this. You'll have to. I've gotten you for your sense of character and the comedy of it.' So Davy and I would order from room service and would sit by the hour working out that scene. We then brought it to Gower who said, 'Thank you. That's just what I asked of you.' He would prune it, fix it, and stage it. But the point is he *got* the people he knew would give him what he couldn't do himself."[136]

The pair devised a routine in which Channing consumed a full-course chicken dinner, and scores of dumplings, while engaging in a rapid conversation with Burns, who, in turn, grew increasingly amazed by her voracious appetite as she piled spoonfuls of unwanted beets upon his plate. The dumplings were actually cotton candy made with a blend of brown and white sugar to give the proper color. When Channing developed hypoglycemia as a result of the daily consumption of the candy, the formula changed to tissue spread over a lightbulb and sprinkled with tea, which she disposed of at the end of the scene while wiping her mouth with a napkin.

A similar example was the scene in which Mary Jo Catlett as Ernestina, a hefty, hootchy-kootchy girl dressed "all in buttercup yellow with baby pink shoes,"[137] met her unsuspecting date for the evening—the merchant of Yonkers. Catlett comments: "When I first entered in Act II singing 'Sweet Rosie O'Grady' to Davy [Burns], he did this wonderful take. When he finally realized that I was actually his date, he pushed out his cheek from the left side of his mouth, and then pulled it in in rapid succession. It got the most wonderful reaction from the audience. It must have been an old vaudeville bit he'd learned. It sounds kind of strange, but Gower loved little things like that."[138]

Though he welcomed bits of business and shtick from performers, Champion edited and refined these contributions until they had the precision of one of his dances. In fact, he orchestrated the actor's moves and business in dialogue scenes almost like a dancer's steps in a ballet. Catlett adds that this specificity "stunned actors at first. But later, it proved most effective."[139] By combining carefully planned segments of shtick, he could reduce dialogue and make movement the chief means of advancing the story.

Characterization also profited from the director's staging practices. For example, he stipulated the posture and attitude actors were to express as part of the physical attributes of their characters. In Channing's case, this meant replacing with her trademark flapper's stance—slouched and casual—for the erect carriage of a woman of the 1890s. "Carol and I worked closely and for a long time," Gower explained. "We worked on her performing style in terms of both character and period—for example, Dolly had to have a 'pulled up' look which is totally foreign to Carol, but it was necessary and she got it. Then, I set the numbers for Carol. After each one was set, I'd turn her over to Marge, who would rehearse her and work on the details. I called Marge the 'woodshed coach.'"[140]

Concerning the details of Channing's physical transformation, Marge provides this insight: "We started with any kind of exercise I could devise to strengthen her abdominal muscles, to pull her chest high and give her just a slight swayback that a woman of that time would have adopted—bustle or no bustle. We worked on her arms and hands and head, because a woman of that period never stood in a relaxed posture. She couldn't slouch in one of those big hats they wore. Carol used to stand with her pelvis pushed forward."[141] The "woodshed coach" also gave the star "a good deal of ballet work to strengthen her legs so she could carry the new posture."[142]

In the closing days of rehearsal, Champion continued to introduce changes. As with *Carnival,* a conventional overture was replaced with a prologue in which Dolly gave a stereopticon slide tour of Old New York complete with advertisements promoting her various yet peculiar specialties ("Varicose Veins Reduced," "Fresh Jersey Eggs," and "Handwriting Analyzed").

The director also had Herman make several changes in the score. "This Time," Horace's pledge to trim the costs of his second wedding, and "Ernestina," the Dolly–Horace comic duet extolling the virtues of the ideal female, were dropped in favor of "It Takes a Woman," the merchant's chauvinistic paean to the opposite sex sung while being shaved by Dolly posing as his barber. Champion made this change because "David Burns was bringing a wonderful quality—the funniness of a W. C. Fields acting like a curmudgeon—to his role. So we dropped certain songs originally planned for his character in order to channel David's special talents into the show, to utilize his great gifts and to exploit his way of building wonderful comedy out of expressions of anger and exasperation."[143] After the Detroit opening, Champion would ask Herman to rework this song once more into what would become the definitive version. The songwriter would also compose "Come and Be My Butterfly" to replace the less humorous "The Man in the Moon is a Lady" (later to be used in Herman's *Mame*) for the floor show of the Harmonia Gardens in Act II, Scene iv.[144]

This same period found Gower in the midst of yet another production number, "Penny in My Pocket," the first act finale, which took place at an auction. As Vandergelder discoursed on the rewards of frugality, Dolly charged scores of unusual but impractical articles to his account that were then placed in a pyramidal formation about him. By the number's end, a stupefied Vandergelder turned to find himself owner of the mountain of knickknacks that engulfed him.

As in *Birdie,* the director dispensed with the conventional big finale, replacing it with an intimate man-gets-woman denouement reinforced by dance.[145] After Vandergelder reprised part of the title song—in effect both an admission of his need for Dolly and a proposal of marriage—a short dance break took place. This underscored not only the bond the couple would share, but also Horace's compliance with whatever Dolly would ask, even if it meant learning to dance.[146] They then concluded the song.

With the last rehearsal at the Mark Hellinger Theatre on Monday, November 11, the company of what was now known as *Hello, Dolly!* (to the delight of women's guilds throughout the country) prepared to travel to Detroit for the debut at the Fisher Theatre on Monday, November 18. "When we went out of town," says Herman, "we weren't ready. It was very rushed because it was a big show and we didn't have enough time. You *never* have enough time."[147] Though everyone, including the director, knew the show was rough, none were quite prepared for the response of the Detroit press.

" 'Hello, Dolly!' Insipid, But Cast Does Well," the headlines of the *Windsor Star* blared the morning after the debut.[148] " 'Dolly' Has Its Moments but They're Not All Good," echoed the *Detroit News.*[149] The show started slowly, ran thirty-nine minutes overtime, and required more excitement in the first act and tightening throughout. Yet despite the discouraging reception, critics recognized its potential as a long-run hit.[150] Gower Champion "will know what to throw out and what to bring in to make *Dolly!* the hit it should be,"[151] predicted Shirley Eder.

First thing next morning, the director met with Herman and Stewart to discuss the feasibility of a thorough revamping. "We had four numbers with pizzazz ["Sunday Clothes," "Dancing," "Waiters' Gallop," and "Hello, Dolly!"], he readily admitted, "and the rest of the show died around them."[152]

"We were so depressed," recalls Herman, "we didn't know what hit us or what the answers were. So, the three of us promised each other in that meeting, that fateful day, that we would just stay up night and day to make the show work. I think Mike said it best. He said, 'I've never worked on a show that had more promising elements than this one. We've got to make this work.' Then we sat down and started to pull apart what was really wrong, very carefully and meticulously."[153]

The team agreed to eliminate superfluous characters and ineffective material and to improve the show with new scenes, songs, and staging that focused on the characters. For the next eight weeks, the three would do nothing but rewrite, recompose, and restage.

That same afternoon, Gower gathered the company on the stage of the Fisher Theatre, complimented them on their performance, and then took responsibility for the weak premiere.[154] After stressing the critics' comments on the show's potential, he outlined plans to overhaul the production. Hartman remembers what the director told the company. " 'We've got a lot of fixing to do,' he said. 'We're going to do it in eight parts and we're going to take them by the numbers between now and the opening in New York. We're going to do one number per week.' As I recall, it was an absolute plan and a plot over an eight-week period [four weeks in Detroit and four in Washington] to fix hunks of the show beginning at the beginning. But he was methodical in that way, fixing one hunk at a time—and he knew what he wanted to do."[155]

He certainly did. New material for the eight troubled sections would be rehearsed during the day, and then gradually phased into the evening performances over the course of the eight-week tryout. If all went according to plan, the final change would be added just in time for the Broadway opening. The cast was united behind him and ready to go to work. Just then an irate Merrick arrived from New York bent on closing the show.

Dolly!'s weak reception combined with the failure of his recent production of Brecht's *The Rise and Fall of Arturo Ui* to put the producer in a terribly foul mood.[156] He immediately launched an inquisition calculated to intimidate the staff. "It was truly the most difficult time of my life," Herman recalls, "because

David Merrick was just crazed. He expected this to be 'the *big* one,' and he read the reviews from the two newspapers in Detroit which were much more negative than positive. He thought, 'Oh, boy! This is going to go down the drain. This is going to be one of my failures.' So he became absolutely crazed and made life very difficult for everybody, including Gower."[157]

The first to suffer his wrath was Wittop. A fierce diatribe scornful of the "Sunday Clothes" costumes left the designer utterly dispirited until Herman convinced him that the applause following the chorus's entrance in the number was *for* the costumes.[158] A similar altercation nearly prompted Stewart to resign as librettist.[159] But it was Merrick's treatment of Herman that was particularly nefarious.

Without informing the songwriter or the director, the producer summoned Bob Merrill to Detroit to supply new songs.[160] When Merrill—then in the midst of rehearsals for *Funny Girl*—expressed misgivings, he was assured that both Herman and Champion *wanted* him to come. The moment he encountered Herman in the lobby of their Detroit hotel, he knew this was not so. In the midst of this tension, Merrill viewed the musical, finding it to be in far better shape than Merrick had indicated. Merrill's diplomatic but important recommendations included a stronger closing for the first act and opening for the second (both of which Gower was already at work on), together with some suggestions for new numbers. He then departed for New York. The tactfulness of Merrill's proposals, however, did little to mitigate the betrayal Herman felt from Merrick, the man who had initially told him, "Kid, the show is yours."[161]

Merrick now turned to Gower. In Philadelphia, after attempting to introduce major changes weeks before *Carnival*'s Broadway opening, the director capitulated to the producer's demand to remove the "improvements" and restore the musical to the critical and popular success it had been in Washington. In contrast, *Dolly!*'s state was tenuous, virtually guaranteeing Champion's submission once more. The producer began to attack Gower's work, declaring to Herman and Stewart, "You've got one number—'Hello, Dolly!'—and that's it."[162] To Marge, he barked, "If this show becomes a hit, it'll be for all the wrong reasons."[163]

His harassment of Gower peaked in an exchange over the "Sunday Clothes" number. He loathed everything about it, especially the train, which he termed "vulgar."[164]

"It's not a good number," he added. "It just holds up the show. Let's cut it out."

"No!" retorted Gower. "In fact, I have such faith in that number that if you want me to buy you out right now, I will!"

Merrick had apparently forgotten that his director and choreographer was also his co-producer and had a controlling interest in the production. Nevertheless, he stood his ground, declaring, "I don't know. I really feel like I ought to close the show entirely."

Once more, Champion offered to buy him out. Finally, Merrick responded, "No, no. I'll stay with it."[165]

Though the producer rescinded his demand, his meddling continued. A few days later, the exasperated director reached his limit, declaring to Marge, "Tell Mr. Mustache that when he leaves town, I'll come back." Only she knew that Gower had gone to Ypsilanti, Michigan, where he relaxed, taking in the latest films, while awaiting Merrick's next move. Only two days later, when the producer withdrew to check on his production of *Foxy* with Bert Lahr in Cleveland, did Gower then return to work in earnest. But Merrick was clearly not pleased. When *Foxy* music director Don Pippin asked him about *Dolly!*'s status, he remarked, "I wish my name wasn't on it!"[166]

In the midst of Merrick's tirade, the assassination of President John F. Kennedy occurred four days into the run. The show was canceled the evening of November 22, but the company, buoyed by the antics of Burns and Reilly, resumed performances the following day.[167] At that moment, however, the shock of Kennedy's death on top of the poor notices dimmed hopes of a warm reception in Washington, where the show was due to open at the National Theatre on December 18. Despite low morale, the performers embraced Gower's plan, and for the next eight weeks dutifully rehearsed a new version of the show (Book Two of the Director's Scripts) by day, while performing the original version (Book One—*Dolly, A Damned Exasperating Woman*) at night.

As part of the plan, Stewart pared dialogue, cut and refined characters, and wrote whole new scenes. "Every day, he came in with new pages," says Herman, "all trimmer, leaner, to the point, and all about Dolly Levi."[168] Naturally, the constant revision of the script affected the performers, who needed to master the new material quickly. In Detroit, the dialogue in the Hay and Feed Store Scene changed so frequently that six-foot-five assistant stage manager Hartman was concealed inside a wooden barrel positioned at upstage left to prompt the players. "They changed the lines every night," recalls Channing, "and we would go back [to ones from] four nights before! So we put Davy Hartman in the barrel with a flashlight and he sat there all through the Hay and Feed Scene. We had pregnant pauses where we would wait and he would give us the next line. But at least we could find out whether the new lines moved the show more toward what we were after."[169]

During the remainder of the Detroit run, Gower launched the initial wave of changes that would begin to strengthen the production. The first centered on a more effective opening. The original—Dolly's stereopticon lecture with its 132 slide cues—was a wild mix of buildings, girlie shots, and drinking scenes designed to show what a wicked city New York was at the turn of the century.[170] This travelogue was explained by way of Dolly's raucous commentary, delivered through a megaphone to an admiring foursome of ladies gathered in her parlor.[171] As the presentation progressed, Dolly's lecture gave way to an overture. The quartet's rendition of "Call on Dolly" followed, which was sung as the matchmaker boarded a horsecar bound for Grand Central Station. En route to the station, she explained the nature of her profession with "I Put My Hand In."

The lengthy and complicated structure of the scene impeded the speedy introduction of the heroine and her goal—"to marry Horace Vandergelder for his money and send it out circulating among the people."[172] Diverse solutions—including one in which Dolly strolled the runway distributing her ubiquitous business cards to audience members—failed until the director created a New York street scene in which various townspeople in stylized poses, moving as if on a treadmill, urged passers-by to "Call on Dolly" for her unparalleled matchmaking services.[173] In the midst of the number, a horse car pulled by a dancing human horse (Jan LaPrade and Bonnie Mathis) entered from stage right bearing several ladies with newspapers in front of their faces.[174] As the townspeople sang the words, "call on," a third time, the woman seated at the end of the car dropped her newspaper and proudly announced herself as Dolly Levi to one and all. Dolly then proceeded with "I Put My Hand In." Afterward, she crossed to the center stage footlights and, in an address to deceased husband Ephraim Levi, stated her intent to marry Horace Vandergelder. In light of the series of similar monologues she delivered throughout the musical, it was a suitable beginning.[175]

It was also in Detroit that the director inserted the eating scene with Dolly and Vandergelder, in place of their duet, "No, A Million Times, No," in which Dolly pretended to object to Vandergelder's marriage proposal while he protested that he'd never made one.[176] The eating sequence, on the other hand, was an ideal opportunity for Channing and Burns to display their comic expertise.

Next, the director tackled "The Goodbye Song," Dolly's farewell to Horace, which came near the closing of the second act. A parody of Tosti's "Addio," it began with a series of six "goodbyes" sung by Channing as she rode down from the flies on a piece of scenery—a prelude to a comic aria ranging from *basso profundo* to crackling coloratura.[177] But not even Channing's deft antics could save it.[178] As Victor recalled, "It was all so terribly funny to us, but the audience sat on their hands. None of it worked."[179] Gower turned to Herman, who supplied "So Long, Dearie," a splendid eleven-o'clock spot reminiscent of the old razzmatazz songs Al Jolson once sang.[180]

Champion now went after the opening of the second act, exchanging the counterpoint number between Vandergelder and a trio of street vendors for one that featured Cornelius, Mrs. Molloy, Barnaby, and Minnie as they sauntered to the Harmonia Gardens in the company of the dancing human horse. The former opening, "You're a Damned Exasperating Woman"/"Please, Sir, Mrs. Levi Sent Me," was an extension of the contrast between Vandergelder's parsimony and Dolly's magnanimity established earlier in the first act finale, "Penny in My Pocket." But here, a shoeshine boy, coachman, and flower lady—all engaged by Dolly— separately approached Vandergelder for payment of their services ("Please, Sir, Mrs. Levi Sent Me"). The merchant's frustration with the matchmaker mounted ("You're a Damned Exasperating Woman") until it exploded in a contrapuntal cli- max with the solicitors' song.[181] Though musically interesting, the number failed to advance the plot.[182]

The second act required an opening that would further develop the romances between the clerks and the milliners. Herman, in league with Merrill, composed a send-up on pretentious manners called "Elegance" to which Gower fashioned a charmingly mannered routine for the quartet with steps that were ideal for this light satire.[183]

"It was stunning," Brennan recalls. "I remember that the step he gave us was again an 'off-center' kind of step, a real odd thing. We all walked with our hands out as the horse danced behind us.[184]

Like the other numbers added to the score on the road, "Elegance" was per- formed only hours after the actors had first seen the music. "What most people don't know about out-of-town musicals," explains Reilly, "is that directors and composers have to try the number right away to see if it works. They can't hang around and rehearse it for three or four days only to find out that it doesn't work. Performers have to 'wing it,' and if it works a little bit, then the authors know to continue developing the number further."[185]

During the musical's Detroit and Washington engagements, new music would appear under the hotel room doors of cast members at 11:30 A.M. with the expec- tation that they would perform it at the 2:30 P.M. matinee the same day.[186] Upon re- ceiving the material, they would immediately meet Howard or musical director Shepard Coleman at a piano in the basement of the theatre to learn the number. This was common practice in the state of emergency known as the "out-of-town tryout." Reilly adds that the first performance of "Elegance" was "very easy. It went in, was there two minutes, and worked. Right away everyone knew that was the way to go. When something is organically correct, you don't have to hover over it in re- hearsal. Gower gave us one basic step and the number stood up by itself on its own feet. He rehearsed it with us during the intermission, and then we went out and performed it."[187]

Toward the end of the Detroit run, the first series of revisions was starting to draw a more favorable response from audiences. Straightaway, Gower ushered in the remaining changes—a more energetic version of "It Takes a Woman," the addition of "Motherhood March" to enliven the Hat Shop sequence, a streamlining of "Come and Be My Butterfly" in the Harmonia Gardens section, and a reconfiguration of the first act finale that would center on replacing Vandergelder's "Penny in My Pocket" with Dolly's "Before the Parade Passes By."

As Champion began to implement this phase of his agenda, assistant director Victor grew more and more uneasy with the way he was pushing the cast, still performing by night and rehearsing every available moment of the day.[188] One afternoon, the sight of their fatigued faces and perspiration-soaked clothing became unbearable and she exclaimed, "It's too much, Gower! You're driving this company into the grave!" Glaring down at her from where he stood in the balcony, the director icily replied, "That's the way it's going to be. We keep working." Victor bore the reproof; no one gave more of himself to a show than Champion.[189]

Under this stress, the director's obsession with curbing distractions in rehearsal reached proportions nearly as comical as the farce he was directing. Huge black screens were placed in front of the wings to keep performers' offstage movements out of his view; the bell of the stage telephone was disconnected and replaced with a flashing light, also kept safely from his sight.[190] Once, when his concentration was disturbed by the subdued clacking of metal needles emanating from the many women who knitted to fill moments when they were not needed onstage, he insisted they use plastic ones to mute the noise.[191] Nothing would thwart his efforts to reform the show.

"You know that number in the beginning that Davy [Burns] sings?" he later asked. "The one called, 'It Takes a Woman'? Well, it was a solo and I wanted a piece where the male dancers could join in as singers. We almost drove Davy out of his mind. It was the toughest thing he had to do, because, although we kept the same words, Jerry wrote an entirely different tune and Davy had all he could do to keep from falling back into the old one."[192]

Though an accomplished comic actor in the tradition of Frank Fay, Bobby Clark, and Bert Lahr, Burns did not have much of a singing voice and Champion wanted it reinforced.[193] Herman's new melody, with the off-the-wall quality the director had requested, now had a vocal and visual counterpart—an instant glee club of men that suddenly sprang from the Hay and Feed Store's beams and posts to accompany Burns each time the refrain was sung until he swept them away with a broom.[194] The number, originally a solo for Vandergelder ("This Time," dropped during rehearsal) and later a duet with Dolly posing as his barber, was now a brawny male anthem in praise of the ideal woman who endlessly toiled to bring her husband "the sweet things in life" like "setting the table, weaning the Guernsey and cleaning the stable."[195]

In the Hat Shop scene (Act I, Scene vii), Cornelius and Barnaby desperately prevail upon a bewildered Mrs. Molloy to conceal them from their employer as they seek refuge under tables and in closets. Despite misgivings, she aids the ruse by mollifying the suspicious merchant who has come with a box of chocolate-covered peanuts ("Unshelled. That's the expensive kind"[196]) to propose marriage to her.

Tedious at the time of the Detroit debut, the scene found new life in the course of the Washington engagement when the director introduced the Herman-Merrill collaboration, "Motherhood March," in which Dolly, Irene, and Minnie attempt to forestall Vandergelder's discovery of the clerks through an appeal to his patriotism that makes malapropisms of every conceivable political rallying cry. So completely mesmerized is Vandergelder by the women's subterfuge that he fails to detect the two clerks as they scurry from table to closet and back again right under his nose. With each move as thoroughly choreographed and strategically timed as a dance, Gower soon had an in-and-out-of-closet scene in the best farce tradition.[197]

Through the tryout period and well into the first year of the Broadway run, the modification of *tableaux vivants,* the floor show segment of the Harmonia Gardens sequence, would trouble the director. This portion of the musical was inspired by a popular turn-of-the-century entertainment, which consisted of a series of scenes, pictures, or paintings illustrated by a group of appropriately costumed performers posing silently without movement. According to Book Two of the Director's Scripts, *Dolly!* initially had three of these living pictures, each representing "a bosky dell, with rocks, trees, [and] fronds,"[198] replete with a female chorus of butterflies, whose gleeful invitation to "Come and Be My Butterfly" ended the scene.

Jess, on board once more as Gower's dramaturge, submits that the butterfly motif was the result of a long-standing private joke between the Champions and himself. "Gower, Marge, and I had always giggled a little bit about the legendary Loie Fuller, an American girl who made an *astonishing* hit in turn-of-the-century Paris as she whirled and twirled in front of colored lights wearing great wings made of Chinese silk. Gower said that he really wanted to get a Loie Fuller number into the show."[199]

A self-proclaimed "artist of the dance" and a forerunner of Isadora Duncan and Ruth St. Denis, Loie Fuller was a native of Fullersburg, Illinois, whose combination of natural movement with colorful visual images created a sensation in London and Paris.[200] In 1892, when appearing in New York as the *première danseuse* in Charles

Hoyt's musical farce *A Trip to Chinatown* (also a precursor of *Hello, Dolly!*), her "butterfly dance," in which she fluttered about the stage using her skirts as butterfly's wings, so captivated audiences that it launched a fad for what became known as "skirt dancing."[201]

The idea of a comic ballet with Vandergelder pursuing an elusive Cornelius and Barnaby through a sea of skirt-dancing butterfly girls proved irresistible. A scenario was devised in which "a large gold picture frame containing closed velvet drapes" was lowered as Ambrose Kemper (Igors Gavon) entered with a female quartet of "muses" to sing of a restful glade far from the city where the fairies dwell. As he described how this setting grew more beautiful through the day, the drapes parted to reveal a morning, an afternoon, and finally an evening tableau of frolicking sprites, nymphs, and butterflies. Caught onstage as the last tableau was revealed, Cornelius and Barnaby posed as dancers, fronds in hand, to dodge Vandergelder. Just as the old man spotted them, the music broke into double time and a chase ensued as the entire host of butterflies spilled out of the picture frame and onto the restaurant floor for the wing-flapping refrain.[202]

While rampaging through this ocean of wings, each of the three characters would surface at key moments for brief remarks. Vandergelder's lines to the butterflies were among the best ("Keep away from my suit, it's rented!" "Why don't you buzz around a flame?" "Didn't I know you when you was a caterpillar?" and "Watch those feelers, Miss!"). The merchant was about to apprehend the clerks when Mrs. Molloy stepped forward in full butterfly regalia and, spreading her wings to protect them, gave forth with a powerful coloratura note that momentarily stunned him. Roused by the wails of his niece Ermengarde, Vandergelder turned to discover her emerging from a silver cocoon as a newborn butterfly haplessly attired in wrinkled flesh-colored tights and limp wings. Throughout this fiasco, Dolly sat before a table placed at downstage right, where she intently downed course upon course of food totally oblivious to the chaos until the restaurant was a shambles and Vandergelder, clerks, and ladies—butterfly wings and all—landed in the city courthouse.

Through the Detroit and Washington premieres, Gower drastically altered the piece, but it evaded his efforts to make it worthwhile. To have it succeed would have meant topping the title number that preceded it—a virtual impossibility. Moreover, because it lacked the invention and energy of the remaining nine-tenths of the show, it was a noticeable flaw—a good idea rendered ineffective through some perversity of the theatre, and the only part of the eightfold plan Gower would not be able to fix before the show landed in New York.[203]

One evening, shortly before the show's Washington departure, he stood in the back of the house with Victor observing the first act finale, "Penny in My Pocket,"

Vandergelder's comical reflection on how his staunch devotion to frugality made him a half-millionaire.[204] The number, which took place at a bankruptcy auction in Joshua Van Groot's Emporium on Broadway, invariably drew thunderous applause as chorus members, perched on crates of varying height, passed a steady array of articles—red feathered hats, bolts of cloth, baskets, grandfather clocks, even rowboats—to each other from downstage to upstage, creating a perfect pyramid around the merchant for the climax. On this occasion, however, "Penny" brought only a sullen expression to Gower's face.

When Victor asked what was wrong, he answered, "It has to go. It doesn't move me ahead to the second act at all. We can't close the first act without something that moves us into Act II, that makes us want to come back and see what happens in Act II."

Ironically, the assignment of the Act I finale to Burns had brought the musical to the very brink of the same precipice into which Wilder's *The Merchant of Yonkers* had fallen: Dolly was simply more intriguing than Vandergelder, and audiences were curious as to the nature of her exploits in the act to come. Though indeed impressive, "Penny in My Pocket" was centered on the wrong character. To dismantle it and then replace it with something equally splendid that emphasized Dolly was the daunting task to which the director immediately applied himself after Burns graciously acquiesced.

Undoubtedly, the deletion would strike some as capricious considering the two weeks of rehearsal taken to stage "Penny in My Pocket," its enormous $100,000 cost, and its multitude of props, three pages long.[205] But Gower was confident that a number celebrating Dolly's resolve "to rejoin the human race"[206] would give the show precisely the boost it needed.[207]

Herman, who had likewise questioned the suitability of "Penny," agreed to compose a new song incorporating Gower's suggestion of a parade—the 14th Street Parade to which Vandergelder referred earlier in the act.[208] Not long afterward, Merrick arrived with Merrill and the team of Strouse and Adams—all of whom he had engaged in an effort to procure an explosive finale for the first act.[209] Apparently, Herman could not work fast enough for Merrick, who seemed bent on partitioning the score among the songwriter's peers. What the producer neglected to consider, however, was the director's response to the Strouse and Adams parade piece. After a single hearing, Gower knew the song would not fit the mood of the scene. He rejected it, telling Herman, "It's up to you now."[210]

Late that evening, following the performance, the songwriter took to his hotel room, sat down at the piano, and, with a fistful of candy bars to stimulate his inspiration, began to compose a march that would become the heroine's anthem to abjure mourning and embrace life anew: [211]

Before the parade passes by
I'm going to go and taste Saturday's high life
Before the parade passes by
I'm gonna get some life back into my life
I'm ready to move out in front, I've had enough
      of just passing by life
With the rest of them, with the best of them, I
      can hold my head up high!
For I've got a goal again
I've got a drive again
I'm gonna feel my heart coming alive again
Before the parade passes by![212]

It was well after midnight when Herman completed the song and, in his eagerness to share his new creation, telephoned a sleeping Channing with a request to come and hear it.[213] Minutes later, the performer, clad in bathrobe and slippers, joined him and quickly mastered it. The two then woke Gower, who also donned his robe and slippers for the debut. "Since the change involved ordering new scenery, costumes, and a whole new staging," explains Herman, "it was important that Gower be thoroughly convinced. Nothing could have done that more clearly than Carol's commitment—singing there in the middle of the night, on top of her strenuous performance earlier that evening. I can't think of too many stars that would be so supportive of their composer-lyricist at three o'clock in the morning."[214]

By the end of the song, Gower was so moved that he led Channing and Herman in a "ring-around-the-rosy" about the room, shouting, "That's it! That's it!"[215] "The number was a turning point for us," adds Herman. "Now we had a throughline, a sustained theme, a firm point of focus throughout. We had a woman who was locked away from the world because of the loss of her husband, spending her life fixing everybody else up, until the moment came when she clenched her own fist and said, 'Hey, it's time for me!' After that the show worked like a dream."[216]

"Before the Parade Passes By" also illustrates Champion's talent for creating seamless transitions from dialogue into song and for building production numbers. As Dolly, spotlighted at the center of the runway, concluded her request of her late husband to let her rejoin the human race, a "sting"[217] from the string section of the orchestra cued her to sing of getting in step with life while there was still time.[218] Suddenly her reverie was interrupted as the orchestra took up the theme of the preceding number, "Dancing," and the stage lights rose on various passersby still reeling from their first encounter with dance. Among them were Mrs. Molloy and Cornelius, who invited her to join them for the 14th Street Parade. Just as she promised to do so, the "Dancing" theme abruptly ended, the lovers disappeared in the darkness, and Dolly was alone once more. Now she started the song again, beginning slowly, then building the momentum as various instruments gradually joined her until the number became a full-out march backed by the whole orchestra.

By the time she started the second verse, the lights had slowly risen on an empty stage relieved by one of Smith's lithographic backdrops depicting a turn-of-the-century 14th Street that receded into the horizon. One by one, representatives of various trades, professions, and associations appeared, each bearing a particular banner or placard.[219] Soon the entire stage was a throbbing panoply of Old New York life, encompassing firemen, waiters from the Harmonia Gardens, seamstresses, policemen, brewers, divas from the opera guild, showgirls from Tony Pastor's Theatre, and gymnasts from the local men's athletic association.[220] Even the dancing horse made an appearance.

Now Dolly crossed from the runway to the stage, where she took a pennant from a parader, raised it aloft, and then weaved in and out of the ranks of the chorus as they reprised the second verse. An instrumental section followed in which she led some of the paraders across the runway from right to left. She then returned to center stage, and her companions to their former places, just as Vandergelder and a huge electrified float carrying three girls and a mannequin (a last-minute substitution for the merchant's date) joined the ensemble for an all-stops-out finale:

I'm gonna raise the roof
I'm gonna carry on
Give me an old trombone, give me an old baton
Before the parade passes by![221]

Launched in the final week of the Washington tryout, just days before the New York opening, the new number's scenery, costumes, and orchestrations—which required all the overtime union regulations would permit—totaled $40,000.[222] "It wasn't until the last performance in Washington that I finally got to see all the costumes together," the director later recalled. "We made New York by the skin of our teeth."[223] Gower would not see the number fully outfitted—with Smith's enlargement of Maerz's celebrated 1882 lithograph of Union Square as the backdrop—until the preview performances in New York.[224]

When the curtain rose at Washington's National Theatre on December 18, *Hello, Dolly!* was still in the process of being transformed from a play with music into a musical.[225] Even so, the audience responded with an unprecedented enthusiasm, embracing it as a means of dissipating the grief still keenly felt in the aftermath of the President's assassination.[226] Though they could not have had a better reception, the company continued to rehearse by day and perform by night until, with the final addition of "Before the Parade Passes By," the transformation was complete. But the strain of restructuring almost two-thirds of the production was taking a toll on the director.[227]

One afternoon, during a run-through of the parade number, he halted the proceedings, sprang to the stage, and beckoned the ensemble from the wings, demanding to know why they were not devoting themselves completely to the number, why it was not working, and what the difficulties were. In his rage, he seized one of the parade placards and menacingly stalked about the stage with it, taking swipes at the backdrop. Only when his trusted assistant dance captain, Nicole Barth, offered him a stick of chewing gum did he realize the total absurdity of his behavior and begin to laugh. The tension subsided, and the rehearsal resumed.[228] This behavior was the result not only of the stress of setting the show aright, but also the fact that having previously led *Bye Bye Birdie* and *Carnival* to triumph, he was now something of a sitting duck.[229] In effect, his reputation as a Broadway director-choreographer was at stake, compelling him to rival, if not, surpass former efforts. To dispel the tension, the company's unstinting dedication and loyalty deserved recognition.

On Saturday evening, January 4, the Champions hosted a belated New Year's party for the cast and crew in the ballroom of Washington's Willard Hotel.[230] In the midst of the festivity, Gower announced a special surprise, then played a recording of "Hello, Dolly!" sung by popular jazz musician Louis Armstrong. Within weeks, it would prove a blockbuster hit not only in the United States, but in Europe as well,[231] and with altered lyrics, it later would become "Hello, Lyndon," the theme song for Lyndon B. Johnson's successful 1964 presidential campaign.[232] However, for the company of *Hello, Dolly!* gathered that night to celebrate what they hoped would be a happier year than the one past, Armstrong's lusty rendition of the song seemed a good omen promising success in New York.

On the morning of the musical's Broadway opening, January 16, 1964, the director gathered the cast for a brief rehearsal to share last-minute concerns and make one final plea to "sell the dances"[233] before the performance that evening. After dismissing them, he lingered for a few moments in the vast emptiness of the St. James Theatre, chatting with his assistant Ed Kresley. "For me," he mused, "this is the saddest moment of a show—when the house is as empty as it was before any of the work began."[234] He spoke of his regrets: how naive he had been about the work and how he wished he had responded better to certain situations. He also reflected on what the past six months had taught him. Afterward, the two parted in silence.

"Don't bother holding on to your hats, because you won't be needing them. You'd only be throwing them into the air anyway,"[235] advised Walter Kerr the next day in the *Herald Tribune*. *Hello, Dolly!* is "a musical comedy dream," he added,

". . . a drunken carnival, a happy nightmare, a wayward circus in which the mistress of ceremonies opens wide her big-as-millstones eyes, spreads her white-gloved arms in ecstatic abandon, trots out onto a circular runway that surrounds the orchestra and proceeds to dance rings around the conductor."[236]

With "qualities of freshness and imagination that are rare in the run of our machine-made musicals," declared Howard Taubman in the *New York Times,* "it transmutes the broadly stylized mood of a mettlesome farce into the gusto and colors of the musical stage. What was larger and droller than life has been puffed up and gaily tinted without being blown apart."[237]

"Top to bottom, the new musical . . . is a funny, melodious, and smashing show," the *Morning Telegraph*'s Whitney Bolton concurred, "with every department contributing confection like throwing ingredients into a prize-winning Lady Biltmore cake."[238] Richard Watts Jr. of the *New York Post* described it as "big, bouncing, handsome, rapidly-paced, and filled with the shrewdest ingredients of successful showmanship."[239]

The opening night was one to stir the heart of even the most cynical observer as applause erupted in the midst of dance numbers, waves of ovations surged through the aisles, and the title number, which stopped the show cold, was reprised again and again. An air of euphoria rare in the theatre had filled the St. James. With universal praise from the press, the powerhouse show was assured a long and lucrative future as a potent touring item, musical stock vehicle, and film.[240]

Chief among the causes for jubilation was Gower's staging. To a production that could easily have been prosaic, he brought choreography with tremendous excitement, style, and compelling theatrical effect.[241] Broadway had not seen such an endless stream of breathtakingly effortless, direct, old-time, knockout numbers since Harrigan and Hart brought down the curtain; critics had not seen a finer corps of dancers turned loose in more exciting dances since Robbins staged *West Side Story.*[242]

Harold Clurman dubbed Gower "the Tyrone Guthrie of musical comedy direction,"[243] and rightly so, for he had shaped the entire production with something far more than technical skill. While combining elements of old-fashioned glamour with a salute to the adventure within the hustle-bustle of urban life, he had directed with affection, humor, and an unerring sense of what amazes, rouses, and deeply touches an audience.[244] Clearly, much of the success of *Hello, Dolly!* was tied to Gower's unique talent for composition in the creation of a musical show.[245]

Certain periodic slips in taste did raise a critical eyebrow or two. Minnie Fay's coarse accent, Ermengarde's grating wail, and Vandergelder's muddled chase of the clerks in the *tableaux vivants* section were considered frenzied touches out of place in a musical of this caliber.[246] Still, these were trifles when compared with the production's numerous assets, especially the performers.

Thanks to Gower, Carol Channing, whose career had been consigned for years to an obsession with diamonds as a girl's best friend, was now outfitted with an entirely new role—one in which she showed an inner strength and power in performance uncommon on the musical stage.[247] With hair like orange cotton candy, a contralto like a mare's neigh, and a form of comedy as unique in scope and physicality as outrageous in behavior, Channing dominated the evening with a talent Lillian Russell would have envied.[248] As Kerr expressed it, "Miss Channing has gone back for another look at that advertisement labeled 'His master's voice,' and she has swallowed the records, the Victrola, and quite possibly the dog. She is glorious."[249]

In one of the top roles of his career, David Burns, as the petulant Horace Vandergelder, upheld his righteous obstinacy in the face of benevolence, roaring nasally like a W. C. Fields resurrected.[250] Together, he and Channing made a superb pair of moonstruck comedians, she amiably wide-eyed and teasing, he growling and grumbling: a Gilded Age version of Harlequin and Pantelone.[251]

Wringing his hands until they dribbled and vaulting into dance like a stammering Nijinski, Charles Nelson Reilly gave a colorful, energetic, and convincing performance as chief clerk Cornelius Hackl, squeezing as much comedy as feasible from the role.[252] Eileen Brennan embraced the part of Mrs. Molloy, the widow/milliner who prefers the clerk to the merchant, like the fitted bodice she wore so gracefully.[253] Her gorgeous voice, charming presence, and come-hither sway greatly aided her comic romance with Reilly.[254] But not all the critics were impressed with Champion's comic emphasis on the Brennan and Reilly roles. Some felt that in contrast to the exaggeration of some of the other performances, a more restrained or underplayed treatment of the lovers was preferable because it would have given greater value to their romance, made them seem more like characters than caricatures, and rendered the overall buffoonery more effective.[255]

Blonde, pint-sized Sondra Lee, whose flair for dancing and mischievous energy contributed much exuberance to the evening in the role of milliner's assistant Minnie Fay, was well-paired with Jerry Dodge's supernaturally agile and wildly comic Barnaby Tucker.[256] The caterwauling of Alice Playten as Vandergelder's niece, consternation of Igors Gavon as her beloved, *Deutschland Über Alles* command of David Hartman as headwaiter Rudolph, and antics of Mary Jo Catlett's Ernestina were among the highlights that also included an outstanding singing and dancing chorus.[257]

With its breezy waltzes, melodic quartets, and bouncy polkas, Herman's hurdy-gurdy score provided songs new yet reminiscent and ideally suited to Stewart's faithful and straightforward adaptation of Wilder's play.[258] Gower's coordination of these elements with Smith's vivid decor, Wittop's eye-filling costumes, and Rosenthal's impressive lighting created the ambiance of an Old New York bathed in wistful sentiment, yet remembered with crackling laughter.[259]

To the company gathered at Delmonico's for the opening-night party in the early morning hours of January 17, the unanimous proclamation of smash hit status from the critics had made the arduous two-month journey from Detroit worthwhile. "I love all the drama critics today," exclaimed Merrick, whose incessant feuds with the press were legendary. "I can just lean back and enjoy this success. I had no idea it would be like this, as I always run scared. This is by far and away the biggest hit I've ever had, and if the response continues, I think it will turn out to be the biggest hit of all time."[260] Channing, "just petrified with happiness," was equally delighted with the notices: "Isn't Walter Kerr heaven? I think I'm in love with him. I've memorized every beautiful word he wrote."[261]

As for the director, although "hysterical with joy," he nonetheless "fidgeted over a few things I want to fix—like that butterfly number, about which a couple of critics expressed deserved reservations."[262] For more than a year and a half *tableaux vivants* would continue to bedevil him until, when Ginger Rogers replaced Channing in August 1965, he replaced it with a brief polka contest.[263] Only then was his work complete. "Even when it was playing to lines all the way down the block to Sardi's," he later confessed, "I was still rehearsing—until Marge literally said 'Stop already' and dragged me onto a plane to Acapulco."[264]

On May 24, 1964, *Hello, Dolly!* became the first musical in Broadway history to receive a total of ten Tony Awards—a record no other musical would rival until surpassed by *The Producers* in 2001.[265] In addition to being designated Best Musical of the Year, it also won in the following categories:

Best Actress in a Musical—Carol Channing

Best Composer and Lyricist—Jerry Herman

Best Author—Michael Stewart

Best Conductor—Shepard Coleman

Best Scenic Designer—Oliver Smith

Best Costume Designer—Freddy Wittop

Best Producer of a Musical—David Merrick

Best Director of a Musical—Gower Champion

Best Choreographer—Gower Champion.[266]

The show was also named best musical of the season by the New York Drama Critics' Circle, and during the same period, the *Variety* Poll of Drama Critics chose Champion as best director, Channing as best female lead, Smith as best designer, and Herman as best lyricist.[267]

By the time it closed on December 27, 1970, it had become one of the longest-running musicals in Broadway history, totaling 2,844 performances, thanks to the host of stars—Ginger Rogers, Martha Raye, Betty Grable, Bibi Osterwald, Pearl Bailey (with an African-American cast), Phyllis Diller, and Ethel Merman—who succeeded Channing, freeing her to rival her New York success with an extensive and lucrative road tour.[268] During this time, Gower coached Rogers for Broadway and launched the first national production with Mary Martin, which later toured Tokyo, South Vietnam, Korea, and Okinawa, before a long-term engagement in London. Thereafter, he entrusted the task of schooling all future Dollys and their companies to assistant director Victor, so he could devote himself to new projects.

Champion's "salvage job," as Merrick called it, had cost $440,000 to produce. During the time it ruled Broadway and the road, it grossed more than $60,000,000 and earned profits in excess of $9,000,000.[269] Yet beyond its popular and artistic success, *Hello, Dolly!* heralded the finale of an era as the last titanic hit in a class of musicals launched over sixty years before by George M. Cohan that celebrated the innocence and boundless optimism of the American spirit.[270] The crowning achievement of that period had been the integrated musical, in which all the elements of production—performers, music, lyrics, book, choreography, orchestrations, scenery, costumes, and technical design—converged to realize a single creative vision. Rodgers and Hammerstein had created the first with *Oklahoma!* (1943), and now Gower was clearly one of its undisputed masters. But in the wake of the President's assassination, as the country plummeted deeper and deeper into the political and social turmoil of the Vietnam War, civil rights movement, Martin Luther King and Robert Kennedy assassinations, and numerous counterculture factions, the common cultural understanding of American society shattered, and with it the populist ritual that the musical had been for many since the end of the Second World War.[271] As a result, the musical changed as abruptly and drastically as the historical events that were changing America.[272]

Hello, Dolly!, whose Broadway run spanned this period, now had to share the street with more cynical and hard-edged shows, like Harold Prince's *Cabaret* (1966) and *Company* (1970), that reflected the disillusionment and alienation felt by many.

In a polarized society where the efficacy of the American Dream was questioned and found deficient, the integrated musical could no longer serve as a ritual for that dream.[273] Without a common reference point, the Broadway musical tried to reinvent itself in an effort to attract new audiences. Rock musicals like *Hair* (1968) and *Jesus Christ Superstar* (1971) appealed to the young, while *The Me Nobody Knows* and *Purlie* (1970) spoke to racial minorities. Throughout the 1970s, Gower, whose work had largely defined the musical in the previous decade, would try his hand at these new forms, as well as those more wry in tone, and fail. Only when he returned to his roots in 1980 with *42nd Street* would he have a success as great as *Dolly!*

At the show's final performance, as he drew cheers while making a brief dancing appearance, the celebrated director-choreographer had no idea that his brand of showmanship had already fallen prey to the musical's struggle for identity in the midst of a country at war with itself.[274]

ELEVEN

Metaphorical Marriage Presentational Style

I Do! I Do!

1965–1966

With the phenomenal success of *Dolly!*, Gower was swamped with directing offers, including one from producer Lester Osterman in March 1964 to replace an ailing Noël Coward during the Philadelphia tryout of *High Spirits*, the musical version of his play *Blithe Spirit*. Gower agreed, with one provision: he was to have a free hand and no interference from the former director, who was also the librettist and reluctant to cut his own dialogue.[1] "Imagine me saying that about Noël Coward!" he confided to Jess.[2] Though he had great respect for the legendary British showman, he could not let it compromise the need to trim the show's lengthy running time. His clear-cut strategy immediately sped pace and scenic transitions. "He had all the blocking planned out in his head," comments Tammy Grimes, who played the flying ghost Elvira. "If you said, 'What if I came on like this . . . ,' he'd say, 'No, I've figured this all out' and he'd walk away. Then you'd say, 'Gower, Gower, never mind. I'll walk from here, I'll walk from anywhere you tell me.' Some directors will say, 'Sure, try it, let's see it.' But Gower knew the stage that way, and it all made sense when you saw the entire scene."[3]

It did not make sense, however, to tamper with the madcap portrayal of Madame Arcati by skittish but beloved veteran Beatrice Lillie (as Coward had tried to do), so Gower had Grimes, Edward Woodward, Louise Troy, and the rest of the cast heighten their characterizations instead.[4] *High Spirits* moved on to New York, where it ran for 375 performances, thanks to the show doctor, who remained anonymous in order to credit Coward as director.[5] Two years later in Boston, he performed similar surgery on Donald McKayle's choreography for *A Time for Singing* (1966), an adaptation of Richard Llewellyn's *How Green Was My Valley*, but it was not enough to keep the show from fading after a brief New York run.[6] Film offers also came his way— directing Barbra Streisand in *Funny Girl* and Richard Burton and Samantha Eggar in a musical version of *Goodbye, Mr. Chips* with a score by Dory and André Previn.[7] When these failed to work out, he focused on fulfilling an old aspiration.

His string of hit musicals had failed to exorcise the bitter memory of the Hellman play that now reignited his determination to win approval as a director of drama. He took on Jerome Chodorov's *Bascom Barlow,* an adaptation of Claude Magnier's *Oscar,* starring Nancy Marchand and Paul Ford.[8] When this domestic comedy, set, like *Dolly!,* in New York's Gilded Age, opened as *Three Bags Full* at Henry Miller's Theatre on March 6, 1966, "I personally got slaughtered," he later stated. "It was an adaptation of a French farce and the critics got mad because they didn't get Feydeau, they got straight comedy instead. I had a background in wild, far-out farce and I didn't want to repeat that. I'm always looking for a new, experimental way to do everything. Anyway, it was my decision to direct it that way and boy, were they ready for me—*zonk!*"[9] When the play expired in less than a month, he turned to his next project—a new musical, which had first come to light in the late summer of 1964.[10]

One afternoon at the New York Athletic Club, he lunched with librettist-lyricist Tom Jones and composer Harvey Schmidt, the authors of the long-running off-Broadway musical, *The Fantasticks* (1960), with whom he was about to launch a long-desired collaboration.[11] After all, it was Jones and Schmidt's little musical romance with its spontaneous theatricality and presentational style that had persuaded him to try a similar approach on a larger scale with *Carnival.*[12] Now free to consider new projects after the debut of their *110 in the Shade,* the songwriters, at Gower's urging, agreed to examine Ludwig Bemelmans' *The Street Where the Heart Lies,* a novel about the Paris underworld and its eccentric inhabitants.[13] Equipped with copies of the book, they promised to draft some ideas during their November work session. The next day, Schmidt left New York for a villa overlooking the Tyrrhenian Sea at Porto Santo Stephano on Italy's Monte Argentario Peninsula, where he would spend the year composing. When Jones joined him in mid-November, work commenced on *Street,* but soon afterward, they received a transcontinental telephone call—a rare occurrence in those days—that was to alter the course of their work.

"We didn't know anyone in Italy," recalls Schmidt, "so, for the phone to even *ring,* it was shocking! We got on the phone and there was Gower calling from David Merrick's office in New York. He had just finished a meeting with David and he was very excited, because he said, 'Forget about *The Street Where the Heart Lies.* David has this great idea! What would you think about a musical based on *The Fourposter?*' At first, he asked if we knew the play and we did. We remembered it. Privately, the immediate reaction of both Tom and me was that it was a *horrible* idea. No one, we thought, could make *this* work, but we didn't say so over the phone."[14]

The Fourposter was a two-character comedy, written by Dutch playwright Jan de

Hartog in 1946, which chronicled one couple's responses to the highs and lows of marriage over fifty years—from the turn of the century to the 1940s.[15] To give the play an intimacy that the addition of a third character would have compromised, de Hartog confined the action to Agnes and Michael's bedroom with its fourposter bed. Shortly after the publication of an English translation in 1947, the play received an unsuccessful London production.[16] Then, in 1950, it captured the attention of actor José Ferrer, who bought the rights and persuaded the husband-and-wife team of Hume Cronyn and Jessica Tandy to try it out on an extended tour of the summer theatre circuit in 1951 under his direction.[17] The successful tour led to a Broadway premiere on October 24, 1951, at the Ethel Barrymore Theatre, where the play ran for 632 performances.[18]

In light of *The Fourposter*'s two-character cast and single setting, the reservations of the songwriters were quite understandable. These were formidable limitations to impose upon a Broadway musical. Gower himself had considered them insurmountable until struck with an idea he now proposed to the team: two major musical theatre stars of the day, Mary Martin and Robert Preston, to play Agnes and Michael.[19] "When he started listing those names," says Schmidt, "it suddenly sounded better."[20] Still, it was possible that the stars might not be available or even be interested in the project. Merrick's failure to engage Ethel Merman at the start of *Dolly!* was just one example of how musicals frequently failed to get the performers initially envisioned. Tempting though the offer was, the team refrained from making a definite commitment until after they had studied the script, made notes, and developed a feeling for the material.[21]

No sooner had their conversation with Gower ended than they began to reflect on how *The Fourposter* might be adapted. "In reality," explains Jones, "we were intrigued. But we didn't know *how* it could be done, *if* it could be done, but we weren't about to turn down the invitation to examine it, because all that we had written— the four or five songs for *Street*—was for a story I felt was very weak. And I knew *The Fourposter* was very strong having the challenge of just the two people."[22]

Intrigued as they were with the play, Jones, Schmidt, Merrick, and Champion were not the first to venture a musical adaptation. A version with book, music, and lyrics by Edward Earle was to have toured summer theatres in 1962 with Robert Rounesville and Anne Ayers, but was canceled shortly before rehearsals began when the producers failed to obtain the rights.[23] A second effort, *No Bed of Roses*, with book and songs by Michael Kalmanoff, was produced by Robert K. Adams and directed by Romney Brent for a summer tour in 1963.[24] With Walter Cassel and Gail Manners as the stars, it played theatres in Alabama, Michigan, Pennsylvania, New Jersey, and even Ontario, but failed to reach Broadway.[25] The Merrick production could suffer a similar fate if its creators failed to find a way to structure it more like a musical than a play with songs.[26]

Days later, after reading the copies of *The Fourposter* forwarded by Champion, the two writers parted company for the weekend. While on a train bound for Rome, Jones received the initial inspiration that would break open the play: a presentational approach designed to acknowledge the audience by having all scenery, costume, and makeup changes take place in their sight and the performers step out of the stage action to directly address them. "It must have been the rhythm of the train," says Jones, "because I began to get ideas sitting in the empty compartment; it was the off-season for tourists and the train was empty. I hadn't brought paper to work on because I hadn't been too enthusiastic, to be quite truthful. So I jotted ideas on a newspaper I was reading, on my train tickets, on anything I could find to write on. And that's unusual for me because I'm usually not an impetuous writer."[27]

Back at the villa, Schmidt was experiencing a similar brainstorm. "I had the same feeling of excitement," he remembers. "While Tom was away that weekend, I sat down and wrote several tunes, almost as if we had agreed beforehand. He liked them—in fact some of them were in line with his ideas."[28] Soon they were working on what they had agreed to call *Man and Wife*. Within days, they conveyed their interest in the project and the idea of its presentational structuring to Gower, who responded enthusiastically.[29]

Later discussions with the director would center on whether to alter the time span of the play. When *The Fourposter* made its American debut, the fifty-year trek from the turn of the century to the early 1950s was still possible for a couple, but no longer so by the mid-1960s. Ultimately, the idea of updating the story was abandoned in favor of a slight reference to the periods indicated in the play. As Schmidt explains, "Agnes's menopause scene in the late 1920s or early 1930s is about as specific as we got. The only clue the audience had was a cloche hat that Mary [Martin] wore in the scene."[30] This approach naturally affected the songs, which would emphasize the characters' moods and situations rather than particular eras. With universality of plot and character as primary goals, it was best not to trap the musical in time.

By mid-December, Jones and Schmidt had composed sufficient material to play for Gower upon their return to New York for the holidays. This included a ten-minute prologue consisting of three songs.[31] Rather than start with the groom carrying the bride over the bedroom threshold as in *The Fourposter*, the musical would commence with a three-part wedding sequence. Part I would take place moments before the wedding as Agnes and Michael soliloquized on "All the Dearly Beloved" gathered for the ceremony and confessed to the audience their mutual apprehension about marriage. This segued into Part II, a musical exchange of vows, entitled "Together Forever," which, in turn, was followed by Part III, "Man and Wife," the couple's celebration of their newfound joy.

Delighted with their efforts, Gower had the team play the songs for Martin, then preparing to head her national and international tours of *Dolly!*[32] She and her manager-husband, Richard Halliday, were interested, but could not be completely persuaded without guarantee of Preston as co-star. Until that was resolved, she would examine other offers—the role of Maggie in *Walking Happy* (1966) and the title role in *Mame* (1966)—upon concluding the tour.[33] Though Martin's reluctance was a letdown, Schmidt returned to Italy in January 1965 to compose the remainder of the score while Jones finished the lyrics and book in New York. Each kept the other apprised of his progress by means of a lively correspondence.[34]

After inaugurating Martin and the national company of *Dolly!* on an eleven-city tour that April, Gower joined Marge for a well-earned vacation in the Greek isles. On their way, they spent a few days in Italy at the villa, where the authors were to debut the score for them. The evening of their arrival, Gower relaxed and enjoyed himself for the first time in months. To the delight of their hosts, he and Marge shared a spontaneous dance together during an after-dinner stroll along the port. "I'll never forget it," says Schmidt, "because it was a real MGM-movie-type moment with Marge and Gower. There were no people anywhere, just this beautiful port with all these sailboats at night, which was so stunning. They just started dancing by moonlight—around and over all the boats."[35]

After returning to the villa, the songwriters performed their latest addition to the score, "I Guess We May as Well Stay Married Now." With the acquisition of Martin and Preston in question, this second act opening was composed with the popular husband-and-wife singing team of Steve Lawrence and Eydie Gormé in mind. "Gower hated it," recalls Jones, "just absolutely *hated* it!"[36] He cut the song at once because it differed so radically from the portion of the score he had heard earlier.

When the Champions failed to show for breakfast the next morning, the songwriters grew anxious. Finally, about noon, Marge appeared and explained that Gower was ill. He had just begun to relax when all the tension from the previous weeks of rehearsal caught up with him. The debut of the score would have to be postponed until the following evening when he was stronger. By then, the weather had suddenly turned cold, so the team quickly improvised an auxiliary heating system for the vast, glass-enclosed, marble-floored room that housed the piano.[37] "I'll never forget the image of Gower," says Schmidt, "on a strange kind of *chaise longue* with heavy blankets, the raging Tyrrhenian Sea behind him, and three bombolas— little portable gas stoves that transmit these intense death-ray heat stings—blasting him in the face, while Tom and I performed the score for the first time in this huge room that echoed like you were playing it in St. Peter's. But, most importantly, he liked what we had done. Whenever I think about this show, however, I always see these three flaming stoves aimed at Gower, who appeared to be on his deathbed, like something from nineteenth-century Europe."[38]

Still too weak to travel, Gower remained behind for a few days while Marge went on to Greece to arrange their tour of the islands with Jess. By the end of his stay, he was fully recovered and ready to resume his vacation after drafting preliminary work plans with the authors. Returning to New York in late June, he began to search for a cast. Yet even after auditioning film star Mitzi Gaynor, he remained set on Martin for Agnes.[39] Shortly before her departure for Asia with the international tour of *Dolly!,* Martin agreed to hear Jones and Schmidt perform the full score in Cleveland, the day after her final performance there. She was completely charmed.[40] "Mary took the tape I made of the music all over the world with her when she toured in *Dolly!,*" said Schmidt. "I visited her once in Brazil, and she played it for me. It was an eerie feeling in South America to hear my own piano playing on a tape I had made in my living room in New York. I felt like Beckett's character in *Krapp's Last Tape.*"[41] On August 3, the *Daily News* announced, "Mary Martin is set for the Broadway musical version of *The Fourposter,* a David Merrick project which will have Gower Champion at the helm."[42]

"I knew those two parts had to be brilliant power-house performances," Gower later explained, "[but] neither Mary nor Bob had liked the play and they thought the idea [of making it into a musical] was preposterous. We finally got Mary to agree, but couldn't persuade Preston for another six months. After he turned me down four times, I gave up. But Merrick doesn't take no for an answer."[43] With Preston's enlistment in the hands of the producer, Gower left for London in November to prepare Martin and the *Dolly!* company, newly arrived from their tour of Asia, for the December 2 opening at the Drury Lane Theatre.

Staging the London production of *Dolly!* was no mere matter of polishing a previously existing company. Some of the cast who had toured the United States and Asia had to return home so producers Merrick and H. M. Tennent, Ltd., could honor union rules requiring them to hire a certain number of British performers. Out of this bicultural cast, the director had to forge an ensemble that was convincingly American in appearance, movement, and sound.[44]

An additional complication was the runway encircling the orchestra pit. Despite Gower's instructions to the contrary, it was incorrectly constructed and its surface waxed. These factors invited injury by increasing dancers' chances of misjudging steps and falling onto the netting over the pit or of losing control and sliding off the stage floor and into the audience. With no time to rebuild, all the director could do was to have the wax removed. While rehearsing the role of Cornelius just a few days later, Carleton Carpenter fell off the runway and injured his back on one of the steel bars supporting the netting over the pit. Fortunately, he recovered fully, but not in time for the opening. Garrett Lewis had to be called in from California to replace him.[45] But even the magnitude of these troubles paled in comparison to the brutal scrutiny the show received from the London press.

"By the standards of *South Pacific, Kiss Me, Kate* or *My Fair Lady*," reported the *Daily Mail*, "*Hello, Dolly!* is sadly non-vintage, indeed mediocre." The *Daily Express* concurred ("A reputation out of all proportion to its engaging but essentially modest merits"), along with the *Evening Standard* ("Not a genuinely amusing line in the entire evening") and the *Sunday Telegraph* ("Obstinately unfunny").[46] While the critics praised Martin's effort, they virtually ignored the direction and choreography. But Gower's disappointment was soon soothed by the production's popular success and its 794 performances.[47] Having his work endorsed by Thornton Wilder himself made him mighty proud, too.

Too ill to fly to London, Wilder sent his sister Isabel to represent him at the benefit preview performance hosted by the Queen Mother. Afterward backstage Miss Isabel took the director aside to convey her brother's approval: "Thornton saw the show in New York and is truly delighted with what has been done. The adaptation, the choreography—everything has realized his intentions. And, oh, he is eternally grateful to you, Mr. *Robbins*."

"Thank you very much," Gower replied without missing a beat. "That makes me very happy."[48]

Following the failure of *Three Bags Full* in early March 1966, he began to take a skeptical view of middle-aged Martin and Preston portraying young newlyweds in what was now called *I Do! I Do!* Since Preston was still dickering over the role, Gower thought it wise to see if a younger pair of performers could handle the middle-age phase of the couple's life. After an unsuccessful attempt to secure Carol Lawrence and husband Robert Goulet,[49] he turned to Florence Henderson and Bill Hayes, who agreed to learn the corresponding dialogue and songs and, later, to perform them in full costume and makeup at the St. James Theatre on a designated afternoon for the songwriters and himself. Though both gave fine performances, the experiment convinced him that the middle-age section—the most extensive part of the couple's life—would be better served by Martin and Preston.[50]

Shortly after Champion reached this decision, Preston refused the role once more. Vapid notices for his recent portrayal of Henry II in the short-lived *The Lion in Winter* (1966) only compounded his previous failures, *We Take the Town* (1963) and *Ben Franklin in Paris* (1964), so the film actor, who had won theatrical renown as smooth-talking traveling salesman Harold Hill in *The Music Man* (1957), opted to take indefinite leave of Broadway. As Jones relates, "Rosemary Harris [Preston's co-star in *The Lion in Winter*] absolutely took all the reviews and Bob was treated very much in a cavalier fashion. So his thing was, 'They're tired of me. I'm going to get off the street for a while.' He also didn't want to be in another show where the woman was going to take all the notices from him again."[51]

Indeed, Preston's fear was not without grounds. With Ethel Merman in semiretirement, Martin now was the reigning First Lady of the American musical stage. Her debut in Cole Porter's *Leave It to Me* (1938), singing "My Heart Belongs to Daddy," had been a prelude to a host of critically acclaimed performances in shows such as *One Touch of Venus* (1943), *Lute Song* (1946), *South Pacific* (1949), *Peter Pan* (1954), and *The Sound of Music* (1959). Although her career briefly derailed in 1963 with *Jennie*, her London triumph in *Dolly!* had restored her standing.

With Preston now out of the picture, Martin's commitment would soon falter unless Gower could quickly find a suitable replacement. He turned to his friend and former MGM colleague Howard Keel, who agreed to audition. In June, Martin, resting from the London run of *Dolly!* at her estate in Brazil, flew to New York for a day so that the director could ascertain the chemistry between Keel and herself in the privacy of his new 79th Street duplex apartment overlooking Central Park.[52] As Martin later wrote: "This man [Keel] could act, he had a beautiful voice, but there just wasn't the special astringent quality of Bob. After the audition, Gower, Richard and I went back to our hotel. We were pretty glum. Gower asked me how badly I really wanted to do the show. I said very badly indeed, but only with Bob. We were all sitting around as at a wake when all of a sudden David Merrick walked in and said, "I've got Bob Preston."[53] At last, after twelve refusals, Preston had given in.[54] "ROBERT PRESTON SAYS 'I DO! I DO!' " quipped a *Daily News* headline the next day, adding, "As has been forecast since his *The Lion in Winter* closed, Robert Preston has signed to co-star with Mary Martin in *I Do! I Do!* The musical goes into rehearsal in August."[55] With the perfect pair of performers finally secured, Gower now searched for a unifying concept that would visually express his fascination with *The Fourposter*.

"No other show I've ever done has gotten to me the way *I Do! I Do!* has," he confessed. "It's unlike anything I've ever tackled."[56] Indeed, minus the forty-plus casts and multiple scenes of his previous works, the staging this time would have to be more unconventional by far: "Two characters, and no more, for a musical? Wow! In a regular musical, if you have a lag or a weak spot, you can throw in a big dance number, or have the lesser characters take up the slack. Lots of ways to jazz things up. But here? And to make things rougher, Mary and Bob go through 50 years together, so you've got problems with changing makeup, clothes styles and such."[57] Yet the challenge of mounting a two-character musical was not the sole reason that attracted him to the project. "It came at a time in his life when we had been married a long, long time with children and everything," comments Marge. "After Gregg was born, Gower's work became more family-oriented beginning with *Birdie*. By then, all the challenges of raising a family had become less scary to him. So his personal life figured into his decision to do the show as well."[58]

Out of Champion's many collaborative sessions with Jones and Schmidt, a unifying concept gradually emerged that would give the musical a form distinct from de Hartog's play. *The Fourposter*'s universal charm sprang from its particularization of the events in one couple's life. In *I Do! I Do!*, however, that same relationship would become more metaphorical by making Agnes and Michael archetypes in a kind of universal marriage. As Schmidt explains, "We wanted the piece to reflect all marriage in a universal way. That is why we didn't go into it any deeper than we did. The play doesn't, either. Some people quarrel with that, saying it's all too surface, too goody-goody, but it also helps make this universal statement."[59]

To stress this universality, the musical would require a sort of blank environment or theatrical arena in which this study of a marriage could take place.[60] Within this setting, the songs and staging could function independent of *The Fourposter*'s turn-of-the-century-to-1950s time frame, allowing the characters to better illustrate what every couple cherishes and tolerates in marriage. In effect, Champion, Jones, and Schmidt were creating a concept musical about marriage and its timeless highs and lows.

Initially, Jones and Schmidt's view of the piece was far more presentational than it became under Gower's direction. They wanted it to be not only a celebration of the archetypal wife and husband, but also a celebration of two great performers—Martin and Preston—who would apply the trappings of age—wigs, makeup, and costumes—before the audience throughout the performance from designated areas onstage. "The only part of that which was left on Broadway," says Jones, "was at the very end when they did the old age thing [putting on makeup, wigs, and coats in front of the audience]. Gower just felt that to do the entire production that way was too *avant-garde*, too off-Broadway, too presentational, and I think he was right."[61] Schmidt adds, "Gower also began to feel that it might be physically impossible for Bob and Mary to try to do all of that at their age."[62]

That summer, the Champions rented a home in Westhampton, Long Island, where Gower continued the preproduction work. At his invitation, scenic designer Oliver Smith and production supervisor Lucia Victor joined him one afternoon to discuss the concept of the show. Upon arrival, Smith showed Gower the realistic design they had previously agreed upon—a box set, complete with a ceiling piece. Now, however, as a result of his sessions with Jones and Schmidt, the director was having second thoughts about this approach. When Smith asked why, he explained,

"Well, the play isn't about a specific family, actually. It doesn't even acknowledge the happenings in the world, like World War I, or anything like that. It's about 'family-ness' and therefore, I just think that the set should not be that specific."[63]

He asked Smith to help him find a solution—"something much more abstract with a feeling of just screens or something."[64] Smith gladly obliged: "That afternoon, I drew while Gower talked, and we redesigned the whole show. The execution then took time—to develop the floor plans and so forth—but actually, Gower and I did it together. We designed it. I mean, he told me what he liked; he showed me on the floor how he wanted people to come in and out, and as he talked, I simply drew. And by the end of a very long afternoon, the show was designed and it stayed that way; it never changed."[65] Smith further commented that *I Do! I Do!* was planned as "an exercise in elegant simplicity. That was Gower's idea of it, and that's what we tried to achieve. It was all very, very, *very* stylized with no clunky means of any kind. Gower assembled it in a balletic, almost dance-like pattern. We worked on it the same as we did in *Dolly*. He didn't want a series of scenes, but a continuous flowing thing."[66]

To achieve this flow, the director sought to animate the set by giving a kind of persona to the inanimate objects that filled Agnes and Michael's bedroom—a four-poster bed that bucked and revolved on cue, auberge-colored, curvilinear, screened panels that flew in to suggest walls, self-propelled furniture that floated on and off-stage, and props that mysteriously appeared, then disappeared without a trace.[67] With no chorus to choreograph, Champion substituted scenery and properties that danced.

Another innovation was placing the members of the twenty-five-piece orchestra on the stage and masking them behind the cyclorama—the huge, curved, opaque cloth stretching the length of the stage—that could be backlit at certain moments to reveal the musicians. This allowed a stage extension to be built over the orchestra pit, permitting greater intimacy between performers and audience. As a result of Smith's animated abstract design, Champion could give the production full Broadway appeal and, at the same time, curb some of the mawkishness a more representational approach might have fostered.

Victor watched the collaboration in utter disbelief: "Oliver asked for a spare area where he could work, so Gower put him on the porch with a sketch pad. I sat there with my jaw falling on the ground as I watched Oliver create that lovely, incredibly diaphanous set. Finally, Gower said, 'That's it! That's what I want.' "[68] Thus, what had begun as a realistic approach had developed into something far more interesting and flexible that would also enhance the concept and style of the production.

I Do! I Do! was costume designer Freddy Wittop's third production with Champion. After studying the script and scenic plans, he noted that the time span of the story would be the primary factor influencing his designs: "I saw all the different years—the fifty years—and my sketches were made following the succession of those fifty years from the turn of the century to the 1950s."[69] Besides representing a variety of styles and periods, Wittop also had to devise a means of facilitating the thirteen rapid costume changes required for both characters. Though the substitution of Velcro for buttons and zippers expedited many of the changes, others required more imaginative solutions. One instance concerned the transition following the first scene of Act I, where Martin, dressed in a nightgown, had to exit the stage, then return pregnant in a maternity smock for the beginning of scene two. Later in that scene, an even quicker repetition of this same change was required for the number "Love Isn't Everything." Wittop's solution was to sew a hidden pouch inside the front of the smock just below the waistline and insert a decorative, accordion-like, papier mâché Christmas bell into it. When Martin unfastened her belt, the bell sprang open to give her a pregnant look. To lose the effect, she collapsed the bell, and then tied the belt of the smock around her waist. Problem solved, the designer wired the star, then still in London with *Dolly!*: "Dear Mary, I just solved your pregnancy. Love, Freddy."[70] Martin was greatly amused.

Another issue concerned acquiring an abundance of Bird of Paradise plumage for an enormously extravagant hat Martin was to sport in "Flaming Agnes"—the faithful wife's reprisal to her philandering husband. The song's specific reference to the feathers made it imperative for the designer to find the authentic item, but with the Bird of Paradise now protected by federal law, Wittop had to devise a way of obtaining these once-common adornments from secondhand sources: "We put an announcement in the *Daily News* and I got thousands of letters from old ladies that still had the feathers. Such funny letters! The address we had given was the David Merrick office, and they were flooded with letters and telephone calls. They were furious! We finally got the feathers from some old costumes in the Brooks costume warehouse. They had some old costumes of Sonja Henie, the ice show performer, and one of them was covered with flanks of Paradise feathers. We had them cleaned and they became the hat of 'Flaming Agnes.' "[71]

Upon viewing the designs for Martin, Gower was particularly impressed with Wittop's wedding gown for the opening, his green satin evening dress with embroidered lace overlay for the argument number "Nobody's Perfect," and a yellow ensemble with black cloche hat for the daughter's wedding in Act II. The designs for Preston contained several humorous touches, including a pair of long johns, and a striped nightshirt and matching nightcap. Most striking were a brown Norfolk suit worn in "Love Isn't Everything," a full-dress outfit with tails, cape, top hat, and cane for "Nobody's Perfect," and a green satin embroidered smoking jacket trimmed in velvet in which Preston strutted for "A Well Known Fact."

As in *Dolly!,* Jean Rosenthal would once again provide polished lighting to blend perfectly with the grand, quality feel of the production that was evolving.[72]

In the closing weeks of preproduction, Jones and Schmidt joined Champion in Westhampton to resolve potential staging problems. "We had several weeks there alone," recalls Schmidt, "where we just went through the script over and over again with Tom and Gower reading the text and me playing the music. Gower would mimic all the costume changes. He'd say, 'I need four more bars of music here because Mary has eighteen buttons on this dress.' He would actually count the buttons while I was playing, to see if Mary could have time to be doing that offstage. That's the kind of preplanning I love, and almost nobody ever does in the theatre. It was one of Gower's great talents; this sense of organization and pre-pinning down of everything before it gets into rehearsal. He said, 'With these two stars, I don't want to go into rehearsal unable to answer any question they're going to ask me regarding how something is to be done.' "[73]

As rehearsals commenced in late August at the 46th Street Theatre (now the Richard Rodgers), Gower explained, "The basic premise we started with in doing this show is that it's impossible to do! . . . The impossible will take four weeks." Thanks to the meticulous preparation, his rapport with the performers remained lighthearted and productive from the start. "I may never work for anyone else as long as I live," declared Preston.[74] Martin agreed, "Our entire rehearsal time was like a three-way tennis game, a love match. Bob would suddenly do something which Gower and I loved. Gower would think up something we couldn't wait to try. I stayed awake at nights dreaming up things to please them. I can't ever remember having such concentrated fun while working."[75] Even the director himself had to admit, "We never want to stop rehearsing. There are so many quicksilver moods. They make a brief exit. Bam! They come back. It's ten years later."[76]

Identifying those moods and bringing them to life on the spot was the rigorous task that Gower helped the performers master during what eventually became a five-week rehearsal period from mid-August to late September 1966. Concerning these demands, Preston observed, "It's the most challenging part I've ever attempted. Only we two on the stage for the entire evening. We never really leave— except for a quick costume change—and I'm finding out I can't use any tricks. Everything has to be real and come out of the moment."[77] Martin expressed similar sentiments. "This was a very demanding musical, two full hours with just two people onstage. No supporting cast, no big production numbers, no chance to vamp while somebody else took over. Both roles required the stamina of boxers. Boxers with enough strength to go 15 rounds."[78]

Contributing to the actors' stamina was the fact that the score, unlike *Dolly!*'s, saw little revision during the rehearsal period. Though four second-act numbers were rewritten during the tryout tour, the first act remained essentially unchanged. Moreover, the score was composed not simply to blend with the staging, but also to be continuous, progressing without pause from the opening to the closing of each act. Although today's "through-composed" or "through-scored" musicals (those in which the music is continuous throughout, as in the later operas of Wagner[79]) had not as yet come into being, *I Do! I Do!* was clearly advancing the cause. With Schmidt's unceasingly musical, dance-centered, Americana score and Jones's moving, lilting, bouncy poetry to keep story and mood flowing, Champion could generate the continuously choreographed staging that by now was his hallmark.[80]

The key was to blend songs with parts of songs throughout while linking them to an ever-changing stage picture. For the first ten minutes not a word of dialogue would be spoken as Martin and Preston wove song into song with ceaseless, deceptively effortless musical staging and dance.[81] This "Prologue" began on "an almost empty stage"[82] with spotlights illuminating Martin as a bride seated upon a *chaise longue* at downstage right, and Preston as a groom seated in a wing-backed chair at downstage left. As a piano sounded a "pulsing beat,"[83] each, unaware of the other, started to sing about "All the Dearly Beloved"—the curious collection of friends and relatives assembled to witness their union. As they sang, the tempo slowed and a projection of a stained-glass window appeared on the cyclorama behind them, indicating their arrival at the church. Now the tempo changed again, becoming more agitated, as the two, still unaware of each other, nervously soliloquized on the words "I do." Their private contemplation was suddenly interrupted by the chime of church bells—a series of three chords played by duo pianists Woody Kessler and Albert Mello—signaling the start of the ceremony. On the third chord, both rose, and, after Martin lowered her veil, she and Preston crossed around their chairs, then turned and slowly walked toward each other until they were face to face. They had arrived at the altar where they now professed their vows ("Together Forever").

During the brief musical interlude following the reprise of the verse, Preston placed a ring on Martin's finger. The music climaxed with a sting, then ceased for an instant, as he raised her veil and kissed her. "A sense of suspension [or] an almost dream-like quality"[84] was then created as the two faced the audience and walked in place as if coming down the aisle. Now the stained-glass window of the church gave way to the brightly hued streamers of the reception hall, which slowly unraveled from above as the newlyweds sang of the bewildering but fascinating new life on which they had just embarked ("I Do! I Do!" replacing the former "Man and Wife").

During a second musical interlude, "a virtual explosion of color and of sound" took place "as streamer after streamer came cascading down upon them."[85] A brief dance break followed, which ended with Martin moving to the edge of the stage where she tossed her bridal bouquet into the audience. "Because I always threw the bouquet from the same spot, with the same gesture," she recalled, "the flowers landed in practically the same place every night. By chance, the area I hit happened to be our own house seats, though I didn't know it. People kept coming backstage to thank me for throwing the bouquet right to them, not knowing that I couldn't see far enough into the dark to aim at anybody."[86]

While the beat of the music quickened, the pair exited stage right as the streamers flew out and the balustrade-shaped walls of the bedroom flew in together with the fourposter bed that gracefully glided into upstage center from the left wings. Preston now reentered from upstage right carrying Martin over the threshold.[87] As she repeated her part of the song, he exited, quickly returned with their suitcases, and handed Martin hers. After crossing to their chairs on opposite sides of the room, they placed their suitcases upon them and then faced each other. On each of the three final "I Do's," they both took a step toward the bed, then turned once more, collapsing upon it face up as the number ended. In effect, Gower's staging of the prologue established the tasteful, imaginative, and fluid style of the production in which the entire stage picture would change almost minute to minute.[88]

Between the prologue and the next number, "Goodnight," Preston had a piece of stage business worth mentioning because it illustrates Champion's penchant for having actors respond with certain movement, business, or emotions on specific beats of music. Preston described this process as " 'Instant Method.' It's theatrical behavior and reactions on the exact beat of the music. You count it out before you make it happen—you say to yourself—'Hold it,' you count, then—'OK, I'm ready—go!' Did you ever change your pants by the numbers? I get out of them and into a new pair while I count. It's very technical."[89]

Just as he had entrusted the specifics of the "eating scene" in *Dolly!* to Channing and Burns, Champion did likewise with Preston, who created the business for a scenario in which he nervously removed his wedding finery and donned a nightshirt while awaiting the return of his bride for the commencement of their wedding night. After creating the scene, Preston brought it to Champion, who polished and refined it before tying it to specific beats of music. "Bob's timing on this mad quick-change was a high spot of the show," Martin explained. "It may have looked easy but it took hours and hours of work. All through rehearsals Bob and his dresser stayed late at the theatre to work on it. I have seldom seen anyone work so hard for just a few seconds onstage, but all the hours paid off in a show-stopping performance."[90]

In "Goodnight," the performers conveyed the couple's awkwardness as they climbed into bed together for the first time. Sitting up in bed, they brought to life the feelings and identities of the characters by means of the subtext the director had devised with the same precision that marked his dances: "There must be a constant interchange [between them] moment-to-moment, [during which their] every antenna is out."[91] He thought that Michael should be especially sensitive toward Agnes: "He must now be terribly careful. Just what does she expect? He is not a boar or a truck driver. Perhaps she needs a period of tenderness? After all, the bed isn't even warm yet."[92]

His subtext for Agnes was equally specific: "What am I going to say to him? I have tried to turn things away from S-E-X twice now—he kissed my feet and wanted to undress me."[93] But just as Michael resigned himself to go to sleep, Agnes brought "things back to topic 'A,' delicately, shyly with true reserve and not sexy or coy."[94] She did this by confiding to her husband that she had never seen a man undressed, to which he reassuringly replied, "You haven't really missed very much."[95] With Michael's response, "they are back on safe ground—except that she hasn't given up—and threads her thoughts right on back (to the subject)"[96] by asking Michael if he has ever seen a girl "without a stitch of clothes?" He intones back, "Well—I must have seen one once, I suppose."[97] The intimacy of the wedding night was now set in motion, with Martin contriving to steal a kiss from a delightfully surprised Preston. After a momentary reprise of "I Do! I Do!" and "Together Forever," they embraced as the lights faded out.

During a brief moment of darkness discreetly designed to convey an interval of connubial bliss, Preston rose from the bed and leaned against its upstage left post. As a spotlight discovered him admiring a sleeping Martin, he sang, "I Love My Wife," the first part of "Transition #1," which linked scene one of Act I—Agnes and Michael's wedding night—with scene two—Agnes and Michael as expectant parents. Jones explains that this was the "one song I wanted to write for my wife. It was to be a present for her. I wrote the lyrics and gave them to Harvey. I told him we'd probably never use it in the show, but I wanted to surprise her. So he composed a tune that we liked so much, we decided to use it."[98] Champion was equally taken with the number—so much so that he told Schmidt that he wanted to stage it with "a real 'Gene Kelly'–*Singin' in the Rain* feeling."[99] To achieve this, he followed Preston's joyful rendition of the song with a dance in which he would spin a drowsy Martin around on the revolving bed before coaxing her into joining him for a barefoot soft-shoe finale.

By the time he neared the final verse of the song, Preston was fairly brimming with enthusiasm. Strolling to the upright side of the bed, he kissed the sleeping Martin, and then began to rotate the bed like a merry-go-round. Before long, she awoke startled to find the bed spinning and stood up before leaning over the headboard to attract his attention. Though apprehensive, she clearly enjoyed the thrill of the ride. After questioning his sanity, she turned back to face the front side of the bed again, balancing herself between the headboard posts. With the two of them on the verge of dizziness, Preston finally ceased the spinning and locked the bed into its former position facing center stage. Throughout this section, the music continued to play beneath their dialogue.[100]

Jumping onto the bed in which Martin still stood, Preston engaged her in a modified fox-trot, dipping her twice. He then jumped off the stage right side of the bed to escort her onto the floor. Crossing to the downright stage area, they began the barefoot soft-shoe hand in hand across the stage and into the downstage left area. With Preston to support her, Martin executed two high kicks—one right and one left. She twirled right, and then broke her spin to cross in back of the *chaise longue* in an effort to return to bed. Playfully, Preston blocked her return by crossing in front of the chaise and jumping up onto her side of the bed. Martin countered this move by unlocking and spinning the bed as Preston resumed the song and brought the number to a close. Martin, who by now had ceased revolving the bed, repositioned it at center stage to rejoin Preston. As both climbed into bed once more, he became "sleepier and sleepier, so that by the end of the number, he is back to bed, and she is left wide-awake, with his head on her shoulder."[101]

Concerning Gower's contribution to the evolution of "I Love My Wife," Schmidt states: "There was a dance section which I had put down on manuscript, but then during the actual rehearsal, Gower would break that open further with orchestral conductor John Lesko and the two pianists to include certain bars of music to accommodate certain bits that were evolving, like Bob's soft-shoe dancing with Mary."[102] Champion began assembling the choreography during the show's preproduction phase. (When he told a reporter that "I've worked for weeks with my wife, Marge, blocking out the dance movements for Mary and Bob," Preston replied, "All of a sudden up there I get the feeling we're Marge and Gower Champion—only I am Marge!"[103]) Likewise, he conformed the choreography to suit not only the characters, but also the specific talents of the stars: "If I see it in rehearsal and it isn't right for the play, or isn't what these people would do at that moment—if it isn't true—it stands out like a dead radish."[104] No matter how long he labored on a particular dance, he would not hesitate to scrap it and start again if it failed to work. Martin remembered that "Gower would make up dances, sketch them in and we'd learn them, only to have him throw them out later. But I'd rather do it that way—before Boston—instead of setting the numbers and having them discarded afterwards."[105]

Once the director set the bounds of the choreography and business for a number, he expected the performers to conform to those limits. "The lyrics and music are so witty and have so many amusing and great ideas," Preston remarked, "you are tempted to do a turn and play the numbers for their sure-fire audience appeal. You know, you get so excited you start showing off. You do a turn. There they go—Mary and Bob buckwinging it! But that's wrong and Gower wouldn't allow us to indulge ourselves. These are two real people who age with subtle growth and many different attitude changes. It's got to look and sound like it's really just happening."[106]

Champion's choreographic design for a number, in turn, affected its orchestration. Again, in the case of "I Love My Wife," Schmidt recalls that "he would say to arranger Phil Lang, 'I want these two bars emphasized strongly to underscore what Bob's doing here.' Gower also evolved the delightful vamp with Bob humming at the top of the number including the 'I Love Agnes' interpolations, which also worked wonderfully later in the dance as an orchestral countermelody to the tune of the song."[107]

As in previous shows, Gower often discussed his view of the production with Jess, who was most impressed with a certain aspect of the staging: "I think I was proudest of Gower for his work in this show because he happened on a kind of wonderful shorthand that I've never seen anybody use in the theatre. It was this: instead of some literal way of saying 'time is passing,' he would collapse time for you. And he did that in about five or six ways during the show—various ways of collapsing time to let you know the years are passing and that these people are growing older together."[108]

The stage directions for "Something Has Happened," the second part of "Transition #1," which immediately followed "I Love My Wife," demonstrate the way in which Champion collapsed the time of Agnes's pregnancy: "Seeing that HE is sound asleep, SHE smiles and puts the blanket over him. SHE then puts away his tie, vest, etc. from Scene 1. As the music becomes slow and gentle, SHE goes [offstage] into her dressing area and begins to change into a maternity costume."[109] Champion covered this change by having Preston briefly stir in his sleep until Martin reentered in the late stage of pregnancy to consider her new status as a mother-to-be with "Something Has Happened."

With the conclusion of this song, "Transition #1" was complete and the action moved right into the second scene, which began with Martin soothing a nervous Preston, bedridden with sympathetic labor pains. In the midst of this, the two reflected upon how their love had grown and flourished over the course of their first year of marriage with "My Cup Runneth Over." Champion staged the number quite simply, with Preston seated in his wingback chair and Martin standing behind him caressing his shoulder.

The song, which later became a popular hit by singer Ed Ames, was almost dropped from the score. "I'm ashamed now to admit it," states Schmidt, "but I was the one pushing to cut it. I was never fond of that song. When I wanted to cut it, Gower said, 'Surely, if you look back to when you wrote this, you must have had some feeling for it.' I said, 'No, I've always hated it.' I hated the music, but I learned to love it when it became a hit. It made a lot of money."[110]

One day during rehearsal, the director gathered the songwriters specifically to address the number and difficulties he was experiencing with its staging. Schmidt again remembers that "Gower said, 'This just isn't working. She's pregnant and about to have the baby, and they're singing this song.' I said, 'Well, cut it. I just never liked the song.' We all talked a bit further and then decided to cut it. But when we presented it to Mary, she said, 'Oh, let's not cut it. It's such a sweet little song. Let's just not hold the long note at the end! We'll keep it real simple instead.' Gower liked that idea. So it was changed to become just a little intimate number which is suddenly interrupted by her having the baby. It didn't even go for applause."[111] Months after the Broadway opening, patrons drawn to the show by the song's popular recording would find its subdued staging and abrupt termination odd. "It was almost like it wasn't there," adds Schmidt. "But because of Mary, that song was saved. Thank God! Otherwise, we would never have had a hit record."[112]

To signal the birth of Agnes and Michael's first child, the director, working with Preston, Lesko, and the duo pianists, created an expectant father sequence that not only helped to break open the narrative, but also served as a transition into the production number "Love Isn't Everything." During the blackout of the previous scene, as Martin went backstage to change, a spotlight followed Preston to the stage extension over the orchestra pit, where he began to pace as a clock started ticking slowly in the background. At length, the ticking ceased, and he pulled out his pocket watch to check the time. The orchestra then sounded an "almost-fanfare"[113] that faltered and faded out. He wound the watch, returned it to his pocket, and resumed pacing as the ticking of the clock became faster and more frenzied. Preston's attitude now changed from "assumed nonchalance" to "the strain and disintegration"[114] of an anxious father-to-be. Once more, the ticking ceased, he checked his watch, the fanfare weakly sounded, then died. "Concerned and slightly angry,"[115] he shook the watch before returning it to his pocket. The ticking resumed a third time, more frantic than ever, reducing him to a "completely disheveled"[116] mess before finally stopping. Out of the silence came a fanfare, "more resounding than before,"[117] building until it became a triumphant march. "Young, virile, rejuvenated,"[118] he strutted to the edge of the forestage and proudly announced in song the arrival of his six-pound-fourteen-ounce namesake.

Champion had perfectly welded his "anxious father" scenario to the beginning of "Love Isn't Everything," where once more he would use his theatrical shorthand to collapse time with even more spectacular results. From the number's 188 measures of music, he fashioned seven strategically planned scenes by means of a vertiginous series of entrances and exits in which Martin and Preston added property upon property to the stage picture. He further festooned the setting with Smith's huge cutouts of toys, suspended from above. As a result, "Love Isn't Everything" had the look and feel of a full-scale production number although only two people were in it.

At the finish of the birth announcement scene, Preston exited left to change. At right lights rose on a second scene in which Martin, now no longer pregnant, entered singing the refrain to "Love Isn't Everything" and carrying a laundry basket while pulling a clothesline to which diapers were attached "like banners in the wind."[119] Crossing down left, she gave the line to a stagehand hidden in the wings, and then pinned on a final diaper before gesturing to hoist the line up high. Love cannot buy the pills, pay the bills, heat the house, or warm the baby's formula, she admitted, but it does make doing all those things "sort of fun."[120] As she exited right with laundry basket still in hand, a third scene commenced with Preston entering from the left laden with toys a three-to-six-year-old boy would enjoy—an Indian feathered headdress, which he wore while pushing a tricycle and carrying a pop gun and stick horse. At the same time an additional line of clothes and huge cutouts of pianos, rocking horses, and tricycles were lowered from the flies. Martin now reappeared from stage right pulling a red wagon, joining Preston to enumerate the costly yet indispensable possessions that parents supply for sons.

An orchestral interlude kicked off the fourth scene, in which more items materialized. From the right, Martin pushed on a life-sized guardhouse with a toy soldier painted on the front and Preston, at left, pulled on a fire wagon with a clanging bell, while more cutouts—a huge building block with the letter "B" and a doghouse—joined the other figures suspended above the stage. As the music peaked, Martin exited right and Preston crossed to the bassinet he had placed at the stage right side of the bed in the previous scene. He was just about to remove it when Martin reentered and crossed in front of him, pregnant once more. To his dismayed "Oh, no!," she nodded and smiled playfully before exiting right.

The intensity of the music and lighting now diminished as Preston exited right and a spotlight picked up a no-longer-pregnant Martin at right, who started the fifth scene by singing of the birth of her five-pound-fifteen-ounce daughter. Reentering from the right, Preston initiated the sixth scene by pushing on a baby's carriage containing a little girl's ruffled parasol, which he opened and twirled while crossing to stage left and singing the refrain once more. While bemoaning love's inability to fill the purse to pay for his daughter's nurse, milk, or party dresses, Preston produced a clothing rack on wheels from the wings and placed a succession of little girl's dresses—ages one through five—upon it. As he hung dress after dress upon the pole, they grew in size. This acted as a visual cue to the audience indicating the daughter's growth through time. Preston concluded acknowledging that despite the struggle to make ends meet, love makes married life worthwhile. The seventh and final scene of the number commenced as Martin entered right carrying an armful of girls' toys and clothing while Preston conveyed a huge gift-wrapped box from the left and then stewed over a pile of bills. The pair now added several new items to their previous list—dolls, safety pins, and Buster Brown shoes—things that bring "the money blues."[121] Crossing from their respective areas, they came to center stage and stood side by side for the song's finish while the clothesline Martin hung at the outset was lowered. Then she crossed to downstage right and took one end of it from a stagehand as Preston went to downstage left and did the same. Reaffirming that love does make everything fun, they pulled the line hand over hand until they arrived at center to plant a kiss on each other's lips on the final note.[122]

The movement behind each scene was choreographed with equal precision. The performers' costumes and properties were laid out in order of use, with Martin's offstage right and Preston's offstage left. Each actor's dressers supervised the arrangement and changes of costume. Assistant stage managers Patricia Drylie and Robert Avian distributed and collected the props. As Preston would exit left from the previous scene, he would hand a prop to Drylie, throw off one jacket, and slip into another with the assistance of his dresser. He then received another prop from Drylie before reentering the stage for the next series of lines. Exiting to his offstage area once more, he would discard the prop and exchange his jacket, trousers, and shirt for a new outfit. Picking up yet another prop, he reentered the stage for the remainder of the scene. Each one of these moves was thoroughly choreographed and rehearsed until perfect.

"Gower plotted the production like a wartime invasion—every moment, every prop, every second,"[123] Martin observed. She further explained what it was like for her offstage right in the tiny dressing room constructed to give her a little privacy: "I had fifteen costumes and five wigs, so I had to hustle my bustle. The moment I went off, Nena [my dresser] and two assistants swarmed all over me, changing wigs, clothes, shoes. Bob would continue to speak his lines to me, or sing, from the stage as I answered him, on a microphone, while dressing."[124] Change made, Martin would rush back onstage, so Preston could exit to do likewise. She added that meeting this challenge required "not only stamina but also choreography. Gower is a master of that. Every move, every change, was made on a beat of the music."[125]

Champion even choreographed the music cues for the orchestra. With the musicians onstage and hidden behind the cyclorama, conductor John Lesko would be unable to see the movement or gestures of the performers that cued certain numbers. At the time, the closed-circuit television technology now used to broadcast the action from out front to the conductor backstage was still a thing of the future, so Gower had to equip assistant stage managers Drylie and Avian with electrical switches connected to a light at Lesko's podium. The light would go on to warn of an upcoming cue, then off when the performers had executed the gesture or movement that was to trigger the music.[126] All in all, "Love Isn't Everything," with its on-and-offstage precision and amusingly rhythmic mixture of action, properties, music, and narrative, would prove to be one of the director's best touches.[127]

With a superabundance of props now everywhere in sight, Gower devised some shtick for Martin, which not only cleared the stage for the remainder of the act, but also rivaled Preston's earlier dressing scene. As Preston pompously lectured the audience on the glories of being a writer, a scowling Martin hauled off prop after prop, growing more and more perturbed by the minute, even disrupting his discourse several times while cleaning up. "Gower was a demon," she recalled. "He loved to see me carry props. . . . Once I asked why Bob couldn't carry some of the props and Gower simply said, 'He has his part and you have yours.'"[128] Finally, she hopped on a tricycle—the one remaining prop—and rode about the stage. As Preston searched for the perfect word to describe his latest novel, she volunteered it—"boring"—then rode offstage without missing a beat. Martin's business with the tricycle developed out of a spontaneous moment of play: "During one rehearsal, just to liven things up or work off some surplus energy, I climbed onto one of the children's tricycles and rode it wildly around the stage. Gower watched for a moment and then said, 'Great. Leave it in. Do it every night.'"[129]

Following Martin's scenario with the props, Champion had "an expensive and elaborate chandelier descend grandly from above and come to rest in the center of the room"[130] to advance the time of the action and indicate the prosperity Agnes and Michael now enjoyed after sixteen years of marriage. While preparing to attend a dinner party in Michael's honor, the couple had their first serious argument, expressed in the song "Nobody's Perfect." During it, each produced a list of the other's irritating habits in hopes of effecting a reformation. (Champion devised a wonderful sight gag for this in which Preston, after producing a modest-sized list of his wife's faults, was topped by Martin, who produced a scroll of his eccentricities that unfurled all the way down to the stage floor.)

Jones relates that the lists of faults comprising the number actually "came out of a game I once played with my wife. I asked her—as a gag, of course—to write down ten of her pet irritations with me, and said I would do the same with her. I admit, this is a dangerous game, but it's better than drinking or gambling. That notion became 'Nobody's Perfect.'"[131] Martin remembered how when Jones and Schmidt were still drafting the number "they kept asking everyone for examples of irritating little husbandly or wifely tricks. One whom they asked was Tom's wife, Elinor, a very successful writer herself. Elinor thought for a minute and then said to Tom,

'You chew in your sleep.' 'I do *what?*' Tom asked. Then he put the line into the song and it always brought down the house."[132]

At the end of the number, the two, now quite agitated, gathered the remainder of their composure and proceeded in silence to the dinner party. Upon their return later that evening, the tension between them erupted into a full-scale row upon Michael's revelation of an affair with another woman. Angry and hurt, Agnes planned to get even by engaging in a little extramarital recreation herself.

Preston's "A Well Known Fact" and Martin's "Flaming Agnes"—two numbers that brought the conflict between their characters to a head—also gave Champion a means of applying the topper principle he had used so successfully in *Dolly!* In "A Well Known Fact," Preston, attired in a blazing green dressing gown and high silk hat, compared his now middle-aged self to "the late October rose," justifying his affair with a younger woman on the grounds that "men of forty go to town, women go to pot."[133] Whirling a walking stick and slithering along the floor one patent-leather shoe at a time, his ludicrously self-deluded rendition of "A Well Known Fact" captured the total James Thurberish absurdity of the moment.[134] Under Gower's guidance, Preston bloomed superbly and suitably for a rake nearing the autumn of life.[135]

In "Flaming Agnes," Martin had a spree to outdo Preston's and, with the director's approval, even supplied some choreography of her own: "While I was learning this number I remembered a crazy dance step that a Texas friend of mine used to perform after she had had one more mint julep than was absolutely necessary. It involved extending both arms with the wrists drooping and prancing slowly from one toe to the other with a little knee bend in between."[136] Gower gave the "mint julep prance" a thumbs-up, then added some choice embellishments of his own. He had Martin tie the ribbons of Wittop's enormous Bird of Paradise hat under her chin, hike up her dressing gown into an instant pantaloon, and then slip into Preston's huge bedroom slippers. From there she took over, summoning that flippant style reminiscent of her 'Honey Bun' number from *South Pacific*.[137] It was a show-stopper calculated to bring down the house.

The couple's furor peaked in "The Honeymoon Is Over," with Martin grabbing the checkbook, packing a bag, and storming out. Before she could leave, however, Preston intercepted her, threw her over his shoulder, and carried her back into the bedroom. His apology won her forgiveness and, as the first act drew to a close, they reconciled.[138]

By the start of rehearsals, Jones and Schmidt had replaced their first attempt at a second act opening, "Guess We Might as Well Stay Married Now," with "Throw It Away," a specialty number in which Martin was to play a violin and Preston a saxophone found in the treasured clutter accumulated over their sixteen-year marriage.[139] But the director had an idea for a new opening that would visually reconnect the audience to the story by a comical domestic scene. His suggestion was a New Year's Eve at home—just Mom and Dad in their pajamas with their paper hats, whistles, and champagne riding in from the wings on the mechanical four-poster decorated with balloons.[140] The songwriters agreed and supplied "Where Are the Snows?" In it, Agnes and Michael, now content to spend every night at home, pondered how the time had slipped by so swiftly.

Only two of the original numbers written for the second act would be retained—Preston's "My Daughter Is Marrying an Idiot" (later called "The Father of the Bride") and Martin's "What Is a Woman?" The remainder would undergo substantial change as the show moved from rehearsal into a two-month tryout period prior to Broadway. Immediately following the Boston debut at the Colonial Theatre on September 26, 1966, Champion initiated a series of revisions in response to the mixed notices of the critics, who cited weaknesses in the second act. This included following "Where Are the Snows?" with something more engaging than the couple's marriage-wise reprise of the title song.

One Saturday morning, the age-conscious performers gathered in Schmidt's hotel suite to hear the darkly funny but dirge-like replacement song. Just as Schmidt started to sing "We're not getting any younger; the days are shorter than in summer," Martin fainted dead away. "It turned out that she had gout," explains Schmidt, "but I like to think it was also a savvy judgment of the song." Martin would require hospital care and a week's bed rest before returning to the show. Until she recovered, performances would be canceled, since both stars had previously agreed not to appear without the other. It was during Martin's convalescence that Champion revived the idea of a comic off-key duet with Martin playing her violin and Preston his saxophone. Jones and Schmidt provided "When the Kids Get Married," a real "foot-stomper" in true hillbilly style.

For Preston, one of those rare individuals who could pick up almost any instrument and draw music from it, producing a respectable saxophone routine posed no problem, since he had studied the instrument in his youth. But this bit of business proved more challenging for Martin, who had received only rudimentary lessons on the violin as a child. So whenever Gower visited her in the hospital, it was no surprise to find her sitting up in bed with a violin crooked under her chin, sawing away. Weeks after the director had set the number and they had performed it several times, both still practiced backstage without fail.[141] With the addition of the new song the pace improved dramatically. "The minute that it went in," says Schmidt, "it really lifted up the second act. So we left Boston feeling good about that, because it worked."[142]

"Thousands of Flowers," which appeared in the next-to-last scene, was panned by Boston critics who found it to be a pictorial intrusion—oddly inconsistent and superfluous compared to what had come before.[143] Inspired by Gower's recollection of a vast Parisian flower market through which he and Marge had once wandered, the song's broad musical range and lyrics with open vowels contrasted mightily with the rest of the score. Moreover, in a production otherwise distinguished for inventive use of props and scenery, the number's decor—four bouquets lowered from the flies accompanied by projections of numerous flowers upon the walls—seemed out of place. So did the sight of Martin and Preston sweeping across the stage ballroom-style. As Gower later explained, "Mary and Bob were not dancers and every time I tried to get them to dance it looked phony."[144] Indeed, Mary and Bob were not Marge and Gower. They needed something tailor-made to their talents, which they got in Washington with the breezy waltz "Someone Needs Me." Gower staged it with Martin seated on a small rolling table that was pushed about the stage by Preston while a series of satin ribbons came cascading down from the flies.[145]

Following the opening of the musical at the National Theatre on October 19, the Washington critics responded only slightly more favorably than those in Boston. Merrick soon arrived demanding greater and quicker changes. "Mary and Bob were working themselves to death," Jones remembers, "but Mary was a very, very slow study, spending six to eight months, even at that point in her career, learning the lines. It wasn't like we could do a new number for the juvenile, the ingénue, or the dancing chorus. It was *just them*. So even though we were writing, it took at least three weeks to get in a new number."[146]

Merrick ushered in a parade of songwriters and librettists—Jerry Herman, Jule Styne, Betty Comden, Adolph Green, and N. Richard Nash—to prescribe a remedy for the ailing show. In the end, Gower himself prescribed the cure by persuading Merrick to send the show to Cincinnati for a three-week extension of the tryout. There, the song "What Can I Tell Her?," Agnes's counsel to her soon-to-be-wedded daughter, would be cut and two new numbers, "Roll Up the Ribbons," and "This House," added as a new finale replacing the series of reprises, "Echoes of the Past."

"Roll Up the Ribbons" set the tone for the scene in which the performers assumed the affects and attitudes of old age before the audience. As the couple prepared to collect their belongings and move to a smaller dwelling, they reflected upon the fullness of their marriage, symbolized by the bed and dwelling they now prepared for newlyweds with "This House." After placing a bottle of champagne on his side of the bed and the "God Is Love" pillow that greeted them upon their wedding night on hers, they crossed to center, where Preston lifted Martin and carried her over the threshold for the exit.[147]

Though the touching yet optimistic finale was effective, it disturbed the director, who questioned why these still vigorous people had to leave home and move on as if they were outcasts. His preference was to let them remain in their home and conclude with a song describing what they would do next. In short, Gower could not let Agnes and Michael complete the cycle of life and die. According to Jones, this controversy persisted until Marge visited her husband in Washington toward the end of the run and attended a performance. Shortly after her departure, the director acceded to the ending as written.[148]

By the time *I Do! I Do!* completed the final three weeks of the tour in Cincinnati, it was properly tuned and polished for the Broadway opening on December 5, 1966, at the 46th Street Theatre. That evening, the performance proceeded smoothly until Martin failed to draw a laugh on a line that had been consistently amusing to out-of-town audiences. Later, when her "Flaming Agnes" also did not get the showstopping response it had received on the road, she froze—abandoning the genuinely funny, wry, and sexy characterization Champion had helped her cultivate for the coyly sweet persona that had dominated her work since *Peter Pan*. Within seconds of the intermission, the director was backstage with her hand in his, reassuring her and restoring her confidence. When the performance resumed, she was once more in command, and by the end of the evening had completely transcended herself.[149]

"*I Do! I Do!* has a steady glow of humorous sympathy and appealing humanity that causes one almost to forget that it is also a brilliantly ingenious feat of craftsmanship," wrote Richard Watts Jr. the next morning.[150] Norman Nadel called it "a happy show, generous with charm and lavish with love" that was "beautifully realized."[151] While admitting that it was "sentimental, determinedly professional, [and] loaded with resourceful gambits and geegaws," Whitney Bolton admitted, "that's what a show is for . . . to accomplish one direct, planned thing—to entertain you. This one is laden with entertainment."[152] Only Walter Kerr took a dim view: "A Santa Claus who shall here be known as David Merrick has hitched a very high-powered Donner and a very high-powered Blitzen to a very low-powered One Horse Shay. . . . Your passion for it is going to depend heavily upon the depth of your devotion to two of the fastest-starting sprinters the contemporary stage knows."[153] The book and lyrics were "barely passable," he maintained, "a sort of carefully condensed time capsule of all the clichés about married life that have been spawned by people married or single."[154]

But everyone relished the staging with its mystifyingly propelled furniture, whirling bed, and extension over the pit making greater intimacy possible with the audience.[155] Still, there was much more to *I Do! I Do!* than technical wonders. Though not really a dancing show, it was suffused with a choreographic design that only a showman of Gower's demonstrated skill could imagine and realize.[156] Simple and theatrically true movement was flawlessly integrated into the action to dramatize the situation, ideas, and emotions of the characters.[157] This "informal choreography," as Martin Gottfried termed it, "never once had the look of a 'number,' " and possessed a "rich, mellow style" consistent with the rest of the production.[158] All in all, Gower's staging for *I Do! I Do!* was judged as his most imaginative to date, brilliant in its inventiveness and timeliness because it favored a simplicity and directness faithful to de Hartog's story and mood.[159]

True performers in the classic sense, Martin and Preston stepped out with the assurance and mindfulness that they were communicating with a big audience, which they held in complete control throughout.[160] Whether spectacularly imitating Preston chewing in his sleep, prancing about as a scarlet woman in the huge Bird of Paradise hat, or pouting up a storm, Martin was in top form, giving the old stuff she first showed in "My Heart Belongs to Daddy" twenty-eight years before.[161] Preston, who played the gray-striped pants off of his straighter and stodgier role, was at his untouchable best when he strutted snootily for "A Well Known Fact" or was delightfully thickheaded, as when a pregnant Martin sighed that her carefree days were over and he cheerfully muttered, "Well, I'll find something to do."[162]

Kerr's assessment not withstanding, many admired the way Jones preserved the romantic flavor of *The Fourposter* while expanding its scope beyond the limits of the double bed.[163] His wise libretto—sentimental, but never schmaltzy—scrutinized the foibles and petty conceits of Michael and Agnes with amused tolerance, creating an entertaining couple whose domestic behavior was both thoroughly funny and extraordinarily touching.[164] His able, insightful, and zesty lyrics also conveyed a natural simplicity and grace perfect for the production.[165] Schmidt composed a gracefully lilting, tuneful score that furnished each character with a cluster of solo opportunities and both stars with numerous chances for lively and occasionally touching duets, all of which captured the proper spirit.[166] Smith's splendidly atmospheric and flexible set with its peripatetic furniture, soaring screens, and cascading ribbons made for attraction, alongside Wittop's amusing and fetching costumes and Rosenthal's expressive and dramatically suitable lighting.[167]

At the Tony Awards in March 1967, *Cabaret* was selected as best musical and awarded most of the major honors with the exception of Best Actor in a Musical, which went to Preston.[168] After a year on Broadway, he and Martin undertook a twenty-seven-city national tour, leaving their successors, matinee performers Carol Lawrence and Gordon MacRae, to bring the show to a respectable run of 561 performances.[169]

Gower Champion as the Sailor and Jeanne Tyler as the Nurse in *Count Me In,* November 21, 1942, their final performance together.

COURTESY OF JEANNE TYLER HOYT

Marge and Gower Champion performing the climax to "Country Fair" (1947), the first story dance he created specifically for the act and their signature piece.

COURTESY OF MARGE CHAMPION

The Champions strut their stuff in "I Might Fall Back on You" from the film *Show Boat* (1951). AUTHOR'S COLLECTION

Trains were a favorite Champion motif. Cut from the film *Mr. Music* (1950) was a production number Gower choreographed with Marge and him as newlyweds preparing to board a train for their honeymoon. Note how the chorus has the raised or pulled-up look Gower has in the previous photos— a distinctive feature of his choreographic style. COURTESY OF MARGE CHAMPION

The prosperity of AT&T clearly and charmingly explained in
"The Telephone Hour" from *Bye Bye Birdie* (1960).

What *Mr. Music* lost, *Hello, Dolly!* (1964) gained spectacularly in Gower's fashion parade on
wheels, "Put on Your Sunday Clothes," a visual expression of the show's theme and a scenic
transition woven right into the plot.

Dolly's dancers and star Carol Channing illustrate the Topper Principle: the number the audience thinks cannot be surpassed ("The Waiters' Gallop") until the next wonder ("Hello, Dolly!") hits them moments later. © 2005 EILEEN DARBY IMAGES, INC.

Carol Channing and company in *Dolly*'s new Act I finale, "Before the Parade Passes By," the throbbing panoply of Old New York that replaced "Penny in My Pocket" days before the New York opening. © MARTHA SWOPE

Gower rehearsing the "I Love My Wife" barefoot soft-shoe with Mary Martin and Robert Preston in *I Do! I Do!* (1966).
COURTESY OF MARGE CHAMPION

Robert Preston as Mack Sennett, leading his bathing beauties from their corkscrew slide in "Hundreds of Girls," an example of Gower's vertical staging from *Mack and Mabel* (1974).

COURTESY OF WILL MEAD, FROM COLLECTION OF J. C. SHEETS

Shadow play in Gower's "Show Business Ballet" for the 1977 Los Angeles production of *Annie Get Your Gun,* with Debbie Reynolds as Annie Oakley being initiated into Buffalo Bill's troupe by clowns Reed Jones (left) and Marc Pluf (right). Ringmaster Gavin MacLeod and Indian Trey Wilson (braided figure on stilts with balloon in back) look on.

COURTESY OF WILL MEAD, FROM COLLECTION OF J. C. SHEETS

Director Julian Marsh (Jerry Orbach) and company of *Pretty Lady* urging a reluctant Peggy Sawyer (Wanda Richert) to listen to the "Lullaby of Broadway" in *42nd Street* (1980).

© MARTHA SWOPE

The underworld meeting the elite in the "Tap Ballet" from *42nd Street*.

© MARTHA SWOPE

Curtain up on the dancing feet of *42nd Street*. © MARTHA SWOPE

Following the opening night performance, the cast retired to a black-tie dinner party at the Rainbow Room, where Gower had appeared with Jeanne almost thirty years before. Midway through the celebration, he and Marge danced for the guests with an impeccable urbanity as dazzling as the city lights below them, never suspecting that it would be for the last time or that their own marriage of nearly twenty years would begin to unravel within the next two.

TWELVE

Memories, IMAX, and a Million Bucks

The Happy Time

1967–1968

Two hit shows running in tandem failed to diminish Gower's loathing for the New York theatre scene, which by now he viewed as no more than a commercial enterprise pandering to the banal expectations of the well-heeled who filled its coffers: "Out in Tulsa or Memphis or wherever the hell, those people come into the theatre because it's an event. Then you come back to New York and see those theatre parties—last night I heard some guy look over the credits at *I Do! I Do!* and say, 'You mean I paid a hundred bucks a seat and there's only two people in the show?' He didn't know where he was. He was there because his wife had joined some committee."[1]

Summoning the prestige and financial autonomy garnered from his four previous triumphs, he went in search of more appreciative audiences: "Listen, I've made a helluva lot of money—every time Carol Channing sings 'Hello, Dolly!' in some place like Greensboro, I get a check—so I've got the luxury to choose what I want to do and I want to bring theatre to people who care about it."[2] But the prospects of unveiling a new project in Greensboro, Tulsa, or Memphis promptly yielded to Los Angeles with its impressive new performing arts center with a 2,100-seat theatre perfect for showcasing a new musical calculated to win the approval of his hometown peers in the entertainment industry.[3]

From its inception, Gower wanted to work in the Ahmanson Theatre. Following a series of conferences with Center Theatre Group director Elliot Martin in the spring of 1967, he was commissioned to direct a production "that would explore new ideas and new areas of the musical theatre, particularly in movement and dance."[4] Pledging to mount a new musical for the inaugural season that fall, the director went in quest of a project that would stimulate his creative vision and satisfy the expectations made of him.

In the meantime, Merrick had won long-sought rights to a musical version of *The Happy Time,* Samuel Taylor's 1950 play based on stories by Robert Fontaine.[5]

Produced by Rodgers and Hammerstein and featuring Johnny Stewart, Kurt Kasznar, and Eva Gabor, it ran 614 performances at the Plymouth Theatre before becoming a successful motion picture starring Charles Boyer and Louis Jourdan in 1952.[6] Seven years later, Taylor did a television adaptation, which Ralph Nelson directed as a pilot for a possible series, but it failed to interest networks. That did not deter Merrick. "What I liked about it," he maintained, "was the French Canadians on the North American continent trying to keep their language and nationality while surrounded by English people. I thought they were fighting an interesting battle."[7]

Although he initially approached Cy Coleman and Dorothy Fields of *Sweet Charity* (1966) to write the songs and French film actor Yves Montand to play the lead, by January 1967 all three had withdrawn to pursue other interests.[8] Not long thereafter, while in London for the opening of his production of *110 in the Shade*, Merrick asked its librettist, N. Richard Nash, to write the book for *The Happy Time*. Nash, who had previously declined the offer because the story was too sentimental for his taste, refused it once again. However, he did suggest an idea for a musical based upon an original story of his own, which he thought held more promise. It concerned a small-town Midwestern photographer who returned home every four or five years only to ruin his family's serenity.[9] Eventually, his father compels him to face the truth concerning the glamorous life he supposedly has led: that he is a liar and a failure who, because he has never found himself, has hung at the brink of dishonesty most of his life. "I made him a photographer," Nash later explained, "because I wanted to find an artist who could go either way, towards art or commercialism. The original concept that I had came from three words: pictures, images, fantasies."[10]

Merrick questioned why the story had to be set in the West: "You're always doing Westerns—why don't you make them a French-Canadian family?" When the writer asked why, the producer responded, "Because I own *The Happy Time*, and I've got to put it to use."[11] An agreement was struck that allowed Merrick to finally make use of his property and Nash to draft his story about a footloose photographer, Jacques Bonnard, whose reunion with his family in the small French-Canadian town of St. Pierre ruptures the relationship between Bibi, the teenage nephew who idolizes him, and Philippe, the brother who resents his interference in his son's life. When Jacques decides to liberate Bibi from Philippe's exacting but well-intentioned parenting, his own father, Grandpère Alexandre, compels him to reveal the truth about himself to the boy. Painful as it is, Jacques's admission of failure ultimately frees both his nephew and himself to see reality without pretense. Thanks to Grandpère's wisdom, Bibi learns a difficult but necessary lesson about adjusting to adulthood, and Jacques wins his dying father's blessing and a chance to begin life anew.

Though Nash's plot had little in common with that of Taylor's play, it did use most of the characters with the exception of Bibi's Uncle Desmonde, the woman-chasing traveling salesman, who became Uncle Jacques, and the coquettish Mignonette, the object of Desmonde's affection, who became Laurie Mannon, Bibi's practical-minded schoolteacher and Jacques's romantic interest. Moreover, Nash's script, purportedly based upon Fontaine's *The Happy Time, My Uncle Louis,* and *Hello to Springtime,* actually borrowed no more than incidental details from these sources.[12] Fontaine's warm, colorful, and frequently humorous vignettes about his boyhood in the city of Ottawa (as opposed to the small town of St. Pierre) with his mildly eccentric but loving family were never actually a part of the libretto. Hence the credits, which read "Based upon the play by Samuel A. Taylor and the book by Robert L. Fontaine" at the time of the Los Angeles premiere, eventually changed to "Suggested by the characters in the stories by Robert Fontaine" by the time of the Broadway opening.

Early in 1967, Nash received Merrick's authorization to present an outline of his plot to composer John Kander and lyricist Fred Ebb, the Tony Award–winning team of *Cabaret* (1966), who admired the touching nature of the story and agreed to do the score.[13] By the spring, the songwriters and librettist presented Merrick with an initial draft. So impressed was Merrick that he immediately forwarded the script to Gower, then flew Kander and Ebb out to Los Angeles, where they performed the score for him in the privacy of his Hollywood Hills home. For Ebb, whose first impression of the showman was that of a "mysterious mystic person who was sort of perfect in action, dress, grooming and style," the astounding beauty of the house on Cordell Drive was no surprise. "I thought, 'Well, that's perfectly natural for somebody like Gower to have the most beautiful azaleas in California.'" The interior of the home was equally impressive: "It was spotlessly clean; the floors were beautifully waxed; every piece of furniture was just *beautiful;* everything was in its perfect place. And when the children were brought in, they looked beautiful and were perfectly dressed with wonderful manners. At that time, everything about Gower struck me as if he was this perfect person who was incapable of being sloppy, buying the wrong piece of furniture or planting a flower wrong."[14] As for Kander, the most surprising sight was that of the director-choreographer's numerous Tony Awards scattered casually about his desk as paperweights—a curious contrast to the perfection in the rest of the house.[15]

After the team performed the score, Gower agreed to stage the show with the provision that it open in Los Angeles as part of the Center Theatre Group's season at the Ahmanson.[16] "This sounds like an about-face for me to do another sentimental musical," he later confessed, "but I fell in love with the score and the idea of combining film projection and live action fascinated me."[17] His Los Angeles option went unopposed. "It's true Gower made a lot of demands at that time," Marge explains. "He had earned the right to make a lot of demands about where a show was going to be. He *hated* living in New York with the kids and all of that. We had moved away from there so many times because we wanted to bring up the kids in California. And it seemed that there was no logical reason [to rehearse and try out on the East Coast], once you could get to the point of demanding otherwise."[18]

That June, while visiting the Quebec Pavilion at Expo '67 in Montreal, Gower discovered a visual metaphor that he believed would powerfully convey the concept of the musical.[19] Like Tennessee Williams's *The Glass Menagerie*, *The Happy Time* would be a memory play, which moved from the present—Jacques's commentary on family times recollected—to the past—his reminiscences relived. Since Jacques was a photographer, what better way to express his memories and bridge transitions from past to present than through Chris Chapman and Barry Gordon's inventive IMAX system? With its larger-than-life motion picture screen and 70-millimeter film projector, the IMAX process not only could instantly fade in and dissolve Jacques's photos of family life past, but also accommodate several images at once, interchanging them with others. Yet, as promising as this theatrical experiment in multimedia seemed, the director advised proceeding with caution to insure "that the film work does not overtake the play, that it does not consequently, become a gimmick show."[20]

Though not exactly the "chamber musical" some have reported, Nash, Kander, and Ebb's initial draft was intended as a smaller and more intimate piece.[21] But after the intimate *I Do! I Do!*, Gower was eager to break new ground and proposed a large-scale production wedded to the spectacular visual wizardry of the IMAX system. The authors and producer considered the idea impressive, if not inspired, but wondered how well the stage and film effects would blend. One trip to the Canadian Exposition was all that was needed to deflect their objections and win their unqualified support.[22] "I don't understand the projections," remarked Merrick. "It's a big gamble; we have very little scenery now. But Gower on the visual side is sensational, and I'm trusting that judgment."[23] "It seemed fabulous," recalls Kander, "and the more Gower described what could be done, we all thought, 'This is really terrific!'"[24] The manner of presentation likewise appealed to Ebb, who not only found it "highly theatrical and quite beautiful," but also remembered how the entire staff "all thought it was extraordinary."[25] Curiously, in the midst of all this euphoria, no one thought to ask if the multimedia format might overpower the fragile story. Within days of receiving the staff's unanimous approval of the IMAX, Champion visited Griffith Park Botanical Gardens in Los Angeles to photograph a series of roses to be used in the opening sequence.[26] As the six-week preproduction period began in the early summer of 1967, the director filled every available moment with matters of casting, technical design, and the staging of the major numbers.

The story goes that Champion wanted singer Robert Goulet, who first won acclaim for his portrayal of Sir Lancelot in *Camelot* (1960), to play the leading role of Jacques Bonnard even though "everybody else was against the notion."[27] The fact was that after the director, producer, and songwriters attended Goulet's nightclub performance at the Latin Casino in Cherry Hill, New Jersey, only Kander and Ebb were in favor of him. "We both liked Bob," recalls Ebb. "I had already seen him in *Camelot* and I knew that he had the possibility of being a fine stage performer. We thought his basic talent would be very well suited to the piece."[28]

Champion and Merrick were initially skeptical, but abandoned their objections once the director found the singer capable of playing the role.[29] As for Goulet, he was immediately attracted to the material and the chance to work with Gower: "Kander and Ebb came to me and showed me the script and the music, which I liked. Then they told me that Gower was going to direct, and I said, 'How wonderful!' I thought Nash's book was marvelous, delightful, and charming and that it fitted me to a 'T.'"[30] The star was signed with the provision that he finish the remainder of his nightclub engagements before starting rehearsals.[31] In the meantime, understudy John Gabriel would substitute for him until the fourth week of the two-month rehearsal period, when he would join the company.[32]

Gower conducted the remainder of the casting process in a similar way inclusive of producer, songwriters, and librettist.[33] Actor David Wayne, who had won Broadway renown as the leprechaun in *Finian's Rainbow* (1947), was chosen to play Grandpère Alexandre Bonnard, the seventy-plus but still sassy patriarch who sported Maurice Chevalier–like charm, sharply waxed mustache, and a predilection for brandy-centered chocolates and photos of voluptuous young naked women. Wayne's versatility had helped him create a variety of characters for the stage (Ensign Pulver in *Mister Roberts* [1948] and Sakini in *Teahouse of the August Moon* [1953]) and screen (*Adam's Rib* [1949], *How to Marry a Millionaire* [1953], and *The Tender Trap* [1955]).[34]

Champion's chief casting challenge, however, was finding an adolescent boy for the featured role of Bibi Bonnard, the third in the trio of characters around whom the plot revolved: "I needed a teenager who could sing well, dance well and act up a storm. It's tough enough to find an adult who can do that. Bibi is the center of three major dramatic scenes, he has several songs and he's a central figure of a ballet number, a lyrical ballet."[35]

As with the role of Lili in *Carnival*, Gower launched an extensive search that not only included scores of auditions in Los Angeles, New York, San Francisco, Chicago, and Dallas, but also Toronto and beyond: "I saw 300 kids in London, all of whom had played in *Oliver!* at one time or another, and nearly that many in Paris.

Useless. For a musical, you have to cast in this country—they simply don't have the training abroad."[36] Nearly a thousand youngsters had auditioned before a twenty-one-year-old performer was chosen who, by the end of the second week of rehearsal, was replaced by boys' chorus member Mike (now Michael) Rupert. Though less seasoned than his predecessor, the fifteen-year-old was the exact age required for the role. "They were a little scared that I wasn't experienced enough," he recalls. "I had only done three plays before this and they were all very short runs in Los Angeles. My work was mostly in television shows like *My Three Sons*."[37] Though impressed with Rupert's singing and acting, his lack of dance training concerned Champion, who needed to be certain that his natural grace and rhythm were indeed true indicators of dancing ability. After leaving the young performer in the care of dance assistant Lowell Purvis to learn the basic steps to "Tea for Two," the director returned for a final look and declared, "Good, you're it!"[38]

When Willie Burke was initially cast as Laurie Mannon, the school music teacher and former love of Jacques, the role was that of a widow in her late thirties struggling to raise an adolescent tomboy of a daughter. However, shortly after the Los Angeles debut, Burke was replaced with Linda Bennett and the widow dimension dropped "to provide a younger romance."[39] Then, just prior to the New York opening, Bennett was replaced by Julie Gregg, a veteran of the national tours of *Fanny* and *How to Succeed in Business Without Really Trying* and frequent guest star on television's *Bewitched* and *McHale's Navy*, who would be making her Broadway debut.[40] Each time Champion recast the role, the entire series of photographs in which Laurie appeared had to be reshot, thereby escalating the cost of the production.

Another performer making her Broadway bow was stage, film, and television actress Jeanne Arnold in the role of Suzanne Bonnard, the eternal mother torn between love of her husband, Philippe, and only child, Bibi. The eldest Bonnard brother, Philippe, Bibi's exacting but loving father and manager of the local vaudeville theatre, was played by George S. Irving, who began his career as a member of the original cast of *Oklahoma!* and subsequently created a host of roles in musicals such as *Gentlemen Prefer Blondes*, *Bells Are Ringing*, and *Irma La Douce*.[41] Charles Durning, later to become an eminent film and television actor, was chosen as Bibi's Uncle Louis, the middle Bonnard brother who never ventures an opinion and drinks wine from an ever-present "water" flask. Durning joined the company following performances with the New York Shakespeare Festival and frequent television appearances on *The Defenders* and *East Side, West Side*.

Felice, Louis's long-suffering, sardonic wife, was played by June Squibb, whose Broadway credits included the title role in *Electra* and one of the three strippers in

Gypsy. The remaining roles went to Kim Freund, Mane Stites, and Connie Simmons as Louis and Felice's three daughters, Annabelle, Nanette, and Gillie; Jacki Garland, Mary Gail Laverenz, Tammie Fillhart, Mary Ann O'Reilly, Vicki Powers, and Susan Sigrist as the acrobatic "Six Angels"; Jeffrey Golkin as Bibi's impish school chum, Foufie; and Dallas Johann as Bibi's archrival, Ganache. The remainder of the large forty-five-member cast was composed of a company of five-to-eighteen-year-old dancers and singers who portrayed the students of the St. Pierre Boys' School.[42]

Simultaneously, Gower addressed the technical aspects of the production. The fixed nature of the giant projection screen precluded the use of conventional set pieces and drops, which would have obstructed the visual effects. So Peter Wexler, scenic designer for the New York Shakespeare Festival and the Center Theatre Group's productions that season at the Mark Taper Forum, devised an alternative— a three-tiered revolving stage with several vertical poles and a snail shell-like mechanism in the center that emitted tables, beds, pillows, china, and assorted props.[43] Wexler's flexible environment gave the director the means to execute his continuously choreographed staging, which sped scenic transitions made in full view of the audience and provided a constantly shifting stage picture with strategically placed performers at different levels. This way a respectable family dinner could erupt spectacularly into the stage of a vaudeville house with the Six Angels in pink tights sliding down from the flies on poles as table, chairs, and family were whisked away.[44] As in *I Do! I Do!*, the orchestra was onstage behind the projection screen, so that the stage could be extended over the pit.

Once more designer Freddy Wittop was on hand to create flashy and colorful costumes subtly integrated to move the play through color phases; so was Jean Rosenthal, who fashioned lighting that complemented the performers, designs, and ever-changing backdrop of images projected by the IMAX system.

Rehearsals began Thursday morning, September 7, 1967, on a soundstage at the Allied Artists Studios in Los Angeles, where the cast, after being welcomed by the director and receiving their scripts and schedule for the coming eight weeks, gathered for publicity photos and costume measurements.[45] That afternoon, Gower conducted a read-through of the script. The title number, which opened the show and established the memory play concept, was staged first because of its technical complexity. Like the prologues in *Carnival* and *I Do! I Do!*, it began without overture on an empty stage representing Jacques's studio. Gradually, colorful images of the photographer's past filled the area, culminating with a Bonnard family portrait precisely duplicated on the revolving stage as each member of the clan materialized for Sunday dinner. Champion's directions relate the details.

A dim figure entering from stage right turned on a spotlight, focused its beam on an empty vase atop a pedestal, and then moved to an opposite light at left to turn it on and adjust its beam.[46] After crossing above the point at which the beams intersected, the figure turned directly to the audience and walked into the light, revealing himself as Jacques Bonnard (Goulet). Selecting a rose from among several objects in his "property pile," he placed it in the vase, adjusted its position several times, then, after refocusing the lights, returned to his camera to commence shooting.

Click! A signal transmitted from Jacques's camera caused a small area of the screen to come alive with a brilliant color photograph of the rose.[47] *Click, click, click, click!* A series of varying views of the rose appeared on different areas of the screen; then, suddenly, to Jacques's bewilderment, the rose unaccountably appeared in a woman's hand! With that, the picture faded to black. Yet, in no time, the screen again came alive with a picture of the rose by itself—exactly as he had photographed it. Relieved, Jacques smiled as if to say, "There goes my imagination again, thinking that the rose was in a lady's hand." *Click!* This time the rose appeared not in a lady's hand, but in the lapel of a man's suit coat!

No longer able to ignore these intrusions, Jacques finally surrendered to the memories they awakened as the "memory music" preceding the number now insinuated itself into his subconscious and was faintly heard by the audience. Next, the face of Grandpère smelling the rose in his lapel appeared on the screen; then, suddenly, the picture went wild—breaking into a number of pieces, jumping about, and reassembling! Flashes of faces, flowers, and scenes of family life past appeared in rapid succession, then vanished as the screen went black. Annoyed and bemused, Jacques turned to the audience and, casually speaking to them, revealed the theme, which the lively projections had just illustrated: "You know, it's a very strange thing. The memory plays tricks. You see, every time I take a picture of this rose, it reminds me of something else."[48] Within moments of the opening, Champion had fashioned the IMAX projections into a visual metaphor for the tricks that memory plays.

As the screen glowed with Grandpère's face, then a big birthday cake topped with many candles, and finally, a huge picture of the man and the cake, Jacques invited the audience in song to be his companions on a journey to a happy time past—his family home in the small French-Canadian town of St. Pierre—and to recall the Christmas mornings, carousels, chocolate kisses, and pale pink skies that formed their own happy times of bygone days. Soon "a romantic sky laced with pink clouds" in which a buoyant boy's kite, "filled with hope [and] dancing with the illusion of childhood everlasting,"[49] appeared behind Jacques as he recalled more memories of dollar bills found, hills skated down, compliments received, and lies believed. While the pace of the music increased and the full orchestra picked up the theme, the dancing kite gave way to the rose again, which was then joined by several more roses and finally an array of different flowers—the "lush blooms of late spring and early summer."[50] Occasionally, the faces of Bibi, Grandpère, Nanette, Gillie, or Foufie would individually peer from the flowers, each "a surprise in the bower."[51]

As Jacques again asked the audience to return with him to St. Pierre, the stage revolved to reveal chairs and a table set for Sunday dinner. Completing the scene by adding more chairs and stools from the property pile, he sang of having the furniture and table in place for this odd but amusing excursion into his past. Now, as the screen filled with a lush color image of the entire Bonnard family poised for dinner, each member entered and, after speaking a line, was introduced by Jacques. One by one, they took places at the table that corresponded exactly with their position in the picture above—Suzanne and Philippe followed by their son, Bibi, then Louis, Felice, and their daughters, and lastly, Grandpère, presiding at the head. At the climax, all froze in place while Jacques finished the song. "Hold it!" he then shouted, and as he snapped the picture of his family, the photo above went out of focus and disappeared while the music drew to a rousing finish. With that, the transition from present to past was complete. With this spectacular and effective opening, the memory musical was off and running.[52]

Throughout the production, Gower would employ similar montages of photographs with equally brilliant effect to clarify relationships or establish a particular mood. Later in the first act, Jacques expressed surprise and vexation when a picture of Laurie riding a bicycle suddenly appeared on the screen. Dismissing the image from his memory by waving it away into the darkness, he then openly denied it with the song, "I Don't Remember You." But like the introduction to "Before the Parade Passes By" in *Dolly!*, it suddenly was interrupted as more pictures of Laurie, captured in various poses during the course of a day at a picnic, flooded the screen. These moments in a past long since forgotten and now rejected by Jacques were the very ones that Laurie would fondly remind him of later in the play.

Attempting to dismiss her face once more, he resumed his song and struggle with the memories of their laughter, dancing, and evenings by the fire. But the stronger his denial, the stronger the memory persisted. Before he finished, the strains of "St. Pierre," sung by the schoolboys' glee club, could be heard in the distance in counterpoint to his song. Now the scene segued into Laurie's classroom where, in imitation of the photographs projected above, the boys' faces appeared one by one as she led them and Jacques in the stirring conclusion of the town's anthem. Using projections in this way not only established the relationships between the characters, but also created a romantic mood.

In the second act opening, "Among My Yesterdays," projections were used to further develop the "memory-that-plays-tricks" theme. Here, Jacques, while developing family photos in the red-orange glow of his studio darkroom, questioned just how closely his recollections corresponded with what had actually occurred. As he sang, the photographs he developed seemed "to float up to the screen as if shimmering out of the hypo and wash waters"[53] in which he placed them. While waiting for the hypo to work, he browsed through "opened telegrams and the contents of a small fancy box—objects [that would] give him a moment of pleasure and poignancy."[54]

For "Without Me," the projections were used to emphasize and comment upon Bibi's appointment as his uncle's photographic assistant. While he and his classmates frolicked about the school gymnasium with its sliding boards, rings, seesaws, swings, and jungle gym, Bibi shot "a sequence of bad pictures" that formed "a photo-montage"[55] that gradually covered the entire screen. As he began to sing, the entire lot of "out of focus, out of frame, lightstruck, too dark and double exposed" photographs faded, "leaving only their outline as a Mondrian-like backing for the number."[56]

With Gower's top-notch choreography, this first-act production number was destined to become the musical's best scene.[57] As Rupert sang the opening verse, each member of the boys' chorus went to an assigned place in the gym and proceeded to work out on a particular piece of equipment in time with the music. After sliding down boards, climbing up ropes, and swinging out over the audience from the bars of the jungle gym, the boys joined Rupert in a series of semaphore-like movements. For the climax, Rupert perched himself on the uppermost rung of the jungle gym to take final shots of the boys that flashed on the screen as they tumbled out of a pyramidal formation and went sprawling in several directions at once until they collapsed, totally spent, upon the floor.[58]

With the orchestra in the wings, Champion could begin the number with chorus member Brian Shyer running, jumping, and then grabbing onto a set of monkey bars that hung out over the audience. "I'd be singing the song while swinging almost right above their heads!"[59] he recalls. Initially, though, not all of the young performers were as enthusiastic about the choreography. Rupert remembers a rehearsal in which one boy, who, after being instructed to lean way over the rail of the jungle gym and sing, blithely objected, "I really can't sing with this bar in my stomach!"[60] Without missing a beat, the director—then under the pressure of the impending premiere and unappreciative of the levity the remark occasioned among the boys—sternly replied, "If Mary Martin can sing hanging on a wire thirty-five feet above the stage flying back and forth, you can sing with a bar in your stomach. Now sing!"[61] Novices and professionals observed the same rules—no excuses and no disruptions—save one.

All the children in the cast had to go to school, so Merrick set one up right in the studios. "I'll never forget the picture of one of those teachers going to Gower," recalls Jeanne Arnold, "and saying, 'I want so-and-so, and so-and-so, and so'; and Gower saying, 'Can't I please have them for ten more minutes?' and she said, 'No!' She didn't care if he was Gower Champion or not."[62]

Ordinarily, his rapport with the youngsters was quite friendly. "He had that capability," comments Shyer, "of really knowing the people that he worked with. It wasn't like, 'Oh, well, you're just another chorus member,' to him. He made it his business to know people personally. I *felt* that. He didn't seem close-minded at all. He wanted what was best for a number and what would make it more exciting, more accessible to an audience. I remember some of the young people showing him athletic things they could do, and some of these he incorporated."[63]

With the help of associate choreographer Kevin Carlisle, dance assistant Lowell Purvis, and dance captain Nicole Barth, Gower devised other choreographic highpoints: "Allez-Oop," a spoof of vaudeville to showcase the acrobatic skills of the Six Angels; "Tomorrow Morning," a festive high-stepping routine for Bibi, Jacques, Grandpère, and the Angels; the stylish "I'm Getting Younger Every Year" for Grandpère; and a song-and-dance duet, "A Certain Girl," for Grandpère and Bibi. There was also the "Chase Ballet," a rapid, impromptu dance consisting of a single ingredient—Bibi's attempt to retrieve from his schoolmates a raft of girlie photos he stole from his grandfather. The movement focused on catching, running, chasing, and finally tossing a great spray of pictures into the air, finally intercepted by Foufie.[64]

Dance music arranger and rehearsal pianist Marvin Laird incorporated Kander's melodies into the ballet as much as possible, but there was little in the score that could be used to produce the effects the choreographer had in mind. [65] So Laird, with Kander's approval, worked with Champion to create new musical phrases. "I remember we did a sort of Prokofiev feel within that ballet," says Laird. "Gower wanted that slightly off-centered, one-key-working-against-the-other sound. The left hand, say, C major; the right hand, D flat, so that you have a slightly dissident sound going on."[66] His climax called for an abrupt change in the music and stage lighting to correspond exactly with the moment Ganache threw the pictures into the air and the action froze as they drifted slowly to the ground like leaves. Thanks to music arranger Don Walker, the explosive sound cueing the throwing of the pictures was achieved by having the brass section of the orchestra blow air through their instruments without engaging the valves. This whooshing noise, coupled with a tinkling sound via harps, cascading woodwinds, piano and guitar plucks, produced the desired effect.[67] The resulting classic ballet struck the perfect emotional tone—the dulcet grace of the Bonnard girls (Kim Freund and Julane

Stites) and the mortified anxiety of the boys creating an extraordinarily sensitive and subtle observation about beauty, desire, and youth.[68]

During the rehearsal period, Kander and Ebb composed four additional songs, three of which, in time, the director would delete from the score. These were "Jeanne-Marie," "I Won't Go," "I'm Sorry," and "Seeing Things."[69] Written in the manner of a French-Canadian folk song, "Jeanne-Marie" was a brief but amusing duet between Jacques and Bibi, which gradually involved the entire family.[70] It followed the opening number and preceded "He's Back"—the family's three-part expression of their ambivalence over Jacques's return. In addition to providing local color, "Jeanne-Marie" established Jacques as a catalyst for family fun and emphasized his camaraderie with Bibi. After the Los Angeles premiere, it was deleted because the director felt it slowed the pace of the production.

"I Won't Go" was a second-act song that came between "In His Own Good Time," Suzanne's gentle critique of Philippe's authoritative rule over Bibi, and "I'm Getting Younger Every Year," Grandpère's celebration of his perennial youth. Staged as a comic production number, it showed the warring factions of the Bonnard clan—torn between Philippe's austerity and Jacques's permissiveness—verging on a boycott of the birthday party Grandpère suddenly gives himself as a pretext for effecting a family reconciliation.[71] One after another, each band of protestors wheeled a huge birthday cake ablaze with candles about a darkened stage while proclaiming their intent to boycott the party. At length, Grandpère himself appeared and, with cake in tow, declared, "I won't go" in protest of the protestors. Like "Jeanne-Marie," this number also would be cut after the Los Angeles debut. The third number, "I'm Sorry," was an apology in song that Bibi, at his father's insistence, delivered to his teachers and peers as punishment for plastering pictures of nude women about the school. The director deemed the song too awkward, and removed it from the score prior to the Los Angeles premiere.[72] Also during rehearsal, Laurie's adieu to Jacques, "If You Leave Me Now," was replaced with the stronger "Seeing Things."[73] In this duet, the pair, after expressing their different views of life, lamented the fact that those differences kept them from acting on their mutual affection for each other.

Champion planned to climax the evening in a manner rivaling the spectacle of the opening. Following the news of Grandpère's death, Jacques was to discover a moveable platform upstage bearing a tearful Bibi seated upon a suitcase all set to run away. After singing the consoling "Being Alive," he would snap a final picture of the boy, whereupon the stage would go dark as the picture flashed upon the screen above them. At the same time, the platform upon which they stood would roll into the wings with them aboard. A seven-minute film underscored with the music of "Being

Alive" would then commence, chronicling Bibi's efforts to live his uncle's words as he matured from age fifteen to eighteen. Bibi's pursuit of various exploits—riding a tractor, chasing a girl through meadows, working the fields, and celebrating a birthday—would culminate with him running over a hill and leaping into midair just as the camera froze the moment in time. The still image of the airborne youth would slowly dissolve as the strains of "St. Pierre" overtook "Being Alive," and the cast reassembled onstage for his high school graduation—the finale.[74]

By Saturday, September 16, almost two weeks after the first rehearsal, Gower completed the filming of the stills and the seven-minute motion picture sequence, which he shot with the cast on a three-day trip in the Northern California wilderness just above Santa Rosa.[75] By the time the week of preview performances neared a month and a half later, nothing had deterred his resolve to give Los Angeles a finished work in time for the November 7 premiere—not the mysterious bleeding of his nose and gums that came and went without warning nor even the death of his mother, who, in her declining years, had suffered a series of stokes, leaving her bedridden and speechless.[76]

Betty's physical deterioration, coupled with her recriminating looks critical of his sporadic visits and inconstant attention, were beyond Gower's endurance.[77] With neither the heart nor the time to seek the quality care that would allow his mother to remain in her home and out of a nursing facility, he turned to Marge, who not only enlisted the help of neighbors and nurses, but also became Betty's emotional support. Though he would spare no expense to ensure his mother's care and comfort, his feelings toward her remained conflicted to the end. Try as he might, he could not dismiss the specter of the exacting discipline she had wielded in his youth. Hence, he could never bring himself to affirm Betty as a talented and intelligent person in her own right who simply wanted his recognition—that is, not until the day of her funeral.

So as not to burden her sons, Betty had planned the service long before her death. The day of the funeral, Gower left rehearsal early and headed to Forest Lawn Cemetery, where he entered the chapel, walked to the front, and seated himself next to Marge. Moments later, when the minister (a complete stranger Betty had chosen to give her eulogy) began to preach, Gower stood up and stopped him cold. "You don't know my mother," he declared. "You don't know anything about her." All were thoroughly stunned. "No!" he continued, "*I* am going to speak because I know what she did." He then stepped to the podium and proceeded to give the most eloquent speech about what Betty had done for him and John at the sacrifice of her own life—as though the bitterness within him was virtually nonexistent. The spontaneous tribute proved that he really understood what his mother had done for him. Sadly, it was a posthumous one because he was never able to acknowledge his debt to her while she lived. The guilt he felt at Betty's passing was enormous; nonetheless, he could not allow it to compromise the task at hand. He returned to work immediately.[78]

Back in rehearsal, his concentration intensified all the more—so much so that to get his attention Goulet would have to stand directly behind his ear and yell "Gower!" before he would acknowledge him.[79] Gower even kept a tape recorder by his bedside to save ideas that would come to him in the night. On more than one occasion, Marge was awakened at two or three o'clock in the morning by the sound of her husband's voice speaking into the machine in a hasty struggle to preserve inspirations he might otherwise forget.[80]

He was also growing unduly suspicious of those around him. Without consulting Kander or even hearing one note of the musical arrangements, he fired Don Walker, considered the dean of Broadway arrangers, who had done the superb orchestrations for *Cabaret, Fiddler on the Roof,* and *Carousel.*[81] Just as Gower was about to summon his customary arranger, Philip Lang, Walker reappeared and politely stated that the termination of his services would cost the production $350,000. He was rehired at once, and his sensitive and original orchestrations became one of the production's best features.[82]

Concern for her husband's overly restless state prompted Marge to express a stronger interest in his work—work she had frequently assisted him with in the past. But her overture served only to alienate him more. He made it clear that she had no business encroaching upon his domain, and even asked her what was so wrong with just being Mrs. Gower Champion.[83] As she explains, "Despite his need and desire for suggestions or criticism, Gower would just shut down on anybody who offered them. I finally learned not to offer a single thing, or to offer it as somebody else's idea, because that was his Achilles' heel."[84]

Beyond the trial of the show itself, there was for Gower the overriding challenge "to keep up his batting average," as Ebb puts it. "His concern was that he maintain his reputation and his status in the theatre, which were enormously high. Essentially, he was quite competitive and anxious to stay 'king of the hill,' which he was at the time. Critic John Simon once called him a genius, and he was really proud of that. Gower wanted that kind of approval, and had every right to want it. He had gotten it fairly consistently and was now this highly successful, very rich fellow, who had incredibly good deals for every show he did. I think basically that's where his head was. And he did the very best he could on every show in the way that he was able to do it—as a showman."[85]

After the funeral, unexpected troubles with the revolving stage greeted him upon his return, forcing him to postpone the premiere by two weeks. As a gesture of faith in the cast, he gave them a week's leave until the obstreperous machine moved with the precision of a 17-jewel Swiss watch.[86] The misfortune taught him a difficult lesson about mounting productions 3,000 miles away from their intended destination: "In some areas, it increases the cost of the production as much as 20%. I've knocked doing shows in New York, but it's still true that the key people you want, particularly the technical people, are all there—you have to bring them out to do a show anywhere else in this country."[87]

At last, on Sunday, November 19, before a star-studded audience that included Natalie Wood, Carol Channing, Julie Andrews, Henry Fonda, Bob Hope, Gregory Peck, Fred Astaire, Lee Remick, and George Burns, *The Happy Time* had its premiere.[88] "What spins out on the Ahmanson's stage on that adroit turntable . . . ," wrote Cecil Smith, "has an almost operatic size, the dimensions of muscular drama. But the play it contains is small and episodic and only fitfully engaging, casually amusing and highly forgettable. The impression you take away with you is of elephantine labor to bring forth a mouse."[89] Los Angeles had expected a *magnum opus,* and had been given a work-in-progress—a fact of which her native son was now all too painfully aware. "An opening in Los Angeles is exactly like a Broadway opening," he admitted. "You are judged by a jury of your peers. The top people in the theatrical world are there—the people for whom you have the greatest respect. You want to show them your best work possible, not a half-finished product. I would never do a musical here that I didn't first try out somewhere else and get all the kinks out before I opened it here."[90]

Poor notices from every critic virtually guaranteed that Merrick would soon appear, sights aimed on folding the show, but by now Gower, who had made an art of avoiding out-of-town skirmishes with him, had already enlisted Kander and Ebb in a plan designed to neutralize the threat. Upon his arrival, Gower would simply disappear, and though the songwriters would know his whereabouts, they were not to reveal it however intense the pressure. If they all stood together, Merrick would eventually back off and return to New York. Just as Gower predicted, Merrick showed up and, after venting his fury over the state of the production and threatening closure, demanded to know where Gower was. As planned, Kander and Ebb replied that they had no idea. Again, exactly as Gower predicted, Merrick soon grew frustrated and quit Los Angeles, yielding the field to the victorious Champion, whose uncanny foresight had rescued the show. "I had never known anyone to be that omniscient," comments Ebb. "Gower had warned us absolutely accurately," adds Kander.[91]

Remarkably, audiences did not share the pessimism of Merrick and the press and were making a sellout of what seemed to them a hit in the making. In view of this, aborting the show seemed thoroughly incomprehensible to the director. Could Merrick not see that *The Happy Time,* like *I Do! I Do!* and *Dolly!,* would be another "salvage job," requiring a series of tactical changes out of town before moving on to Broadway for a prosperous run? Did he not realize that the current work was merely a play with songs with the potential of becoming a dazzling and distinctive musical? With just a few deft touches, Champion was certain he could deliver what audiences really wanted—a happy time, devoid of the soulfulness of Nash's libretto, which he blamed for keeping the musical earthbound.

Nash, who left the Los Angeles rehearsals early on to open his *Keep It in the Family* in New York, returned for the premiere only to have his worst fears confirmed—his poignant little story had been sacrificed to eye-popping spectacle.[92] Never mind that Champion's sleek staging had brought deeper dimensionality to the delicate plots of *Lili, The Matchmaker,* and *The Fourposter;* the application in this instance was jarring to Nash. Desperate to preserve the integrity of his work, the author confronted the director, who, in turn, confronted him with the critics' unanimously negative appraisal of the book. Against a mandate from the press challenging the director to rectify this flaw, Nash's protests were futile. Soon after, Champion, on the advice of certain Hollywood friends, began to eliminate what remained of the libretto's sardonic touches.[93] "Gower was being fed what I now have come to understand as 'real Hollywood advice,'" explained Ebb. "There were many famous Hollywood names attending the show who felt that Goulet was too good-looking to play a cheat, a rascal, and a phony. They thought we should change him into a fellow who was simply a misunderstood desperate person who kept up this pretense, not because he was a liar and a sham, but because he wanted his nephew to love him. These were slight changes, but basically, enormous ones. Richard [Nash] was extremely unhappy about the changes being made through the offices of Gower's confidantes out there."[94]

To lighten the mood, Champion first approached his three-time librettist Michael Stewart, whose talent for comic dialogue was sure to enliven things.[95] But Stewart was unable to oblige, so the director went to work himself, substituting dialogue for action. These changes included removing some songs intended to develop the characters and their relationships, like "Jeanne-Marie," "In His Own Good Time," and "I Won't Go," and revamping others like "A Certain Girl," the grandfather-grandson duet, which now became a trio with the addition of Jacques. By featuring three generations of Bonnard men, Gower could now emphasize how the song was something distinct for each—the old widower, the lady-killer, and the adolescent.[96] Certain production numbers were also replaced with stronger ones. "Allez-Oop," which introduced the Six Angels, became the more naughty "Catch My Garter," and Grandpère's "I'm Getting Younger Every Year," too reminiscent of

Maurice Chevalier's "I'm Glad I'm Not Young Anymore" from the film *Gigi,* was replaced with "The Life of the Party."

The stage design was also reconfigured. To rid the orchestra of its mechanical, pre-recorded sound, the extension over the pit was ripped out and the musicians put in their usual place rather than onstage behind the projection screen.[97] As the production moved on to previews in New York, Cecil Smith's disparagement now turned into confident assurance of a hit thanks to Gower's "extraordinary dentistry."[98]

To give the director more time to implement changes, the New York previews were extended and the opening postponed from January 8 to January 18, 1968. On the evening of the first preview, Jess joined Gar for dinner before the performance. On this show, he had declined his customary role as dramaturge to devote himself to the novel he was writing, but the truth was that he considered *The Happy Time* a weak subject for musical adaptation because its dramatic content was negligible.[99]

Though the two friends had not seen each other for almost half a year, their rapport was especially warm that evening. "We took a walk before the show," remembers Jess. "Gower pointed out that we had been close friends for twenty years; and that this was unusual in his life. I admitted that it was unusual in mine also. Then I went to see the show. I can remember my reaction. I just sat there amazed that it was as stupid as it was. The audience seemed to be enjoying it, but I kept putting my head in my hand and closing my eyes. Everything was flashy and spectacular and none of it touched me, none of it meant anything, nothing surprised me."[100]

Afterward, Jess went to a small bar next to the Broadway Theatre where Gar and his agent, Lester Schurr, awaited him. "He knew from the look on my face—I guess, he knew five minutes before I came in—that I hadn't liked it. I sat down at the table and he said, 'Well?' I was tactful, and he saw right through it. He said, 'What did you do—hate it?' And I said, 'Yes, I did.' And he retreated, as he always did when he was angry or hurt, and became cooler and cooler."[101]

Jess explained that none of the characters held his interest because there was no genuine dramatic conflict to engage them. If he and Gar could uncover significant elements of friction between the characters as they had on previous shows, perhaps they could find a solution to rivet the audience's attention. Rising from his seat, Gar replied, "Listen, I don't doubt that you have a lot of good suggestions, but I just can't listen to them tonight." With that, he walked out of the bar, his agent trailing behind.

Next day, they squabbled on the phone, hung up on each other, then, after recouping an hour or so later, finally began a constructive dialogue. At that point, it was safe for them to meet face to face for more in-depth discussion. "I asked if I could come and see the show that night," Jess explains. "Gower said, 'Come tomorrow night. Maybe I'll have some changes.' And he *did* have changes. Wonderful changes! I saw it again maybe three weeks along, and acknowledged that it was better. But something had happened to our friendship in the meantime, and I'm not sure that it ever recovered."[102]

Among the last-minute changes was "The Life of the Party," the replacement for "I'm Getting Younger Every Year." Starting with Wayne's Grandpère, a tall ladder, and a lavender piano on which schoolboy Shyer and the elfin Golkin plunked out the beat, Gower gradually built a showstopper that never compromised the initial simplicity of its ingredients. While Wayne ascended the ladder and sang, the boys diligently played the piano that slowly began to revolve around him. Soon the entire chorus of schoolboys filled the stage, climbing rather than dancing, as they mounted poles and rope ladders to hang Grandpère's birthday party decorations about the gym. In a world where choreography tended to be planimetric, Gower's vertical showstopper was an astonishment, climaxing with Wayne's marvelous slow descent down the ladder in red coat and red paper top hat.[103] Comparisons can be odious and the similarities between "Life of the Party" and its predecessor "Hello, Dolly!" would not go unnoticed by critics. ("Hello, Davy!" one would quip.[104]) Still, there was far more distinction than resemblance between the two.

In the midst of previews, the long-anticipated seven-minute film chronicling Bibi's journey to adulthood finally arrived—the director's crowning touch. What it became was a technical nightmare, with its shimmering beauty clashing severely with the live action of the high school graduation finale.[105] Thousands upon thousands of dollars had been spent on a visual marvel that could not be used because it dwarfed the stage action, rendering it dull and colorless by comparison. Now, with only days to the opening, Gower scrapped the film and contrived a new ending that landed Goulet in the most abrupt marriage since the invention of the shotgun.[106]

Still, because it was guided by the most commercially successful director of musicals then working, *The Happy Time* promised to be the one legitimate hit in a season of flops like *Hallelujah, Baby!*, *Henry, Sweet, Henry*, *Illya, Darling*, and *How Now, Dow Jones*.[107] Just as the musical was poised to take on this challenge, on the night of its debut, Thursday, January 18, the curtain at the Broadway Theatre was held half an hour for *New York Times* critic Clive Barnes, late arriving from a lecture in Pittsburgh.[108] Afterward, disgruntled critics, delayed by the tardiness of their chief competitor, scrambled to meet deadlines as the cast gathered at Sardi's for the party. Midway through the festivities, Gower called for attention as young Brian Shyer read the notices.[109]

"Did you ever hold a polished, beautiful red apple in your hand and then bite into it only to discover that there was a worm inside?" asked Whitney Bolton. "I cannot avoid thinking this about *The Happy Time* . . . Here is a polished, beautiful production with a libretto that . . . leaves some considerable holes in its story. The consequence is that handsome, active and colorful ballets are staged to cloak the deficiencies."[110] Julius Novick described it as "alternately, and sometimes simultaneously, repulsive and superb,"[111] while George Oppenheimer added that it "has the feel of a ship without a rudder, going in circles without direction or goal."[112] Lastly, John Chapman advised, "If I had this show to do over again, I'd keep the fine cast, the fascinating production and the score, throw out the book and start over again with Samuel Taylor's original play."[113]

Barnes, who missed the opening number even with the curtain's half-hour delay, gave a more circumspect assessment: "Style in a musical is a very precious but intangible thing. *The Happy Time* . . . has a certain style, a certain charm, even a certain distinction that put it above the rest of this season's so far sadly sparse crop of Broadway musicals."[114] It is bad enough when your show is described as the best of a bad season, but worse is hearing that as a choreographer you are essentially washed up—precisely what Barnes said of Gower: "When Mr. Champion attempted a proper ballet he came a sore cropper for his quite lengthy ballet does nothing to advance the plot and merely shows the ironic poverty of his actual choreographic abilities."[115] But the suggestion that he "might do best to stick to staging at which he is a master and leave choreography to someone else"[116] was what really infuriated Gower. The rest of the critics hailed the choreography as a virtuoso job that was not so much an exhibition of complex dance movements as a telling comedic commentary on character and circumstances, using positions and postures to relate a tale without pretense.[117]

Generally, the use of the IMAX system was considered impressive and effective. Only Walter Kerr thought it distracted attention away from Goulet during his singing, and created a cavernous effect that made the stage action seem dark and gloomy by comparison.[118]

Goulet was praised as an elegantly unaffected singer whose charm and sincerity carried conviction in a bravura performance perfectly suited to the feckless photographer he played.[119] Wayne proved an indisputable delight as the old father, half-saint, half-scoundrel, and all show business.[120] As the adolescent in awe of his sophisticated uncle, Rupert was outstanding—the kind of young performer W. C. Fields spent a career shunning; and Gregg's enchanting voice, looks, and personality made her Broadway debut as the winsome schoolteacher a memorable one.[121] The small-scale but genuine characterizations by Charles Durning, Jeanne Arnold, George S. Irving, and Kim Freund were recognized as assets as well as the unusually good-looking Six Angels with their honky-tonk exuberance.[122] Lastly, the delightful and thoroughly winning kids were praised for their wonderfully effective dancing.[123]

Kander and Ebb produced a varied, melodious, and literate score that functioned gracefully—rousing or touching as the plot required.[124] Nash's libretto bore the brunt of the criticism, berated as a dubious homage to the blessings of the simple life in French Canada because of its lack of humor and bogus sentimentality.[125] Wexler's straightforward and remarkably flexible setting with its giant turntable that wondrously moved the large cast and props about was also noted, as were Wittop's admirably right and colorful costumes and Rosenthal's atmospheric lighting.[126]

Gower now had three Broadway musicals running simultaneously—two hits and one that teetered precariously between success and failure. "If it were a dead hit, I could go home; if it were a dead flop, I could go home," he admitted. "I'm still working on *The Happy Time* with the scissors. I slice a little here, change something there. It's a much better show than opening night."[127] But no amount of trimming could correct the basic flaws that still remained. Nevertheless, his direction and choreography, together with Goulet's performance, were recognized as the best of the season at the 22nd Annual Tony Awards. On that evening of April 21, as he bounded to the stage of the Shubert Theatre to accept the choreographer's award, he blithely commented, "I don't know how to break this to Clive Barnes." Later that night, he received a telegram from the critic, congratulating him on both awards and admitting, "Even critics can be wrong at times."[128] Yet neither the distinction of its three Tonys nor Merrick's heavy promotion and bargain rate of two tickets for the price of one could keep the show running beyond 285 performances. It closed on September 28, 1968—the first musical in Broadway history to lose a million dollars.[129]

His work concluded, Gower returned to Los Angeles a different person. Weeks later, he asked Marge for a separation, to which she reluctantly agreed. After a short-lived reconciliation, the Champions would finally divorce in December 1973, leaving a bewildered Marge to ponder the irony of the inscription inside the wedding band Gower had given her twenty-five years before—"More than happy time."

THIRTEEN

A Most Peculiar Lady

Prettybelle

1969–1971

The personal consequences of Gower's one-man assault on Broadway were escalating perilously. He wearied of the bicoastal existence that kept him madly shuttling between his professional life in New York and personal life in Los Angeles, and in time, two months away from home became four, and four, six. "That's very dangerous for two people who are very involved and have started out more as partners in everything," concedes Marge. "Each time they get back on the same side of the country, it takes a little bit longer to meld because each one has filled in those periods of separation and loneliness with other activities. At that point, you really don't see what's important and what isn't. You become very defensive of your own identity. Then there are expectations from both sides as to how much you're going to meld again before there's another six-month separation."[1]

When Gower finally returned home, Marge, Gregg, and Blake had barely adjusted to having him back when he was off once again. With Gregg at the age when a son especially needs his father's guidance, Gower struggled to find a way to bridge the miles to hearten him. "Hey, son. Go to the window and look out at the moon," he urged during one long-distance chat. "See it?" It glowed golden and full. "Gregg, we're looking at the same moon and we're together."[2] Thereafter, the sign of the moon would fondly link father with son no matter how far the distance between them.

In February 1968, after a month's worth of tweaking *The Happy Time*, Gower was London-bound to ready *I Do! I Do!* for its May 17 opening at the Lyric Theatre with stars Anne Rogers and Ian Carmichael—not to return for another six months. Though far from the usual raves, his work this time was viewed more positively than it had been when *Dolly!* opened there two and a half years before.[3]

His occasional emotional withdrawals were becoming more frequent and pronounced. Even when home, he was often far away. While he was gardening, swimming, or simply sunbathing, Marge would approach in hopes of discussing family matters tabled during his absence, only to be told that he was "mulling over things" related to his current enterprise and should not be disturbed.[4] "He was really used to being taken care of by me," she relates, "and having everybody understand that there would be a time when we could communicate. But there were other factors that we couldn't prevent—like his getting to be fifty, and his feeling that things were getting topsy-turvy and out of control. When life began to present him with things that made him out of control—physical things as well as emotional things—that was a very serious problem."[5]

The stomach ulcer that first appeared during his post–Coast Guard days reduced him to a bland diet, but worse was the strange sporadic bleeding of his nose and gums that doctors could not explain. In Arrowhead, a vacation area in the mountains above Los Angeles, the family had a summer home that they eventually sold because of his frequent and unpredictable bouts of bleeding that doctors believed were linked to altitude or a lack of Vitamin C. These were early signs of a fatal condition that would not be pinpointed for another ten years.[6] These problems commingled with the advent of age fifty; the sudden death of Lester Shurr, his longtime agent, mentor, and first line of defense against Merrick; and his mother's death to produce a potent mix—one that now stirred up deeper issues long dormant and unresolved. "He had such a need to change his lifestyle," explains Marge, "as he got into that male menopause phase: to change his lifestyle and maybe taste all of the things that he had not tasted when he was a teenager because his mother had kept such tabs on him and had really raised him to be this perfect gentleman. But he really felt the need for all kinds of experimentation that he'd never done in the appropriate years. If you walk before you crawl, you have to go back and crawl."[7]

Ernest Belcher's "Boy," the nimble youth with head-turning looks and boundless vigor, was no more—gone with the road shows, supper clubs, and Hollywood musicals in which he had made his mark. His successor, the distinguished Broadway showman, had basically remained a stranger to him—someone he was coming to terms with only now. Sadly, his terms for coming to terms excluded Marge and Jess, his greatest allies, whom he regarded with suspicion and kept at a distance more and more. "I think that Gower was pretty sure of Marge and myself," Jess remarks, "and was always very aware that I was not going to shake loose of him, which is something I had to do. Margie, of course, loved him, so she wasn't going to abandon him. So he knew he was on pretty steady ground. He could treat us both poorly and knew it wasn't going to have any particular effect."[8]

Fearful of becoming dependent upon Marge's assistance on productions, Gower gradually eliminated her role. Her coaching duties on *Dolly!* were reduced to pre-production dance work for *I Do! I Do!* As *The Happy Time* got under way, he made it clear that there would be no place for her. With the boys now in school, she set her sights on reviving her career and soon landed a featured role in the film *The Swimmer* (1968) with Burt Lancaster. She also began to socialize again. "If I hadn't had some outlets," she explains, "like going out with gay guys or married couples, I would not have gotten out at all. Even when Gower was back, he was not all that anxious to socialize because he was not the most comfortable in social situations. So I became the best single-married lady in town."[9]

By fall 1968, Marge and Gower had agreed to a trial separation, but, in hopes of reconciliation, neither initiated divorce proceedings. She remained in their Hollywood Hills home. He moved to Topanga Canyon, high in the Santa Monica Mountains above Malibu Beach, where he took up the freewheeling lifestyle of the hippie counterculture, shedding his clean-cut conservative dress and musical tastes for caftans, rock bands, and experimentation with drugs and sex. Unlike Marge, Gower faced this time of deliberation alone without counseling, which he tried but abandoned because he could not bear anyone—even a therapist—knowing the specifics of his private life.[10]

The work continued. In December 1968, he accepted the invitation of American Conservatory Theatre's (ACT) founder-producer, William Ball, to stage Georges Feydeau's classic French farce, *A Flea in Her Ear*, for his San Francisco company. From start to finish, the unconventional staging was thoroughly choreographed, with sets and costumes entirely in black and white to conjure the farces of silent movies. Each act began with a tribute to that era as the characters mutely dashed about before wildly flickering strobe lights. In February 1969, *New York Times* critic Howard Taubman caught the show and called it "a gem of light, fantastic buffoonery" that "should have wide currency beyond its home here at the Geary Theatre."[11] With that endorsement, director and producer launched preparations for a fall opening at New York's ANTA (now the Virginia) Theatre. Champion flew to New York to make the arrangements and check on *Dolly!*, only to become a victim of the major snowstorm of the season when struck on the head by a chunk of ice that fell from a building at the corner of Sixth Avenue and 59th Street.[12] After a brief recuperation back in Los Angeles, he launched his return to television, staging the 41st Annual Academy Awards and then a special with Julie Andrews and Harry Belafonte.[13]

The awards ceremony, always a dull and indolent affair, sorely needed streamlining to improve pace and style. To stage the overhaul, Academy president Gregory Peck had one person in mind, and Gower, after taking five months to give him an answer, finally agreed to do it gratis provided the show was moved from the Santa Monica Civic Auditorium ("a dreary barn" he dubbed it, to the dismay of the city fathers) to the new Dorothy Chandler Pavilion at the Music Center in downtown

Los Angeles. Peck and Leonard Goldenson of the ABC network concurred, and at once he initiated a series of innovations designed to give the evening the intended lift. In so doing, he "was putting his neck on the line,"[14] risking the ire of the Academy's old guard, who, up to this time, had resisted change.

Because the Chandler had no middle aisle for winners to reach the stage, he added a runway that extended into the house from the center of the apron. A mobile backdrop of panels, mirrors, and rear projections replaced the former setting, which "always used to look like Tara."[15] To host this "very high-price super-intimate revue"[16] with its less formal dress code (black tie instead of white, and no tails) were ten "Friends of Oscar" substituted for perennial emcee Bob Hope, who sighed a "Thank God" when Gower broke the news to him.[17] But when the director advocated eliminating the forecourt activity because "it seemed very Hollywood Boulevard,"[18] the Academy and the Los Angeles Police Department drew the line, insisting that bleachers were necessary to keep in check the 2,000 fans expected to eyeball the stars.[19] No loss. When the evening of April 14, 1969, arrived, the Champion touch was in evidence everywhere.

Beginning outside the Chandler Pavilion with *Oliver*'s Fagin (Ron Moody) and Artful Dodger (Jack Wild) threatening to "pinch one of them golden Oscars" if they did not win, Peck welcomed viewers to the new site of the Awards. The program then moved indoors for a quick introduction of the ten hosts before Sinatra's rendition of "Star," the first of the five nominated songs. While he sang, the cameras panned the auditorium, picking out some of Hollywood's most distinguished female celebrities decked out in their finest.[20] Ingrid Bergman and Sidney Poitier's amusing demonstration of the absurdity of the words to another nominated song, "Chitty Chitty Bang Bang," was followed by a stirring march version of the song performed by the UCLA Marching Band and dancer Paula Kelly, who delivered "the best visual and musical number the Oscar cast had presented in many years."[21]

Champion's ingenuity was also evident in the presentation of the Oscar for best costume design. As Jane Fonda announced the nominees, a pair of dancers entered performing a popular dance to the music of the rock band Soul Rascals, while modeling the outfits worn in the films. *Romeo and Juliet*'s "star-crossed lovers" did the Jerk, *The Lion in Winter*'s Henry II and Eleanor the Frug, and *Star!*'s 1920s fringe-draped showgirls the Shimmy as *Oliver*'s namesake and Fagin bopped about until one of the apes from *Planet of the Apes,* seated in the orchestra pit, bounded to the stage to thrash among the other dancers.[22] Champion also moved the Best Actor Award to the middle of the program, with Burt Lancaster making the announcement of Cliff Robertson's win for *Charly*.[23]

The standing ovation the director received later that evening from his peers at the Governor's Ball was well deserved,[24] for as Joyce Haber reported the following morning, "From the logistics of rearranging props and sets to the simple but brilliant notion of having the presenters memorize the nominees in various categories instead of reading (and frequently mispronouncing) them, Champion proved a champ. The show was new and lent dignity to the new Hollywood."[25] In the end, the magnitude of the show with all its technicalities had been an agreeable task for the director, who remarked, "I really had no trouble. Everyone was a pro. And no one even asked for a change. This is a TV show. You put it on once and that's it. It was a great challenge and I wouldn't do it again. I like to keep jumping around—from shows to pictures to TV."[26]

That is precisely what he did. Following the critically acclaimed Andrews-Belafonte television special that spring, he rejoined Jones and Schmidt to prepare the screenplay for the film version of *I Do! I Do!* he was to direct with Julie Andrews and Dick Van Dyke for United Artists in 1970. (Still having misgivings about the way the musical ended with Agnes and Michael abandoning their home of fifty years to seek a smaller residence elsewhere, he modified his version of the screenplay to have them adopt twelve Korean children and remain in their home!)[27] Scouring the studio's lot, he found a suitable location for his office, decorated it in soft hues of beige and gray, and then went to work drafting a production schedule and preparing the shooting sequences.[28]

Marge marked her fiftieth birthday in September 1969, and Gower threw a huge celebration for her that held promise of better days ahead. The spouses had reunited, and Jess, seated next to Gar for the occasion, was especially pleased for them both. "Toward one o'clock," he remembers, "when the candles on the cake had been blown out and the rock combo temporarily silenced, Gower lifted his glass and spoke quietly, ardently, in tribute to Marge. It had been a love affair, he said—was a love affair still."[29]

Along with domesticity, respectability returned to Gower's life. On Sundays, Debbie Reynolds with her children, Carrie and Todd, would arrive at the Champions' home on Cordell Drive to take the family to services at the Bel Air Presbyterian Church. "I used to pick up Marge, the children, and even Gower, who didn't like to go to church," she explains, "because I always thought that everybody needed to have faith. Gower thought that everybody needed to have talent. I didn't get to talk to Jesus about it, or God, but I think both are very, very important."[30] So did Marge, who by now had become an active member of the congregation, responsible for inaugurating a special Sunday liturgy that used alternative forms of worship—multimedia, folk music, and dance—to illustrate a particular theme. The popularity of the twenty-one liturgies she co-authored with former all-American football player Pastor Don Muma and fellow church member Marilee Zdenek author of *The Right Brain Experience,* led to performances in faith communities as diverse as synagogues and Roman Catholic monasteries. This inspired the publication of *Catch the New Wind,* soon the guidebook for the burgeoning liturgical dance movement of the 1970s. Though Gower admired Marge's faith and its creative expression, he continued to remain ill at ease with organized religion (possibly because of his mother's unbending religiosity) and attended services only sporadically.[31] But for Marge, the dance ministry was a prayer answered—a redis-covery of the resourcefulness that had recently helped her win featured roles in the Blake Edwards film *The Party* (1968), *The Swimmer* (1968) with Burt Lancaster, and the TV movie *The Cock-Eyed Cowboys of Calico County* (1969).

Once more Gower was off to New York, this time to ready *A Flea in Her Ear* for its October 3 opening. His previous attempts at non-musical plays—*Hemingway and All Those People, My Mother, My Father and Me,* and *Bascom Barlow*—had failed because of inherent weaknesses or irascible authors. But *A Flea* was a well-made play, a classic farce—ideal for fulfilling his longstanding need for recognition as a director of pure drama, and it already had Taubman's *Times* endorsement. How could it miss?

Reviews were mixed. In the *Times,* Clive Barnes, perhaps easing the sting of his criticism of the choreography in *The Happy Time* a year and a half before, rhap-sodized over how Champion had "directed the proceeding with precisely the right mixture of charm and gusto," expressing admiration for "the general look and feel of the production," its "style" and "class."[32] "This was champagne," he added, "and, with all respect to this California company, champagne that was blissfully not do-mestic."[33] The *Post*'s Richard Watts, Jr., felt quite differently, calling it "shockingly flat and deadly . . . merely sound and fury, signifying nothing in the way of enter-tainment,"[34] and pinned the blame on Champion. "His intention was probably to choreograph the comedy," he observed, "and it might appear an excellent idea. The result, however, was to make the actors show their awareness that they were sup-posed to be funny, and that is the surest way to remove the humor from their an-tics. The fun disappeared, and what was left was a straining for effect."[35] The run was disappointing, and he was soon back in his Los Angeles office preparing to take *I Do! I Do!* before the cameras.

Work progressed well into spring of 1970 when United Artists suddenly dropped the project—a bitter disappointment to the director, whose one and only film, *My Six Loves,* had debuted more than eight years before. Over that time offers had been ample, but for one reason or another, circumstances had never been right. Ulcers prevented his taking on *Birdie,* MGM backed out of *Carnival,* and he turned down *Dolly!* because he thought Barbra Streisand completely wrong for the role. He withdrew from *Goodbye, Mr. Chips* after songwriter-friends Dory and An-dré Previn were replaced by Leslie Bricusse at the request of Rex Harrison, who, after taking over the leading role from Richard Burton, was later replaced by Peter O'Toole. But the recent blow to his film career was eased by the reconciliation with Marge now in full swing.

With his personal life back in order, Gower agreed to accept Merrick's invitation to reunite with *Dolly!* colleagues Herman and Stewart for *One of the Girls,* a musical version of *Some Like It Hot* (1959)—film director Billy Wilder's classic 1920s romp about a pair of male musicians who pose as women in an all-girl band to evade a pack of Chicago mobsters. Merrick had secured the rights to *Fanfares of Love* (1951), the German film on which Wilder and I.A.L. Diamond had drawn, but the rights to their screenplay were held by the Mirisch Company and remained firmly out of his reach. To get the project under way, Stewart agreed to supply an original libretto based on *Fanfares,* and Gower began drafting ideas for the production. In the late summer of 1970, Bob Merrill phoned to ask if he would read his script for a new musical called *Prettybelle* that he and Jule Styne had composed for Angela Lansbury. It was now ready for production, and also in need of a director.

Initially, director Gene Saks, who had steered Lansbury to triumph in *Mame* (1966), had taken on the project at her request following her appearance in the short-lived *Dear World* (1969), a casualty of weak direction.[36] "He invited us to his house in Connecticut to work," Merrill remembered. "After a couple of weeks, I thought we were doing well, but suddenly Gene said he didn't want to do it. Angela was disappointed, but I told her, 'I once had a good experience with Gower Champion.' We sent it to him: he called right back and said, 'I want to do it.'"[37]

"It grabbed me,"[38] Champion later stated. Without a doubt, he found the book for *Prettybelle,* which he read in autumn 1970, "comedically wild" and refreshingly different from scripts received since *The Happy Time,* all of which he had rejected because they were either repeats of what he had done or set in "never-never land"—the fantasy world of the musical itself.[39] *Prettybelle,* in contrast, grabbed him because of its ironic message: the insane attempting the sane, an alcoholic schizophrenic attempting to rectify the atrocities of her deceased husband.[40] Coupled with this was the means he foresaw for visually expressing this message: adapting the techniques and abstractions of avant-garde cinema for the musical stage. This also was what had first roused the interest of the show's librettist-lyricist.[41]

After the failure of his *Henry, Sweet Henry* in 1967, Merrill returned to the West Coast to do some film writing. "I was looking for a novel that could be adapted for the screen," he said, "and found *Prettybelle* in the library. I was suddenly smitten with the idea of it becoming a musical."[42] So was his *Funny Girl* (1964) collaborator, composer Jule Styne. Together, they approached Lansbury, who took to their vision of an intimate show for a small theatre and instantly accepted their offer to play the title role, which she found intriguing. "It's a charming study of a woman's dilemma and how she decides to solve it," she explained. "I would say Prettybelle is a bit of every woman in the South. Her problems sum up a lot of situations women must feel . . . [She] behaves in many curious, funny and delightful ways."[43] Both star and creators agreed to receive reduced pay for their work out of devotion to this unique experiment with its mature material that could stretch the bounds of musical theatre.[44] Alcoholism, schizophrenia, bigotry, and revenge—the stuff of Jean Arnold's sardonic *Prettybelle: A Lively Tale of Rape and Resurrection* (1970)— were likewise echoed in Merrill's darkly comic, unapologetic, and unrestrained adaptation.

As a folk singer (Michael Jason) croons the melancholy title ballad that introduces the heroine, the Piciyumi State Asylum of Louisiana and its most controversial patient, Prettybelle Sweet, widow of the late Sheriff Leroy Sweet (Mark Dawson), appear. Directly, Prettybelle reveals that she is an alcoholic schizophrenic who has chosen to make the best of her confinement by writing her memoir, *Rape and Resurrection,* which she hopes to sell to the *Piciyumi Gazette* as a newspaper series. She begins to narrate the events that have led to her hospitalization—a form of therapy unfolding in stream-of-consciousness fashion with the audience as analyst. The life of this genteel, somewhat madcap, small-town Southern belle has been plagued with trouble. The trauma of her precarious mental state and husband's sudden death is soon deepened by the revelation (via flashback) that Leroy was a brutal bigot who took pleasure in murdering black activists, terrorizing Mexican migrants, and carousing with New Orleans poon (prostitutes). Finally, there is Prettybelle's dysfunctional family—her senile, sex-starved mother-in-law (Charlotte Rae) and unattractive, obese daughter, Lovey (Renee Lippin).

To expiate Leroy's atrocities, Prettybelle first sends personal checks to the National Association for the Advancement of Colored People (NAACP), then, prompted by a *Reader's Digest* article, consents to a series of "therapeutic rapes" by a Mexican delivery boy (Bert Michaels), a Jewish psychiatrist (Richard Kuss), and finally, a white liberal lawyer (Peter Lombard) with whom she falls in love. Word of her NAACP checks and taboo trysts reaches her white supremacist neighbors, who pelt her and her house with garbage. A race riot ensues and shots are fired, causing Prettybelle to relive the day when her thirteen-year-old son, John (Dean Crane Jr.), now likewise institutionalized, shot three men resembling his father while concealed in a tree on Lapeer Street. The recollection fades and she decides to plot another remedial liaison—this one with Willie Thomas (Joe Morton), her black houseboy—which is suddenly interrupted by the appearance of Leroy's ghost. Incensed by his attempt to intimidate her, she takes revenge on Leroy by exposing his corrupt deputy and best friend, Ray Schaeffer (Jon Cypher), who once seduced her.

Accusing him of rape, she takes refuge in the asylum where, after the successful publication of her memoirs, she chooses to remain to help others pen their stories.

Producer Alexander H. Cohen, a renowned force in New York and London theatre (*The Homecoming, At the Drop of a Hat, Beyond the Fringe, The Price, 1776,* and the annual *Tony Awards* TV specials), now became part of the mix following duties on *Dear World.* With his addition, however, Merrill's idea of a small production quickly vanished. Cohen saw no reason why the show could not be bigger or the creators receive full royalties. "If you have Angela and Gower," he told Merrill, "ticket buyers are expecting a big show."[45] The writer never intended to go commercial. He thought of *Prettybelle* as a labor of love; after all, no one working on it was exactly poor.[46]

Cohen and Champion were good friends. In 1966, Gower's out-of-town doctoring helped ready Cohen's ailing production of *A Time for Singing* for Broadway, but their relationship actually dated back twenty years before, when as producer and choreographer they joined forces on *Make a Wish.*[47] Even then, Cohen realized that if Gower had been in charge from the start, the struggling show might have been the smash that most of his later productions—all large-scale—had been. Cohen's insistence, therefore, that *Prettybelle* be a big show made sense, but not to the director, who had something quite different in mind. "Up to this point," says dance captain Bert Michaels, who also played Mexican delivery boy Jesus, "Gower was known for glitz and glamour, but he wanted to show that he was a more versatile director and had other things in him. He wanted this one to break away to express other parts in him that weren't fulfilled in the glitzy Gower musicals, and this was a *very* dark piece, especially at this juncture in our history."[48] This "no-glitz approach" was precisely what was reflected in the set he commissioned from scenic designer Oliver Smith: a permanent unit platform with curved ramps and stairways that could accommodate the forward-backward movement of the story and his twenty-seven-member, smaller-than-usual cast.

"I remember that the design for *Prettybelle* was a unit set," Smith recalled, "and had to take on a lot of different aspects—indoor-outdoor thing—and wasn't too complex. It had many levels and Gower and I worked on it together very much like we did for *I Do! I Do!* He'd tell me what he wanted, and I'd draw and change."[49] The result was a flexible environment perfect for developing the cutting-edge staging he had in mind. By jumping to and fro in time through rapidly moving scenes backed by Nananne Percher's tight area lighting and Ann Roth's crisp and colorful costuming, he aimed to widen the musical's scope at a time when *No, No, Nanette,* "the New 1925 Musical," was engulfing Broadway in a wave of nostalgia. *Prettybelle,* by contrast, would be the New 1971 Musical, "a Gower Champion Production" conceived, directed, and choreographed by him as an avant-garde stage work—the concept that would inform its every aspect.

A chief component of the avant-garde cinema of the day was the visual depiction of the harsh truth about life, capturing the dark, grimy underside of reality as only the camera could with little or no reliance on dialogue. Like the directors of these works (Bergman, Fellini, Antonioni), whom he admired, Champion had sought to minimize dialogue in this show by telling the story visually through choreographed staging and dance. But harnessing the conventions of musical theatre in service of a decidedly caustic plot was something altogether different. For the generally triumphant showman who only eight years before had carped about angry young writers flooding Broadway and Hollywood with "their narcissistic nonsense, defeatist philosophy, four-letter word vocabularies . . . and sophomoric, overlabored, trashy output,"[50] *Prettybelle* would mark a radical departure from the Hollywood "sweetness-and-light" approach that had largely defined his film and stage work, precisely why he found the idea of creating an avant-garde musical so intriguing.

Up to this time, his works, notwithstanding their commercial and artistic merit, had had nothing significant to say—not unusual, perhaps, considering that they were musicals. But now, the political, the intellectual, and the literary were finding a place in the musical as never before, chiefly due to director Harold Prince, whose *Cabaret* (1966) and *Company* (1970) had succeeded in exposing the dark side of life and commenting upon it aptly. Champion's chief strength, on the other hand, had been to reconstitute the musical, tired as it was, and make it soar to the heights on the adrenaline boost he gave it. Yet for all its invention, his work had been pure entertainment, and that was no longer enough. Now he had to *say* something, too. *Prettybelle* was the perfect platform because there was valor in its rage against brutality and substance in its compassion for gentle people, for the Prettybelles of life. If he could devise techniques as distinctive as those of avant-garde cinema to tell the story visually with nominal dialogue, he could launch the Broadway musical— and his career—in a whole new direction.

Something else about *Prettybelle* grabbed him. With the sexual revolution now in full swing, the face of Broadway had changed radically since the arrival of *Hair* on April 29, 1968, just three and a half months after the opening of *The Happy Time*. Provocative language, situations, and actions (gratuitous nudity) were now in vogue, exploited more for the sake of controversy than for humor or interest. Shock for shock's sake was in and with it, the deconstruction of the integrated musical through loosely episodic or almost formless plots that stressed imaginative, dazzling staging over concise librettos and elemental integration. Staging, rather than story, was defining the musical—indeed, a movement he inadvertently helped set in motion with *The Happy Time*. In light of these trends, the continuously choreographed staging, dramatic flashbacks, and psychological symbolism he envisioned for *Prettybelle* seemed ideally suited to Merrill's shocking episodic script and bawdy lyrics and Styne's diverse, satirical score.

A few days after Christmas 1970 in a conference room atop the Rivera Theatre at Broadway and 97th Street, Champion began the first rehearsal by apologizing to the huddled group of overcoat-clad performers before him for the lack of heat. "I was here three times before deciding whether to use this theatre, and each time it was warm," he told the cast, who responded with good-natured chuckles and applause.[51] Cohen, in turn, urged everybody to take the flu shots the management was offering to preserve the health of the company in the weeks ahead. Then the process of fleshing out *Prettybelle* unfolded, with the director calling attention to the $3,000, wood-framed, five-tiered working replica of the set that filled the stage of the building's rooftop playhouse.

"The script you now have," he continued, "already has some changes. But I would advise you to work with a loose-leaf binder since there will be additional changes. But we think we will have a tight script."[52] In the days ahead, assembling a tight script would prove an elusive task as he struggled to animate the stark but raucous tale with staging as far-reaching as his vantage point from the center of the house on the specially built rehearsal ramp that extended down the aisle around the pit and onto the stage.[53] This position provided a vast periphery from which he could expand the plot through action in preparation for the five-week run at Boston's Shubert Theatre to begin February 1. There he would further hone the show prior to its New York opening, slated for March 15 at the Majestic Theatre. Until then, rehearsals would be conducted behind closed doors with no one but the cast admitted, lest someone peer over his shoulder and judge his work before completion. Merrill and Styne resented the restriction, but reluctantly accepted it.[54] Cohen, though he quickly tired of Gower's hard-to-get tactics, kept his rage in check pending results.

As rehearsals progressed, book problems surfaced. "The story was very weird, very strange," observed music director Peter Howard. "Basically, the story was a very simple one, and I think Gower was trying to expand it. It probably had the makings for a one-act musical, but he had some innovative things in it. In a way, I think he was trying to make a statement totally opposite *Dolly!* or any of his previous shows."[55] Gower went to work composing his statement, drawing upon Styne and Merrill's unconventional contemporary-sounding score with its mix of folk ("Prettybelle"), Dixieland ("You Ain't Hurtin' Your Ole Lady None"), patter

("Manic Depressives"), honky-tonk ("When I'm Drunk I'm Beautiful"), and romantic ("I Met a Man") numbers to produce some very resourceful staging.

He put together a real showstopper in the satiric "I Never Did Imagine." While singing the praises of a *Reader's Digest* article on therapeutic rape, Lansbury and Mexican delivery boy Michaels hilariously demonstrated the benefits by way of their riotous kitchen fandango. At times, Champion had the uppermost reaches of the towering set throb with the bumping and grinding of wild half-naked women sporting tangled hair or Afros: extensions of the heroine's unconscious that suddenly appeared, then vanished. By way of strategically placed choreographed flashbacks, he revealed the extent of the brutality of Sheriff Leroy Sweet and partner Ray Schaeffer. The first followed "You Ain't Hurtin' Your Ole Lady None," in which the villains and their cronies (Igors Gavon, Robert Karl, and Jan Leighton) boarded Leroy's station wagon for a "poon safari" boasting of the beer-swigging revelry they kept hidden from their wives and children. They arrived at a go-go dive where Ray replied sadistically to the enticements of a topless dancer by drawing a switchblade from his pocket and slashing an "S" for slut on her breast. Later, the same pack of rednecks entered a pool hall, where this time Leroy taunted a Mexican patron (Chad Block), killed him with a pool stick, and, with the help of the gang, disposed of his corpse by tossing it over a bridge. Finally, there was a bizarre tragicomic ballet that fused pathos with violence as the young boy with the rifle in the tree targeted men resembling his father and claimed them as victims one by one. It was a study in the absurdity of trying to coax surrender from a child oblivious to the gravity of his play.

"It was the type of number," states Robert Karl, who played one of the deputies, "that worked in reverse. If it worked, there shouldn't be any applause. If it got applause, then you knew it wasn't dramatic enough, that it wasn't working. And it was done, of course, without dialogue. There was no dancing. It wasn't a dance number, per se; there was just movement—dramatic movement."[56] The ballet began with thirteen-year-old John Sweet (Dean Crane Jr.), son of Prettybelle and the sheriff, receiving the gift of a rifle from his father. Leroy attempts to teach John how to shoot animals and fails. The boy is repelled by the lesson and his father's delight in the kill. They argue bitterly, and in protest John runs from Leroy, concealing himself in a tree on Lapeer Street where he fires on three deputies resembling his father (Chad Block, Robert Karl, and Joe Nilan). "The whole thing was to get the gun away from him," states Karl. "We had a basketball to distract him and worked off all the levels of the set with it, passing it around while moving all around. We used the whole stage with the ball, trying to get closer and closer to him so we could grab the gun. And it was all part of the [show's] plot."[57] Finally, one deputy produces a yellow balloon on a stick and, while slowly luring the boy's attention to it, eases closer and closer toward him. Now only an arm's length from the boy, the deputy extends the balloon to him. He reaches out to take it, but quickly reconsiders, firing the gun and popping the balloon. Frightened, he drops the gun. In an instant the standoff ends as the deputies gently take him into custody, lead him to Prettybelle for a final embrace, and then off to the asylum.[58]

As her son was led off and she took his place in the branches, Lansbury profoundly captured the shock of his violence with "I'm in a Tree," in which she regressed from a middle-aged woman into a timid adolescent girl. "Gosh, it was incredible," recalls Michaels. "I was no more than fifteen feet away from her offstage when she was doing this number. I looked at her and she was seventeen. I can't tell you *how* she did that magic, but she *did* it. No makeup. No lighting. Nothing. You believed she was seventeen. She just *tore* your heart out. What an incredible talent!"[59] Lansbury had equally marvelous moments like "The No-Tell Motel," a rouser with the male chorus in which she jumped in and out of scene as participant and commentator; the affecting "To a Small Degree"; and the high-kicking eleven-o'clocker "When I'm Drunk, I'm Beautiful." Clearly this was not *Till the Clouds Roll By,* the MGM musical in which she and Gower had appeared almost twenty-five years before. *Prettybelle* had a different set of assets—all calculated by the director to unfold nonstop without the slightest break for applause. But what was it saying?

The opening night audience couldn't have cared less, so angered were they by the show's content. Clearly, Boston was not the place to open an unconventional musical like this one. "What I remember most," acknowledged Merrill, "was that first-night Boston Theatre Guild audience hearing the four-letter words and those old ladies hobbling up the aisles."[60] Lansbury gave a electrifying performance in a role that first nighters found totally unsympathetic, especially when Act I climaxed with a race riot in which she was pelted with garbage from the fly gallery. "Angela is a beloved musical artist," noted Smith. "People just don't want their artists pelted with garbage, and the audience absolutely resented every moment of it and just booed and hissed and carried on. It was just so awful!"[61] The response was especially devastating to the star, who later observed: "I really thought we had something big in *Prettybelle,* a biting musical about the South, rednecks, and magnolia blossoms, plus Gower Champion. When you are in a project like that, you get so immersed in it that you don't realize you are going too far. We just didn't realize how far out we were."[62]

The critics were as derisive as the audience. *Prettybelle* "is pretty bad," quipped Kevin Kelly; "a collection of ethnic slams and four-letter words," snapped *Variety*; "a kind of sick cartoon," cracked Roderick Nordell.[63] "It wants to please," added Samuel Hirsch, "but can't quite make up its mind exactly how to go about it."[64]

Champion's statement was awash in the wave of avant-garde staging he had let loose. As Kelly noted, "Now what is being tried here is a musical with something to tell us, . . . but what are we being told? Will the South rise again through the liberated fantasies of a Prettybelle? Is that the hope there is? If that's the message, or part of it, it comes to us sideways and spurious."[65] Only Elliot Norton, the dean of the country's drama critics, while admitting that *Prettybelle* was "not a pretty story," recognized the show's potential, countering in defense: "If Gower Champion, as director, can bring it into sharp focus and give it a little more muscle in the next three or four weeks, this bold new show at the Shubert could become a memorable American musical play. It could and it should."[66] So confident was Norton of *Prettybelle*'s merit that he began to attend rehearsals, contributing his expertise to ensure the show's success. "He re-reviewed it," Merrill remembered, "saying this was something ground-breaking, a new pioneering of what musical theatre should be, and I hope they succeed."[67]

The innovation was due in no small part to the inventiveness of the actors. Norton described Lansbury's Prettybelle as "surely the most extraordinary performance she has ever given and one of the richest, most artful and understanding some of us have ever seen in any show of the kind. She is absolutely magnificent."[68] Mark Dawson's burly and belligerent ghost of a sheriff was excellent and Jon Cypher's Ray Schaeffer fittingly villainous.[69] Peter Lombard did well as Mason Miller, the disingenuous white liberal lawyer.[70] As senile sex-starved Mother Sweet, Charlotte Rae maintained the kind of equilibrium between lampoon and character that the show largely lacked, while Renee Lippin, as her granddaughter Lovey, was perfectly repulsive and unhappy.[71] Bert Michaels's spry Mexican delivery boy savored every ounce of his wayward pleasure, and Michael Jason sang the folk song theme with sensitivity.[72]

Days later Jess arrived in Boston to visit Gar and take in his latest work, which he found to be a real shocker so unlike his ever impeccably dressed and barbered friend. "Nothing about that show seemed 'Gower,' " he observed. "I thought it was ugly. Angela Lansbury was extraordinary. She spent most of her time in an ivory-colored satin slip and high heels. It was a cagey performance and she was marvelous. But the show was ugly!"[73] Like the critics, Jess could find no value behind the dark, convulsive staging that seemed more Bob Fosse than Gower Champion. However, unlike the coarseness in Fosse's shows, *Prettybelle*'s seemed baseless. "If you're going to be ugly," notes Jess, "then it's got to have a purpose. I couldn't see any purpose for it; this seemed to me to be little more important than graffiti on walls. And yet, the dances were marvelous and it was full of invention. But the figures that kept sweeping across the stage were sleazy. For all the money spent on it, it was sleazy."[74]

Like Norton, Jess was impressed with what Gar was trying to do and anticipated the discussion sure to be part of their reunion after the show that evening. During their conversation back at the hotel, he offered a suggestion, which was welcomed; then, just as he was about to raise another, he was abruptly cut off. "I don't want to talk about it," Gar protested. The admonition failed to cool Jess, who continued to comment eagerly. Gar then turned on him abruptly, exclaiming, "I *said* I don't want to talk about it. Now shut up!" and walked out of the room. "It was like a family quarrel," Jess mused. "Nobody said anything about it. But I had the feeling again I'd been trespassing on property that wasn't mine anymore. I saw the show again and found no way it could be improved or saved."[75]

Once Gower sensed negativity—imagined or real—he recoiled from it instinctively, for he was utterly aware of its power to stifle or, worse, kill the creative force needed to resolve the challenge at hand. In his view, criticism—however well intended—had a dark side with potential for marring the work in progress.[76] For that reason, he shunned it unfailingly, even if it meant alienating friends and collaborators. He was certain he was on the right track with *Prettybelle*. Day by day, the show was revealing itself to be a viable entity with a life of its own. To succeed, he must listen with rapt attention to what it was saying. This was not *Dolly!*, but its antithesis—a radical new work with a peck of troubles that defied the kind of strategic planning he had used so advantageously in Detroit and Washington seven years before. But though he lacked a specific plan, he was never at a loss for ideas, and that, at times, posed difficulty. "The problem with Gower," admits Michaels, "was that he was so darn inventive. He always had something, and it wouldn't work, or part of it would work. A plethora of things would come out of him, and to try to find the one that was going to work, that was Marge. She had that eye for picking the right one that would work."[77]

Gower chose to forge ahead alone, trying forty-two different variations on a new scene or number however time-consuming for him and costly for Cohen, growing more impatient by the minute. As the cast rehearsed changes by day and implemented them onstage by night, Gower dropped Lansbury's "I'm in a Tree" and inserted a new second act opening, "God's Garden," for the chorus of social outcasts helping to clean the debris from Prettybelle's home following the race riot that ended the first act.[78] A refocusing of Joe Morton's "Give Me a Share in America," the mock-patriotic protest he sang as Prettybelle's houseboy, and the completion of "Back from the Great Beyond," the big production number marking Mark Dawson's entrance as Leroy, were also in the works.[79] Despite Gower's insistence on trying every idea, progress was being made. Still, there was one other factor slowing the completion of *Prettybelle*.

Next to the Shubert was a hotel with a ballroom that served as a rehearsal hall during the run. There, Champion gave Michaels carte blanche to attend all rehearsals. The performer, also an aspiring director-choreographer himself, was learning from Gower, studying his methodology and appreciating his efforts, not judging him. Once, after a long work session on a particular number that required him to start from scratch several times, Gower picked up a chair, threw it across the ballroom, and started swearing at Styne and Merrill—mostly at Styne. Afterward he came over to Michaels and said, "Whenever something that you work and work on doesn't work, it's because it's *wrong*. Your interior voice is giving you that, but not telling you how it got there. It's saying, 'Don't do that.' And you say, 'Why shouldn't I?' It's already gone through the process of why you shouldn't."[80] Gower knew the number was wrong for the scene on which he was working, but asking the easily bugged Styne to do a rewrite was an ordeal.[81] With no other choice, he ignored his intuition and forged ahead, only to waste time and effort on a number that had been wrong from the start.

Remarkably, as a consequence of Norton's positive press and Gower's ceaseless tinkering, audiences were now doing an about-face; even numbers that had previously generated only a halfhearted response were raising the roof.[82] Indeed, it seemed possible that both *Prettybelle* and *Follies*—the newest Prince-directed show, around the corner at the Colonial Theatre that likewise treated reality, fantasy, and self-delusion—might be contenders for Best Musical that year. But *Follies* had glitz and glamour; *Prettybelle* did not, and Champion was determined to keep it that way whatever the cost. At last, audiences were responding favorably to the avant-garde nature of the show, and the cast was behind him one hundred percent. Another couple of weeks in another town far from uptight Boston would do it—provided he could accelerate changes, get Merrill and Styne to deliver the goods, and Cohen to extend the tryout.[83] But the star remained wary. "I'm not going to let them bring it into New York unless it's fixed,"[84] confided Lansbury to her dresser, Dolores Childers. Meanwhile, an exasperated Cohen fumed over the turn the show was taking as Gower scrambled to finish it.[85]

At length, Marge arrived from the West Coast. *Prettybelle* impressed her at once: "I remember it was innovative. I saw things in *Miss Saigon* that I saw Gower do in *Prettybelle* twenty-some-odd years before. He was really coming into a much more mature way of working. It was *definitely* a New York show. Everybody from out of town who saw it just said, 'Wow! Wait till this gets to New York!' People I really respected. And I couldn't change my feelings about it, either."[86] By March 1, though, Cohen had had enough. After four weeks' worth of performances, he issued a formal press statement declaring: "I have decided that the show is not in shape for Broadway, so I am closing it this Saturday night in Boston."[87] The cast was stunned. The sudden surge in audience support and influx of theatre cognoscenti from New

York, Chicago, and Canada had convinced them that they were on the cusp of a ground-breaking effort. "We thought, 'Okay, Gower's on the right track and we're going to go to the next town,'" Michaels states. "We really thought we had something that was going to come in and electrify New York. Alex freaked out. I think that's what it was. It came out of the blue. *Out of the blue!* That's why we were so shocked. It was an abortion. It was that reprehensible, and that's the way we all felt—that a child was killed."[88]

Cohen's refusal to explain his decision concealed his contempt for the one person whom he held accountable for barring his access and taking things in a direction he did not approve. "He was a dictator and a fascist," he said of Gower years later, "and he had strange sexual alliances. First Marge, then a girl in the show, than a guy in the show. And he wouldn't let anyone into rehearsal, wouldn't even speak to anyone about it."[89] For Cohen, the turning point had come less than twenty-four hours before in a conversation with Merrill. "*I* closed the show," Merrill later declared. "I have always had a conscience about people who invest in the theatre, and told Alex that the best we could hope for was a cult following, and we wouldn't get that at the Majestic. Alex put his arm around me, almost wept, and said, 'You're the most level-headed man in the theatre; you are my brother.' Postscript—I never heard from him again."[90]

After the conference with Merrill, Cohen went backstage to tell Lansbury of his decision; at the news, she threw her arms around his neck in gratitude.[91] "The show wasn't ready for Broadway," she commented months after, "and I'm glad the producer had the sense not to bring it in."[92] Moreover, by now even the civil rights overtones of the story no longer seemed topical. "It was a little late for that," she later reflected, "and we couldn't circumvent the basic horror of the subject. It didn't seem possible to temper it with humor. So we scuttled it."[93] The next day Cohen assembled the production team to relay his decision prior to issuing official notice of the closing. "That's when I really blew my top," Marge declares. "I don't know whether Gower was very pleased or not. But when they were all there, I said, 'How *can* you do this!' It needed another couple of weeks."[94] David Merrick flew in from New York, took one look at the show, and was so thoroughly convinced it deserved a reprieve that he offered to buy it on the spot, but Cohen flatly refused. What if his archrival extended the tryout to another town, and then brought it to Broadway a big hit? Given their mutual scorn for each other, he would be a fool to give Merrick that chance. No. *Prettybelle* was history; case closed.[95]

The shock of the betrayal had greatly angered and hurt Gower. By the week's end, he had retreated to a dressing room within the recesses of the Shubert's backstage, where he vainly worked to pry his show from Cohen's grasp. A knock

sounded, then the voice of the trusted performer with whom he had shared the se
crets of his craft.

"Gower, can I talk to you?" asked Michaels.

"Yeah, Bert. Come on in," he replied.

"Listen. Obviously I have a stake in this, but nowhere near what yours is. So I talked to my cousin, Sidney."

"Sidney? Sidney Michaels? The author? He's a great book writer."

"Well, if you need help . . . No obligation. No nothing. He's on the next train."

"Oh geez. That's so great," responded Gower warmly.

"And if you need money to go on," insisted Michaels, "Tommy Valando, the music producer who does all the big records? He's interested in it."

He smiled faintly. "I don't know if I can manipulate that because Merrick is also interested in it, and that's not going to happen."

A deafening silence pierced the air before Michaels spoke again.

"Gower, the number you gave me? . . . I could never repay you for it."

The response was quizzical, as if to ask, "What are you talking about?"

Then Michaels quickly added, "If there is anything, anything I can do, any plan that I can help you with, you know . . ."

"I'm thinking, Bert." sighed Gower. "I'm thinking."[96]

Try as he might, Champion could not salvage *Prettybelle*. Cohen's obduracy had rendered him powerless, and there was no escaping his first out-of-town closing. All he could do was sit through the remaining performances and wait for the curtain to finally descend on Saturday, March 6, 1971. "The closing was almost a religious ceremony," recalls critic Peter Filichia, "especially during the final moments, when Lansbury sang, 'Prettybelle, Prettybelle,' and could not finish; she just lifted her arm in a what-can-you-do gesture and let it fall."[97] Afterward, columnist Rex Reed drove the weary star back to New York into the dawn, stopping only for gas and to eat fried clams at a Howard Johnson's restaurant at three o'clock in the morning.[98] "I always figure that it was the material's failure, not mine," she later reflected. "I know that Hal [Prince] thought that *Prettybelle* was some of the best work I had ever done in the theatre, and it probably was, but it was just an unfortunate root idea for a musical."[99] That was not the opinion of the director, who insisted, "I think the show could be fixed. It was Cohen's determination that there was no point in going ahead."[100] And it was Gower's determination never to speak to Cohen again.[101]

FOURTEEN

Confections New and Old

Sugar and *Irene*

1971–1973

After the humiliation of *Prettybelle,* crafting the musical makeover of film director Billy Wilder's farce *Some Like It Hot* (1959) was just what Gower needed to restore his status and just what Merrick needed to generate a smash equal to *Dolly!* Having already struck gold with *Promises, Promises* (1969), derived from another Wilder hit, *The Apartment* (1960), the producer now aimed to make a long run of the even more popular *Hot* by reuniting the *Dolly!* team of Champion, Herman, and Stewart. All three were ideally suited for adapting the Wilder–I. A. L. Diamond screenplay about the misadventures of two male musicians who witness the St. Valentine's Day Massacre, and then dodge a gang of Chicago mobsters by masquerading as female sax and bass players in an all-girl jazz band. The film was a coup permanently etched in the public consciousness thanks to the high jinks of Tony Curtis's Joe/Josephine, Jack Lemmon's Jerry/Daphne, Marilyn Monroe's voluptuous Sugar Kane, who falls for Joe, and Joe E. Brown's Osgood Fielding III, an aging millionaire who woos an ecstatic Daphne. Indeed, this was prime material for Broadway and would have been another Merrick brainstorm, except for one catch—the Mirisch Company, which produced the film, also owned the rights and refused to part with them.

Unfazed, Merrick kept on, convinced the company would eventually give in. He already had the rights to the film's source—*Fanfaren der Liebe (Fanfares of Love),* a 1951 German film adapted from a story by Robert Thören and Manfred Logan that they, in turn, had adapted from a 1935 French film, *Fanfare d'Amour.* So while Gower took on *Prettybelle,* Herman and Stewart moved ahead on turning *Fanfaren* into *One of the Girls.* Frustrating though it was not to have the vastly superior Wilder-Diamond screenplay, it seemed possible that *Fanfaren,* with its more than casual resemblance to *Hot,* might provide as much fodder for Broadway as it had for Hollywood.

Set in postwar Germany before the rise of the Berlin Wall, *Fanfaren* comically exposed the underside of the country's recovering showbiz industry and mocked the national fascination with American Big Band music by focusing on Hans and Peter (Dieter Borsche and Georg Thomalla), two unemployed musicians. Desperate for bookings as pianist and bass player, they pose as Hungarian Gypsies and even black jazz musicians before boarding the night train to Ingolstadt as Hansi and Petri for a gig at a classy hotel with the Alpine Violets All-Woman Band. Although falling in love with band members Gabi and Lydia complicates their scheme, they keep their ruse intact by scrambling in and out of drag as the occasion demands. In between, Hansi evades the advances of an old man and Peter is roughed up by a hoodlum on whom he later takes revenge as Petri. Gabi is soon wise to the boys' hoax, but plays along until they are forced to reveal their true identities just as the band lands a recording session with a major record producer.[1]

For *One of the Girls,* Stewart moved the action to 1945 postwar America, where Eddie and Harrison, two GI musicians gone AWOL, ditch military police in New York by boarding a train for Chicago as bass Harriet and tenor sax Edna in Dixie Trotter's All-Girl Band via their slimy agent Stanley Wezelle (a character Gower cut from *Birdie*). In the process, they befriend fellow band member Precious Lane, with whom they form an Andrews Sisters–type act that gets booked for a birthday party at the Newport, Rhode Island, home of Old Man Mellonbach, the world's richest person. There the boys inadvertently capture a master German spy, assumed dead but actually living in the United States as capo mafioso Antonio "Gumdrops" DeLuca. Herman's contributions included three numbers later rewritten for *Mack and Mabel*—"This Time," "The Lights of Broadway" ("When Mabel Comes in the Room"), and "One of the Girls" ("Hundreds of Girls").[2]

When Gower returned to the project after *Prettybelle* in spring 1971, it was clearly in distress. If Merrick's dream team used even an iota of the plot—especially Monroe's Sugar Kane persona—legal consequences were guaranteed. As Herman wrote to Stewart, "Gower told me that one of the Mirisches told him there'd be trouble if any essence of the Monroe character or any of the Wilder film were used. How can I work on anything with that kind of fear of infringement hanging over me?"[3] No one could. Earlier, the same hazard had forced *Mame* and *Sweet Charity* producers Fryer, Carr, and Harris to drop plans for their version, *Doing It All for Sugar.*[4]

After reading the first draft, Merrick tore into Stewart for abandoning the 1920s milieu. He demanded a rewrite and then flew to Los Angeles for the opening of Herman's *Mame,* where he let it circulate that he was losing interest in the project because the authors had not done a good job.[5] If he was that negative, figured Herman and Stewart, then it was certain death to continue working. Under his glare and that of *Hot*'s owners, things could only get worse, and anything less than the plot of the popular film itself was sure to disappoint. Then, to everyone's amazement, Merrick came up with the rights, but it was too late. Herman and Stewart had resigned. *One of the Girls* now became *Nobody's Perfect* (a play on the final line of *Hot*'s script, which also gave away its biggest laugh).

As news of his rights conquest spread through Broadway's grapevine, Merrick briefly entertained director-choreographer Michael Bennett's pitch for an all-black version with Diana Ross as Sugar Kane and Flip Wilson as Daphne before finally opting to stay with Champion, who, despite the exit of Herman and Stewart, had remained committed.[6] In better times, Gower would likely have stood with his friends in protest of their poor treatment, but the calamities of *The Happy Time* and *Prettybelle* left him no choice but to stick with Merrick, who was all too aware of his shaky footing. Reshuffling the deck, they came up with George Axelrod, who had penned stage and screen hits like *The Seven Year Itch, Will Success Spoil Rock Hunter?, Breakfast at Tiffany's,* and *The Manchurian Candidate.* Nearly twenty-three years before, he and Gower had worked together on *Small Wonder,* and that rapport provided a foundation for this project. But when Merrick proposed Styne and Merrill for the score, Gower protested furiously. Moreover, the songwriters themselves were just as mulish about working with him, but after extensive negotiations, all three agreed to put aside their *Prettybelle* differences and move forward—if ever so cautiously—because each was desperate for a hit.[7] Both Styne and Merrill had had their last in 1964 with *Funny Girl* (their first collaboration, thanks to Merrick who had teamed them before withdrawing early on[8]), and Gower in 1966 with *I Do! I Do!* Even Axelrod was overdue for one.

By the beginning of October 1971, *Nobody's Perfect* was only ten weeks from the first rehearsal when Gower prevailed upon an old acquaintance to "do something about *Some Like It Hot.*"[9] Peter Stone—librettist for *1776,* the Tony Award–winning Best Musical of 1969—agreed on condition they return to *Hot*'s plot, hardly used by Axelrod. "I like George and I like his writing," Stone later commented. "It turned out he'd made the changes at Gower's instigation. As was always the case with Gower, he leads you someplace, he gets to a point where he hates it, and he turns on it. I came in and said, 'Why try to improve on what's already terrific?'"[10] This was sound advice from the practiced librettist *(Kean, Skyscraper, Two by Two)* and screenwriter *(Charade, Mirage, Arabesque),* who also suggested a new title for the $750,000 venture—*Sugar.* The first musical to premiere at the Opera House of Washington's new Kennedy Center, it would move to Toronto's O'Keefe before arriving at the Majestic on Broadway.[11]

In translating an unforgettable movie into a stage musical, Champion, Stone, Styne, and Merrill could not disappoint audiences by failing to deliver the film's best remembered moments, which included the St. Valentine's Day massacre; the all-girl band; Jerry, Joe, and Sugar's romps on the train and at the beach; Osgood's worship of Jerry-as-Daphne; and especially his famous last line in response to her revelation that she is a man—"Well, nobody's perfect." But perfect was what the casting had to be, and Gower was determined to find a Jerry, Joe, and Sugar who together could deliver the kind of triangular symmetry that had made the film performances so delightful. By November, he had his trio—Robert Morse, Tony Roberts, and Elaine Joyce.

Morse first landed on Broadway in the original production of *The Matchmaker,* followed by roles in Styne's *Say, Darling* and Merrill's *Take Me Along.* A skilled performer and gifted comic, he was best known for his Tony Award turn as the misleading but lovable ladder-climbing executive of *How to Succeed in Business Without Really Trying.* As *Sugar's* Jerry, he was following in the line of such distinguished leading ladies of the theatre as Bert Lahr in *The Beauty Part* and Ray Bolger in *Where's Charley?*[12] His costar, Tony Roberts, won the part of Joe after a score of first-rate performances in plays *(Barefoot in the Park, Don't Drink the Water, Play It Again, Sam)* and musicals *(How Now, Dow Jones* and *Promises, Promises).* With actress of preference Joey Heatherton unavailable, Broadway newcomer Elaine Joyce, wife of actor Bobby Van, was selected to play Sugar Kane after a series of television *(Hawaii Five-O, The Carol Burnett Show, Here Come the Brides)* and film roles *(Bye Bye Birdie, Christine, Such Good Friends).*[13] From *The Roar of the Greasepaint, the Smell of the Crowd* came Cyril Ritchard to take on aging playboy Sir Osgood Fielding. A highly regarded actor both here and in London, his career spanned the classics, opera, and musicals, like the Mary Martin *Peter Pan,* in which he played the most beloved of all Captain Hooks. Singer Johnny Desmond, another *Say, Darling* and *Funny Girl* alumnus, signed on as mobster Spats Palazzo, Sheila Smith left her featured role in *Follies* to lead the Society Syncopators All-Girl Band as Sweet Sue, and Alan Kass became Bienstock, the band's harried manager. Also among the twenty-eight-member cast were Ted Beniades in the dual roles of booking agent Poliakoff and rival gang leader Little Bonaparte, Connie Day as Poliakoff's secretary Nellie, and associate choreographer Bert Michaels as Bonaparte's lieutenant Joker Gomez (a role later cut).

Creators, cast, and crew gathered for the first rehearsal on the afternoon of December 13, 1971, in the studios George Balanchine had built along upper Broadway years before. "Well," declared Bobby Morse, "Alexis Smith will have to move over if she thinks she's going to get a Tony for the best female musical performance of the year [in *Follies*]. I don't know about you, but I'm going after that category. And after all the shows I've played in as a man, never, never, never have I been so fussed over by the costumers, make up people and wig experts as I have for this. And girls get their costumes paid for."[14] Ritchard added, "I am a far cry from Joe

E. Brown, but I am getting a title (Sir Osgood) AND I'm going to tie up Bobby for our scenes together."[15] Conspicuous by his absence was Merrick, who earlier that day expressed complete confidence in his team, remarking, "Oh, I don't think I need go. They know what they're doing."[16] There was the read-through by Stone, Styne, and Merrill with the cast listening dutifully, the usual measurements for costumes, and, within twenty-four hours, Gower's ironclad rule that barred everyone but performers from rehearsals. To enforce it, he had a revolving red police light installed outside the studio that when lit warned "Keep Out." The authors bristled. "I can smell trouble ahead for me," Styne told Merrill.[17] Until the light was off, Gower was inaccessible, secure inside with the cast, arranger Philip Lang, and music director Elliot Lawrence. Meanwhile, Stone, Styne, and Merrill just waited. Merrick, too.

On one occasion the producer was seated outside the studio bathed in the red glow of the warning light as Bert Michaels arrived to enter. "How come *you* get to go in?" grumbled Merrick. "He likes me, David," replied the associate choreographer, smiling brightly before closing the door behind him.[18] Champion's tight rule likewise exasperated Merrill. "Gower is the type of man who will take a show away from you," he once declared. "He'll battle producers, actors; anyone. He'll disappear for two days to get his way. He's perfectly capable of taking David Merrick for a fall. Example—'All right, fellows, if you have something to say, let's have breakfast at eight o'clock.' The trouble is that Gower doesn't show. He doesn't intend to show."[19]

Was Gower's by now legendary control any different from how other director-choreographers worked? "I have to tell you Agnes de Mille wouldn't have anybody around when she was choreographing," explains producer Biff Liff, also Merrick's production supervisor on *Sugar*. "I've seen this happen with Michael Bennett. They wanted their freedom to be able to do things, and try things, and the authors often felt put out by it. So it was always that way and that was Gower's way. He was a very private man. I mean, *private*. He was also a very creative guy who wanted to create by himself. Look at how successful he was! So maybe he was right."[20]

Inside the rehearsal studio Champion was creating, but not with his customary clarity. The overriding idea, the concept crucial to framing the production, had been dealt a severe blow. Originally, the show was to open with the closing scene of Greta Garbo's *Camille* (1937), giving the audience the sensation of being in a vast movie palace as the stage show portion of the bill was about to begin.[21] Once the film ended, they would hear the band tuning up and see the pink chiffon curtain descend and the bandstand rise from the stage floor bearing Sweet Sue and her Society Syncopators. The blare of their "brass with class" and the glare of their sequin-spangled shocking pink gowns combined with Sue's energetic conducting and hot sexy dancing would be an unmistakable takeoff on "The Blonde Bombshell of

Rhythm" Ina Ray Hutton and her Melodears, who from 1934 to 1939 created a sensation with their all-girl swing music.[22] Throughout the evening, the remainder of the story would be filtered through similar parodies of 1930s entertainment icons such as Busby Berkeley, Carmen Miranda, and Jeanette MacDonald and Nelson Eddy. It was an era Gower knew well, from movie palaces to Pullman cars. The problem was, he could not get the rights to *Camille*. Without that hook, he was forced to rely on his performers for a sense of style, which he now was having trouble defining. Work on the "look" of the show with eminent costume designer Alvin Colt *(On the Town, Li'l Abner)* was progressing well, but the equally eminent scenic and lighting designer Jo Mielziner *(South Pacific, Death of a Salesman, Gypsy)* had his blue velour-themed scenery, which Gower had approved, roundly vetoed by Merrick, who was insisting on his favorite color—red. In the end the designer, not in the best of health, proposed a compromise that was accepted: a neutral color that he could alter with lighting as the scenes changed. But when the company finally saw the set on the Kennedy Center's Opera House stage just hours before the Washington premiere, they were utterly stupefied.[23]

It was brown—a russet brown—the worst possible color for a comedy made even worse against the red plush interior of the Opera House. "You have to understand," Stone explained, "that Gower worked in utter secrecy and no one saw the drawings for the set. But the set goes up at the Kennedy Center, and it's terribly unattractive and drab. We all looked on in astonishment and said, 'How can you be funny on a brown set? How do you get light and happy on a brown set?' "[24] An enraged Merrick turned on Gower blasting: "I am going to junk every piece of scenery on that stage. It will be redesigned and you will pay for it."[25] He did, but not until Merrick persuaded Robin Wagner to redesign the show on the pretext that Mielziner was not only aware of but also appreciative of his intervention. Astonished to find Wagner in Washington, Mielziner, prevented from setting the lighting, was still greatly relieved—particularly after shouldering the brunt of Merrick's wrath, which now began to assume epic scope.[26]

"The show's a disaster and I'm closing it," Merrick ominously confided to Stone at the final preview performance.[27] The next night the show opened as planned, the bluff doing little to scare anyone into accelerating progress. The reality was that Gower had *Sugar* up and running, but, as the reviews of the January 18, 1972, premiere made plain, it was neither the dazzler Merrick intended for the equally dazzling new Kennedy Center nor the phenomenon with which he planned to mesmerize Broadway. The program listed three numbers and three characters that never appeared—evidence that *Sugar* was very much a show in progress, with Gower's cutting and pasting still under way. Sweet Sue and the Society Syncopators'

"The Girls in the Band," Joe, Jerry, and Nellie's "All You Gotta Do Is Tell Me," and the characters of Nellie, Poliakoff, and Little Napoleon never materialized.[28]

Still, potential abounded in the sparkling professionalism Gower had crafted into the proceedings, including the opening with Smith as Sweet Sue leading her Society Syncopators in the manner of Ina Ray Hutton. There was also rapid-fire staging with a stop-action raid on a speakeasy concealed as a funeral parlor, Michaels's gangster lieutenant Joker Gomez plunging to his death in a hail of mob bullets for "The Massacre," and "Penniless Bums" Roberts and Morse artfully threading their way to the front of an unemployment line full of starving musicians before reappearing as Josephine and Daphne with their burlesque-inspired "The Beauty That Drives Men Mad." For the Offenbach-like "November Song," Ritchard led a chorus of aging Palm Beach playboys in a riotous wheelchair ballet conducted like an amusement park dodgem ride. In the second act, the priceless Jeanette Mac-Donald and Nelson Eddy parody, "Beautiful Through and Through," had Ritchard, decked in his dashing best, espying a wistful Morse clad in billowy gown, giant floppy hat, and golden tresses. This was capped by Morse's madly adept portrayal of an infatuated young lady that had first-nighters rolling in the aisles.[29] Champion suffused each scene—even ones that hindered the show's general progress—with that splendid dance sense that only his continuously choreographed staging could produce. But there were problems, and a major one was finding an effective way to showcase Desmond and his gangsters.

Before casting the singer, Gower had tried several approaches—even recruiting film Spats George Raft, only to find he was too ill.[30] At length, he hit upon a newsreel sequence that established the law-breaking of the mobsters, but, like the original opening to *Dolly!,* wasted time on pointless exposition. When the thugs finally appeared, they were no more than recycled *Guys and Dolls* types with none of the menacing traits of Raft and his cronies.

"What we need is an old-fashioned machine-gun tap dancer," volunteered Michaels one day during rehearsal.

"What?" countered Gower, staring straight at him.

"A machine-gun tap dancer," he repeated, this time punctuating the idea with a burst of rat-a-tat steps. Michaels danced on, the director's gaze riveted on his feet. Clearly, the wheels were turning in Champion's head. A dancing capo with a band of mobsters, violin cases in tow, who communicate through spurts of machine-gun-like tap might work.

"That's not regular tap dancing," Gower observed.

"No, it's not. It's rhythmics."

"Who can do that kind of stuff?"

"Steve Condos."

"Condos? Where is he?"

"Florida. He works nightclubs. Call the union down there."[31]

It was sound advice. Michaels had studied with Condos and even had performed a nightclub act with him, so their vocabulary was virtually identical. Condos's start in the business was similar to Gower's, too. In the 1930s when Gower was touring the road show circuit with Jeanne and the Wayne King, Eddie Duchin, and Hal Kemp orchestras, Steve and his older brother Nick, now deceased, were doing the same with the Benny Goodman, Duke Ellington, and Jimmy and Tommy Dorsey orchestras as the Condos Brothers. While dazzling vaudeville and Hollywood *(Wake Up and Live, Happy Landing, In the Navy)* with their teamwork, they also insisted on improvising their solos so that each performance was unique and challenging. Since those days, Steve himself had earned nightclub, Broadway *(Heaven on Earth, Say, Darling)*, and international repute as a consummate tap artist with lightning speed, spellbinding rhythm, and spectacular precision.[32]

But despite Michaels's recommendation, Gower hesitated. Finally, Marge coyly nudged, "*That's* the route to go, and if you don't, I'm divorcing you."[33] Three days later Condos's feet had barely hit the floor of the Opera House stage when Gower yelled, "Stop! You're hired." Now he had to figure out how to slowly phase in the dancer and the showstopper he envisioned for him while phasing out Desmond, the singer still waiting for his role to gain heft and a song of his own beyond "Spats-s-s Palazzo," a meager salute by his goons. Until the switch could be made, Condos would lead the gangsters as Desmond's second-in-command. To his credit, Desmond, who could see what was coming, stuck with the show until no longer needed. When Condos finally took over as Spats, Gower wisely gave him the freedom to ad-lib the steps in his solo spot every night. It would be the high point of the new gangster number he was planning to reveal near the end of the Toronto run—"Tear the Town Apart."

Because it relied more on rhythm than melody, "Tear the Town Apart" was not the kind of number Styne was accustomed to writing. "Can't be done. Can't be done," he carped no matter how much Michaels, Condos, Lang, and Gower insisted it could. Only when Michaels finally brought the drummer to the stage to demonstrate the required rhythms did Styne finally capitulate. Even so, he hated the number, but for Gower, it was a conceptual breakthrough and just what the show needed.

The gangsters' initial appearance was calculated to mesmerize: a growing silhouette of weapons and men beneath a skylight above the tops of car stalls in a Chicago garage. In due course, they assumed a kaleidoscopic series of formations, all the while tapping with violin cases in hand. Off-stage the *pow! pow! pow!* of Condos's machine-gun tap rose in intensity until he exploded on the scene in pinstripe suit, white tie, and fedora. At that moment, with the rest of the gangsters still tapping on, the spotlight hit his spats and he drove across the stage declaring, "You gotta find those guys! I want 'em dead! You understand me? I don't care what you gotta do. Just tear the town apart!" Then he pounded out instructions to his hench-men in bursts of improvised precision tap to which they replied in simple rhythms counterpointing his maneuvers. It was a breathtaking feat of skill that kicked every-thing into high gear. When the effect was repeated at key moments throughout the show, it would deliver the exact measure of menace and mayhem needed.[34]

As Gower worked on, Merrick turned to Stone, Styne, and Merrill. Though the score was high among the problems critics cited, he nevertheless targeted Stone for what he deemed undistinguished work. "Three days after the Washington open-ing," Stone remembered, "we're working well, we're all in an up mood, and I'm there with Styne and Merrill and I get told that Merrick's on the phone for me. I say, 'David, how are you?' He says, 'You're fired. Get out of town.' Hangs up. Of course I wasn't fired—my contract didn't allow it."[35] As a lawyer, Merrick knew that pro-ducers could not sack writers without submitting to a laborious legal process. It was far more practical to make things so unbearable for Stone that he would have no choice but to quit. Merrick did his best—planting, in Stone's house seats, play-wright Neil Simon (who averted a clash by handing his revisions of the early part of Act One to Stone before a hasty return to New York), shipping in by special Amtrak rate the entire writing staff of Rowan and Martin's *Laugh-In,* and, in his daily morning invective to the creative staff, singling out Stone as chief cause for the show's mediocrity.[36] The writer stood firm: "Neil Simon came in and wrote a cou-ple of scenes, which were not used. I didn't let them be. I owned the show [the li-bretto], and Merrick could not change a word of it. All he could do was pressure. Neil didn't know I was there. Merrick had told him I had left."[37]

Styne and Merrill were next. They were lodged at the Watergate Hotel at the height of the Nixon White House wiretapping intrigue—the perfect place for Mer-rick to stage his own. Across the street was a Howard Johnson's where the song-writers met daily to commiserate over the latest song Gower had cut from the show by easing their frustration in a comfort food therapy session of pancakes with ice cream, pie à la mode, root beer floats, sundaes, and whipped cream desserts. One of these feeding frenzies came to an abrupt halt one evening when Biff Liff arrived with a message from Merrick. "Stop eating," he advised them. "You're off per diem. I'm not about to tell you that. I didn't see you." Old hands at Merrick's psychologi-cal warfare, they recognized the admonition for what it was: a means of prodding them into doing their best work. The pair smiled shrewdly, then Merrill offered, "Have some ice cream, Biff."[38] These were pros; Liff respected them. But after three days' worth of Merrick's refusals to take their calls, they took an entirely different tone. Without access to the producer, the show would soon grind to a halt. They entreated Liff to arrange a truce.

"David was unhappy about something I can't remember much about," states Liff. "He holed himself up in the Watergate Hotel, and wouldn't talk to anybody. Just stayed there. And it became a big problem because we needed things and he was the only one who could say, 'Okay,' and he wouldn't do anything. He kept saying to me, 'I'm not doing anything until they come to me.' "[39] It was a standoff. Breaking it required the intervention of one person and Gower was not about to be trapped into begging for what the show needed. He told Liff that a meeting was out of the question. Within twenty-four hours, Liff called again, his panic obvious. Unless Champion agreed to meet, no one would be able to do anything. Liff was certain that all Merrick wanted was a meeting. Nothing more. But the producer wanted *Gower* to take the first step.[40] "Gower was pragmatic, practical, and wise enough to forget all of that, and to say, 'Okay.' " Liff adds. "So he called Merrick and they had the meeting. It wasn't but two minutes after that call that Merrick called me and said, 'You see? You see? They finally came to me. They finally came to me.' It just shows all the problems that Gower was able to take care of. He was quite a guy. He had the end in sight all the time."[41]

Far from over, the Merrick-Champion rivalry was about to take a decidedly different turn. One afternoon, Gower returned to rehearsal visibly agitated. When Michaels asked what was wrong, he explained that he had just returned from lunch with Merrick and his *Promises, Promises* director Robert Moore, with whom, he surmised, Merrick had been discussing a new project. During the course of the meal, Merrick suddenly produced the script to *Sugar,* and tossed it across the table to Moore with the order, "Work on this." Moore was utterly dumbfounded. He thought he was being consulted about some problem with the show. Gower's instinct was to punch Merrick out; instead, he rose brusquely and left.[42]

The mishaps of *The Happy Time* and *Prettybelle* had profound consequences, and Gower was oblivious to them. He was truly vulnerable—a fact *Sugar*'s tap-dancing mobsters and wheelchair ballets for elderly playboys could not conceal from Merrick, whose next volley carried an inconceivable ultimatum. No longer could he continue as both director *and* choreographer; it was one or the other. Once he set on doing the choreography, Merrick called in directors Robert Moore and Gene Saks. Days later, when he opted for director, Merrick went in search of other choreographers. Though ultimately Gower remained in both positions, it was at Merrick's pleasure—just to make sure the director-choreographer knew who was in charge.[43]

By the end of the second of its three-week Washington run, *Sugar* had been refined significantly, the result of Gower's round-the-clock work with the cast. With the massacre, speakeasy, and newsreel sequences gone, it now moved quickly from the curtain raiser of the all-girl band to the entry of Joe and Jerry as the band's new members whisked off by the Miami Express seconds before the gangsters' arrival at the station. The actors were in better form, too. Morse and Roberts moved with greater ease through their roles, seeming to improvise business on the spot, and Joyce's Sugar was more subtle and nuanced.[44] Despite these improvements, the show was only beginning to achieve focus. New numbers were still in process and construction of the new set barely begun. Upon completion, the cast would need time to adjust to it. Evidently, *Sugar* would not be ready in time for its February 29 Broadway premiere, so Gower convinced Merrick to extend the tryout.[45] Following Toronto, the company would spend two weeks in Philadelphia and two more in Boston before an April 9 opening in New York.[46] For Merrick, the tour was lucrative—a box office jackpot in every city despite mixed reviews. For Gower, it was a grueling task as he strove to cut, tighten, and improve the show.

"What I saw him cut," says Sheila Smith, "were things that I thought were really wonderful dancewise. I'm an old hoofer from the time I was a kid. I admired his work in all his shows and his own performances, too, but it kept getting less and less. The dancers were doing less and less. He was cutting his better stuff, his best stuff."[47] One case was the "Kooka Rooki Bongo," in which Joyce, Morse, and Roberts popped out of a huge cake to lead the cast in a send-up of Carmen Miranda. Styne and Merrill had written a hysterical song for an equally hysterical bit with Morse in drag as Miranda. In addition, Gower's working experience with "the Brazilian Bombshell" on *Streets of Paris* gave it the perfect note. Still, he was uncomfortable with the idea. "He didn't like it," explains Michaels. "After he put the number on its feet, I was standing nearby. He said, 'All right, Bert, what do you have?' I said, 'You should do that. I think you're on the right track. It's hysterical. And it's gonna stop the show cold.'"[48] Perhaps Gower thought the idea too obvious or unoriginal. (Nearly twenty-two years before, Mickey Rooney had done a similar bit in the film *Strike Up the Band*.) Next to closing night in Washington, he substituted a new finale, "When You Meet a Man in Chicago," with Smith leading Joyce, Morse, Roberts, and the all-girl band as a regulation 1930s chorus line dressed in frock coats, canes, and top hats. It was a subtle, elegant, and delicious commentary on gender-bending from both the male and female perspective.[49]

Merrick meant what he said about scrapping Mielziner's scenery. The show arrived in Toronto with hardly a flat and would continue that way through Philadelphia and Boston. "We had a train and a bandstand," states Smith. "Everything else was velours and scrims with tiny trains all around them. The bandstand looked like sixth graders had constructed it. It was in two pieces that wiggled as they came in from the wings, then bumped when they hit center jiggling all the girls. If it weren't for my clothes, there almost would have been no show because I had really gorgeous beautiful things to wear. Really stunning."[50]

As Merrick summoned a phalanx of show doctors to Toronto and rumors spread that *Sugar's* ills were being diagnosed by everyone from Neil Simon to *Marcus Welby,* Gower spiraled into indecision—unable even to determine whether script revisions should be given to actors before or after they were in makeup. Director Moore arrived to lend a hand, as well as choreographer Saddler. Ritchard's performance was restricted by gout, he and Morse were not getting along, and the girls in Smith's band wanted to go home to their husbands. Dissatisfied more than ever with the book and score, Gower contrived to get Stewart to rewrite Stone's work and Herman to replace Styne and Merrill. Stewart never intervened, but Herman came to Toronto as a favor to Gower, who now was calling on him to "assist" Merrill the way Merrill had assisted him on *Dolly!*[51]

Styne soon learned of the plan and also that Herman was in town at a hotel some distance from the theatre. Figuring the meeting he was to have with Gower later that evening could have only one purpose, he determined to fight his dismissal. He phoned Herman and discussed the show and Champion. Arriving late at Styne's suite because of an earlier meeting with Herman on the other side of town, Gower stormed in quite incensed that the composer had spoken with Herman. Styne admitted he had—and to his lawyers as well.[52] Gower was saddled with him, like it or not.

At length, the severity of Gower's nosebleeds increased and Marge arrived in Philadelphia to help him undertake the unavoidable. Moore worked on the book scenes while Saddler, at Gower's request, choreographed two numbers: "The People in My Life," an interim solo spot for Joyce eventually replaced with "Hey, Why Not!," *Sugar's* dream of marrying her Shell Oil tycoon-boyfriend who is actually Joe. Through it all Merrick kept insisting, "This is it. This is the way we open."[53] For all Merrick's bluster, Gower knew that freezing the show at this point would be disastrous. "Tear the Town Apart" had just gone in and "Sun on My Face," a send-up of Busby Berkeley's "Shuffle Off to Buffalo" from *42nd Street* (1933), was in progress. With them, the remainder of the first act would be fortified considerably. The momentum began to improve along with the reviews in Philadelphia and Boston, and while Merrick's visits became less frequent and malignant, the dread of opening the stage door and finding his trademark homburg hat hanging on the hat tree just inside was more palpable than ever. Everyone cowered when he was in town.

In Boston, Wagner's new set pieces, which used Mielziner's original floor plans to avoid reblocking, gradually replaced the old.[54] The exception was Gower's signature motif—a train that actually traveled across the stage and broke open to reveal the occupants in their Pullman berths. Because it would not be ready until opening night in New York, the old train set remained in the show while a mock-up of the new one was assembled in the ballroom of the Bradford Hotel next door to *Sugar*'s home at the Shubert Theatre. There Gower and the cast rehearsed new staging for the sleeper car sequence and the tongue-in-cheek "Sun on My Face," a ballet of wiggling legs and playful faces popping out between the closed curtains of the berths in various combinations of twos, fours, and sixes—bedlam staged with charm. "The train number went in on our one day off," Smith comments, "our last Sunday in Boston before we came into New York. On opening night at six o'clock, Alan Kass and I had a rehearsal for lines we were singing in the number for the first time. It was an interesting opening because we also didn't have that much time on the new set, which was terribly small, terribly cramped."[55] The opening was interesting in other ways. Earlier that day of April 9, Merrick had contacted every major Broadway producer to discourage their attendance that evening for fear they might "dampen enthusiasm."[56]

Gower arrived at the Majestic escorting Mary Martin on one arm and Ethel Merman on the other. As the lights went down and the curtain rose, he knew *Sugar* was not the show he wanted it to be. The organizing principle of the 1930s showbiz spoofs worked only partially; an unremarkable score and strict adherence to screenplay dialogue compromised fluidity, as did the lack of chemistry among the three leads. Despite a noble attempt, Joyce could not deliver the Monroe magnetism needed to balance the trio. Hence, the emphasis had gone to the men—Morse and Roberts, especially Morse—both hilarious, but worlds from the magic and incandescence Joyce needed to project and Gower needed to infuse into the rest of the production. The result was an unsatisfying hodgepodge of modern musical innovation, like the Expressionistic tap dancing gangsters, and the passé book-and-songs structure of the old-fashioned musical.[57] Beneath such weight *Sugar* could never soar because it was never free to dance, something Gower knew long before the critics.[58]

They were as divided as they had been throughout the tour. "Rarely in show-business history has so much been done by so many for so little,"[59] exclaimed Clive Barnes. Douglas Watt contended that *Sugar* "spends two hours trying to catch up to the movie. It never does. It just winds up breathless."[60] Others, like John Simon, deemed it "the best nonmusical musical I have ever seen. Consider it straight comedy—fast, funny, unassuming—with incidental, or accidental, music, and all is well."[61] Harold Clurman concurred, "The show is well paced, the movement adept. As for the rest—who cares!"[62] That was the popular opinion, too. *Sugar* ran for 505 performances, with audiences relishing the vitality of Gower's choreography,

Morse's masterfully droll clowning, Roberts's youthful joviality, and Joyce's engaging charm. When combined with Ritchard's rakish elegance, Condos's incredible hoofing, and Smith's feistiness, it made for an agreeable evening of fun and spectacle, which Colt's costumes, Wagner's sets, and Martin Aronstein's lighting added to greatly.[63] At the 27th Annual Tony Awards on March 25, 1973, Gower was nominated for best direction and choreography. Bob Fosse won both awards for *Pippin*.

Gower returned to California with Marge. Their reconciliation was fleeting and had failed to rekindle the marriage; as a result, they agreed to divorce. "Out of the twenty-five years that we spent together," Marge explains, "there were three—at the most four—which started to be rocky and then, impossible. No matter how difficult things were, they always got to a better place two or three months from then. We got back onto some kind of footing for a while, but our marriage was beginning to flounder. There was never any mention—any thought—any hint of what eventually happened."[64] The divorce was "catastrophic," adds Jess. "They had it within them to destroy each other."[65] Happily, good sense prevailed and they remained friends to the end of Gower's life.[66]

Back in Topanga Canyon, Gower relaxed from the rigors of *Sugar* by roaming his much-loved span of Malibu Beach. In the works was a film version of *The Fantasticks* for Paramount. The studio put up research money and that summer he, Tom Jones, and Harvey Schmidt spent a month scouting film locations in Sicily.[67] Upon returning, he leisurely worked on the screenplay through the fall. One afternoon in late December 1972 while peacefully basking in the sun with a girl half his age named Debbie, he received a call from another Debbie.[68] Immediately he knew what it meant.

"Gower, I'm in Philadelphia dying," sobbed Debbie Reynolds. "My show stinks, and my life is going down the proverbial john. I need you."

"No, Debbie! You got to be kidding! I'm lying on the beach with the most beautiful girl and just having a wonderful time. I don't need to do this."

"Well, I didn't ask you that. I need you. I am dying! That younger Debbie—you'll have time for her later. Get the old Debbie back on her feet, Gower."[69]

By January 2 he was in frosty Philadelphia to assess the $800,000 musical *Irene* that had been getting equally frosty reviews since beginning its pre-Broadway tour in Toronto just weeks before. It was a revival of the 1919 Harry Tierney–Joseph McCarthy hit that produced "Alice Blue Gown" and recounted James Montgomery's Cinderella tale of modest Irene O'Dare, an upholsterer's assistant from New York's Ninth Avenue, sent to mend cushions at the Long Island estate of Donald Marshall, who falls in love with her despite their class differences.[70]

With a new book by Hugh Wheeler that made the heroine a piano tuner and added a good measure of other Tierney-McCarthy gems, producer Harry Rigby aimed for a hit as stupendous as the previous season's *No, No, Nanette*—the phenomenon that had fueled the comebacks of Ruby Keeler, Patsy Kelly, and Bobby Van; the cash cow he had conceived, initiated, and almost co-produced. Just days before the opening, his co-producer, Cyma Rubin, wife of retired Fabergé founder, president, and multimillionaire Sam Rubin, had herself designated sole producer, then removed Rigby's name from the billing. While his reinstatement underwent arbitration, the nearly destitute Broadway gadfly with big ideas but little business acumen doggedly pressed to make a similar blockbuster of *Irene*.[71] Rigby flew to London and finagled an audience with Sir John Gielgud, stating with characteristic charm, "I have Debbie Reynolds to star in a 1919 show called *Irene,* and I'd love for you to direct it."[72] For Gielgud, acclaimed director of plays and operas who had always longed to take on a musical, the offer was as auspicious as it was for Reynolds, who, after turning Rigby down for two years, finally consented *after* learning Sir John would be steering her Broadway debut.[73] Rigby may not have had a nickel to his name, but he now had Gielgud and Reynolds, and, in short order, backing from co-producers Albert Selden and Jerome Minskoff to get *Irene* on the boards with an equally stellar supporting cast—Ruth Warrick, Patsy Kelly, Billy De Wolfe (later replaced by George S. Irving due to poor health), and Monte Markham.

Yet almost from the first rehearsal, the show was destined for trouble. The plot was much ado about nothing, the director was treating it like *Hamlet,* and the whole thing was becoming a comedy of errors. Sir John worked on the book in one studio while choreographer Peter Gennaro staged the dances in another. At the disastrous Toronto premiere, the lack of integration was obvious to all, especially the critics, who applauded the star, scenery, and costumes, but faulted Gielgud's slow-paced, unfocused direction.[74] Rewrites were needed at once, but librettist Wheeler had to depart for *A Little Night Music,* so *Fiddler on the Roof*'s Joseph Stein stepped in.[75] Four weeks later, the relentless pace of daily rehearsals atop performances caught up with the star—laryngitis. With her understudy unrehearsed and management unwilling to cancel the performance that evening, Reynolds braved an increasingly hostile capacity crowd incensed by a hastily improvised synopsis in which she careened from number to number as Gielgud read her lines and lyrics while the rest of the company scrambled to keep up.[76] In Philadelphia, the chaos grew worse and so did the reviews. Rigby was livid with Sir John. Cuts he had made were restored by the director, whom he impudently chewed out for insubordination.[77] Reynolds, down from 112 to 97 pounds, was frustrated, miserable, and tired.[78] Then the show doctor got her SOS and sped to the rescue.

Rigby was as happy to see his *Make a Wish* choreographer as Reynolds, and offered Gower the show moments after the curtain came down on January 2. With Paramount no longer interested in *The Fantasticks,* Champion was free to accept, but would do so only on condition he be listed as production supervisor; Gielgud's name was to remain as director.[79] The next day Sir John returned to Philadelphia from an overnight stay in New York utterly amazed by the news that television commitments in London had required his being replaced by Gower Champion.[80] His ignominy, however, was at least partially lessened by a payoff of £40,000: "I kept telling them all in rehearsal how very little I knew about musicals, and I suppose that was a mistake because eventually the producers concluded that I was right, and they had better bring in someone who did know a thing or two about how to stage them."[81]

The most delicate scene of *Irene*'s offstage drama played out a few days later at the Bellevue Stratford Hotel where Gower met Sir John to discuss the transition.[82] Though neither had ever spoken with the other before, both were cordial as they focused on how best to word the announcement that Gower was taking over. Then they rode down the elevator together: "I remember thinking: Here's John Gielgud, for God's sake, and we're riding down in the elevator together—and it's not even the big one. Then, I think, I said, 'The theatre can be a terrible place sometimes, though it can be a beautiful place, too.' Neither of us showed any great feeling about what was happening. After all, we're theatre people. These things happen all the time."[83] They did not happen to Sir John, who was quite devastated at being fired for the first time in his life by the very person who had originally cajoled him into taking on the show.

Gower demanded absolute control and got it. Repairs had to be phased in gradually, so four weeks in Washington were added to the tour prior to previews in New York. Right off, he junked several big scenes, including a huge fountain for a dancing waters grand finale that leaked all over the stage and drenched the cast. "It was tacky," Gower concluded. "Ruth Warrick [who played dowager snob Mrs. Marshall] always said it looked like Mrs. Marshall's bidet."[84] In Washington, sweeping changes occurred that clarified focus and improved pace. Comedian Eddie Phillips's character (a foil for Kelly's) was dropped, lengthy dialogue compressed, scene-to-scene transitions accelerated, a new opening staged, and the title song expanded from a duet to a production number.[85] "In six weeks, we opened on Broadway, and it was a smash due to Gower," states Reynolds. "We never stopped rehearsing. We did fourteen endings and ten openings. If he didn't like one, he'd throw it out and start another the next day. He was killing himself. I was killing myself. We both were just raving lunatics to make this work."[86]

Essentially, Gower's doctoring of *Irene* was about converting it into a dazzling showcase designed to perfectly highlight Reynolds—its biggest asset and box office draw. "He was trying to land Debbie as a Broadway star," says dance music arranger Wally Harper. "I thought it was very smart because the show was all over the place.

It wasn't focused on her, and I think his decision was, 'I've got to do everything to land her—to show what she can do.' And he sure did that. Boy, did I learn something. He really understood how to do that without violating anything with the show—how to put her out front."[87]

From the first scene, Reynolds had to be out front with an opening number that packed a punch. After several tries including everyone from Ed Kleban to Sheldon Harnick, Gower turned to Harper one day in rehearsal and simply said, "I know you can write this." The remark surprised and delighted the young arranger: "I was kind of a snot-nosed kid, but Gower was so excellent to me—really supportive and encouraging."[88] With a lyric from Reynolds's friend Jack Lloyd, Harper spent the night on "The World Must Be Bigger Than an Avenue." Finally hitting on something, he played it for Champion and Reynolds, who were elated with the results. Two days later it was in the show.

Not everyone welcomed the show doctor with equal enthusiasm. Reynolds's *Unsinkable Molly Brown* choreographer Peter Gennaro was worried that Gower would want his own stamp on the dancing. Their first rehearsal, Champion put him at ease: "Look, Peter. I want to choreograph just one number—an opening number for Debbie. I think I know how to do it. Everything else, do your thing."[89] Gennaro relaxed. But as Gower's ongoing centering of the show progressed, one other change in the choreography became necessary—a reworking of the title number in the middle of the second act. Gennaro had designed it as a thoroughly charming duet in which the romance between Reynolds and Markham unfolded amidst four upright player pianos in a Ninth Avenue music store. Each time Reynolds fingered the keys of one, it would play a different part of the song that Markham would then sing. Gradually the pianos formed a tinkling quartet that was joined by the orchestra as Reynolds, carried to their tops by Markham, danced with a broom for a cane before jumping into his arms for the finale.[90]

Much as he admired the number, Gower had to cut it. Reynolds was hoping for a big number with the male chorus, and the sensational celebration she received bore all the classic Champion traits. It started with Markham's solo as before, but when finished, he and the orchestral accompaniment faded away as from behind the pianos in different areas of the store the male chorus popped out parts at a time to serenade Reynolds in four-part harmony. The pace accelerated, the orchestra came back in, and they lured her into a dance. She appeased them with a dainty soft shoe, the pace diminished, and then it rapidly picked up again as the men rolled the tinkling pianos one by one downstage, lined them up side to side, and climbed onto the tops, forming a chorus line. Then they lifted her from the stage up to the center of the line to join them for an explosive high-kicking finish.

Irene opened in Washington less than a month after the second inauguration of

President Nixon, who in the midst of the Watergate scandal was rarely given to public appearances. February 22, 1973, was an exception when he, the First Lady, and their daughter Tricia attended that evening's performance. Afterward the President called it "a great show," predicting that it would be "a big hit in New York, perhaps not with New Yorkers, but with the out-of-towners," and praised Reynolds as a "superstar" who showed "real range" as a performer.[91] Nixon's presidential publicity was the kind money could not buy. The next morning, his review made every paper and newscast in the country. By the tryout's end, the show had racked up a record $1.5 million in out-of-town business and was heading to New York with another $1.5 million in advance ticket sales—and no director![92]

Gielgud no longer wanted to receive billing and asked that his name be removed as director; Gower still wanted to be credited only as production supervisor because *Irene* had not been his from the start. Just days before the Nixons attended, Merrick saw the show, and was so impressed that he personally phoned Gower (something he rarely did) to tell him, "You'd be a fool not to put your name on it."[93] With that, the show doctor became *Irene*'s director.

Gower's tinkering was unstoppable—right up and into the New York previews. "Debbie, if I could just have two more days—two more days—I could fix the 'Palais Royale' number," he confided to the star. It was the first act finale, a grand ballroom scene with wonderful costumes and Gennaro's electrifying "Riviera Rage," which plainly needed to be tightened and better framed. Both realized the producers would oppose any further delay of the opening. The playful glint in Reynolds's eyes was a giveaway; she was plotting mischief and Gower was delighted to aid and abet it. "Let's rehearse the street scene where I have to jump down and do the front flip," she proposed. "When I flip, I will knock myself out. But know this. I really won't be out. Everyone will think I'm out, and you will have two days. They'll think I have a concussion. They probably will think I've died. So don't be frightened, but get down close to me at one point when you're insecure about whether I'm alive or dead, and I will open one eye."[94]

Reynolds did the front flip, earning a huge bruise on her head in the process. While she resorted to yoga to slow her breathing and assume a semiconscious state, everyone panicked, sirens roared, ambulances arrived, and paramedics applied CPR before shuttling her off to the hospital where a bevy of doctors examined her: "Now I'm in a private room. I'm still out. Gower leans over close to me, and I can tell. I knew it was Gower, and he said, 'Debbie. Debbie, are you all right?' And I opened one eye, and he went, 'Ah! Oh! Oh! Oh, dear! Oh, dear! She's just out. You know, we're going to have to take at least two days. This is so serious.' "[95] Two days later, when Reynolds returned, "Palais Royale" had its facelift and previews had also been extended from one to two weeks.[96]

Gower kept the changes coming. "We had an overture that was stunning and stopped the show," recalls conductor Jack Lee. "The audience just loved it, and it's on the recording. Gower—and rightly so—said, 'Jack, I'm going to have to cut the overture because it upstages our star. She comes on right away at the top of the show, and it's killing her. She has no number to counter it and I want her to be strong. So what we're going to do is play a little game here.' "[97]

No curtain. The audience would enter the theatre with the stage dimly lit and set as a Ninth Avenue street scene circa 1919. Things would gradually get under way with a single clarinet playing one of the tunes twice through while house lights remained full, not dimmed as was the custom. Then came a break before the clarinet joined an alto sax for a little jig. Another break, then a third tune with the trumpets coming in like a street band on a corner of Ninth Avenue. Again, a break, before a fourth sequence started with two reeds and a banjo. A final break before a young lady, Jeanne Lehman, entered to sing the opening verse to "Alice Blue Gown." House lights dimmed and went dark; Meg Bussert joined Lehman for a duet before Penny Worth arrived to make it a trio. Now the stage lighting dimmed and went dark as a spot picked up the girls. Toward the end of their song, Ninth Avenue reappeared behind them, brighter and more colorful than before. The number ended, and Reynolds made her entrance and received the first hand in the show—just what Gower wanted. All Lee had to do was to wait for the stage manager to cue the start via the red light attached to his podium in the pit.[98]

Opening night, March 13, 1973, the light went on and he immediately cued the clarinet soloist to begin. The orchestra was just reaching the end of the fourth sequence when the conductor got a tap on the shoulder and turned around to find Gower, who had crawled down the aisle on his knees in full tux to avoid being seen, laughing as he leaned into the pit from above. Lee continued to conduct as Gower explained, "Jack, you're not going to believe what happened. I'm going to ask you, when you finish the banjo section, to go back to the top. Stay in the first reed solo, just have him keep repeating. When I think everything is ready to go, I personally will give you the red light. Then go on through each section and start. I'll tell you later what happened."[99] Then he disappeared, crawling back up the aisle once more. Lee did as requested. During intermission he learned that the stage manager had been giving his family a backstage tour and when he reached the highlight—the button he pushed to start the show—hit it by mistake!

Nixon's prediction proved true. Though *Irene* opened at the new Minskoff Theatre to mixed but fairly positive reviews, it became a box office bonanza thanks to a steady stream of out-of-towners who reveled in its star, spectacle, and good old-fashioned fun. Gower's intervention had not only saved the show, but also helped it earn a highly respectable run of 605 performances.[100] Reynolds, Kelly, and Gennaro received Tony nominations and George S. Irving won the Best Supporting Actor in a Musical Award for his Irish-dandy-turned-French-couturier Madame Lucy.

Long after opening, controversy continued to haunt *Irene*. Though Broadway's highest-grossing show for a year, it had yet to return a fraction of its $800,000 investment to backers because of an additional $700,000 loaned by Selden and Minskoff to cover revamping expenses on the road. Until that loan was repaid, investors would see no return on the musical that actually had opened on Broadway to a tune of $1.5 million.[101] In February 1974 *Irene* again made the news when Gower refused to return to New York to groom Reynolds's replacement, Jane Powell, for her Broadway bow—a major disappointment to the star, adrift with no one to coach her. Days before her successful debut, Powell's *Girl Most Likely* choreographer finally called with an explanation: "Gower told me he didn't like this show, he didn't like musicals, he only wanted to do movies. He said he only had a few minutes to give me. He was doing it as a friend of mine. I told him, 'I don't see how you could consider yourself a friend of mine after that, and I won't consider myself a friend of yours. Your ego has gone too big for you.'"[102] His callousness was typical of the postproduction fault-finding he often applied to his collaborators, but rarely to himself.[103] For Rigby, the solution was simple. He just did to Gower what Cyma Rubin had done to him—removed his name from the billing. (Those who purchased the souvenir program would find a piece of white adhesive tape over Gower's name.) Once more *Irene* had no director—little consequence to Gower, now back in Los Angeles directing George C. Scott in a new film comedy.

FIFTEEN

Bathing Beauties, the Bard, and Bitterness

Mack and Mabel and *Rockabye Hamlet*

1974–1976

Post-*Irene*, Gower retreated to beachcombing and his Topanga Canyon home, delighted to be commencing work on his first film in twelve years, *The Bank Shot*, an offbeat comedy about a bank heist starring George C. Scott that also featured old friends Max Showalter and Bibi Osterwald. Spring and summer 1973 were occupied with laying the groundwork in preparation for filming in the fall. By then, *Dolly!* collaborators Merrick, Herman, and Stewart were offering him a new musical about the relationship between silent film director Mack Sennett and his ill-fated star Mabel Normand called *Hundreds of Girls*. But he was fed up with the New York theatre scene and bent on the film directing career that had eluded him until now. Moreover, the failed reconciliation with Marge and the aftershock of the divorce were too fresh. With a new life taking root, it was vital to remain in Los Angeles for the sake of Gregg, now living with him, and Blake, living with Marge. He declined the offer.[1]

As filming of *The Bank Shot* got under way, the daily commute from home to studio soon became taxing. His solution was to move closer to the city, trading Topanga Canyon bohemia for Beverly Hills respectability with the purchase of Charles Boyer's enormous estate in Beverly Grove—replete with tennis courts, indoor swimming pool, retractable dining room ceiling, screening room, and guest house, which he converted into a film editing studio.

To help furnish the sprawling residence, he called upon longtime friend and interior plantings specialist Karla Robertson Russell. When Gower first met her seventeen years before, the bright, amiable, poised brunette had been a technical assistant on the TV broadcast of *3 for Tonight*. Over the years, she and husband Norman Russell had become friends of the Champions and often socialized with them. Now wise herself to the effects of divorce, Karla helped the new homeowner expand his living space from two furnished rooms to the rest of the house and also replaced his diet of junk food with nourishing meals—just the kind of support he needed. "It was a natural segue," she explains. "We were friends. I was in the plant business at the time, doing interior designing with plants. Gower was a *huge* plant person. It was a passion we shared. He had bought the Beverly Grove house and wanted me to help him fix it up. I guess he was going through his Hollywood period. He even filmed a party scene for *The Bank Shot* there. It was a gloriously fun time."[2]

Supplying a new décor soon included a remodeling commensurate with the mansion's style. In the process, a romance developed. His personal life was on the rebound, but not his film career. *The Bank Shot* bombed at the box office. The reason, reveals Jess, was because "he made it up as he went along. I know that to be true because he borrowed a lot of stuff from the book I had written, *Baby Boy*—which made me none too happy, even though before that I told him anything I had he was welcome to. But I kind of liked it better when he asked. He didn't have any concept where it was going—no ending."[3] Jess attended the preview with Gar and was amazed at the film's discrepancies: "All the shots didn't match. I mean, it was supposed to be the same scene and one shot would be at 6:00 at night and the other would be at noon. You'd sit there and say, 'Well, why is this so strange?' And he would say, 'Oh, don't worry about it. We can fix it or doctor it up.' But there was no way it could work. It was a mess. I don't know how they got any bookings out of it."[4]

In January 1974, the offer to do *Hundreds of Girls* resurfaced. He read Stewart's first draft, intrigued by its tale of thwarted romance between work-fixated Mack Sennett (1884–1960) and talented, feisty star Mabel Normand (1892–1930): his typecasting and inability to express affection the source of her frustration and decline. The backdrop was Hollywood's silent era, when Sennett presided over the popular two-reelers that filled the silver screen with the antics of Normand, Fatty Arbuckle, Chester Conklin, Charlie Chaplin, and his own Keystone Kops and Bathing Beauties.

Beyond the appeal of staging the pratfalls and pies in the face of Sennett's comedies, there was a greater attraction for Gower—a progressively sinister plot that treated Normand's desertion of Sennett for director William Desmond Taylor, her descent into alcohol and cocaine addiction, her charge and acquittal in Taylor's unsolved murder, loss of popularity, and death at age thirty-seven from a drug overdose. (Those who knew the real Normand would later criticize the way the musical played fast and loose with the facts of her life, especially her relationship with Taylor, substance abuse, and cause of death—actually tuberculosis.[5]) Not since *Prettybelle* had this kind of material come his way and, with the support of his *Dolly!* teammates, he resolved to make the most of it. "Mike, it's *so* good," he wrote Stewart after his first read. "It would work as it is. But with work and fleshing, it'll be fantastic . . . Congratulations! What a show we have!"[6] Gower was entering his "Chekhov period," as Herman calls it, emphasizing the book's abrasive elements, especially its dark finale, much to the composer's dismay: "Gower insisted that we go to Mabel's death. *Absolutely* insisted on it. He liked the idea. He wanted to be a little bit like Hal Prince, who was doing darker musicals at that time. Everybody was. And I felt that *that* hurt the show."[7]

In the screening room at Beverly Grove, Gower spent hours analyzing Sennett's work to do it justice: "Sennett was a genius. He carried the pratfall to surrealism and really introduced comedic violence. I don't know how those Kops survived some of those routines. Take the scene where the girl's taking a bath. The pipes break and the bathtub floats downstairs and up the street. He was wild."[8] But capturing that wildness and planting it firmly on the musical stage meant adapting a silent medium to a talking one—tricky business indeed, but a challenge he was determined to tackle nonetheless.

Sensing a megahit in the making, he had certain provisions built into his contract to advance his film directing career—a West Coast debut and a guarantee to do the screen version. It was a timely move. By opening night four studios would be vying for the rights—which not only pleased him, but also Merrick, Hollywood's newest producer, now preparing a major release, *The Great Gatsby*.[9] But despite his Los Angeles link, Merrick insisted that rehearsals remain in New York. Gower complied, but not without Merrick's assurance that he would not undermine his efforts as in *Sugar*: "Merrick and I have a special arrangement. We keep out of each other's way. I respect him. Who else is producing, for God's sake? In *Dolly!*, he didn't like the 'So Long, Dearie' number. He even refused to order Carol's costume for it. I went and bought and paid for it. In time, Merrick paid me back."[10]

By the time of Gower's signing, *Hundreds of Girls* had undergone a very odd journey dating back to 1971, when Edwin H. Lester, general director of the Los Angeles Civic Light Opera, seeking to debut a new musical for his upcoming season, chose Herman to write the songs and Leonard Spigelgass the book based on Gene Fowler's biography of Mack Sennett, *Father Goose*. A year later, when Lester abandoned the project, Spigelgass moved on to pen a biography of Edward G. Robinson, retaining credit for the "idea" of what Herman and new librettist Stewart soon renamed *Mack and Mabel*. By 1973, Joseph Kipness and Lawrence Kasha had agreed to produce, but problems securing rights to the source and preoccupation with their production of *Seesaw* finally forced the authors to turn reluctantly to Merrick. With three of the original four members of the *Dolly!* team now in place, another blockbuster was within reach provided the fourth could be won over. But while Gower deliberated, Kipness, who had agreed to sell his interest in the show, fumed over Merrick's delay on settling the percentage of profits he was to receive and billing he expected to share. To speed the decision, he hired a team of thugs who paid an after-hours call on Merrick's offices, ransacking one of them. Though the New York Rackets Bureau launched an investigation, the matter was ultimately settled out of court, with Kipness receiving a ten percent share of the profits on his $30,000 investment (nothing) and no share in the billing.[11]

The peculiarities multiplied. *Mack and Mabel*'s world premiere was scheduled to take place at San Francisco's Curran Theatre on May 7, 1974, but just as New York rehearsals were getting under way in mid-March, Gower had to return to Los Angeles to have his wisdom teeth extracted. To reduce the risk of provoking his bleeding condition, the procedure was performed in a hospital surgery room, and he was ordered to bed afterward as a further precaution.[12] There were no complications save the second thoughts he now had concerning the leads he had cast—which changed immediately after he returned to New York, accompanied by Karla.

For the role of Mack, he had chosen Jerry Orbach, whom he hastily replaced with Robert Preston only days before rehearsals began at the Belasco Theatre on May 6, 1974.[13] At the time Preston had more star power than Orbach, which may have been a deciding factor. The fifty-six-year-old actor, whose last Broadway bow was seven years before in *I Do! I Do!,* had recently appeared in the film version of Herman's *Mame.* The songwriter's score for the new show attracted him, as did the personality of its central character. "Mack Sennett, king of comedy," he noted, "was a tragic, lonely figure, a driven man, with one idea: to make people laugh. Everything else was secondary, friends, money, food, even love."[14] Positive that Preston would deliver the humanity necessary to warm the audience to the blustery self-absorbed Mack, Gower went in search of a Mabel—a search even more bizarre than the one for *The Happy Time*'s leading lady.

Auditions were not held because the role seemed destined for *Applause*'s Penny Fuller; then suddenly auditions *were* held, with Marcia Rodd (*Your Own Thing, Last of the Red Hot Lovers*) emerging as the top choice after five weeks of testing. Before going to work on a big hit she was likely to be with for two years, she took a vacation. Upon her return, Gower, just back from California, called to say that rehearsals were beginning sooner than planned. "That was weird," she observed. "And from that second on, I knew something was wrong . . . The two days of rehearsals weren't rehearsals, but setups so he could justify firing me . . . I was stunned. I've never been fired in my life . . . When he wanted me, he could not have been nicer. He was kind of like an uncle; we had a nice, open relationship. But when he got scared, everything closed up."[15]

Rodd was first and foremost an actor, and that intimidated him. She sang and danced well but, like all actors, worked from the inside out, examining the character and focusing on the whys and wherefores of movement.[16] Gower worked from the outside in, and although he borrowed from what performers brought him and suited it to his purposes, he generally prescribed the staging as he saw fit, expecting them to replicate it exactly each time. Whatever internal motivation the movement required was for them to decide, and definitely not something to be explored with him. To work with Champion, actors had to think and respond like dancers, and those who could not were rebuffed. To conceal his Achilles' heel, he spared no effort.

"She's a dynamic performer," he remarked of Rodd, "but Mabel Normand has to have a broken-wing quality."[17] He thought he had found it in singer Kelly Garrett the night he saw her in *An Evening with Sammy Cahn*. She signed on with the understanding that an assistant director would coach her in the dramatic training necessary for the role; yet after less than a week rehearsing with Preston, she, too, was let go. "That one broke my heart," explained the director. "That face, that voice. But this role takes a lot of deep acting."[18] Deep as it was, he didn't want any directorial assistance.[19]

Four weeks into rehearsal, Bernadette Peters, who up to then had declined to audition because of a recent move to California, arrived on the scene. While in New York to do TV's *$10,000 Pyramid,* she also did a cold reading for the director, who still seemed sold on Garrett. But just as she was ready to depart for home, something strange happened: "I was ready to leave, I was on the plane, on the runway, and suddenly the engine goes *pffft* and we have to get off. I called my lawyer in California to say I'd be on a later flight, and while he was talking to me, his other phone rang. It was Merrick's office, calling to say I'd gotten the part. It was fate; I really believe that."[20]

Monday morning, when the cast arrived at the Belasco for rehearsal, there, to their surprise, was Peters. "Hi, I'm the new Mabel," she said with a smile. "The show's now called *Mack and Maybe*."[21] Not for the director, who at last had found a leading lady with that requisite broken-wing quality: "She's terrific. She makes you want to laugh and cry. When she walks out on stage you sense her destruction before it happens. Now, I can't imagine anyone else up there on that stage."[22]

Pairing an established star with a new one had its advantages. Song-and-dance man Preston brought a commanding vitality and suave professionalism; young, honey-voiced Peters an affecting vulnerability and plucky comic sense. But the chemistry central to their relationship would be complicated by the thirty-year age disparity between them—which further distanced the show from historical fact (Sennett was only eight years older than Normand).

The featured performers remained unchanged: Lisa Kirk *(Allegro, Kiss Me, Kate)* as Lottie Ames, a vaudeville chanteuse who advances from Sennett's troupe to talkies, and James Mitchell as director-playboy William Desmond Taylor, Mabel's faithless lover. Supporting players included Jerry Dodge as screenwriter Frank Wyman (a takeoff on young scenarist and soon-to-be-director Frank Capra),

Christopher Murney as cameraman Charlie Muldoon, and Tom Batten and Bert Michaels as investors Kleiman and Fox. Robert Fitch played performer Wally, Nancy Evers pianist Ella, Marie Santell wardrobe mistress Iris, and Stanley Simmonds studio watchman Eddie. A chorus of bathing beauties and grips completed the forty-one-member cast.

Onto the canvas of Robin Wagner's attractive yet functional movie studio with its diagonal thrust, lofty vaulted ceiling, sliding panels, and configuration of lights, ladders, and catwalks, Gower imposed impressive effects like Sennett film montages, a multicolored corkscrew slide for a bathing beauties frolic, and a splashy tinsel-draped tap sequence evoking a Warner Brothers musical of 1929—all in the shadow of an omnipresent camera boom that swung Mack over the audience.[23] Patricia Zipprodt's colorful costumes and Tharon Musser's top-notch lighting beautifully set off the design.

But the V-shaped unit set literally backed Gower (and Wagner) into a corner because its permanent walls prohibited use of the flies. As a result, changes had to be made by means of cutout scenery tracked on and off with little background variation throughout. Despite this adaptation, the stage action always seemed to be happening in the same place. "Gower wanted a set that had us in a brown wood corner all night," states Herman. "The show never really changed colors and tones. When Mack's troupe sings 'Big Time' and sees their first palm tree, I wanted the entire stage to turn from Brooklyn grays and browns to Hollywood Technicolor. That never happened. At the end of the evening, we were still in the brown corner. There was just a lot that we didn't see eye to eye on."[24]

Herman's tuneful score, generally considered his best, was a collection of bright choruses, touching ballads, torch songs, and showstoppers impeccably suited to the era. But it contrasted mightily with Stewart's top-heavy libretto, a memory play that opened with Mack in 1938 bankrupted by the talkies and alone in his studio, about to be sold from under him. Recalling his past glories and love for Mabel, he narrated the story, popping in and out of the action as it flashed back to 1911 Brooklyn and moved forward. But as much as Stewart tried to perfect it, the drama remained bogus, with the comical events of the first act mired in the sobering trials of the second and the characters lacking in depth.

Gower's challenges escalated. Now not only did he have to invent staging that fused a dynamic score with a dismal story while effectively evoking Sennett's comedy, but also avoid comparison with Jerome Robbins, whose "Mack Sennett Ballet" from *High Button Shoes* had made a lasting impression on many theatergoers. This seaside romp of mistaken identity that featured Keystone Kops madly pursuing bathers in and out of lockers was a classic. Gower greatly admired Robbins's work, but did not want his own measured by it. Though the Kops were central to Sennett's comedy and Gower's desire to do a ballet with them was great, he dismissed the idea altogether as rehearsals got under way.

Once more he was up on the rehearsal ramp striding back and forth between house and stage assessing every detail of the production. What would be the organizing principle, the overriding idea unifying the show this time? A tribute to silent film comedy as Prince's recent *Follies* had been to the Ziegfeld revue? If it was, he failed to communicate it to the company—an uncharacteristic slip for the ordinarily meticulous showman. "I never heard Gower ever make any kind of statement about what the show was going to be or what he was aiming for," says musical director and vocal arranger Donald Pippin. "I don't think *he* knew. He was totally confused about the show. I think he saw it as the real glitzy, motion picture kind of show, but never a serious, tragic love story between two people. He was running around with a lot of energy, but was very unfocused."[25]

The opening, "Movies Were Movies," was a stellar piece of work but, like his set, another self-made trap. It began with Mack, alone in the darkness of his once-thriving Hollywood studio, salvaging his battered director's chair from a pile of junk and then slamming it down into a pool of light, where to the tune of a tinkling piano he sang of how movies were movies when he ran the show. Near the end of the first two verses, the full orchestra came in, a huge scrim was lowered, and instantaneously its every space was filled with a vibrant collage of Mary Pickford, Francis X. Bushman, the Gish sisters, and moments from *The Great Train Robbery, Greed,* and *Way Down East.* With that, the silent age of the cinema sprang to life once more in all its silvery splendor. When Mack reached the climactic "Movies were movies were *movies,*" a shot of a Tin Lizzie filled with Kops about to soar off a cliff suddenly froze for his final *"When I ran the show!"*[26]

No musical could have had a more impressive start, but after this glorification of the real thing, Gower literally spent the rest of the time trying to top the opener that firmly established Sennett's genius and challenged his own. "Every time he tried to do anything that was reminiscent of those old films," explains Herman, "we already had seen the real thing. He was fiddling with a ballet called 'Beauty and the Burning Hospital,' trying to put on the stage what Sennett had put on the screen. It just wasn't funny with real people. Gower didn't need to be told; he knew it wasn't working. Of course the disappointment was enormous because of all the time wasted."[27]

"Beauty and the Burning Hospital" and "Beauty and the Buzz Saw" were choreographed comic sequences done to themes from the score. In the first, which came after the troupe's arrival in Hollywood, Mack's "I Wanna Make the World Laugh" was literally interrupted when Charlie and Frank entered to warn him to get to safety because the local hospital they were about to pass was on fire. He responded by grabbing the camera, boarding the dolly, and riding out over the audience to direct an improvised scene using the real fire as a backdrop. From the wings, a cutout of a hospital shot out and burst into smoke and flames just as an enormously pregnant Peters about to deliver quadruplets ambled inside. In seconds a fire truck arrived with a pack of firemen flailing arms, tumbling over stretchers, and frantically spinning old ladies around in wheelchairs in a search for the heroine, whom they discovered giving birth on the uppermost floor and delivered to safety after their slapdash rescue of each baby.

At first the erratic and ludicrous running, falling, and reverse action moves—which mirrored Mack's slowly cranked camera work—seemed to come off.[28] But the dissimilarity between the stasis of the stage and the dynamism of the screen soon became painfully clear as Gower discovered that what had made the films work "were incredible mechanical gags—buildings falling down, horses riding through living rooms, cars going off piers. That was Sennett's madness. The biggest frustration is not being able to do it in this show. The mechanical age is what he used. And what do I have? One adorable fire engine. But I can't tip it over, and I can't run it through a wall."[29]

While negotiating pitfalls, Gower did manage to fill *Mack and Mabel* with some fabulous effects and numbers. Transitions and staging employed the dissolves, freeze frames, iris effects, cross-cutting, and even superimposing of film. When Mack sang "I Wanna Make the World Laugh," scenes from Sennett's films were projected onto the scrim before him while he stood dimly lit behind. Later, the cast, their faces thick with custard from a pie-throwing frenzy, gave a delightful reprise of the number lined up on the forestage.[30] Mabel's astonishment at seeing herself for the first time on film, expressed in "Look What Happened to Mabel," began with her standing beside a flickering projector looking up at an imaginary screen and led into a humorous dance with four boys that mixed joy with speed.[31] He used "Big Time" to musically transition the ensemble from Brooklyn to Hollywood via his trademark train motif. For "Wherever He Ain't," Mabel's breakaway from Mack, replacing the earlier "Today I'm Going to Think About Me," four waiters steered her about on a restaurant cart. In "Hundreds of Girls," a huge corkscrew slide appeared and down it glided a bevy of bathing beauties who then formed a spectacular diagonal kick line on the corner of the stage extending into the audience.[32] There was an ingenious entry into "I Won't Send Roses" with Mack, inside a narrow Pullman sleeper, winding up the cylinder phonograph that accompanied his song to Mabel. Later, when Mabel reprised it, the railway car turned inside out, revealing her at a tiny lighted window, her starry-eyed dreams soaring out into the vastness of the night.[33]

In anticipation of the grim finale, Herman had written the rousing eleven o'clocker "Tap Your Troubles Away" for Lottie and the girls to perform as a big talking picture routine for the *Vitagraph Varieties of 1929*, but Gower did not want it to climax and then stop the progress of the plot for applause. Just as the number peaked at center, he suddenly shifted focus to the diagonal thrust and the terrace of Taylor's home to show Mabel's dependence on cocaine, Taylor's affair with another starlet, and ultimately his murder while the chorus bitterly tapped to tense, nonmelodic rhythm. Five rapid pistol shots rang out, the tinsel backdrop for the number crashed to the floor, and Taylor stumbled out of the doorway clutching his stomach. Blackout. Shouts of newsboys broadcasting the crime pierced the darkness before lights rose again on Lottie and the girls for the song's conclusion.[34]

"Tap dancing on the stage is boring," he commented. "You've seen *No, No, Nanette*. But by staging a murder simultaneously, it works."[35] Yet it mattered little to him that Taylor's murder occurred in 1922, seven years before the fictitious *Vitagraph Varieties of 1929*. Regardless of the facts, he was bent on creating a musical drama in which "Tap Your Troubles Away" served as an ironic commentary on the tragic but untrue climax Stewart was daily helping him to evolve. By calculating the number for dramatic effect, rather than applause, he intended to succeed. "Gower was playing with the audience's expectations," says Bert Michaels. "If the number got applause, it would have broken the momentum. So he kept trying to fix it by factoring out the applause to make it work."[36] With associate choreographer Buddy Schwab, he eventually achieved the desired effect. "The whole 'Tap Your Troubles Away' segment was wonderfully done," says Herman, "and really did what we set out to do—use a pastiche song, a cheer-up song of the period, to play against the heaviest drama of the piece. Boy, did that work, and he staged it magnificently."[37]

The huge production number that came at the top of the second act, "When Mabel Comes in the Room," was a source of controversy between director and songwriter. For Gower it was too reminiscent of "Hello, Dolly!" "I fought tooth and nail to have that song left out," he told a reporter. "I thought, oh, goddam it, here comes that whole thing about 'if the star comes back, let's sing her song.' I'll never do it again, and I've already told Jerry that."[38] Herman, despite Gower's protests that he had been misquoted, was completely stunned by the remark. He had written the song merely as a greeting to Mabel by seven of her friends—Mack, Lottie, Iris, Ella, Eddie, Kleiman, and Fox—to lift the scene where she returns to the studio after a five-year absence. "I saw it as the family just greeting her," he explains. "Gower made it a production number. He said, 'Wait till you see what I'm going to do here. I'm having her slide down a pole at one point.' He went absolutely crazy with it. If Gower had ever come to me and said, 'I'd like you to write something else for that place in the script,' he knew I could do it overnight. So that's why that comment was very unfair."[39]

Unfair as it was, the remark epitomized his behavior of late—as insensitive and distracted as Mack, unsettled and impulsive as Mabel, and so unlike him. The similarity between his issues and those of the characters was indeed ironic. "Psychologically, it was a very bad period for him," explains Pippin. "He was on drugs and always reacted to things compared to how he was feeling at the moment. I found him very distant, mean and controlling. Not that you saw it in the way he acted, but that's what was underneath. He wanted to come across very glamorous, very 'Isn't he a dashing person to know?' All the time underneath he was so protective and almost paranoid about revealing anything of himself. That must have been exhausting."[40]

The comic sequences consumed him to the neglect of "When Mabel Comes in the Room," which remained untouched. With only days to go before the San Diego premiere, Pippin, frustrated with funneling requests to him through production supervisor Lucia Victor, breached protocol one morning to express his concern and get the time with the cast he and Herman needed to lay out the vocal arrangement. Gower provided the time and the session that morning was productive, but the number was only generally sketched in and not yet ready for staging. Still, that very afternoon there was Gower staging away—without even hearing what had been written and rehearsed earlier. The director-choreographer was now also choral director, deciding who was to sing what and when. Pippin left the rehearsal, taking a seat in the back of the theatre.

Some time later, Victor approached, relaying, "He says you're needed down there."

Pippin replied, "Tell Gower he doesn't need both of us. If he wants to do the vocal arranging, he doesn't need me. Would you please tell him exactly those words?"

"Oh, no. No." Victor knew better. She never would give Gower any message that would irritate him. She shielded him from everything.

"Lucia, I don't want to go down there. He hasn't even heard the number. Now if he wants to hear it, I'll be glad to run it for him."

Victor went back down to the stage and spoke with Gower, who could see that the musical director was not buying his long-distance treatment. He asked to hear the number that Pippin then demonstrated with the cast. Now aware of how the arrangement was shaping up, Gower proceeded with the staging.[41]

The number certainly started out as Herman had imagined it, with Mabel arriving at the studio early in the morning before any of her old friends were there. As she chatted with the night watchman, her friends entered, saw her, and then disappeared to arrange a welcome-back celebration. Moments later, they were all onstage—the seven at first, but then gradually the entire company flipping "Welcome Home" banners above her head, joining hands in a circle of celebration around her, and finally sending her aloft on a crane with a red balloon in her hand, the balloon, rather than the crane, seeming to float her skyward. After joining the dancers for a cakewalk on the catwalk, she leapt from it onto a scaffolding pipe that she descended for the finale.[42]

Mack and Mabel had all the makings of success when it opened in San Diego on June 17.[43] "The audience adored it," recalls Herman. "I was positive, and I mean *positive* that it was a big hit."[44] That news also made Gower's fifty-fifth birthday on June 22 an especially happy one, as did the more manageable beachfront house on Atlantic Oak Shore Drive in Los Angeles that he was now renting thanks to Karla's prompt and efficient move after a realtor asked to purchase the Beverly Grove estate.[45]

Three days later, on June 25, *Mack and Mabel* opened in Los Angeles to encouraging but guarded reviews warning of the excessive comic sequences, uneven book, and, most especially, the dark ending.[46] "I could tell that audiences were not pleased by that," notes Herman. "When Preston said the words, 'And then in 1930, Mabel Normand died,' everyone went, '*Huh?*' It sounded like balloons deflating and kind of hit them in the stomach. Historically, it was untrue because Mabel had married another man [Lew Cody] after her affair with Mack and was with him for four years before she became ill and died."[47]

It was no way to end a musical, so Gower came up with an idea to lessen the negative impact of Preston's announcement—a elegant wedding sequence in which each chorus girl entered in a different-colored gown to form a vivid rainbow across the stage. The purpose was to fulfill what the show's final song, sung by Preston, foretold, "I Promise You a Happy Ending." But to determine whether the number would work, Gower had to see it in all its glory—costumes, scenery, the works—at an exorbitant sum, one of the reasons why the show's initial cost of $750,000 soared to $900,000 by opening night.[48] "The fancy wedding went in and out of the show very fast," says Pippin. "All I remember was the pressure of getting it orchestrated, scored, and in so fast. He simply couldn't run that thing to see if it was going to work. It surprised me that he had to have this complete finished thing and spend thousands and thousands of dollars to have it go in and out in practically two nights."[49]

His color-coordinated costume parade, so effective in *Dolly!*'s "Sunday Clothes" sequence and even more so later in *42nd Street*'s "Dames," fell flat on this occasion as he tried to create Sennett's vision of how the story should have ended. For Patricia Michaels, Lisa Kirk's understudy, "It was embarrassing doing something that was so wrong for the show. We couldn't even take it seriously, we were so uncomfortable with it. They spent a fortune on those costumes which just sat here."[50]

While Gower substituted a slapstick if-life-were-a-movie wedding fantasy, Marie Santell substituted for an ailing Peters, going on cold with less than twenty-four hours' notice at the request of the director (who never assigned or trained understudies) and playing the next ten performances to raves. With Peters back in form and Gower's ceaseless tinkering at full throttle, the show moved on to St. Louis and the huge outdoor stage of the Municipal Opera.

The stopover, Merrick's way of making money while killing time before the final tryout in Washington, generated further complications.[51] New scenery had to be built suitable for the environment, and performers had to adjust to an audience of 11,000. "It was the most destructive thing that happened to *Mack and Mabel*," states Herman. "A lot of the nuance of performance was lost on an open-air stage in the middle of the summer. It pulled the show completely out of shape. We never got back to the intimate musical that it was. It was at its peak in Los Angeles and went downhill from there, falling apart in front of our eyes and getting worse with every sitting."[52] Fixing the show was one thing, reconfiguring it for a venue for which it never was intended was something else entirely. But that was precisely what Gower had to do in St. Louis—reconfigure the entire show and then reconfigure it once more in Washington in time for the opening at the Kennedy Center on September 3.

For all the critical optimism and brisk box office business, the efforts of his team failed to impress Merrick, who told a Washington reporter, "We hit solidly in California and in St. Louis, but I wasn't entirely happy with it. And good reviews don't make writers and directors work very hard."[53] But bad ones did—something he learned back in 1960 when he cajoled *Washington Post* critic Richard Coe into giving his *Do Re Mi* a thumbs-down prior to Broadway. This time, however, Coe needed no cajoling: "*Mack and Mabel* landed on the Kennedy Center Opera House stage Tuesday night with all the zip of a wet, very dead flounder . . . Whoever urged these experts of our musical stage to get serious and artistic did them and the rest of us a dreary disservice. The run is for four pre-Broadway weeks but if anything's to salvage *Mack and Mabel*, it'll have to be from scratch."[54] With that, Gower accelerated the changes.

"He started to try things," says Herman. "I think he was absolutely brilliant at what he did, but he was also a man who had to keep trying things. That was just part of his nature. By the time we got to New York, there never had been a musical so fiddled with."[55] Once more the finale was revamped. The slapstick wedding fantasy appended to Mack's announcement of Mabel's death was dropped in favor of a short but sincere expression of his regret to Mabel. In this way, the evening concluded as it began, with Mack alone in the studio. Then, with his "So long, Kid," he exited through the door as the music rose to a crescendo and ended.

The ending was still gloomy and less than satisfactory. For a time, the director fixed the blame on the low-key "I Promise You a Happy Ending" sung by Preston. His intention was to cut it because he felt the sentiment was too plainspoken and long. This time, Herman stood his ground. "That's the most *necessary* song in the show," he told Gower, "because it shows a change in Mack, who comes out at the top of the show singing 'Movies were movies when *I* ran the show' and is a bully. At the end he has gone through a journey and is able to sing to her, 'I can promise you a happy ending that has you loving me loving you.' You can't take away what I know is the right song for me to have written there."[56] The song stayed.

From the start Gower was unhappy with the overture, which he now wanted to scrap. In the end, he agreed to a compromise—a "Prologue" with a series of stills from Sennett films to be shown during its performance by the orchestra. (Without the recording of the overture on the cast album, the British ice-skating team of Torvill and Dean would never have had the music for their gold medal performance in the Free Dance competition of the 1982 World Championships. Later, when they did the routine during the BBC broadcast of the 1984 Olympics, it brought *Mack and Mabel* to the attention of the British public who demanded a re-release of the album and then catapulted it to #6 on the charts, making the show a cult classic ten years after its appearance.[57])

In San Diego, Champion had briefly toyed with a Keystone Kops number entitled "Call a Kop," which he quickly cut. Just before the Washington premiere however, he gave in to the idea once more, staging "My Heart Leaps Up," a soft shoe with a perfectly off-center chorus of light-footed flatfoots. Yet the Kop chorus was there and gone in an instant, never running riot with the celebrated ineptitude of Sennett's Keystoners. The number it replaced, "Hit 'Em on the Head," an amusing catalog of Sennett slapstick bits impeccably matched by the antics of Preston, Batten, and Michaels, was funnier by far, and eventually reinstated. Despite the modifications, Coe's pronouncement confirmed Gower's worst fear: "A fire scene of total confusion and a routine of Keystoners are bound to be unfavorably contrasted with Jerome Robbins's similar but triumphant number of *High Button Shoes*"[58] With the show finally getting off the road after nearly four months, it was the last thing he wanted to hear. Even "if I had a Jerry Robbins ballet with the Kops," he asserted, "it still wouldn't work. In my play, the Kops are real, and they're not funny people on-stage. Sennett's kinetic action is what makes them funny on screen."[59] That was exactly what he and Stewart were still trying to infuse into the script.

Stewart's foot-and-a-half-high stack of changes testified to the many rewrites he had done over the lengthy tryout—more than he ever had made for a show: "We've been on the road a long, long time, and I don't like that. I wouldn't mind so much if we changed cities more often. You're in one place for a few weeks, so you write for that city. And as sophisticated as L.A. or Washington are, they're not New York. I'm longing for the New York opening, to have it decided. I can't stand waiting for the jury. Come in, and say, 'Guilty,' or 'Not Guilty,' and get it over with."[60]

After the opening night performance at the Majestic on Sunday, October 6, as everyone joined the soirée hosted by Merrick for the cast on the fiftieth floor of the Tower Suite, the verdict was handed down at long last.[61] "It would have been so great for *Mack and Mabel* to be a success," lamented Martin Gottfried. "New York is in the mood for a hit Broadway musical . . . and why not this one? . . . Because in the graduation of a musical from idea to production . . . more is involved than hard work. The show's feel is basically noise trying to pass for enthusiasm . . . and [its] quality is professionalism without identity."[62] Douglas Watt called it "an amiable fool of a musical so desperately anxious to tickle our funny bones and touch our hearts that it succeeds in doing neither," and George Oppenheimer added, "I had the feeling almost throughout of seeing a revival. There was something so familiar about it all that it bred, not contempt, but *déjà vu*."[63]

Most of the fault-finding centered on Stewart's libretto and Champion's obvious attempts to bolster it. "We have all seen a musical with book trouble before," wrote Clive Barnes, "but this one has book trouble so bad that it is practically library trouble . . . Never have so many props propped up so much show."[64] Yet beyond these weaknesses, Barnes, like many critics, felt that *Mack and Mabel* had sufficient merit to keep it running through the season. So did Preston: "I've been a realist in this business for over 40 years. This will build. Our notices weren't great in Washington either, but we had full houses all four weeks we were there, and in St. Louis we did $235,000 in one week. This will build."[65] *Mack and Mabel* was an audience show.

If the story was a letdown, there was still much to savor in Preston's ill-tempered bull in a celluloid china shop, Peters's tough but luminous waif turned broken-down star, Kirk's show-biz flair, Mitchell's corrupt suavity, and the vitality of the other performers, who were well served by the designs of Wagner, Zipprodt, and Musser.[66] Last, there were Herman's lush and catchy songs and Gower's dynamic, if brimful, staging. Other shows ran longer with far less. Why, then, did *Mack and Mabel* close after only sixty-six performances?

"It used to be that you'd bring a show into New York," stated Merrick, "and if it got terrible reviews you closed it; if it got mixed reviews, it cost money to keep it running. I've done that with a lot of shows. But it can't be done anymore. Now it's hit or miss completely."[67] But it seems the producer had doubts about the show's ability to sustain a respectable Broadway run long before New York. "He never invested in advertising," says Herman. "He never came to the theatre. He had made his mind up. I've never seen a producer *less* interested in a show. If he only used quotes from John Simon and Clive Barnes, it would have looked like the biggest hit had come to town. And it had *two* big names in it. He stood behind a lot of shows that didn't have half as much going for them."[68] Not this one. While Gower was directing a series of TV commercials to push the show out of its borderline status and into the hit column, Merrick was directing the box office to kill it.[69] As far back as Los Angeles, he had advised one of the stagehands to "find another job by Turkey time" and, sure enough, the show folded by Thanksgiving.[70]

Merrick's ruse caused a major rift with the creators. Herman refused to write another score for a Merrick show ever again; Stewart parted from the producer just as bitterly. So did Gower, undone by Merrick worse than ever. After the opening he returned once or twice, but never gave notes. By then, he had given all he could give.[71] Weeks later, while in Dallas to check on the national company of *Irene,* he told Jack Lee, "I think I just fussed and fussed. What we had in Los Angeles was terrific. We went to Washington and I started adding and adding things. I just did too much. And I think that hurt the show."[72] At Tony time, *Mack and Mabel* chalked up eight nominations—Best Musical, Director, Choreographer, Actor in a Musical, Actress in a Musical, Scenic Designer, Costume Designer, and Book (the *score* was overlooked)—but received none. Its successor at the Majestic, *The Wiz,* was Best Musical and swept most of the awards.

Back in Los Angeles, Gower eased the failure by launching a home remodeling business with Karla, and even took an active role in the renovation of the house they had recently purchased on Bentley Circle, working side by side with the foreman. It was a time of reflection and reassessment. "He really started life all over again," explains Karla, "and totally different aspects of him came out. He was his own person. He never looked back. He chose the friends he wanted, went out and made a concerted effort to court their friendship. There were a couple of holdons—Max Showalter, Lisa Kirk and Bob Wells [her husband]. But he was quite a different person than in the previous decade. Quite a different person."[73]

In June 1975, he staged *Lyrics by Ira Gershwin,* a benefit for the Reiss-Davis Child Study Center, with Tony Bennett, Ethel Merman, Rock Hudson, Liza Minnelli, Bernadette Peters, Frank Sinatra, and Marge. Then Cliff Perlman of Caesar's Palace made him an extraordinary offer to direct an opening extravaganza—with a practically limitless budget—for a first-class theatre the casino was planning to build in Las Vegas. Though initially reluctant, Gower was soon imagining vast choruses and astonishing technical effects that, for the moment, were eclipsed by plans for his next musical.[74]

That July, at the invitation of producer Lester Osterman, he and Karla went to Prince Edward Island, Canada, to attend the Charlottetown Summer Festival revival of *Kronborg: 1582,* a rock opera inspired by Shakespeare's *Hamlet* that had premiered there the previous summer after its radio broadcast by the Canadian

Broadcasting Company (CBC) in December 1973. (Shakespeare was the first to associate the Hamlet legend with Elsinore and its famous castle, called Kronborg.) Osterman had first learned of the show through actress and island summer resident Colleen Dewhurst, who, after seeing the audience's phenomenal response, pressed him to bring it to Broadway under Champion's aegis. Young Toronto native Cliff Jones, a TV script and radio songwriter for the CBC's top shows, penned the two-hour soft rock score in the styles of pop vocalists Todd Rundgren, Carole King, Elton John, and Carly Simon, as well as groups like the Eagles and Bread.[75]

With only minimal scenery and orchestration, *Kronborg* generated such a stir at its premiere that even *Variety* took notice: "Its chances beyond this professional and hard working festival, given some extra touches, are immediately apparent"— reason enough to restage it with nominal revisions the following summer after a sold-out tour of major Canadian cities and for the superstager of the Broadway musical to come all the way from California to assess its potential.[76] Such dabbling was quite a reversal for Gower, who years before had greeted the arrival of rock with disdain, banning it from his act with Marge and satirizing it thoroughly in his first musical. But with the recent reassessment of his life had come a similar reassessment of his musical tastes. "Gower loved the contemporary music scene," recalls Karla, "and was very much into the music of the Eagles. Most of his friends were younger people. I was sort of in the middle, but our close friends were younger. That's how it got started. So he was totally intrigued, and excited about the idea of doing a rock musical."[77]

Apart from his own interest in the music and the urging of younger friends raised on it, he also felt the need to address the ever-widening chasm between rock with its mainstream appeal and Broadway in danger of becoming a purely elitist entertainment: "It's so damned ironic. There's been this incredible proliferation of music, but not one note of it has made it to the Broadway stage. If Joni Mitchell or Carly Simon could only be persuaded to write for the theatre, that would be the fresh input the theatre needs. But those people don't need the hassles, the incredible complications of the theatre."[78] Indeed, since the 1950s, the preeminent cultural status the musical enjoyed had gradually given way to rock, from which Broadway generally had distanced itself save rarities such as *Godspell* (1971) and *Grease* (1972). "Neither the music nor the dance of the Sixties and Seventies is reflected on the stage," Gower lamented, "except for a few freak shows, like *Hair* (1968) and *Jesus Christ Superstar* (1971). Now there's a show that excited me—*Superstar*. [Director Tom] O'Horgan did it almost like a Las Vegas electronic light show. It was an experiment, something really different for a change, a new way to go."[79]

Much as he admired O'Horgan's style and the fresh direction in which he had taken the musical four years before with his "sensational, trashy, splashy, crazy show,"[80] Gower frankly acknowledged that it was not his style. "I'm ill suited to it," he professed just ten months before his trip to Canada. "A little too disciplined, maybe. Besides, if you had given me *Hair* I wouldn't have known what the hell to do with it."[81] Probably not. But as he sat in the theatre at Charlottetown watching *Kronborg*, somehow this show seemed different.

The works of Shakespeare had long been sources for musicals (*The Boys from Syracuse* [1938], *Kiss Me, Kate* [1948], *West Side Story* [1957]), even rock ones (*Your Own Thing* [1968], *Two Gentlemen of Verona* [1971]), and what is more, Fosse had already shown what a director-choreographer could do with a rock musical in *Pippin* (1972), just as Robbins had with a jazz one in *West Side Story*. But Gower, who at this point saw the conventional musical as a dying form, considered rock the means that not merely could save but also transform it: "I feel that traditional musical comedy has almost run its course because the musical comedy doesn't relate to where the music is today. But I really think the rock musicians are breaking new ground."[82] So why not get in on the excitement with a high-tech staging of an audience-tested rock opera based on the most famous of Shakespeare's tragedies?

His newly acquired interests in rock and unconventional staging were about to converge with his ongoing quest for serious subject matter in a pull-out-all-the-stops, no-holds-barred production more avant-garde (and ultimately controversial) by far than *Prettybelle*. But unlike that show, this one he would complete and unleash on Broadway with an unbounded and unapologetic force that dared to express visually what the Bard had poetically: the madness of the hero unraveling in the most corrupt of courts, in this case the quintessential rock concert with flamboyant, sometimes outrageous, effects rivaling those of the Rolling Stones or Alice Cooper.[83] This was his own unique telling of the classic drama—contemporary, irreverent, audacious, and totally unlike anything he had ever done—the breakout directing feat needed to save a fading career. Never did he have so much riding on a show as with *Rockabye Hamlet*.

"It is not Shakespeare and it is not a revival," he informed the press on the first day of rehearsal, December 15, 1975, as they gathered with him and the forty-member cast in a rehearsal studio atop Radio City Music Hall. This was not Shakespeare indeed, at least not in the traditional sense; one look at the young, hip, racially diverse cast made that clear. Black actors portrayed Denmark's royal family. *Two Gentlemen of Verona* and *Hair*'s Larry Marshall won the title role (over British rock star Paul Nicholas and Broadway's Ben Vereen), Leata Galloway (*Don't Bother Me, I Can't Cope, Hair*) was Gertrude, and Alan Weeks (*Hallelujah, Baby!, George M!*), Claudius.[84] "I think Gower really took a chance making the royal family a black family," says Weeks. "That was really going out on a limb. And the white girl

Ophelia strangling herself with a microphone cord over a black guy? C'mon. I will always hold up Gower on a pedestal for that."[85]

White actors took the parallel roles: soon-to-be film actress Beverly D'Angelo was Ophelia (from the Canadian production), Randal Wilson (*Jesus Christ Superstar, Your Own Thing*), Polonius, and Kim Milford (*Hair, Your Own Thing*), Laertes. Winston DeWitt Hemsley (*Hallelujah, Baby!*, Pearl Bailey's *Hello, Dolly!*) and Christopher Chadman (*Pippin, Chicago*) played Guildenstern and Rosencrantz, and future rock sensation Meat Loaf (*Hair, The Rocky Horror Picture Show*), the sinister Priest. Irving Lee took the role of the First Player, and Rory Dodd, Horatio. "I'm the only one, along with the producers, who is over thirty," the director joked.

Rockabye Hamlet was no mere revival of *Kronborg*, either. Since late summer, when he first joined Gower in Los Angeles, Jones had continued to develop and expand the score, which now consisted of thirty-six songs in various styles: blues, ballad, country-western, vaudeville, gospel, calypso, boogie-woogie, even newly arrived disco.[86] His rock opera stuck closely to Shakespeare's plot except in the details of the murder of Polonius (stabbed by Hamlet not behind the arras of Gertrude's bedroom, but at a Midnight Mass) and Ophelia's suicide (not by drowning, but self-strangulation with a microphone cord—the climax to the title song, a lullaby that built to a screaming lament *à la* Janis Joplin).[87]

As rehearsals progressed, music director and vocal arranger Gordon Lowry Harrell gave the score a fuller and more dynamic sound than its Canadian production in accordance with the director's requests, which never were too specific. "Gower's vocabulary was not really in rock," Harrell explains. "He could tell us dynamically if we were right or wrong or if something had to be of some quality, but he couldn't say that what you need here is a good strong guitar riff on top of everything else to carry it over. Not that he threw up his hands, but he let us know right away that we were going to have to work it out and he was not going to be able to give us much input."[88] Perched upon Kurt F. Lundell's bilevel set for the duration of the show, Harrell's band with its massive Moog synthesizer delivered the sound essential to the ambiance and staging Gower was crafting.

"I have abdicated the dancing to Tony Stevens who knows all the steps from rock to boogie to calypso," he declared.[89] Stevens, an assistant choreographer for *Irene*, was appointed co-choreographer for this. Ever since *The Happy Time* and Clive Barnes's admonition to stick to staging and leave the choreography to someone else, Gower had done just that, ceding the creation of the actual steps to assistants in order to focus more on the concept and general design for each number. Moreover, Stevens's dance language was current, something essential in a production as cutting-edge as Gower intended this to be. A range of styles would be used to mock institutions, social conventions, religious ceremonies (a wedding, Mass, and funeral—each one more resplendent than the other), and literary classics, including *Hamlet* itself. There was an incestuous ballroom turn (kiss and all) for Hamlet and Gertrude; a high-kicking entrance down the huge center stage ramp for Rosencrantz and Guildenstern as a pair of bowler-topped, wing-collared, shirtless vaudevillians; a slinky Cher-like lament for Gertrude, sung atop a piano in a silvery, slit-down-the-leg gown; and a high-stepping country-western romp for the play-within-a-play sequence with the chief player, a black singer (Irving Lee) in "white face," leading his troupe clad in electric blue cowboy outfits. Even the handing-over of microphones from performer to performer was intricately choreographed.[90]

Most impressive was the swashbuckling finale with Hamlet grabbing hold of the castle entry's huge grated portcullis as it rose above the drawbridge-like ramp jutting from upstage into the house. High atop the rising ramp, Hamlet battled Laertes, and then Claudius, in a stunning act of swordsmanship staged by Larry Carpenter, Gower's assistant. Laertes went tumbling head over heels to his death; Hamlet and Claudius fought to the finish with the bravura derring-do of Errol Flynn and Basil Rathbone in *Robin Hood*. "It was *that* choreographed, *that* perfect, *that* astonishing," recalls Jess. "John Gielgud later told me, 'There were things about it that were breathtaking.' And when Hamlet died and there was the 'Good Night, Sweet Prince' part, it was touching and moving."[91]

The rock concert environment called for technical artists who were experts in this form of entertainment and people upon whom Gower could rely to chart a new course in musical-making. Jules Fisher's multitudinous lights flooded the stage with sensational effects, including a laser-induced ghost of Hamlet's father. Lundell's bilevel set with its huge ramp laterally surrounded on the forestage by scaffold platforms and flights of steps was alive with levitating staircases, towering pulpits, and flashing signs the size of Times Square billboards that miraculously appeared and vanished. Joseph G. Aulisi's costumes, ranging from contemporary denim to Hollywood gothic, also ridiculed the outlandish capes, masks, and heavy eye mascara popularized by rock stars.[92]

Directing *Rockabye Hamlet* was the best time Gower ever had in his career, he told Karla, and it was likewise that for the cast, especially Weeks: "My association with Gower was always fun. One thing I had to do was shave my head. He came to me one day and said, 'Look, the skullcap isn't working, so shave your head and you'll look mean,' and I did. That was a big deal for me, but the character really came alive once I did it because the look was established and wasn't fake. It became a thing of life. I carried myself differently. I also had a Fu Manchu—and it was good to be the king."[93]

Part of the fun for Gower also stemmed from not having to take the $750,000 production on a lengthy road trial as with *Mack and Mabel*. This show, as the Canadian staging had already shown, was stageworthy, and given the present production's costly and complicated effects, the producers opted to forgo an out-of-town tryout and open directly on Broadway at the Minskoff Theatre following two weeks of previews. Turnout was poor when previews began, but soon wildly enthusiastic SRO crowds presaged a hit in which NBC was especially eager to invest. The cast was ecstatic. By the time it was ready to open on February 17, 1976, the show seemed to have found its audience.[94] Even so, certain factors were already influencing the outcome, though neither Gower nor the company were aware of them.

The Canadian production had appeared during the Vietnam War at a time when the social order in the United States was under fire by numerous dissenters critical of its injustices and failures. For many, especially American youth, social protest was a way to express dissatisfaction with a nation seen as rotten with war, injustice, and political intrigue as Denmark itself. A cynical distrust of institutions was pervasive and played out on the stage in the guise of *Hair* and *Jesus Christ Superstar,* which mocked everything from governmental indifference to religious haughtiness. But since the climax of Watergate, with President Nixon's resignation, and the fall of Saigon, which ended the war, the era of social protest was rapidly drawing to a close as the nation put behind itself over a decade of unrest in preparation for its Bicentennial. Almost overnight the cultural climate changed, activism faded, and skepticism toward the establishment now seemed as misanthropic as it once was *au courant*. Although Gower's revolutionary musical had not yet opened, already it was an anachronism, and Jess was one of the few who noticed.

"I saw *Rockabye Hamlet* three times and sweated through all of it because I knew it was going to be a flop and I was resisting it being a flop, too. That's what's known as 'flop sweat.' But it was a success in that there was nothing sweet or family value about it. My God, the raw creativeness of it! It was as if *Rockabye Hamlet* was Hamlet's madness and where it was good, it was electric, imaginative beyond belief."[95]

Gar was decked out in his customary red jacket when Jess arrived backstage on opening night to thank him for the tickets and congratulate him on the show. Yet from the lukewarm greeting, it was clear to Jess that their friendship was every bit as bankrupt as he had feared. No sooner had he started describing what he admired than Gar stopped him flat, hand raised in a standoffish gesture. He wanted no praise or criticism. This was it, and if people didn't like it, they could go to hell.[96] Excusing himself from Jess and the cast party, he returned to his hotel room, where he and Karla waited for the reviews. At last the phone rang and Larry Carpenter started to read, Gower listening all the while with mounting unease.[97]

"Cliff Jones' *Rockabye Hamlet . . .* might just as well have been titled *Hamlet Goes to Las Vegas* for the things that impress one about the production—directed,

alas, by Gower Champion—are effects with lights, with neon, with stage gim-
mickry of the sort one associates with Las Vegas girlie shows,"[98] reported Howard
Kissel. "To watch *Rockabye Hamlet*," added Douglas Watt, "a gaudy and anachro-
nistic exercise in musical kitsch that flopped about the stage of the Minskoff last
night like a dying swordfish, is to marvel at the heights of folly attainable along
Broadway."[99] With all the parody seeming more like ripoff than takeoff, Martin
Gottfried asked "Where did Champion ever see the sense in a rock *Hamlet*?" and
"Where is his taste?" He also counseled, "Champion needs to pause and look back
over his previous accomplishments; to see what he did that was right and true for
him, what was wrong and done for misguided or mistaken reasons. He must find
his artistic personality. I believe it to lie in showmanship, raised by invention to a
classy level."[100] But to the director, so intently focused on what he wanted to become and so completely uninterested in what he had been, the words seemed glib.
"What a pity, what a pity," he responded as Carpenter read on.[101]

Jones suffered slings and arrows of outrageous fortune far worse than Gower—
his score was called everything from "a libel on the Bard and a complete bore"[102] to
a "shabby, unpromising, . . . insulting patchwork";[103] his talent, as Clive Barnes put
it, that of "a second-rate musician with a third-rate mind."[104] The lyrics—there was
the rub. Slangy rhyming couplets like the one substituted for Polonius's farewell
speech to Laertes ("Son, you must return to France/Keep your divinity in your
pants") sent critics reeling so much that they failed to notice the songs that did directly incorporate Shakespeare's text, like "That It Should Come to This," "Tis Pity,
Tis True," and "Get Thee to a Nunnery."[105] There were also some songs well-suited
to their moments: Hamlet's breakthrough, "If My Morning Begins," which came
shortly before the tragic end, and Gertrude's low-moaning farewell, "The Last
Blues."[106]

Mercifully, the perfomers fared better. There was praise for Larry Marshall's
dashing, dignified Prince, stirring in movement and voice, Beverly D'Angelo's gorgeous Ophelia, like a Botticelli painting sprung to life, Leata Galloway's intrepid
Gertrude with a dash of hysteria, Alan Weeks's brash boogeying monarch, cun-
ningly fused to Yul Brynner and Genghis Khan, Kim Milford's agile preppy Laertes,
Chris Chadman and Winston DeWitt Hemsley's animated Rosencrantz and
Guildenstern, and Meat Loaf's eerie, base cleric.

Dining with Karla, Jess, and Jess's friend Leo Revi on the evening of the show's
seventh and final performance, Gower bitterly concluded: "The only thing left for
me is to go out to Vegas and do a 'tits and feathers' show."[107] But now Vegas was out
of the question, too. Lack of funding had killed plans for the new Caesar's Palace
Theatre and stage spectacular Cliff Perlman had promised. One more dream
crushed.[108]

SIXTEEN

Reworking, Doctoring, Capitulating

Annie Get Your Gun, The Act, and *A Broadway Musical*

1976–1979

It had rained nonstop ever since their arrival ten days earlier at the Holiday Inn in Jupiter, Florida, but that mattered little to Gower and Karla. Anything was preferable to a New York February, especially one as bitter as this had been. With beachcombing out of the question, they made a grand time of just being together, relaxing and unwinding with the countless sessions of gin rummy Gower loved to play. The weather passed, but Karla worried if his disappointment would also. As their road trip resumed, she tried to boost his spirits, reminding him of how *Rockabye*'s staging had impressed some critics. It was useless. "I'm responsible for everything on that stage," he insisted. "If the show doesn't make it, I let the kids down because they don't have jobs."[1] Much as she admired his accountability, how could he possibly have predicted the hostile critical response given the screaming, cheering crowds that had filled the house with the emotion of a revival meeting right up to closing? Anyone would have thought *Rockabye* a sure bet.[2]

Within days, though, Karla noticed something remarkable. He had stopped talking about the show. Quietly his resilience was returning, growing stronger as they continued through New Orleans, Tucson, and Palm Springs. Shortly after arriving back in Los Angeles he purchased a house in Mandeville Canyon, in the western suburbs. Once again he was starting over, cleaning out years of accumulation—every file, every script from *Prettybelle* to *Rockabye*—and putting the past behind him. "You'd never get Gower talking about what was over," says Karla. "He *really* was not into the past, which he called the waxworks. He lived very much in the moment and for the future. He really wasn't interested in what he had done before. He was a very here-and-now kind of guy, which I loved about him."[3] This time, however, all the cleaning out and moving had a greater purpose. On July 23, 1976, he and Karla were married during a ceremony he personally directed with great care in their new Mandeville Canyon home.

He also had a new production of Irving Berlin's *Annie Get Your Gun* under way for producers Cy Feuer and Ernest H. Martin of the Los Angeles Civic Light Opera, and to help him get it started he asked Will Mead, one of his replacement dancers for the 1965 national tour of *Dolly!*, to be his assistant. For the former dancer, now teaching deaf students at a local junior high school, this was the opportunity of a lifetime: "I was rather flabbergasted that he would ask me. I always had felt a very strong connection with Gower, and wrote to him every once in a while. His work was something very close to my heart. So I just felt that I belonged in his world. And of course I said yes. It was a dream come true. I would have been very happy just to sharpen pencils and go get coffee, and do whatever he wanted me to do."[4] Mead, who had not danced for almost seven years, quit his job, went back to dance class, and prepared to become "Assistant to Gower Champion."

The first day of preproduction at the rehearsal studios in the Dorothy Chandler Pavilion, Gower took the script, opened it rather officially, and asked his assistant, "Well, what shall we do with this?"[5] With that began Mead's tutorial on how to reenvision and rethink an old warhorse of a show. Brainstorming was what Gower was doing: finding ways to make anonymous characters definite individuals, like the four daughters of the hotel manager, whom he compared to a Picasso print of four different flowers, each a little different from the other. There was also much discussion about how to make scenes blend into each other, where to place numbers, and whether they should be repositioned in keeping with the redefined characters that were emerging.

Mead's research also aided the brainstorming and stimulated the director's imagination. Books on Native Americans resulted in a rethinking of how they would be portrayed in this production—not as "filthy redskins," but as a center-point stabilizing the raging egos of all the showbiz characters. As a result, the character of Chief Sitting Bull became the nucleus of the show's spirit. A Dover book containing reproductions of fifty original Buffalo Bill Wild West posters helped to establish the look of the show's scenery, costumes, and lighting.[6]

Gower confided to Mead that this would be his last musical and his staging of its anthem, "There's No Business Like Show Business," his parting salute to the theatre. For that reason, the production would be no mere revival, but a total reworking of the original 1946 play. Berlin's personal endorsement gave him the required flexibility to rethink the entire show. Instead of the usual unspecified prairie setting, he rooted the production in late-nineteenth-century Cincinnati, Ohio (one of the Eastern cities the Wild West Show would have toured), with a choreographed prologue that added substance and depth.

The curtain rose on the lawn and gazebo of the Wilson Hotel on the outskirts of the city, where from up right a scruffy, road-weary cowboy entered, to the strains of "There's No Business Like Show Business," carrying a hammer and a poster rolled up under his arm. After taking in the scene, he crossed to the gazebo, nailing the poster to one of its posts. Members of the Buffalo Bill Wild West Troupe—a mix of cowboys, showgirls, Indians, stagehands, rope twirlers, clowns, cooks, and helpers—then followed him. As a whole, their showbiz coarseness contrasted markedly with the bucolic setting they desecrated as they proceeded to set up camp for their stay in this town and the music grew in intensity. All the paraphernalia of a traveling wild west show—wardrobe trunks, prop cases, banners, posters, ladders, teepees, and show wagons—transformed the Wilson Hotel meadow into a garish setting. At the peak of the pandemonium, Charlie Davenport came forward, ringing a triangle for attention. As he addressed the audience, Dolly Tate and the members of the troupe joined him in "Colonel Buffalo Bill" while the setting-up activity continued.[7]

The third week of preproduction, Gower brought the designers aboard—*Bye Bye Birdie*'s Robert Randolph for scenery and lighting and *Sugar*'s Alvin Colt for costumes—who expected him to give them his master concept for the production. Instead he surprised them by asking, "Well, what do you think we should do with this show?" Soon the designers, too, were engaged in the brainstorming process.[8]

Once musical and vocal director Jack Lee and co-choreographer Tony Stevens arrived, there was much talk about the "There's No Business Like Show Business" ballet, a unique feature and centerpiece of the production. "I said to Gower, 'What are you going to do with the ensemble?'" Lee recalls asking. "That's when he came up with the idea of making the ensemble to be the Buffalo Bill troupe. In the original show, the ensemble consisted mostly of spectators, and the Buffalo Bill troupe a handful of people. Gower replied, 'I want the whole company to be that troupe. And I want the audience in the theatre to be the spectators.'"[9] From that point, preproduction was about how to make the ensemble into members of the troupe for each scene.

The idea would peak with the "Show Business" ballet. "Gower figured if Annie got enwrapped in the story the three guys [Charlie Davenport, Buffalo Bill, and Frank Butler] were telling her about what show business is, she would become so excited that she would want to *be* in show business. He was thinking it all out, 'How is she going to do that? I know. We'll get a putty nose, put the nose on her face, and that'll make her a clown.'"[10] The putty nose was the centerpiece of the ballet about Annie's initiation into show business. It united the first part—Annie as spectator-explorer—with the third part—Annie as troupe member-performer.

Gower began the ballet with the song staged as a competition among Buffalo Bill, Frank, and Charlie, with each of them vying for a chance to explain to Annie what show business is really like. By the song's end she is drawn into their spell. They direct her attention to the right portal, from which pops a white gloved hand in a spotlight as the music diminishes. The men encourage her to investigate. As she pulls the hand from the wings a line of dancing show business types slowly emerges—a clown, then various cowboys, showgirls, a ballerina in tutu and cowboy boots, a minstrel, acrobats, and so on. Buffalo Bill, Frank, and Charlie now depart, leaving the chorus to instruct Annie on the glories and disappointments of show business through pantomime and dance. The music builds as the chorus becomes a moving backdrop for a series of turns by different artists—a strongman with barbells that the clowns comically attempt to steal, a ballerina who completes thirty-two fouettés before collapsing as "the dying swan," a "Gibson Girl" with a swing built into her costume who crosses the stage rocking back and forth. Annie, who has been wandering through all this with amazement, now exits with the clowns.

The entire stage picture is now reconfigured as more dancers pour on, with tambourines forming a backdrop for acrobats who madly tumble down center as a very tall Indian (on four-foot stilts) with long braids enters upstage carrying a yellow balloon. Just as Annie reenters with the two clowns, the music builds to a climax and stops. Suddenly the stage is empty except for the three of them captured in a spotlight. As the music very slowly begins again, Charlie Davenport now enters dressed as a ringmaster and takes the balloon from the tall Indian. He watches as the clowns put a big red putty nose on Annie in slow motion and teach her clowning. The ringmaster offers the balloon, and the clowns pass it before Annie. Just as she reaches to take it, the ringmaster pops it. Annie pantomimes tears; a Chinese magician consoles her with flowers he pulls from the air. A belly dancer shakes her torso haughtily at Annie, and a Chinese dragon drifts in and out of the spotlight. Downstage of Annie a minstrel dancer begins a marching step, and the orchestra goes into a military tattoo. Now silhouetted behind the cyclorama that fills the height and breadth of the stage, the dancers one by one pick up the step until they are all pulled into a circle of rhythm and life. The circle explodes into the light as they fill the entire stage for the song's final verse—some stretched before the footlights, others moving on bended knee toward the audience, Jolson-style—where they are joined by Charlie, Buffalo Bill, and Frank, who alone sings the final "Let's go on with the show" as the music diminishes and all blow a kiss to the audience. Blackout.

The casting was as inspired as the staging. Debbie Reynolds played the feisty Annie Oakley and Harve Presnell, her leading man from the film *The Unsinkable Molly Brown* (1964), Frank Butler. The remainder of the cast included Bibi Osterwald as Dolly Tate, Gavin MacLeod, later of TV's *The Love Boat,* as Charlie Davenport, and Art Lund as Buffalo Bill.

As preparations commenced for the opening, the technicians of San Francisco's newly refurbished Orpheum Theatre had trouble delivering the exact effects Gower wanted when he wanted them, so he simply grabbed a ladder and made the adjustments himself. But as the show neared its debut, Gower appeared to be slowing down and Lee was concerned: "Something was wrong—I knew he was ill. Sometimes he'd be late coming into rehearsals. He'd say, 'I'm so tired.'"[11] Mead, who became a dancer in the show when James Mitchell later succeeded him as director's assistant, noticed something, too: his skin appeared to be easily bruised, as the purple blotches on his arms showed.[12]

The rave reviews *Annie Get Your Gun* received upon its opening on May 10, 1977, so delighted Gower that at the party Reynolds later hosted that evening at Trader Vic's, he celebrated like she had never seen him do in all the years they had known each other: "We just danced and sang our hearts away, and Gower had such a good time and he was not one to do that. That was the only time I've ever known him to break down and just be one of the gypsies. The show was such a smash, and just everybody, even the press, was so crazy about it. Never did I ever see Gower so high that he was dancing so tipsy; I remember that very fondly."[13]

Annie went on to Los Angeles, Dallas, and Miami. Rumors of a Broadway run cooled, however, once Reynolds decided to decline: "I never took it into Broadway, which was my mistake. I was tired at the time; I was raising my children, and I just couldn't face doing eight shows a week. But it was the most staggeringly brilliant *Annie* ever."[14]

Broadway did come knocking for Gower, though, in late September 1977 via a request from producers Feuer and Martin and songwriters Kander and Ebb to doctor their Liza Minnelli vehicle *The Act,* then struggling through its Los Angeles run with only a month to go before opening in New York. Minnelli, fresh from filming the Kander and Ebb–scored *New York, New York* for Martin Scorsese and in the midst of a greatly publicized affair with him, agreed to star on condition the brilliant young filmmaker direct.[15] "Well, it was a crazy time," explains producer Cy Feuer, "what with the rampant counterculture and the omnipresence of drugs. No one was behaving rationally. Liza offered her own explanation for her demand: 'Marty and I are in love and we're going to spend the rest of our lives together. We are together in everything we do. Therefore, he is going to direct the show.'"[16] Feuer and his partner were stunned, but what could they do? Even though Stanley Donen had been under consideration, they acceded to their star's wishes and hired the filmmaker of *Mean Streets* and *Taxi Driver,* who had never directed a musical and quickly became lost in its arcana.[17] "Liza felt grateful to him," Fred Ebb later explained. "I think Marty, himself, went out on a limb to do a Broadway show: I don't think he had any desire to do it; it was his affection for Liza that made him want to do it. And the fact was he was not qualified to do the show. His genius was in another medium."[18]

In July 1977, when *The Act* opened in Chicago as *Shine It On* (after first being announced as *In Person*), the reviews were terrible. They were worse in San Francisco, and hideous in Los Angeles.[19] "At worst, the dumbest backstage musical ever, to the point where you figure they've got to be kidding," scoffed critic Dan Sullivan. "*The Act* needs help and it won't help."[20] Minnelli was virtually running a musical decathlon, belting out twelve of the musical's thirteen songs, dancing up a storm, and darting off only twice all evening for costume changes.[21] Yet in city after city, a dull production with no central vision was undermining her electrifying sellout effort. Scorsese, simultaneously refining *New York, New York* and editing *The Last Waltz,* had no time to nail down specifics with designers regarding the degree of operatic gloom he visualized for the show, and this was evident in Chicago when Tony Walton's scenery and Tharon Musser's lighting first met Thea Van Runkle's "sadistic" costumes (as one critic described them), which were quickly replaced with new ones by Halston.[22]

George Furth's book, said to be loosely based on the life of performer Shirley MacLaine, tried to be inventive with the plot about a movie star determined to revive a flagging career by turning Vegas nightclub entertainer, but its sketchy, episodic scenes, purposely unrelated to the numbers, only compounded the difficulties.[23] So much did audiences resent the disparate and intrusive dramatic flashbacks of Minnelli's Michelle Craig struggling to steer a career through quarrels, physical abuse, abortion, infidelity, bankruptcy, and death that half of them were walking out at intermission.[24]

The lack of coherence in the plot and the production at large stemmed from a lack of direction—the price of putting the star's wants ahead of the show's needs. "Certainly Marty couldn't figure it out," explains Feuer. "He was either locked away in his dressing room fighting his running nose, or completely baffled about how to fix the problem. And he was missing shows. Finally, it was clear to me that he was the problem. *The Act* needed a real director. He had to go. The only person who could fire him was Liza, and I had to tell her . . . She understood."[25] Feuer went in pursuit of his *Annie Get Your Gun* director who, after catching a Saturday matinee, turned him down. While he liked the star and the score, Gower wasn't attracted to the show itself and doubted it could work.[26] But when Ebb pleaded with him to come back to watch the evening performance, he did. Afterward, before joining the authors for dinner, he met with Minnelli privately in her dressing room to discuss what he could do. An hour later he emerged declaring, "She is a *temptress*."[27] The temptress had agreed to *allow* him to take over the show and arrange to bring it to Broadway in respectable shape provided Scorsese retained billing as director.[28] "Granted that Liza was very seductive and that Gower enthralled her," explains Kander, "but he was also somebody who was very definite in rehearsal. Even though the show was never wonderful, he made it immensely better and made her immensely better because she had somebody strong at the helm. He turned it into a show, and we were extremely grateful to him."[29] With the production's suicide averted, the show doctor began to apply the therapy essential for a healthy Broadway life.

On Sunday, September 25, he rehearsed the company and implemented several changes that considerably lightened the Monday night performance. Out went the eleven-minute overture and several scenes—the one dealing with Craig's abortion, another in which she was slapped about by her lover until she subdued him with karate, and two in which she twice lost the Academy Award. In went a new opening, a tag on the second act showstopper "City Lights," and a score of minor modifications that made everything seem effortless.[30] As work progressed, the unconventional structure that avoided linking numbers to book was discarded.[31] "When Gower came in," notes Kander, "he made it clear that we had to connect it, and he was absolutely right. It was for the best."[32] In time, a thematic relationship between *The Act*'s songs and story was forged through Champion's use of color-coded index cards with one color for songs and another for scenes.[33] In this way the authors, director, and choreographer Ron Lewis could examine different combinations of the two and decide which might work best. "Gower saved our lives with that,"[34] acknowledges Kander, who also noticed a change in the director's approach: "He was totally different than he had been on *The Happy Time*, when he kept us out of rehearsals. When it came to *The Act*, he wanted us there all the time."[35]

By the time of the opening at New York's Majestic on October 29, 1977, Gower had essentially restaged the whole show, with the exception of Lewis's dances, placing the band on a moveable stage that separated and moved off (as in *Sugar*) as the scene shifted to Craig's dressing room. In the interest of timing, he also devised a costume change for Minnelli that kept her on stage while a group of dancers surrounded her and a gown floated down from the flies to drape itself over her waiting form.[36] As for the dances, he was delighted that they were in such great shape: "I didn't change one single step of Ron Lewis's choreography. Lewis is brilliant. When you walk in as a show doctor and the dancers are in trouble, you're really in trouble. Then it's just horrible."[37]

Concerning his fixing of *The Act*, Gower was as tight-lipped as he was methodical, closing ranks with Scorsese (now in Rome discussing a film about street gangs) and distancing himself from the press: "I have inherited a sick child, and I can't talk about it right now."[38] When the show opened to generally favorable notices, the New York critics were not fooled by Scorsese's billing as director, for evidence of Gower's "polish as sleek and cool as chromium,"[39] as Gottfried put it, was everywhere. As a result, *The Act* went on to run for 233 performances and Minnelli won the Tony for Outstanding Performance by an Actress in a Musical. "It turned out to be quite a substantial hit, thanks to Gower, who came in and actually saved us," stated Ebb.[40] Even ten years later, when the libretto was finally published, the authors warmly recalled the show doctor's contribution, writing, "This play is lovingly and gratefully dedicated to Gower Champion."[41]

The success of *The Act* as well as *Annie Get Your Gun* also saved Gower while allowing him to remain rooted in California. So when Feuer and Martin, now managing directors of the Los Angeles and San Francisco Light Opera Association, asked him to become the company's artistic director and offered him yet another production, he eagerly accepted. He chose Rodgers and Hart's *Pal Joey* as the April opener for the 1978 season. Like *Annie Get Your Gun,* it would tour the West Coast for twenty-six weeks as a totally revised production. A new book by Michael Stewart and Mark Bramble traded the 1930s nightclub setting of John O'Hara's original for a 1970s disco club and an interracial cast led by Lena Horne, an inspired choice for the world-weary, sophisticated Vera. But by January 1978 the production was so badly mired in casting and conceptual disputes that he withdrew—a rare thing for the intensely committed director, now in search once more for enduring work in California. (Under replacement Michael Kidd, *Pal Joey* became a vehicle for Horne with an all-black ensemble that relied on O'Hara's original libretto after Stewart and Bramble also resigned.)[42]

He decided to do something completely different. At the prompting of young film director and friend Robert Greenwald, he took on a small acting role as a dance instructor in the TV movie *Sharon: Portrait of a Mistress* with Trish Van Devere, Patrick O'Neal, Mel Ferrer, and Gloria DeHaven. He flew up to San Francisco, shot the sequence, and returned the same day. When Karla picked him up at the airport that evening, he seemed full of himself as he strode toward her wearing his ubiquitous sunglasses. Getting into the car, he remarked, "You know I believe that people should change careers about every ten years. So, I think I'd love to be an actor." Karla was amused. Having a director in the family was one thing, but what would it be like having an actor? She was about to find out.[43]

In May 1978, when *The Act*'s co-star Barry Nelson took leave to do a film in London, Gower took over for him in the nonmusical role of Minnelli's producer and ex-spouse Dan Connors. "I haven't been on a stage for 22 years, since *3 for Tonight*," he admitted, adding, "I'm doing *The Act* for the fun of it, the challenge, the stretch."[44] With Karla and stage manager George Boyd serving as drama coaches, he handily rose to the occasion, receiving complimentary notices for his grace and conviction as a slightly battered but totally unbowed former husband.[45]

Whether performing as an actor, rescuing new shows from disaster, or totally reconceiving classics like his acclaimed choreographed staging of Thornton Wilder's *Our Town* (with music by John Kander) for the Long Beach Theatre in

October 1978, he was having the time of his life. Clearly, *Annie Get your Gun* had not been the farewell to the theater he had once predicted, but rather a fresh start he never could have foreseen. The proof was in the agreement he had signed in September 1978 (under his company name "Champion VII") with authors Michael Stewart and Mark Bramble detailing the specifics of his full-scale return to Broadway.[46] *42nd Street* would be a summation of his work; a confident review of everything he knew and cherished about the musical theatre. Already negotiations were under way with Merrick, the only producer in an age of minimusicals with enough cash and clout to give it the classy extravagance required.

Based upon the Bradford Ropes novel and featuring songs by Harry Warren and Al Dubin, the 1933 Warner Brothers film starring Ruby Keeler, Dick Powell, Bebe Daniels, Warner Baxter, and Ginger Rogers recounted chorine Peggy Sawyer's meteoric rise to stardom via her last-minute stand-in for the ailing leading lady of a Broadway spectacular that reverses the fortunes of its down-and-out director, Julian Marsh. Produced by Darryl F. Zanuck, it featured the spectacular kaleidoscopic dance sequences of Busby Berkeley, master of the Hollywood musical. Gower, mindful of his trouble with the Keystone Kops in *Mack and Mabel,* endeavored to steer clear of heavy-handed references to Berkeley's work. His plan was to graft his own spectacular staging onto the slender tale to create a concise history of the ways movement had stirred audiences since musical theatre began.

After finishing preliminary work on the show just before Thanksgiving 1978, he was about to leave New York for California when *Bye Bye Birdie* songwriters Charles Strouse and Lee Adams asked him to look at their troubled satire about white-created black musicals then in its fourth week of a test run at the Theatre of the Riverside Church in Harlem.[47] Strange as the site was for a Broadway tryout, it was the perfect forum for producer Norman Kean *(Oh! Calcutta!, Don't Bother Me, I Can't Cope)*, who usually worked on a shoestring, and maybe thought the show could profit from the prayers, too.[48] Since the sensational *A Chorus Line* (1975), producers were opting to "workshop" productions in smaller off-Broadway venues rather than risk expensive out-of-town tryouts. *A Chorus Line* also reintroduced the backstage musical, with *The Act* the most recent addition to a genre popularized years before by the film *42nd Street*. Like them, *A Broadway Musical* was a backstage saga and, also like *42nd Street,* a musical about the making of a musical. The ailing show, due to open in less than a month at the Lunt-Fontanne, hardly seemed in condition for Broadway, but Kean, aided by Cineplex Odeon movie theatre mogul Garth H. Drabinsky, was determined to get it there by any means. (The careers of both men had unfortunate ends: in 1988, Kean jumped to his death after murdering his wife, actress Gwyda DonHowe, who had played the producer's wife in *A Broadway Musical;* Drabinsky, who later produced *Show Boat* [1993] and *Rag-*

time [1998], went bankrupt and faced criminal charges from leveraging far too much projected income against expenses.[49])

Chief among the show's ills was the slapdash book by William F. Brown (*The Wiz*) about an acerbic white producer's exploitation of a young black author and his locker-room basketball drama "about the exploitation of a human being" called *The Final Point*. In the end, crass Broadway commercialism triumphed as *The Final Point* got subverted into *Sneakers* the musical, and the playwright traded his pen for the starring role. What satire there was surfaced only randomly in tunes about "Lawyers" with ironclad contracts and the "Yenta Power" of Jewish theatre party ladies—hardly enough to entice Gower into taking over from George Faison of *The Wiz* with less than a month to work his magic. "It was a mess, a mishmash," states musical supervisor and vocal arranger Donald Pippin, "and made no sense at all. If George had been together enough to bring it together, he could have made it really innovative. He had such marvelous, exciting ideas, and there was so much talent running around. Then I heard Gower was coming in. I couldn't imagine why he would do it. It was a show you felt like closing."[50]

Karla took in an evening performance with Gower. Although she never expressed an opinion on matters of his career, this time she had no qualms.

"Based on what you saw tonight, are you *really* going to put your name on this?" she asked. "I just don't think you should."

"Well, not at least until I see it's up on its feet," he assured her.

She knew it was not up to his standards; so did Fred Ebb, who likewise counseled against it.[51] Ignoring their advice and his better judgment, he buckled under pressure from his business office, agreeing to come aboard provided he was billed not as director, but as "production supervisor."[52] Maybe there was something he could do for this "musical about the making of a Broadway musical" that would pull together its wild mix of coarse producers, opportunistic lawyers, gullible writers, pretentious Vegas stars, theatre party yentas, and lampooning of the current rage for black musicals.

Another consideration was the talent. In addition to Strouse and Adams, there were gifted performers from past shows like *Make a Wish*'s Helen Gallagher and *Rockabye Hamlet*'s Larry Marshall and Alan Weeks. "One of the reasons I think Gower came to do this show was because Larry and I were in it," reflects Weeks. "I played a black, spaced-out rock 'n' roll composer, so I got to sing rock again. Gower was brought in to fix the book. What book? In a nutshell, it wasn't very good. It was something that could not be fixed."[53]

That did not dampen the atmosphere of expectancy among the predominantly young cast, many of them recent recipients of Equity cards, gathered to greet the show doctor on his first day. Champion was a legend to the newly initiated, a consummate showman to the pros, and to all a savior who would do for them and their show what he had done for Liza Minnelli and *The Act*. Then, suddenly, there he was in all his casual elegance. "I'll never forget it," recalls production associate Jake Weisbarth. "A cashmere blue blazer, a pair of jeans, an open shirt with a kind of ascot. He looked like someone out of the pages of Ralph Lauren. Gorgeously dressed, immaculate, well put together. A good-looking man. And those white Hollywood Chiclet teeth. He smiled and 'Boom!' "[54]

The reception was effusive. "Thank you for your warm welcome," he responded graciously. "I just want to tell you, we have a tremendous amount of work to do with very little time. I've come in and saved some shows before. The last one was *The Act*. But I have to say, I come to this with a lot of trepidation. *The Act* had Liza Minnelli, you don't."[55] Horrified, Weisbarth watched the morale of the cast deflate before him: "It was a shameful thing to do, a jab, and very obvious. He could have kept that to himself."[56]

Gower was pulling no punches, although he did pull out all the stops, mounting an entirely new production with four major cast replacements (Warren Berlinger for Julius LaRosa, Patti Karr for Helen Gallagher, Irving Lee for Ron Ferrell, and Tiger Haynes in a new role) and entirely new dancing with co-choreographer George Bunt. Among the highlights was "The 1934 Hot Chocolate Jazz Babies Revue" with the masterful Tiger Haynes, Tin Man of *The Wiz*, entering as an old stagehand sweeping the stage and pausing to recall the golden era of his youth. From out of nowhere a clutch of old-time Cotton Club-like "ponies" entered to join him in a showstopper that combined jazzy moves of the period with Gower's signature choreography.[57] There was also the second act rouser "You Gotta Have Dancing," with Karr leading the entire ensemble in a flashy pastiche of various show dances.

Not everyone was pleased with the changes, especially Anne Francine, who played a theatre party lady and had the showstopper. "It was fabulous, me and the ladies that helped me in the theatre parties, called 'Yenta Power'—this great Yenta and her little Yenta-ettes. He insisted on putting the men in it, and it just ruined the number. I was sick about it."[58]

At the month's end, when the curtain went up, it seemed that Gower had worked another miracle. "The opening [number] was dynamite," remembers leading player Patti Karr. "They were cheering and screaming, and I went to change, and I heard it again over the loudspeaker. Then it was like someone let the air out of a balloon; it never came back. They got hostile. They said, 'What is this?' "[59] On December 21, 1978, *A Broadway Musical* closed after scorching notices—and one performance. Cliché characterization, all-too-obvious satire, and superficial treatment of the theme—exploitation of blacks by whites—were to blame.

For Gower, getting over its failure was easier than getting over the flu that had persistently gripped him throughout rehearsals.[60] By the time he and Karla returned to California his condition was worse, and his physician ordered a five-day stay at Scripp's Institute for a battery of tests. Finally, he received the diagnosis—Waldenstrom's macroglobulinemia, a rare malignant disease that affects the plasma cells, which are formed from white blood cells known as B-lymphocytes. It occurs when aberrant uncontrolled plasma cells proliferate and attack the bone marrow, lymph nodes, and spleen, secreting excessive amounts of the antibody known as IgM, which coats the platelets and prevents them from clotting. Overproduction of IgM causes the thickness or viscosity of the blood to increase, greatly hindering the flow through small vessels and triggering many of the symptoms of the disease. These include fatigue (commonly from the anemia caused by too few red blood cells), easy bruising of the skin, a tendency to bleed easily, especially in the areas of the nose or gums, headache and dizziness, various vision problems, weight loss, night sweats, mood changes, and pain or numbness in the extremities.[61]

Identified in 1944 by Swedish physician Jan Gosta Waldenstrom, the syndrome occurs in 5 out of 100,000 people, mostly in those over 50, and its cause and prevention are unknown. Generally, diagnosis is determined from the results of blood and urine tests and a bone marrow biopsy. The intensity of treatment depends on the thickness of the patient's blood. In advanced cases plasmapheresis, which reduces or removes the high concentration of IgM from the blood, keeps in check symptoms caused by hyperviscosity. Here, in a procedure similar to dialysis, the patient's blood is removed and circulated through a machine that separates the plasma (containing the IgM) from the rest of the blood—red blood cells, white blood cells, and platelets—which in turn is reconstituted with a plasma substitute or donated plasma. The reconstituted blood is then sent back to the body as in a blood transfusion. A critical procedure calculated to swiftly manage symptoms, in one session plasmapheresis almost seems to miraculously eliminate fatigue and restore the patient's vigor. That can be misleading, for even as the blood is being cleansed, the abnormal plasma cells continue to proliferate and overproduce IgM. In time, the patient returns fatigued as before, requiring the procedure again. Chemotherapy may also be prescribed—Leukeran, Alkeran, Cytonan, or corticosteroids. Today the median survival time after diagnosis is about five years; at the time of Gower's diagnosis, it was three.[62]

The erratic gum and nosebleeds, easily bruised skin, and fatigue now made sense, but an incurable disease did not, especially at fifty-nine and in the throes of a major Broadway comeback that seemed less likely each day. Karla drove him down to San Diego for a second opinion and a bone marrow biopsy, but the results only confirmed his earlier tests. Eventually the trips to Cedars of Lebanon Hospital in Los Angeles for plasmapheresis became routine—three times a week, twice a week, once a week until he finally reached maintenance level, once every two weeks.[63] In a matter of months, with the combination of plasmapheresis and chemotherapy (Leukeran), his symptoms had virtually disappeared and he was feeling the best he had in a long time. Pleased as they were with his response to treatment, doctors warned him to avoid anything stressful. Physical exertion could aggravate his condition. "That year was doctors, doctors," remembers Karla. "They told him to stay out of the sun. Then he got this law saying he shouldn't exert a lot of physical energy: he can't go on the beach, he can't dance. He loved the beach, his walks on the beach. So it was grim. Very grim."[64]

For months he carefully took stock of his life, pondering the doctors' warnings and discerning what he really wanted. Apart from *42nd Street,* he had three home-based projects in the works—two films and a stage show—all small, manageable, and guaranteed to keep him near the plasmapheresis that was keeping him alive. With all this, did he really need to conquer the city again with another big show that Merrick could possibly undo?[65]

In early spring 1979, he phoned Mike Stewart and told him about his diagnosis and the treatment he was receiving. With doctors counseling against arduous activity, directing *42nd Street* was now regrettably out of the question. He resigned.[66]

SEVENTEEN

Going into His Dance Once More

42nd Street

1979–1980

While Gower reluctantly retired to a summer of beachcombing and gardening, his former *42nd Street* colleagues vainly scrambled to enlist other director-choreographers—Michael Bennett, Bob Fosse, Ron Field. By fall, the project was still without a guide, and the first backers' audition to raise the seed money was nearing. Obliging Stewart's request to help with the audition, Gower flew to New York on October 25, 1979, unaware that the event had been calculated to win him back.[1]

"Sure I want to do something that excites me," he confided to scenic designer Robin Wagner at the audition, "but I wonder sometimes if any of it matters, whether Broadway matters."[2] The speculation was understandable. Attempting a comeback after three straight flops seemed as desperately absurd to him as it undoubtedly would to theatre cognoscenti.

"Gower, it's what we do," replied Wagner. "It's our way of reaching people and feeling good. If we matter, Broadway matters."[3] Wagner knew full well just how much Gower Champion mattered. No one could reach an audience, command the mad practice of musical-making, and put every element of a production in service to a total vision like him. *42nd Street* needed the visionary director-choreographer, and he needed it every bit as much. "Gower," Wagner continued, "you made the American musical theatre what it is today, and you tell me you've been in California trimming hedges. How dare you!"[4]

The words hit their mark, "I was retreating from life," Gower later admitted. "Suddenly, I needed the tension and pressure of New York and the immediacy of the theatre—the fact that you're opening next Thursday and have to be ready. That's where I feel at home."[5] His illness? That was a confidential matter and, as long as it remained so, could not diminish his kinship with the character of the showman struggling to make a comeback. Apart from being hospitalized twice for a fever of unknown origin, he had generally responded well to the biweekly blood-cleansing treatments begun over ten months ago. Providing he continued the regimen, he could be anywhere—even New York.[6] The risk of staging the biggest show in decades—a summation of all he knew and loved about the American musical—would be worth it if he could take Broadway by storm once more. Into his dance he was going heedless of doctors' advice.

Back in California he told Karla of his plan to resume work alone, without her company. "It was the first show on which I didn't go with him. We were going through some interesting times and were ostensibly separated. It was a period where he had to shed a lot of things and prove he could stand on his own. And he went off and did the show."[7] Karla was as firmly rooted a person as Gower was peripatetic. Much as she wanted to be with him and tend to his needs, it was freedom, not stability, that he wanted. She could only offer to be there for him, if needed.[8]

He was scouting talent even before departing for New York. On a trip to Las Vegas in late 1979, he paid a call on Debbie Reynolds, then appearing at the Desert Inn: "I get a call that Mr. Gower Champion wants to come backstage just to see me. That was very peculiar because he was a loner and didn't really visit. Gower came back after the show, sat down like he never did, put his feet up, and started telling me about *42nd Street*. Who were the really great tap dancers I knew that were willing to go to New York? This was odd; why would he ask *me* that?"[9] Reynolds gave him a list of five of the best dancers she knew, but soon perceived a deeper intent to his surprising two-hour stay: "He talked about the good days, the children, and going to church; how very nice it was that I picked him and Margie up and would share my faith with them. That it had proven very, very good to him in his own quiet way. Then we both said good-bye, and somehow, I felt I wouldn't see him again."[10]

By January 1980 he had moved to New York, setting up residence in a newly renovated condominium at the corner of Sixth Avenue and West 56th Street that he decorated in flawless taste around a grand piano centerpiece.[11] The city was bracing and the thrill of conquering it with a new musical equally so. As preproduction got under way, he plotted the dances with the aid of two assistants, Karin Baker and Randy Skinner, both specialists in tap. Although they contributed most of the specific steps, Gower took their material and sculpted it until it conformed to his choreographic plan for each number. He had seriously studied tap in 1946, but its intense hard-and-fast style so contrasted with his elegant airborne technique that he could never use it.[12] Even so, the language of tap had never ceased to fascinate him. No wonder it became the vernacular of *42nd Street*.

From the moment he first tackled the dances with Baker, Skinner, and pianist-arranger Donald Johnston, he was scoring the rhythm of not only the music, but also the taps: "Talk to each other with the taps. That's it. A conversation with taps. Faster, now slower. . . ."[13] Much of Ernest Belcher's "Boy" was quite evident. Still and serenely poised on a blue stool, his tall trim figure suddenly leapt to the floor to illustrate a step with all the agility and grace of a dancer half his sixty years. Late in the afternoon, when his collaborators seemed weary and stressed, the old prankster in him surfaced.[14]

"Can we use this?" he asked in a cagey tone. "It was the first step I ever learned." He was back in Norma Gould's dancing class—step with the right, touch with the left, dip the body forward, step back with the left, touch with the right, dip the body backward. Then he grinned as the dancers roared with laughter at the most ridiculous steps they ever had seen.[15]

But there was nothing frivolous about the vocabulary he was assembling from almost fifty years' worth of dance. He drew on everything: road shows with Jeanne, story dances and films with Marge, every musical he had ever staged. More than once he shouted, "Hey, I used to do this step with Marge. Let's put it in somewhere."[16] In it went, time after time. The Warren-Dubin score was quickening his step as much as the treatment keeping his chronic fatigue at bay.

Looking for a way to visually restrain the sentimental plot, he thought a wide, low-framed stage would provide a documentary aspect in contrast to the romantic one the tapered higher-arched stages of the older theatres conveyed.[17] The Winter Garden was ideal and likewise the curtain-raiser he was designing to fill its frame that was rooted in his "Folies Labiche" number for *Make a Wish* almost thirty years before. It began with the sound of a rehearsal piano banging out the title tune, soon joined by the thunderous beat of dancing feet slowly revealed by a rising act curtain that paused on them before continuing to ascend on a forty-member chorus madly competing at a Broadway musical audition circa 1933. It would be a colossal start to a colossal production in which the American musical itself would be the concept, the dynamic driving every component—a forty-eight-member cast, 400 stunning costumes by Theoni V. Aldredge, scores of gorgeous lighting effects by Tharon Musser, and a dozen dazzling symmetrical sets by Wagner to dress sixteen musical numbers, all with that distinctive Champion touch.[18] Gower took the magnitude of it all in his customary stride: "Each time you start a new show, you always feel nervous. You ask yourself, 'Can you do it? Can you come up with it again?' It's always scary in the beginning, but then you get in there, and it's just work. It's always like getting a sick elephant up on its feet."[19]

42nd Street was also going to be a mighty expensive elephant; veteran property supervisor Leo Herbert knew it as soon as he saw Gower's enormous prop list with its mirrors, trampolines, and strolling Atlantic City Boardwalk deck chairs: "This man can drive you nuts. He throws out entire routines costing thousands in costumes and props at a moment's notice. He tries everything until he has his colors. That's what he does, paints pictures on the stage. There's nobody like him. The man's a genius."[20] The genius was planning a ceaseless array of bodies, colors, and clothing that unfolded in scene upon scene in carefully coordinated hues, constantly enhancing and expanding the palette of Wagner's pink/mauve scenery. So vast was the number of costumes that it would take the effort of two companies to construct them in time.[21] Bankrolled at $1,869,500, the cost of the most lavish musical seen in forty years would jump to $2.5 million by opening night in New York.[22]

"When you already have $2 million riding on a show, you protect the investment," explained Merrick, absent from Broadway nearly four years and whose affinity with the character of the comeback showman was as absolute as Gower's. "I'm thinking of how to create the sort of lively, lavish, frivolous musical I believe people have been missing. I think the musical public is fed up with these solemn ones and those tiny little ones of a half-dozen people, skimpy sets and squeaky orchestras. I think it wants what I call this—a song-and-dance extravaganza."[23]

Gower began casting it in April. Initially, the starring role of director Julian Marsh was a straight acting part intended for Kirk Douglas or Richard Harris.[24] Once it was decided the character should sing, Merrick and Champion approached Jerry Orbach: "I was interested in doing *42nd Street* and liked the whole idea of it. But at that point we had had a history—Mr. Merrick, Gower, and I—in one case, of me being told I was all set for something, and then having it fall through at the last minute."[25] Five years before, as rehearsals were beginning for *Mack and Mabel*, Orbach suddenly lost the role of Mack Sennett to Robert Preston, and so he was naturally wary. But this time things were different. "Gower and I talked about the role, and we decided there should be nothing campy about it, that if I played it straight, the laughs would come." Orbach's poker-faced earnestness guaranteed them. But the suitability of this approach was lost on Merrick, who tersely observed: "I could have played that role 10 years ago—and you're too nice to play it."[26]

Though she initially refused the nominal leading role of aging temperamental star Dorothy Brock, Tammy Grimes agreed once Gower assured her that it would develop more in rehearsals. *Applause* and *Lorelei*'s Lee Roy Reams wanted to audition for young leading man Billy Lawlor, but was told by casting directors he was too old and should aim for dance director Andy Lee instead, a dancing role with no solo spot.[27] He was so angry he almost skipped the audition: "I went right into the ballad and then segued into the tap dance without giving them the chance to say, 'Thank you, Lee Roy.' I put on a performance. When I finished, there was dead silence. Then this very elegant gray-haired man started coming down the aisle.

" 'You're really not right for the role of Andy Lee,' Gower Champion said.

" 'I know that.'

" 'But you are very right for Billy Lawlor.' "[28]

Danny Carroll signed on as Andy Lee, and Joseph Bova and Carole Cook as the writers Bert Barry and Maggie Jones. Don Crabtree became Brock's sugar daddy and *Pretty Lady*'s major investor Abner Dillon, James Congdon Brock's true flame Pat Denning, Karen Prunczik the wisecracking chorus girl Anytime Annie, and Robert Colston and Stan Page stagehands Oscar and Mac.

One role remained—Peggy Sawyer, the demure valise-toting chorine whose meteoric rise to stardom was the crux of the famous fable. To fill it Gower launched a nationwide search for a fresh appealing talent who could tap up a storm. Lisa Brown of TV's *Guiding Light* was favored and already in rehearsal two weeks when the director spied a winsome twenty-two-year-old honey blonde in red leotard and skirt carting a purple suitcase—the last dancer to amble onto the stage of the dilapidated New Amsterdam Roof for that day's open call. Michael Bennett had hired her for his national tour of *A Chorus Line,* in which she played every role from tone-deaf Kristine to sophisticated Cassie. Days before, at the Chicago auditions, she had caught the attention of dance assistant Baker, who had been trying to reach her without luck ever since.[29]

An assistant casting director was calling out the names of the final group of dancers auditioning; hers was the last. "WANDA RICHERT! WANDA?" he gasped. "Where have you been? We've been trying to find you!" A communications glitch had kept her from receiving notice of the New York audition, which she later learned of while visiting friends in Buffalo. Summoning her *chutzpah,* she flew to New York to convince them to give her another try, which they willingly did; then, for the next five hours, she outdanced everyone else on stage. When the audition ended, Baker introduced the exhausted dancer to the director.[30]

"So, you're the girl from Chicago I heard all about."

"Yes."

"From the time you walked in the door, I couldn't take my eyes off of you. The unfortunate thing is, the role that you're right for has already been cast. But I'm not married to her. What is the color of your hair naturally?"

"Blonde. I'll dye it."

"I just don't see Peggy as a blonde." That could change. He wanted to consider her anyway. Handing her the script, he told her to expect word from the Merrick office concerning an audition for the producer. She was flying home to Chicago for the weekend. Then, like a latter-day Peggy Sawyer, off she traipsed, purple suitcase in tow. Gower wasted no time speaking with Bennett, who vouched for Richert's dependability. By Monday, she was back in New York auditioning for Merrick and by day's end had signed on as the new Peggy. Lisa Brown (later to take over the role after Richert's departure) returned to daytime TV.[31]

As preproduction drew to a close, Gower made the final choices for his thirty-six-member chorus, selecting a broad spectrum of people—some fresh out of high school, some seasoned pros with scores of credits, and some in between. The younger dancers would bring the energy and excitement that comes from being in a Broadway show for the first time. They would also care less about being in fewer numbers than those who had been around and were likely to receive greater exposure.[32] All the same, there were no guarantees. Before assigning roles in the big "42nd Street Tap Ballet" that would end the show, he thought it wise to let the curtain-raising "Audition" help him decide who should be featured. The chorus learned it the first day of rehearsal for the full company, May 6, after gathering in the studios that formed part of Broadway's new Minskoff Theatre complex.[33]

"I want you to feel the tension, the anxiety—'Am I gonna get that job?'" he gently instructed as they wildly tapped away. "Remember that the early part is dead serious; it has to escalate into fun." To one dancer improvising his own steps, he spoke encouragingly: "It works fine for me, I like it a lot." To another he benignly cautioned, "Remember, you've got tap shoes on and I gotta hear the dialogue."[34] A break; then he wanted a word with them.

He explained that he had a rare blood disease. He didn't have a name for it, but from time to time it would require him to have transfusions.[35] "He was on medication," Reams recalls, "but it was never presented to us as anything serious. Then he would have blood transfusions, and come back feeling fine."[36]

The rehearsal was nearing its close, and there was still something important he had to show them, something that would give them an idea of what the style of the show would be like—the duet Richert and Reams had been rehearsing with him for the past two weeks. It was the heart of the tap ballet in which each and every one of them would have specific roles.

A perfect fusion of the intensity of tap with his own silken style, the duet had all the gripping sensuality of the "Challenge Dance" he and Marge did amid the rooftops of Manhattan in *Give a Girl a Break,* but with a heightened fervor and sense of urgency only the staccato effect of tap could deliver. That staccato was the essence of the duet, which he had personally orchestrated as "a conversation with taps" between a sweet young girl and the soldier boy with whom she finds excitement and quickly falls in love. As the jazzy upbeat tempo of the orchestra slid into a bluesy seductive one for their dance, the pair erotically talked to each other with the taps. This was dance as dialogue, with the two falling deeper in love as their movement became more intricate, intertwining, and sophisticated. But the duet was also part of a larger story, a ballet that would be as vast, colorful, and character-filled as any MGM could ever produce.

He saw it unfolding before an array of vintage theatre marquees lighting up the Great White Way and trailing off into the distance with Peggy standing center in a blue sequined dress before a scrim, only her face bathed in light. Enter three cops from right pounding their beat to the bleating of a lone saxophone. A street musician enters from down right in muffler and cap playing his fiddle. As the cops exit left, a sinister pickpocket in black zoot suit, red gloves, and red-banded black fedora steals on around them, slinks to center, and gestures for the scrim to rise above him. Then he vanishes into the wings right along with the fiddler left. Peggy comes forward for a brassy vocal, suddenly cut short as the music shifts into a busy pace and the chorus enters from up right and down left in character groupings of various numbers. The distinctly stylized movement of each group is tailored to its characters and contrasts markedly with the others. Yet as a whole, they are a cross-section of the American social scene—a newsboy, a trio of soldiers, two Bowery thugs in tweed suits each with a gun moll, six high-toned hookers, seven nifty working girls, and four pair of high-society elites attired in evening wear. Where else but 42nd Street would such a collection be found side by side?

They encircle Peggy, who runs from them to down right just as the music surges and stops. For a spilt second she panics and almost retreats, fearing she cannot do the number, but then quickly recovers, starting the song once more to the beat of dancing feet. When finished, she joins the strollers as the number breaks into full dance, with some characters mixing with others and some aloofly parading with their own kind. The pickpocket reappears, ominously weaves among them, and departs. A young soldier dancing past Peggy beckons her to take in the scene with him, and she does. Soon they are one with the revelers as the music slows and the soldier invites her to dance with him. She is reluctant and retreats. He follows, inviting her again. Again, she shuns him. This stepping-to-confront and turning-to-escape pattern signals the duet that establishes their love. When it concludes, the pace of the dancers quickens and the music grows agitated at the reappearance of the pickpocket, who steals the purse of one of the prostitutes. Immediately, she points him out to a thug, who aims his pistol and fires. The bullet misses the escaping pickpocket, but kills Peggy's soldier by mistake. One of his buddies speeds to his side as the thug darts off, but is pushed away by a cop, who is pushed away by the third soldier. Moving toward the body, Peggy is blocked at once by the third cop, and can only watch helplessly as the two soldiers carry off their friend. She stands at center, lost without love as the impassive strollers now merge into a massive tapping corps—the faceless crowd of 42nd Street sweeping her up into its relentless rhythm. Blackout.

The highly stylized movement of the strollers that Gower had used to lighter purpose in *Dolly!* produced a dramatic effect here, further enhanced by the pick-pocket character—a variation on his jewel thief from the "Fashion Show" sequence with Marge in *Lovely to Look At,* but danced in the hunched, down-low style of Bob Fosse. Likewise, the street fiddler at the beginning of the number was a tribute to Jerome Robbins; as for Michael Bennett, well, one of his dancers was the central figure of the ballet. "He saw everything in his head first," explains Richert. "He put it on the people right there, and it all just worked. It just worked! It could have been a major train wreck and never was. None of the numbers were."[37]

Though the ballet would consume about a fifth of the six-week rehearsal time, Gower knew it was worth it. But not all the dancers were sure, especially the tall blond boy playing one of the high society types who remained mostly in the back row facing upstage center throughout. His name was Jon Engstrom, and he had been a featured dancer for Fosse, Bennett, and Saddler. Sensing that Gower was not particularly crazy about him, he determined to make the best of the situation: "I just kept working as hard as I could, giving him the best I could, aware that he was a very sensitive man who could read people's bodies—their body language. He could tell who was unhappy or who was thinking negatively. I'm sure that was it because as good as some dancers were, their positions never got any better."[38]

Engstrom, a big fan of Gower's who had incorporated much of his style into his own work, was advised by friends who had danced in Champion's shows always to dance full out for him, never to "mark" or just go through the motions. There were occasions when Gower would tell dancers to mark, forget he had done so, and then seconds later assume their lackluster performance to be indicative of how they actually danced. Engstrom never marked once. One day, he was directed to change lines and move to the front. After that he started getting additional numbers and soon noticed that he was in every one.[39] Then came the icing on the cake: "He gave me the 'Shadow Waltz,' where I was the boy who danced with the shadow of Dorothy Brock. I remember walking into the rehearsal hall one day and seeing on the list of what was to be done, 'Tammy Grimes and Jon Engstrom with Gower: 2 hours.' I was just out of my mind because I knew that I'd gotten a featured dance role."[40]

In *Carnival* and *Sugar* Gower frequently used shadows for atmospheric effect, but here he devised an increasingly hilarious interplay of them for a whole number in which Marsh puts Brock to the test. Her trial is complicated by two "shinbuster" lights wheeled back and forth by stagehands that project a shadow effect behind her, but also blind her head-on as she tries to sing. As the number progresses, she and the stagehands move behind the scrim while the girls' chorus enters and lies before the footlights, their faces resting on their hands. Behind them the drama of

Brock's audition plays out in shadows projected on the scrim: her gigantic image dances with the tiny one of a man's (Engstrom's) that gets lost in the voluminous sleeves of her ungainly gown, but then returns a giant as her image diminishes and cowers before him and a pack of dancers leaping madly above her until colliding midair. At length, she struggles from behind the scrim to the front of the stage for the finish, completely disheveled and more petulant than ever.

This was a lighter moment in what initially was a darker and more sinister show, with a pair of menacing gangsters who grimly assailed Brock's boyfriend Pat Denning as the cast of *Pretty Lady* transitioned from New York to Atlantic City (later Philadelphia) during "Getting Out of Town" in Act I. The grim perspective would allow Gower to construct more numbers on the order of the tap ballet, like "We're In the Money," which also had an edge at first. During the final dance audition, Champion demonstrated a step to be used for the men's entrance in the number. "It looked like a piece of cake, but wasn't because he was very specific about the turn of the hand, the cock of the head and everything," recalls Engstrom. "I thought, 'Where did you ever come up with this?' It was really strange."[41] Where the choreographer was going became clear a few days later in rehearsal when he instructed the chorus to sing the lyrics with a desperate, almost diabolical edge while performing the audition step learned earlier.

One afternoon after a particularly exceptional rehearsal, Engstrom, still keyed up and excited, ran into the director in the washroom.

"I just love the show," he raved, "All this dancing—I love all the darkness of it and everything. There's such a dark thing about the Depression stuff."

Gower paused and looked at him intently, taking in every word. Within days the mood of the show lightened and "We're In the Money" literally bounced with abandon as four down-and-out urchins elated over unearthing a dime gave way to a procession of star-spangled platinum blondes bearing giant-sized dimes that converted into foot-high platforms on which they tapped and whirled. It climaxed with skyscrapers made of dimes and dollars rising from the background while the boys danced in among the girls and Billy Lawlor, in a money-colored costume, did his stuff atop a big three-foot-high coin at center.[42] So much for Depression darkness.

But on the road from vision to realization there were frequent detours, and "Money" had its share, with Gower spending days changing or extending the counts and trying different endings. In the heat of its construction, the performers would often hear him say, "I'm having a problem with this. Here's what I'm trying to achieve . . ." or "Okay, I'm working on this, and it's a difficulty. I don't know how I'm gonna go about this." Was this an invitation for a group effort in problem-solving? By no means. He did not want suggestions. Rather, it was his way of explaining to the cast why he was making them do certain sections over and over, like the ending of "Money," which he eventually solved himself.[43]

The shorthand he invented to compress the time span of Agnes and Michael's fifty-year marriage in *I Do! I Do!* he now used even more impressively. It was most evident in the staging for "Dames," *I Do*'s "Love Isn't Everything" supersized. Here a big production number passes through various stages of dress, growing more dazzling by the second until it bursts forth fully outfitted for the final dress rehearsal. Upon the cast's arrival at the Arch Street Theatre in Philadelphia, Marsh announces that rehearsal will commence immediately despite the delayed scenery and costumes, which will be added as they become available. He signals the conductor, who cues the orchestra while the performers, still clad in street dress, scramble to find their places. In the chaos, Billy Lawlor bends over the apron of the stage to get his starting note for the song from the conductor while stage manager Mac calls for quiet. Billy begins the opening verse to "Dames," joined by four chorus men in rehearsal clothes bearing top hats and canes as the entrance to the "Maison des Dames" (Beauty School) flies in behind them. Near the end of the first chorus, they gesture toward the Maison and dance off as it flies out, revealing a chrome Art Deco jungle gym full of chorines in short, pink, tunic-like outfits stretching their legs, bouncing beach balls, and hanging from poles and swings.

Now the entire structure revolves into a multilevel mirrored setting on which the girls continue to frolic like figures on a gigantic music box. Again the Maison drop flies in as Billy and all sixteen male chorus members enter in full burgundy tuxes with tails and top hats to sing the final chorus. The doors of the Maison open and through them pour a seemingly endless stream of beautiful dames in striking evening gowns—first a trickle, then a gush—each a distinct color from pale yellow to midnight blue. The set revolves one last time into massive mirrors curving the width of the stage, reflecting into infinity the panorama of the chorus in final pose. The women, one arm raised, the other lowered, form a spectacular rainbow while the men, with one hand poised on the brim of their hats, line up across the upstage area shoulder to shoulder. Through them, Dorothy Brock, dressed all in white, passes at center moving straight downstage to where she is greeted by Billy at left, who extends hat in hand to salute her as she raises her arms high for the final note. Blackout.

Like "Love Isn't Everything," all costume changes had to be coordinated to the second. But it was one thing to do it for two performers, another for a chorus of thirty-six. "We have 20-second changes from head to toe. It's extraordinary," remarked costume designer Theoni V. Aldredge. "All the clothes are pre-set on the floor. The girls step in. The dresser zips you up. The shoes are there. And, the hat is there.

The change is totally choreographed. And it is black backstage, because Gower doesn't want any leakage of lights."[44] It was essential that every section of the number be as thoroughly choreographed backstage as it was out front.

Even so, the director was far from pleased with "Dames." The middle section, the jungle gym/music box part, continued to annoy him right up and into the New York previews. The problem was that it lacked the dynamic progression of the opening and closing segments. There was movement, but it was static and fixed—the result of stage mechanics rather than the vibrancy that an unfolding story gives. Among the proposed solutions was the interpolation of "Stay Young and Beautiful" from the 1933 Eddie Cantor film *Roman Scandals* with five girls in fat suits who, at the end of the first section, pass by the five men and through the doors of the Maison to undergo a transformation via steam cabinets, exercise cycles, and gym equipment until they emerge sleek and trim in beautiful gowns. The gym setting was too stark, so other motifs were substituted, but they all clashed with the Art Deco setting. Out went "Stay Young and Beautiful" and its awkward admonition to remain that way if you want to be loved.[45] In the meantime, Gower tinkered away, certain he would find a solution.

The phone was ringing in Jack Lee's apartment. He had just arrived in town after touring the revival of *Peter Pan* with Sandy Duncan and was now preparing the show for its Broadway opening. The cheer in Gower's voice was evident. "Jack, I'm having the best time doing *42nd Street*. We've started rehearsals. Just wanted you to know I'm thinking of you. I got a very good conductor, John Lesko. I'm very happy with him and having a very wonderful time here. I just wanted you to know that."[46] Lee was delighted for his friend; how sweet and dear of him to think to call and tell him that.

Gower was having a wonderful time indeed. It was the end of May with a month to go before departing for the Washington tryout and already he had his next show in place—a musical version of *Sayonara*, James A. Michener's novel about a U.S. Air Force hero who falls in love with a lovely Japanese actress from the all-female Takarazuka Theatre near Kobe. The polar opposite of *42nd Street*, it was a romantic musical in the Rodgers and Hammerstein tradition. "We're in the mood for that now," he told a reporter. "At least *I* am." Work was under way. Jerome Minskoff had agreed to produce, George Fischoff was penning the score, Hy Gilbert the lyrics, and William Luce of *The Belle of Amherst* the book. In September, he was flying to Japan to cast the two leading ladies. "I've never done two shows in one season, but my mood now is *go*. I've pulled back from the theatre too long. Being back is a very emotional thing for me."[47]

The emotion was perfectly understandable. The musical stage had always been his creative home, and this was his homecoming. He was back where he belonged, doing what he did best—being a Broadway showman. "Before *42nd Street*, Gower had done *Rockabye Hamlet* and all that; he went through that drug thing," explains Reams. "Then one day, he told me, he was walking the beaches of California stoned, and suddenly he realized what he truly was: an old-fashioned song-and-dance man. And rather than try to compete with what was happening culturally at the time, he decided to go back to what he knew best: the old-fashioned musical."[48]

Having him back was an emotional thing also for the cast, who were in awe of working for him. Veteran dancer Danny Carroll especially liked the way he suited the dance to the dancer: "Champion will say, 'Dance around and show me.' From that he takes it and makes it his own; he fits it to the person."[49] Carole Cook, after touring for two years as Dolly in the Australian-New Zealand company, was thrilled to be working with him firsthand: "He's terribly disciplined and expects us to be. The theatre's not a democracy. You must have someone say, 'This is the way it will be!' It gives you great security but he's also open to anyone in the company. He will listen and hear everyone and the answer may be 'no,' but he'll hear you out."[50] To Reams, working with Gower was compensation beyond par for Merrick's meager wages: "He paid us very low salaries. His feeling was, if you don't like it, you can be replaced. But I was working with Gower Champion, so who cared? I would have paid Gower to let me work with him. It was like Gower and I had met in a previous life. I knew instinctively what he wanted."[51] His ability to find the balance required to work harmoniously with people was what impressed Richert: "He has every quality needed to gain respect, the sternness when it needs to be shown, the 'please' and the 'thank you.' He's really 'into' everybody here and everybody feels that way. No one's worried about stepping on his toes. He's incredible."[52]

All the same, newcomers had much to learn. Ever focused, driven, and time-conscious, Champion demanded a clean environment, with dancers' bags and personal belongings swept to one side out of his vision. Each person was to be in the rehearsal room at all times, accessible on a moment's notice—no calling down the hall after people. Most emphatically, he wanted everyone's undivided attention every moment. When one dancer, fresh out of high school, took to reading a newspaper during Gower's discussion of a number in which he was not involved, the director blew up. "It shocked me," notes Engstrom, "but I understand now. He wanted everybody to understand the show completely, not just the numbers they were in; that you should understand the purpose of every number whether you're in it or not."[53]

Much of what the cast was learning about Gower, Orbach had experienced himself during *Carnival* almost twenty years before. But something that was lacking then was very much in evidence now—an approachability and receptivity that were quite apt: "I could talk to him. I could give him an idea, discuss it, and invent things, like pulling out Peggy's lucky scarf at the end; whereas in 1961, everyone was deathly afraid of him. But now, he was much more approachable and would exchange ideas. Of course, none of us knew how sick he was. I still don't know to this day if *he* knew how sick he was! I think it was one of the great acting jobs ever."[54]

Near the end of the two weeks prior to his next treatment, Gower became increasingly pallid and anemic until the day of the blood-cleaning procedure, when he quietly stole away from rehearsal, returning hours later vigorous, glowing, and ready for work.[55] And work he did—nonstop. But the spectacular numbers pouring out of him were also testing the limits of the Minskoff Studios, so rehearsals moved to Michael Bennett's more spacious Quadrille Studios near Union Square.[56] There he added Brock's "You're Getting to be a Habit with Me," a variation on his old men's wheelchair ballet from *Sugar,* though more elegant by far, with couples gracefully gliding along Atlantic City's Boardwalk in old-fashioned rattan deck chairs. "Habit" was a handsome addition to Act I, which now consisted of "Audition," "Shadow Waltz," "Dames," and "We're in the Money." It was soon joined by three more: "Getting Out of Town" and "I Know Now," which also worked as scenic transitions, and "Young and Healthy," a solo that presented Billy and progressed into a duet to introduce Peggy.

In "Getting Out of Town," the cast quits New York's 42nd Street Theatre, dons street garb, and, luggage in hand, boards a giant turntable forming an astutely arranged pyramid of travelers and trappings. The backstage set flies out and then, just as they complete the circuit, back in again. Boom! Like magic, they are backstage at Philadelphia's Arch Street Theatre, preparing to take their places for the "Dames" rehearsal.

"Dames," the top of the first act, is later topped by "We're in the Money," right before the finale in which Brock's rendition of the title song is suddenly aborted by the fall she suffers when Peggy accidentally collides with her. Linking the two is "I Know Now," which takes place on the bilevel set of the Regency Club, where two scenes play out simultaneously—a cast party at the piano bar below and Brock's reunion with Denning in her hotel room above. Beginning as a romantic solo for Brock, it becomes an upbeat tune for the party crowd until the scene ends and fades out, with the piano giving way to the orchestra for Billy's lively stage rendition at the out-of-town opening of *Pretty Lady* (looking very much like a parody out of *Lend an Ear*'s "Gladiola Girl," with women in crinolines traipsing about with flowered hoops). At the end a cross-fade through a scrim reveals backstage and the cast scrambling into place for "Money."

42nd Street never stood still; even singers' solos were choreographed. "Young and Healthy" established Billy as a "wolf" of a tenor determined to impress a reticent Peggy with his moves—stage and romantic. Gower "didn't like actors to stand still while they were singing a song," explains Reams. "He always had to have something going on. It was all very cinematic: scenery just moved on and off, and there was never any real break in the action. There were a lot of fade-outs and fade-ins."[57]

The second act opening, "Sunny Side to Every Situation," began with a fade-in on a series of dressing rooms at the Arch Street Theatre—twenty-one multihued domed niches à la *Bye Bye Birdie*'s "Telephone Hour," each with its own chorus kid positioned as if before a mirror and lit singly, in groups, or all at once depending on who was singing. It faded into a crossover: the stage of the Arch Street Theatre, where the cast convinces Marsh to save *Pretty Lady* by replacing the injured Brock with Peggy. Then it, too, faded out as Broad Street Station, Philadelphia, faded in for "Lullaby of Broadway."

Before staging it, he did "About a Quarter to Nine," a duet that put Peggy and a wheelchair-bound Brock on friendly terms thanks to some amusing arm choreography, and a high spot, "Shuffle Off to Buffalo," a *Pretty Lady* production number to precede and be topped by the tap ballet finale. Like *Sugar*'s "Sun on My Face," it bore his trademark train motif in the form of a Pullman sleeper, but began with Annie and Bert outfitted as newlyweds (shades of not only *I Do! I Do!*, but also the big train number with Marge cut from *Mr. Music*). From there, it segued into a pajama party hide-and-seek with Bert searching for Annie among the occupied berths and the pair reuniting atop the car, where they dance a barefoot soft shoe before scrambling down to the center berth for the finish. The train splits in two and separates them. As the pieces trail into the wings, Bert, via strobe effect, scampers frantically across the stage from his section to the other, joining Annie just in time for the blackout.

Gower would close *42nd Street* in the same low-key manner he had often ended other shows: a simple reprise of the title song by Marsh, who, finding Peggy's lucky scarf in his pocket, exits to join her at the cast party.

By mid-June the show was nearing the first run-through, and its keystone was not yet in place. The last number to be added prior to Washington, it was a quintessential Champion showstopper with that energy that builds and builds until it explodes in sheer jubilation—"Lullaby of Broadway."

In "Hello, Dolly!" the heroine descended a central staircase in a heart-shaped gown to rally the chorus; but here the chorus descends a double staircase forming an inverted heart to rally the heroine and avert her intended return home on the next train to Allentown. But "Lullaby" is far more than "Dolly!" in reverse. It is the heart of the plot itself, with Marsh and Peggy attaining the reconciliation that restores their relationship beneath the golden glow of the station's huge clock. Fundamentally, "Lullaby" is an expansion of "Underneath the Clock," Gower's railroad station reconciliation with Marge of twenty-five years before. Like that story dance, it is autobiographical and centers on a theme common throughout his work—the power of one heart to attract and move another. That same mystique or "Gower power" was mighty palpable here—the force behind Marsh's spellbinding opening solo, his beguiling plea that literally sways Peggy to spurn heartache, "come along" with him, and "listen" to the hip-hurray, ballyhoo, rumble, and rattle of Broadway—the heartbeat of life itself.

On the landing above them from which the stairs extend, Billy dashes in to launch the second chorus, joined by Annie. Bert and Andy arrive, then three of the girls, each bounding down the stairs and over to aid Marsh down left, still trying to woo Peggy, perched glumly on her trademark valise. While the chorus springs down the steps, Maggie pauses at the landing for a third reprise accompanied by Abner, while beneath them Peggy tries to avoid the ever-growing crowd encircling and closing in on her. Slipping free, she grabs her valise to go, but turns back. Their powerful plea persuades her to surrender at last. She marches over to the com- pacted crowd, who still think she is among them, and taps one of them on the shoulder. The music stops, and they all bend toward her as one. "I'll do it," she cries. The show is on; so is her romance with Marsh. The ensemble roars its approval, and the music soars into the climax as Marsh takes Peggy by the hand, leading her in a cakewalk strut across the stage that Billy, Andy, and Bert join one by one. From top to bottom, Broad Street Station now becomes a pulsating panorama of open- heartedness, a spirited homecoming of one heart welcomed by others. The feeling is infectious, attracting and rousing the heart of the audience itself.

With "Lullaby" finally in place, he could now do a run-through. It turned out to be a shabby affair with missed cues, gaps in continuity, and little of his customary flow. Still, he was pleased. The essence of a terrific show was there, which he yearned to see burst forth in the shapes and colors he imagined. The job was unfin- ished until he was all over the stage—every step, every detail, every performer.

"Most of his concentration was on the dance numbers," recalled Orbach. "The time given to work on the scenes and the acting was very limited, sometimes by his health. But he knew that he had people who were professionals who could get it done right. With certain people like me, it was a case where, if he had me standing in the right place and moving in the right direction, he knew I'd say the words right." Orbach needed little direction. He was playing Champion playing Marsh. Gower's no-nonsense style, clear-headed vision, and high-flying spirit were all there, right down to his classy stature. Nowhere was it more apparent than in "Lullaby."

"What is Peggy thinking right now?" Gower asked Richert after viewing the number at the run-through.

The poignant question overwhelmed her as much as the number did. She had been fighting back tears all through it. Summoning her poise, she replied: "She's falling in love with the director. And he's come to get her."

"That's it," he confirmed, grabbing his sunglasses to mask the emotion in his eyes. Then he turned and was gone.

Wanda decided to write a letter to thank him for making her dream of originating a leading role in a big Broadway musical come true, and to explain precisely what she had been feeling as she watched him watching the run-through. He had been so giving, so openhearted, making rehearsal itself a homecoming. That truly moved her. The cast might not understand it, but she hoped he would. Then, paraphrasing Marsh's compliment to Peggy at the end of the show, she ended, "You're quite a man, Mr. Gower Champion! Quite a Man!"[58]

The next day in Washington, she delivered the letter to his house man; then, a day later, while showing her and Karen Prunczik the huge art deco Plexiglas set for "Dames" on the Kennedy Center's Opera House stage, he handed her an envelope, remarking casually, "Oh, by the way, I have notes for you." Back at the hotel she discovered not notes but a reply to her letter, which he began by thanking her for writing.

"I am at an extremely exposed position in my life, creatively drained, physically exhausted, and on the thin edge of emotional splintering," he wrote.[59] Yet despite the personal cost, this show meant more to him than any before it, and no matter how desperate things got, he was determined to see it through to the end. After all, he had survived this far. Yes, of course he understood what she was feeling during rehearsal, he felt it just as deeply, and if no one else did, so what! Once more he thanked her for writing and encouraged her to keep bringing Peggy Sawyer to life as only she could "because you're quite a girl, Miss Wanda! Quite a girl! Love, G."[60]

They started dating. As the romance deepened, they grew less concerned about concealing it. "At first, we both thought it was outside the realm of possibility," said Wanda. "You know, our age difference, and the wondering if we were attracted because, well, he was the director and I was the leading lady. I finally said to myself no, we were very much in love. He referred to me as 'my lady.' "[61] Soon they were living together in Gower's suite at the Watergate and constant companions holding hands in public. The press played up the relationship. They were unperturbed, but Merrick was indignant. For once, the publicity was not to his liking. "He was very jealous," explains Wanda. "Gower had hired an understudy for me out of the chorus, Mary Cadorette. All of a sudden, one day in Washington, Nancy Sinclair shows up as my understudy. David had gotten her from Los Angeles. Gower was livid. He said, 'Merrick couldn't get *my* Peggy Sawyer, so he had to get his own.' So, there was *that* tension."[62] The next day, Gower was forced to introduce Sinclair to the company.

On June 24, 1980, *42nd Street* debuted at the Kennedy Center to mixed reviews. The cast was sullen, but Gower gave them no time to wallow in disappointment. For the next six weeks he made changes that seemed set and ready to go, almost as if he knew what the critics would say beforehand. Chiefly, there were two problems: getting the audience to warm up sooner to the leading lady and scaling down the unwieldy plot. Wanda was receiving good notices but needed a number that would help her win over the audience early on by showing her dancing expertise to best advantage. "But You Gotta Know How to Dance," a whimsical solo Gower had choreographed for her around a director's chair, was exquisite but too intimate for the spot. "Go into Your Dance," a friendly tap competition with three of her chorus mates (Karen Prunczik, Ginny King, and Jeri Kansas) and dance director Andy (Danny Carroll) that transitioned from the theatre to the Gypsy Tea Kettle Restaurant and back, was just the thing.

In the second act, Gower planned "Lulu's Back in Town" as an eleven-o'clocker for her and twelve male dancers. But the athleticism of its derelicts-turned-dandies and ingénue as femme fatale dancing atop a revolving bar in a magenta-fringed dress greatly contrasted with the rest of the show. It was in one night and gone.[63] "Know anybody who wants to buy a Lulu dress?" asked Merrick as he passed Reams.[64]

The mixed reviews were actually a blessing. Shows declared hits out of town often received lukewarm receptions in New York. The nature of Gower's changes almost seemed calculated to prevent *42nd Street* from becoming a hit prior to Broadway. "When Gower started making the changes," recalls Engstrom, "word of mouth got around Washington that the show was really phenomenal. He gathered us together and said, 'When you talk to your family and friends in New York and they ask you how the show is going, don't tell them it's going really well. Say it's going fine; be ambiguous about it, but don't tell them it's great.' He was adamant about that."[65]

He also explained why he had missed four performances in a row over the second weekend. He had fallen ill and had to be taken to the National Institutes of Health in Bethesda, Maryland, for what he dismissed as "a flu virus" that had aggravated his anemia. With "periodic transfusions," he asserted with a smile, "I'm going to be fine, maybe just go a little easier."[66]

That certainly would be difficult with the frequency of his treatments increasing to every other day and Merrick constantly yapping at his heels with demands for quicker and greater improvements: "If Gower doesn't start doing what I want to do, there's going to be trouble around here."[67] Suddenly the producer in his dapper Panama suit was "like a helicopter always hovering," as one leading player put it.[68] Once more old Mount Merrick was poised to blow, but for Gower there would be no escaping to Ypsilanti this time to wait out the impact. He stood his ground. Constantly chilly and feverish, he wrapped himself in heavy sweaters and coats and had the air conditioning turned off during rehearsals, determined to make the most out of what remained of the tryout time.

"Plot developments fly in and out with the suddenness of meteorites," one critic had carped.[69] That was the result of compressing a film musical with five songs into a stage musical with sixteen, so Champion, Stewart, and Bramble worked to simplify the plot. The role of Brock's lover, Pat Denning, was greatly downsized, but when Peggy's love interest was shifted from Billy Lawlor to Julian Marsh, the old tale really got a boost.[70] Life imitating art imitating life. "Yes," observed Wanda, "Gower and I had to laugh about the onstage–offstage parallels."[71]

Merrick had a method for reducing the book. Wasn't the slender tale merely an excuse for what he had advertised as a song and dance extravaganza? Why not prepare the audience for it beforehand by resorting to what the musicals of the 1930s termed "lead-ins and crossovers," rather than "book"? For the time, the writers reluctantly agreed to the billing "Lead-Ins and Crossovers by Michael Stewart and Mark Bramble," but would later force Merrick to restore their status as authors of the book.[72] Gower, so uneasy with dialogue he would frequently comment that there were "too many words," left the matter in the hands of the producer and authors.[73] By now, it was clear to all that his staging was propelling the plot, not the book, which he had no intention of rehearsing. People raised the issue of his directing book scenes at their own risk.

During one Washington rehearsal, Joe Bova and the other principals waited for Gower to arrive while Merrick passed the time doing his crossword puzzle. "I was feeling kind of flip that day, and I said to him 'Ask Gower when he's going to rehearse the book.' It was a very saucy thing to say, and I could see David's pencil come down, and my face started to flush, and he sort of glared at me, and all the principals were staring. The next day, we were running through something, and I did some little thing that was different. And Gower jumped all over me."[74] Later Bova learned that Merrick had seized on his remark to challenge Gower, who was angry that the actor had tattled on him. "A few days later," adds Bova, "he came to rehearsal and said, 'I've left the next three afternoons just for book rehearsal.' We all arrived the next day and Gower wasn't there. He had gotten ill and gone into the hospital. At that time we joked that he just didn't want to rehearse the book."[75]

It was no laughing matter; Gower's absences were becoming more frequent and pronounced, giving performers no choice but to resolve problematic book scenes themselves. Orbach did precisely that on one occasion when he and some of the other principals ran into traffic difficulties negotiating chairs and tables for a scene (later dropped) in the Gypsy Tea Kettle. Everyone agreed that his solution would work.

The next day, as the scene unfolded with the new blocking during a run-through, Gower went wild with rage.

"Who's been directing around here while I was away?" he screamed. Dead silence. Finally Orbach spoke.

"Well, I'm sorry, Gower, but you weren't here and we had this problem and I fixed it by doing this."

Fuming as if about to storm out of the room or, worse, fire his leading man, he pulled a cigarette out and fumbled for a match. "I gave him a match and lit it for him," stated Orbach, "and then he laughed. We both broke up. He said, 'Next time, ask me first.' But that little incident was part of a continuing thing where we were sort of on our own as far as the scenes went because he was so busy with the musical numbers. Putting things in and taking them out."[76]

But he was never too busy to appreciate the numbers that were working, and most especially, the performers making them work. After a matinee Engstrom, the last person out of the dressing room, was preparing to head back to his hotel when he heard someone by the door clearing his voice. He turned to find Gower. For someone so charismatic, there were times when he was quite shy. Entering the room, he kind of shuffled around before warming to his point: "Jon, I just want you to know that you really do a terrific job in 'Shadow Waltz.' You know, you get applause every single night? That's terrific!"

"Obviously, you haven't seen it every single night," he answered self-effacingly, "because it hasn't gotten applause every single night."

"Well, every time I've seen it, it has gotten applause," replied Gower with a smile. "I just want to tell you that I really appreciate the work you put into that, and thank you." Then he disappeared. Ill as he was, Gower had come all the way down into the dressing area to speak with him—all the more reason why the compliment made a lasting impression on the dancer.[77]

As the Washington tour neared its end and New York previews loomed closer, masking the true cause of his declining health and frequent absences became increasingly complex. He finally decided to disclose the gravity of his condition to Merrick, who immediately assumed autonomous control of the production and shrouded it in a mantle of secrecy.

"Anybody want some 'Habit' chairs?" Merrick asked after cutting "You're Getting to be a Habit with Me" just before the final Washington performance. A set of wheelchairs had been customized to look like rolling Atlantic City Boardwalk deck chairs and that is precisely what they looked like—wheelchairs posing as deck chairs. Out they went and the stylish choreography with them. After the company's arrival in New York on July 28, Gower restaged "Habit" as a rehearsal number with Brock and Billy comically hand-shaking their way through it after *Pretty Lady* investor Abner objects to having his girlfriend kissed by another man. The chorus enters for the dance section as a famished Peggy staggers, spins, bounds, and rebounds all over the stage in frantic pursuit of her partner, never once popping up in the right place—getting to be a habitual annoyance to everyone, especially Brock, a perfect setup for the Brock–Sawyer conflict.

Gower's instructions to Wanda about how the role of Peggy was to be played were quite specific: "If you don't play the show for real, the audience is going to be laughing *at* you, not with you. I don't want you to ever break down that fourth wall into the audience. I want this to be *real*."[78] There was to be no camping; Wanda played it straight. By now, it was impossible to play it any other way.

In the evenings after the treatments and transfusions, they would head to Rumplemeyer's near the St. Moritz Hotel for ice cream before strolling Central Park South back to Gower's condominium.

"Our relationship is bittersweet. I'll be dead by the time you're forty," he said matter-of-factly.

"Oh, please. Don't talk like that," she protested.

"This damn thing could kill me." The secret was out. She wondered how he had managed to conceal it for as long as he did. Each day the walks home became slower and more labored for him.

Merrick canceled previews scheduled to begin August 2, as well as the August 11 opening, postponing both indefinitely. On August 8, he released this statement: "The Great Man way up there has said that this show is very important for people all around the world to see in these gloomy times. He wants to be sure that the show is ready, that it can be a memorable musical. He will give the word when He feels the show is ready. I am waiting for the courier to arrive. When he arrives and gives the word, I will place an ad for the show and promptly open it."[79] Despite Gower's noticeable decline, Merrick brought the show back into rehearsal, insisting on revisions. "Dames" was his pet peeve. In the afternoons, Gower would continue to revise it and polish other numbers; in the evenings, a "technical rehearsal" (for which Merrick was not required to pay theatre rental) was staged—full orchestra and all. One night as the first section of "Dames" concluded and the Maison drop rose on the jungle gym–music box part, Gower gasped, "What is *that!*" Merrick, assuming a directorial prerogative that wasn't his, had dressed the entire scene as a tacky Grecian spa replete with draped fabrics, urns, and *cherubs!* That did it. The two were no longer on speaking terms; Wagner served as intermediary, delivering the producer's scribbled notes on little scraps of paper to the director, who responded in kind.[80]

Finally, Merrick announced a benefit performance for the Democratic National Convention to be held on Sunday, August 10. Paranoid that the press would review a preview rather than the premiere performance, he established strict security measures, posting armed guards at the entrance to the theatre and compelling every member of the company to wear clip-on photograph IDs.[81] As an added precaution, he hired five bouncers dressed in black business suits to scan the audience for interlopers. *New York Times* freelance reporter Cliff Jahr, who not only had an invitation, but also a ticket purchased as insurance, was denied admission and muscled out to the street by two bouncers. Two days later, out of the blue, four hundred tickets arrived at the half-price ticket booth on Times Square for a sneak preview that evening. Right before curtain the audience was told that the performance would be cancelled due to "technical problems." The next morning Merrick complained that "a snake was loose in the audience."[82] Jahr again.

Through all this, Merrick's "technical rehearsals" continued unabated, with the company performing night after night without an audience. "I'm so damn tired of playing to an empty house, let's do *something* that makes us happy to be doing this every day," Wanda told the cast. "Everybody, tomorrow, bring in a stuffed animal."[83] They did. The next evening when Merrick arrived to take his seat front and center and found Big Bird and friends in the first several rows, he was ticked, but even more so the night after, when the cast danced "Dames" in the pink pullover *schmattes* they used backstage to cover themselves while running from one side to the other for quick changes.

Three days before the opening, Will Mead, friend to Gower and also Wanda, with whom he had worked in *A Chorus Line,* was preparing to fly to New York for the event. Eager to hear how the show was progressing, he called Gower, who never tolerated any disparaging remarks about Merrick but who was, on this occasion, quite direct about his behavior. "David has gone way over the edge. He will not open this show," he told Mead. "This man has really flipped out. I don't know what's funny. George Abbott doesn't know what's funny. I have to have an audience." Gower was quite beside himself.[84]

One evening following a dinner break, Wagner returned to the Winter Garden to discover Gower sitting alone in the darkened house. Merrick had just postponed the opening once more, his boundless zeal amassing more artistic control by the second. Irate but helpless, Gower resigned himself to ride out the storm. "I don't know how Gower kept showing up," says Wanda. "I really don't. I saw him walking into the theater for the picture calls, to the dress rehearsals and he was *slow* and shutting down."[85] He could only watch as Merrick went after Stewart once again over changes in the book.

The producer had written a one-liner—"My wallet's so thin it looks like an elephant sat on it"—and phoned Stewart to have it inserted into the show.[86] When the writer flatly refused to use it, Merrick threatened: "Look, Buster, I'm in charge of the book and if you don't make the changes the way I want you'll be thrown out tomorrow. As a matter of fact, don't show up at the theatre because I'll have the security guards throw you out."

"I will show up, David."

"Then, I'll have you thrown out tomorrow and he's next." The reference was to Gower.

"Good-bye, David," repeated Stewart until Merrick ended the conversation by replacing the receiver.[87] He made notes of the conversation and called his lawyer. The next day, when he showed up with a hired bodyguard to escort him through the stage door, Merrick made no effort to evict him. Even so, the incident so embittered the author that he announced his intention to cease writing musicals just hours before the curtain went up on opening night, lamenting, "I don't love it anymore."[88]

At last "the Great Man way up there" spoke to Merrick, who announced that *42nd Street* would open on Monday, August 25, following preview performances on Friday, August 22, and Saturday, August 23. On Wednesday, August 20, five days before the opening, Marge, in town for preproduction work on a TV special, joined Gower for a sneak preview. Since their divorce she had enjoyed much success as a choreographer for film *(Whose Life Is It Anyway?, The Day of the Locust)* and television, winning the Emmy Award for *Queen of the Stardust Ballroom*. Now married to TV film director Boris Sagal *(Masada, The Diary of Anne Frank)*, she warmly accepted Gower's invitation to the preview and for input on the show's trouble spots.[89] She sat in utter amazement, *42nd Street*'s every step echoing their years together: "I was just bowled over by it. He had an overall vision for making a classic show work in the 1980s. It was absolutely one of the best things Gower did in his entire life."[90]

42nd Street was ready to open, Gower declared, and nothing was to be changed. Afterward, he went backstage and ambled about chatting with the cast, something he had never done before. "How'd the show go?" he asked. "Did you have a good time? Enjoying it?"[91] Then he went home.

"Karla, I'm really not feeling great. You know how to take care of me." His calling was not unusual—since leaving California he had called and written several times, sharing updates on the show and his health. But the tone in his voice was most unusual. "I'd like you to come to New York." She would come.[92]

Thursday morning, when he missed rehearsal and failed to call, Wanda called him. No answer. Through lunch and early afternoon she called, and still no answer. Finally, on her way home after the run-through that evening, she stopped at his apartment. It was dark, with an unsettling air that intensified as she moved to the bedroom and quietly called to him. He replied that he was just resting, his breathing quite labored. Alarmed as she was, she did not want to alarm him, but action had to be taken. She called Marge, then Karin Baker and Larry Carpenter, Gower's assistant, who called for an ambulance to take him to Sloan-Kettering Memorial Cancer Institute. Overnight he had hemorrhaged severely—the evidence apparent when the lights in the bedroom were finally turned on.[93]

It was early Friday morning by the time the ambulance arrived at the emergency room. Wanda joined Gower there for a while, his frailty all too apparent. Later that day when she returned, he was in a private room, Marge and Gregg by his side. Then it was back to the theatre for rehearsal and the first preview that evening.

Karla arrived later in the day. By then his condition had deteriorated so greatly that he had been moved to the intensive care unit. Fighting three infections at once, his immune system was taxed to the limit—a side effect of the medication that he had been taking. His plan was to return to California, where his physician was ready to take over treatment. He had even purchased the plane ticket. Doctors told Karla that the infections were so severe that even a healthy person would have trouble fighting them. Still, they were cautiously optimistic that he would pull through, and they would do everything possible to help him do so.[94]

Jess was out the door and halfway down the path to pick up Saturday's mail when Leo ran out calling after him, "Margie's on the phone. Gower's dying." It was unthinkable. Sure, he had heard Gar was ill when the show was in Washington. That was not unusual. His health was always testy, especially during out-of-town tryouts when he became gaunt as a skeleton. But by opening night he had always gained back a few pounds, looking handsome as ever in his customary red blazer. This seemed like more of the same; even so, he told Marge he would come.

When he arrived late that afternoon, the ICU was off limits to visitors. For some time, he remained in the waiting room where Musser, Wagner, and Merrick were keeping vigil with Karla, Marge, and Gregg—Blake was in transit from school in New England. He stayed with them awhile, then departed. Inside, doctors worked vainly to cleanse the patient's blood, which the syndrome was quickly overcoming.

Between rehearsal and the second preview that day, Wanda visited again and Gower smiled when she told him how well the first preview had gone. He was also pleased to hear Karla's news that previews were selling out and lines were encircling the box office.[95] Yet despite the gravity of the situation, Marge found a kind of amusing surrealism to the way Gower's relationships with the three women in his life were playing out: "It was like something out of a Bob Fosse movie, the ex-wife, the present wife, and the girlfriend."[96] The surrealism was just beginning.

Sunday, as Gower went into kidney failure and his vital signs began to decline, Merrick insisted that the impending outcome be kept private and out of range of the media and cast, who surely would be devastated by the news and unable to perform. Everyone present in the waiting room—both family and friends—agreed that it was the best way to proceed. Afterward, he stood sentinel by the pay phone, awaiting personal calls but also ensuring that no one from Gower's room called outside.[97] That evening when Wanda arrived, she took Gower's hand, and though he barely opened his eyes, she knew he was aware of her presence. After the opening tomorrow night she would stop on her way to the party wearing the dress he had chosen for her. Before leaving the room, she paused at the door, waving goodbye to him, and wondered if she would ever see him again.[98]

The morning of the opening, Monday, August 25, Karla was the first to arrive at the hospital. She had been with Gower only briefly when his blood pressure plummeted abruptly. Immediately a team of doctors appeared and asked her to step outside the room. As they worked to stabilize him, she called Gregg and asked him to call Marge and come to the hospital at once. Moments later, at about 10:00 A.M., Gower died.

Merrick arrived shortly afterward. Upon receiving the news, he cautioned the gathering group of family and friends to remain silent about the death, and then requested hospital authorities to withhold the announcement until after the opening. To keep the cast from learning the news prematurely, he summoned them early to the theatre for "notes."[99] In the afternoon he and his assistant met with Karla to discuss arrangements for the memorial service she was planning to have family friend Robert Greenwald direct.[100]

In her dressing room, Wanda sat before the mirror applying her makeup. "I gotta do this for him tonight," she told herself. Then a note from Gower she had taped to the wall fluttered to the floor. He was dead; she just sensed it.

Opening night evoked the kind of old-time Broadway splendor New York had not seen in years, with floodlights scanning and criss-crossing the facade of the Winter Garden and limo upon limo arriving with a host of the theatre's most distinguished celebrities—Ethel Merman, Garson Kanin, Ruth Gordon, Joshua Logan, Carol Channing, Joseph Papp, Bob Fosse, Neil Simon. At 6:15, just before the house lights dimmed for the overture, Merrick appeared onstage, requesting critics to remain in the theatre until after the final curtain call.[101] Then the curtain rose on *42nd Street's* dancing feet, and for the next two hours the audience roared with approval as Gower's power wove its spell. Number by number, the performers were returning him to the peak of his craft, unaware that with each step they were also dancing his epitaph and immortalizing him.

The curtain had barely descended on the finale when the audience shot from their seats as one, wild with applause and cheers. A dozen curtain calls! The cast was ecstatic. On the twelfth, as Merrick appeared from the wings, hand raised to chin and face downcast, the ovation surged. Once more the impresario had defied the odds and landed a megahit certain to run for years.

Shaking his head, he raised his hand for quiet: "I'm sorry to have to report . . ."

Again the house went mad. Sorry? Sorry for what? He was baiting them by acting like he had a flop. A typical Merrick ploy. They lapped it up.

"No, no, it's very tragic," he insisted, raising his voice against the persistent laughter.

"You don't understand. Gower Champion died this morning."

Elation froze in midair. A collective gasp, then stunned silence as he turned from the audience to embrace Wanda, dazed and distraught. With the grieving cast standing helpless on stage and mayhem about to break loose on both sides of the footlights, Orbach called out to the stage manager, "Bring it down. Bring it down."[102] With that, the curtain fell on the opening of *42nd Street*—the orchestra's bouncy exit music strangely dissonant against the audience's funereal silence.

Backstage, chaos erupted, with some fleeing into the wings in search of a private corner and others remaining onstage to embrace and console each other. Respectfully, a young girl weaved quietly among them with a tray full of invitations that read simply: "The family of Gower Champion requests the honor of your presence this evening for a celebration in his memory at the Starlight Roof of the Waldorf-Astoria Hotel."[103] Uncertain about what to do, Wanda struggled up the stairs to her dressing room, utterly devastated. Finally, she decided to put on the dress Gower had chosen for her, pretend he was with her, and go to the party escorted by Will Mead.[104]

Through the early part of the evening, the mood at the Waldorf was somber. Merrick sat at a table, silently drinking wine while members of the cast slowly materialized first in twos and threes, later in larger groups. Many of them disapproved of the way he had informed them of Gower's death. Others maintained that Gower, showbiz veteran that he was, would have appreciated the drama.[105] "David had a lot riding on the show," explains Reams, "as did Gower's estate, and all of us. If he had to announce the death before the show, it would have affected everything. It was a very smart business move on David's part. The papers got a better story, and we got a lot of publicity all over the world."[106]

The evening progressed with the *All That Jazz* Fosse-like nature of Gower's death reflected in the three tables reserved for each of the women in his life and their friends. (Marge did not attend the party or the show. She spent the evening with husband Boris Sagal at their hotel while Gregg and Blake attended on her behalf.) Yet the biggest and most ironic parallel was the one Fosse himself noted. As he later told Reams, "Gower once again did me one better. I filmed my death. Gower Champion had the nerve to do it on opening night."[107] Even in death, Gower was to be envied.

Near the evening's end, a distinct Broadway tradition, of which Gower was an incontestable part, prevailed. Heeding the strains of Woody Herman's Band, some of the partygoers rose up and gave him a tribute he would surely have applauded. They danced.

"Okay, everybody who's done *A Chorus Line*. Let's go down on the floor," Wanda directed. She asked the band to play "One" and they complied. A Michael Bennett number as a Gower Champion tribute seemed odd to some, tasteless to others. But for those on the floor, who knew it reflected the late director-choreographer's signature Broadway style, it made perfect sense. With "every little step he'd take," Gower Champion indeed was "one singular sensation."

The critics unanimously agreed. "This brilliant showman's final musical is, if nothing else, a perfect monument to his glorious career," observed Frank Rich. "As it fortunately happens, this show not only features his best choreography, but it also serves as a strangely ironic tribute to all the other musicals he has staged over the past two decades."[108] "One of Champion's finest achievements, full of imagination, full of the old-fashioned showmanship for which he was justly celebrated," declared Howard Kissel.[109] "The staging—not only of the dances but also of the entire show," wrote John Simon, "has an intensity and sweep that transcend both nostalgia and camp. It grabs you by the throat or entrails—sometimes, indeed, by the heart—and carries you beyond razzmatazz, beyond even pizzazz, into elation."[110] The elation was in no small part due to a stellar collaboration of talented artists—Phillip J. Lang's phenomenally fresh treatments of old standards, Wagner's flashy settings, Aldredge's eye-filling costumes, Musser's splendid and sensitive lighting.[111]

There was ample praise, too, for Orbach's edgy director with his gruff pep-talking and expressive singing, Grimes's haughty stiletto-tongued grande dame, and Richert's modest ingénue who ably belts out songs and madly hoofs her way to stardom. The contributions of Reams's brash breezy tenor, Cook and Bova's zesty writer-performers, Prunczik's cheeky chorine, and Carroll's fleet dancing were likewise noted.[112]

The next evening, just before curtain time at eight, all Broadway theatres observed the request of the League of New York Theatres and Producers to dim their lights for one minute in tribute to the late showman. At noon on Wednesday, August 27, the theatre community gathered at the Winter Garden for Gower's memorial service. During the ninety-minute homage Marge spoke about the boy she had met in ninth grade who became her dance partner and husband and Gregg about the father whose love became present whenever he looked up at the moon. Among those warmly recalling their sixty-one-year-old colleague and friend were Charles Strouse, Fred Ebb, John Kander, David Hartman, Carol Channing, and Jerry Herman.

The final word went to Merrick, who began by reassuring everyone, "I was just talking with Gower. He's quite pleased." Then he spoke of a journalist he had met some years before who wanted to know who was responsible for the artistry of the Merrick-Champion musicals:

"Who chose the songwriters?" asked the reporter.

"Gower Champion," Merrick replied.

"The designers?"

"Gower Champion."

"How about the color and movement?"

"Gower Champion."

"And what did you do, Mr. Merrick?"

"I picked Gower Champion."[113]

The producer's impeccable taste was undeniable. He called for the finale and, while the cast's recording of "Lullaby of Broadway" filled the house, stood against the proscenium, arms folded in the manner of *42nd Street* showman Julian Marsh. When the song ended, he waved grandly to the audience, declaring, "Gower says thank you for coming." Crossing to center, he turned upstage, disappearing into the darkness as the curtain fell.[114]

EPILOGUE

Late Summer 1980

In keeping with family wishes, Gower's body was flown to Los Angeles and cremated. Weeks later, at a spot near his favorite stretch of Malibu Beach, Karla arranged a private service for family and friends, Marge and Jeanne Tyler among them. Actor Max Showalter spoke of Gower's love of azaleas, the anticipation they both shared as blooming season neared, and how, only the day before, he had awakened to find every plant on his porch—many of them gifts from Gower—in brilliant bloom months out of season. Then James Mitchell gave a reading before Merrick, in formal black suit and black shoes, addressed the casual barefooted assembly as Gower's medium.[1] Now that Gower was speaking directly through him to them, couriers from the Great Man way up there were no longer necessary—showman as shaman.

Merrick's mysticism was fleeting. Just a few months later, he had Gower's name removed from the marquee. Not until Gregg Champion threatened to sue to have his father's name restored did the producer comply.[2] Merrick's exploitation continued as he moved the show from Gower's theatre of preference—the Winter Garden—to his—the St. James, where the actors playing Julian Marsh gradually resembled the director less and him more. Even so, Gower's spirit prevailed. It may have been "David Merrick's *42nd Street*," but it sang and danced Gower Champion start to finish.

At the 35th Annual Tony Awards in June 1981, the show received nominations in eight categories, with Richert, Reams, Aldredge, Musser, Stewart, and Bramble among the nominees. It won Best Musical and Gower, posthumously nominated for Best Director and Choreographer, won the choreographer's award.[3] One of Broadway's longest-running musicals, *42nd Street* totaled 3,486 performances over eight and a half years before closing at the St. James on January 15, 1989.[4]

. . .

The car climbed up and up, passing through Malibu and beyond to a serene and unspoiled seascape perfect for the final farewell that Karla, Gregg, and Blake were about to give Gower months past his death and the services. Blake chose the spot— a giant rock. Urn in hand, he climbed to the top, Gregg and Karla behind him. He paused a moment; then, opening the urn, he released his father's ashes to the sea. Silently they watched as the waves slowly bore them beyond sight.[5]

AFTERWORD

On August 25, 1980, Michael Stewart was en route to England aboard the *Queen Elizabeth II* when he received word of Gower's death. Immediately, he penned this tribute:

> Gower Champion was my friend for 21 years. We did shows together. There's no experience more shattering, and we came out of each one better friends than we were before. His talent and his taste took me from where I was to where I wanted to be. I owe everything to Gower. And I'm not just saying it today—I always said it.
>
> I say his name and so many things come to mind. Gower in rehearsal quiet and perfectly contained, then suddenly moving sharp as a knife—cutting through space with that extraordinary elegance and grace. The bold initials "GC" approving costume sketches. Gower in his red jacket at the first openings.
>
> The day I left New York, Gower asked to see me and I went to the hospital. The doctor had given a cautiously optimistic report and we were both relieved and elated. I told him that this show (*42nd Street*) was exactly as he set it and that David (Merrick), the actors, and the authors were all determined to keep it that way. Gower was so pleased and told me what he was going to do when he got out of the hospital—go back home to California and just walk on the beach. Just walk and walk with the sun on one side until he got as far as he wanted to go, then back again. That morning, we both thought he'd be there in a few weeks time. Because life isn't always fair, he didn't get his wish. But as long as I'm around, I'll see my old friend—tall, slender and sharp as that knife—walking on his beach.
>
> I am deeply sad to lose Gower as my director. I find it unbearable to lose him as my friend.[1]

Yet for all his originality and distinguished contributions to the theatre, Champion remains undervalued by scholars and critics alike who blithely dismiss him as an anomaly, thereby fueling the bias that has denied him parity with Robbins, Fosse, and Bennett in the pantheon of director-choreographers. Scholar James Winston Challender excluded him from his 1986 study of *The Function of the Choreographer in the Development of the Concept Musical* on the premise that "he was a product of Hollywood" whose work reflected its "nostalgia and shtick."[2]

Critics likewise have consistently failed to give him his due. While admitting that he "kept alive the old-fashioned tradition of bravura show-business extravaganzas . . . by mixing dazzling staging with subtly artistic craftsmanship," Ken Mandelbaum denies his innovation, stating only that he "brought the staging of conventional musicals to its highest peak."[3] Likewise, former *New York Times* critic Frank Rich concluded that Gower essentially ". . . was an anachronism. He was no innovator, like Jerome Robbins or Michael Bennett. He never created his own distinct choreographic style, like Bob Fosse. He didn't try to tackle daring subjects, like Hal Prince. And yet Mr. Champion's body of work is as much a part of the history of the contemporary musical as that of his talented peers."[4]

A simple reflection from Marge is all one needs to answer all of Gower's critics: "I remember once a parking lot attendant at Chasen's saying as he opened the door, 'Are you *the* Gower Champion?' Gower replied, 'No, I'm the *other* one.' But in the history of the American stage, I don't think there can be any doubt about who *the* Gower Champion is and what he has done to make the musical dance."[5]

Gower Champion's artistry made Broadway's golden age all the more golden because of the dazzling musicals he created—streamlined, dance-propelled musicals each unique in concept and choreography. In one after another, he filled the stage top to bottom with a ceaseless array of sights and sounds that seamlessly unfolded to thrill, delight, and deeply touch audiences. His artistry was also his legacy—one that continues to shape and inform our musicals twenty-five years after his death. In the history of American theatre he stands apart as the quintessential showman, who, to his dying day, literally lit up Broadway, the nation, the world, with a rare and incandescent genius never seen before—or since—the parade passed by.

Acknowledgments

I began this journey with Gower Champion thirteen years ago as a doctoral student at New York University under the extraordinary mentorship of the late Lowell S. Swortzell, cofounder of the Program in Educational Theatre with his wife, Nancy. Lowell's insightful guidance of my dissertation on four of Gower's musicals—*Carnival, Hello, Dolly!, I Do! I Do!,* and *The Happy Time*—was a blessing and something for which I will always be grateful. For that reason, this book is dedicated to him.

Stepping in where Lowell left off were two new guides, likewise gifted, who patiently led me through the world of publishing: editor Michael Flamini of St. Martin's Press, whose brilliant idea for the title for this book at once clarified Gower's life and provided focus, and agent Eric Myers, right beside me at every turn from proposal to publication. Mapping the course was also helped by the work of the late David Payne-Carter, the first Champion scholar and a fellow NYU alumnus.

Gower's friends and colleagues took me inside the world he shared with them (behind the closed doors producers dared not enter), detailing his genius, the secrets of his craft, and the stories that have enriched this work. They have been wonderful tutors, and my gratitude and admiration go to them for the lessons they have taught me about life in the theatre. A special thanks to Karla Champion, Jon Engstrom, Jess Gregg, David Hamilton, Jerry Herman, Jeanne Tyler Hoyt, Will Mead, Patricia and Bert Michaels, Don Pippin, Debbie Reynolds, Wanda Richert, Sara and Alan Weeks, and most of all, Marge Champion, who generously answered questions and opened their personal archives and hearts to me.

No less essential to this work was the wonderful assistance I received from Carol Turley and the staff of the Department of Special Collections at the Research Library of the University of California–Los Angeles, where Gower's scripts and notes are archived, and Bob Taylor, curator of the Billy Rose Theatre Collection of the

New York Public Library for the Performing Arts, and his staff, especially Jeremy Megraw and Louise Martzinek. My gratitude to Marge Champion, Andy Hovick and Eric Skipsey of MPTV, Jeanne Tyler Hoyt, Will Mead, Gabriel Pinski of Fred Fehl Photography, J. C. Sheets, Martha Swope, and Alex Teslik of Eileen Darby Images for the wonderful illustrations of Gower's work used here.

Many friends read or listened to the work as it developed, lent valuable support, or provided getaways where I could work in quiet: Cathleen Albertus, Chris Druse, Margie Duncan, Reverend Thomas Fenlon, Gene Gilvey, Joseph Glancey, Rita Hamilton, Dorothy Kelly, Dee McDevitt, Sister Loretta McGrann, Nick Miraflores, Don Pierce, Roger Repohl, Marc Ricciardi, James Santos, Lee Stuart, Alan Thomas, and my students and family, most especially Fran and Dad.

Along the way, there also has been great support from the communities in which I live and work. St. Joseph's College, New York, and its president, Sister Elizabeth Hill, who provided grants to fund research; the parish community of St. Augustine's Church, Bronx, New York; and my confrères and teachers, the Oblates of St. Francis de Sales, who long ago had the foresight to stick me in the chorus of *Bye Bye Birdie* as a high school sophomore. But before that, my first instructors in the arts, my parents, sparked my interest: the mother who took her six-year-old son to see *The King and I,* the father who later schooled him in what show albums to purchase for the family record collection. Their contributions I cherish best.

Notes

Prologue

1. Letter from Gower Champion to Michael Stewart, 7 June 1979, Michael Stewart Papers, "42nd Street," Series 11, Box 32, Folder 7, Billy Rose Theatre Collection, New York Public Library for the Performing Arts; and Notes from Michael Stewart, Michael Stewart Papers, "42nd Street," Series 11, Box 33, Billy Rose Theatre Collection, New York Library for the Performing Arts.

One: The Young Prince

1. Lloyd Shearer, "Something to Dance About," *Redbook*, August 1953: 70.
2. Karla Champion, personal interview, 28 July 2003.
3. Karla Champion interview.
4. Beatrice Carlisle Champion in Shearer, 70.
5. Jess Gregg, personal interview, 9 November 1998.
6. Gregg interview, 9 November 1998.
7. Jess Gregg interviews.
8. Jeanne Tyler Hoyt, Marge Champion, and Vera Fern Innes interviews.
9. Gregg, Karla Champion, and Marge Champion interviews.
10. Beatrice Carlisle Champion in Shearer, 70.
11. Marge Champion and Jeanne Tyler Hoyt interviews.
12. Hoyt interview.
13. Shirley Temple Black, *Child Star* (New York: Warner Books, Inc., 1989), 40.
14. Black, 40.
15. Black, 386.
16. Marge Champion interviews.
17. Jess Gregg interviews.
18. Marge Champion interviews.

Two: The Dance to Fame

1. "Gower and Jeanne Scrapbooks," private collection of Jeanne Tyler Hoyt, Redlands, California.
2. Jess Gregg interviews.
3. "Met, Boston," *Variety*, 11 February 1937: no pagination.
4. Jeanne Tyler Hoyt interview.
5. Hoyt interview.
6. Morgan Powell, "Normandie Roof Opens at Mt. Royal Hotel," *Montreal Daily Star*, 18 June 1937: no pagination.
7. William D. O'Hara, "Mount Royal's Normandie Roof Open Last Night," *Montreal Daily Herald*, 18 June 1937: no pagination.

8. Morgan Powell, "Normandie Roof Show Continues to Attract Enthusiastic Patrons," *Montreal Daily Star,* 20 July 1937: no pagination.
9. Beatrice Carlisle Champion in Vera Fern Innes interview, 14 July 1999.
10. Innes interview.
11. Beatrice Carlisle Champion in Lloyd Shearer, "Something to Dance About," *Redbook,* August 1953: 71.
12. Gower Champion in Shearer, 71.
13. Morgan Powell, "Normandie Roof Still Coolest Retreat from the Pestiferous Heat," *Montreal Daily Star,* 20 July 1937: no pagination.
14. "Gower and Jeanne at the Normandie Roof a Continued Sensation," *Montreal Daily Star,* 27 July 1937: no pagination.
15. Hoyt interview.
16. "Gower and Jeanne Scrapbooks."
17. Stanley Green, *Encyclodedia of the Musical Theatre* (New York: Da Capo Press, 1976), 7.
18. Stanley Green, *Ring Bells! Sing Songs! Broadway Musicals of the Thirties* (New Rochelle, N.Y.: Arlington House, 1971), 183.
19. Gower Champion in Innes interview.
20. Gregg interviews.
21. Gregg interviews.
22. Innes interview.
23. Hoyt interview.
24. Will Davidson, "Phil Regan of Movies Singing at Chez Paree," *Chicago Tribune,* 4 May 1942: no pagination.
25. Innes interview.
26. Walter Winchell, "On Broadway," *New York Daily Mirror,* 3 November 1942: 10.

Three: Story-Dancing Champions

1. Sidney Skolsky, "Hollywood Is My Beat," *Los Angeles Citizen-News,* 27 February 1953: 17.
2. Gower Champion in Rex Reed, "A Champion—Almost Always," *New York Times,* 19 February 1967: D3.
3. Lloyd Shearer, "Something to Dance About," *Redbook,* August 1953: 70; Ephraim Katz, *The Film Encyclopedia* (New York: Perigee Books, 1982), 88.
4. Shearer, 71; Ruth Eleanor Howard, "An Interview with 'The Ballet Master to Movieland,' " *The American Dancer* (*Dance Magazine*), June 1927: 22.
5. Skolsky, 17; Shearer, 72.
6. Champion in Reed, D3.
7. "Champions Live Up to Their Name," *Cincinnati Citizen Magazine,* 31 July 1951: no pagination.
8. Jess Gregg interviews.
9. Gower Champion, "And How They Dance!" *Philadelphia Inquirer,* 27 August 1961: no pagination.
10. Marge Champion interview.
11. According to Philip D. Morehead, "A pastoral song or dance of the sixteenth century." *The New American Dictionary of Music* (New York: Dutton Books, 1991), 42.
12. Chris Randall, "Two Scrubbed Kids Who Really Dance," *San Francisco Chronicle-This World Magazine,* 12 February 1950: 22.
13. Marge Champion interview, 3 February 1993.
14. Randall, 22.
15. Jeanne Tyler Hoyt interview.
16. Betty Fromm, "Just Right for Each Other," *Photoplay,* April 1953: 103.
17. Gower Champion in McClay, "Howard McClay," *Los Angeles Herald and Express,* 9 June 1952: no pagination.

Four: Broadway, Televisionland, Hollywood

1. Marge Champion interviews.
2. *Lend an Ear,* souvenir program.
3. Marge Champion interviews.
4. John Chapman, "*Small Wonder,*" *New York Daily News,* 16 September 1948: no pagination.
5. George Curry, "*Small Wonder* Too Modestly Names Itself on Broadway," *Brooklyn Daily Eagle,* 16 September 1948: no pagination.
6. George Freedley, "*Lend an Ear* Is Amusing, Tuneful, Not To Be Missed," *New York Morning Telegraph,* 18 December 1948: no pagination.
7. Walter Terry, "Dance: Operatic, Ethnologic, and for Night Club Patrons," *New York Herald Tribune,* 17 December 1948: no pagination.
8. Jack Gould, "Television in Review," *New York Times,* 6 February 1949: no pagination.
9. David Payne-Carter, *Gower Champion and the American Musical Theatre* (Ph.D. dissertation, New York University, 1987; Ann Arbor: UMI, 1988, #88-01561), 128.
10. Ethan Mordden, *Broadway Babies: The People Who Made the American Musical* (New York: Oxford, 1983) 173; Payne-Carter, 128.
11. Kate Cameron, "Marge and Gower—They're Champs," *New York Sunday News,* 17 June 1951: II, 2.
12. Marge Champion interviews.
13. Gower Champion in Rex Reed, "A Champion—Almost Always," *New York Times,* 19 February 1967: D3.
14. Lee Zhito, "Mocambo, Hollywood," *The Billboard,* 3 September 1949: no pagination.
15. Louella O. Parsons, "Ava Helped Fernando Lamas Get Fat Contract with MGM," *Los Angeles Examiner,* 10 September 1949: no pagination. Marge Champion in Scott Eyman, *Lion of Hollywood: The Life and Legend of Louis B. Mayer* (New York: Simon and Schuster, 2005), 378.
16. "Give Marge and Gower Champion a 'Live' Audience Any Old Time," *St. Louis Globe-Democrat,* 1 December 1954: no pagination.
17. "Give Marge and Gower Champion a 'Live' Audience Any Old Time."

Five: MGM

1. Marge Champion interviews.
2. "News of the Screen," *New York Herald Tribune,* 12 September 1949: no pagination; Reed Porter, "Pilots and Pans," *Los Angeles Mirror,* 22 September 1949: no pagination.
3. Frank Quinn, "Super De Luxe *Show Boat* Is Rare Treat at Music Hall," *New York Daily Mirror,* 20 July 1951: 26; Wanda Hale, "MGM's *Show Boat* Is a Magnificent Movie," *New York Daily News,* 20 July 1951: 50; Bosley Crowther, "Rollin' Along," *New York Times,* 22 July 1951: no pagination.
4. Marge Champion in Scott Eyman, *Lion of Hollywood: The Life and Legend of Louis B. Mayer* (New York: Simon and Schuster, 2005), 440; and personal interview, 22 June 2005.
5. Marge Champion in Eyman, 440.
6. Marge Champion in Eyman, 440.
7. Gower Champion in Gary Paul Gates, "Broadway's Champion," *Holiday,* February 1964: 92.
8. John McClain, "*Make a Wish:* Fine Ballet and Music Offset a Dull Story," *New York Journal-American,* 19 April 1951: no pagination; Brooks Atkinson, "Nanette Fabray Stars in New Musical Comedy, Entitled, *Make a Wish,*" *New York Times,* 19 April 1951: 38; Richard Watts, Jr., "Speaking Particularly of a Ballet," *New York Post,* 19 April 1951: no pagination.
9. Gower Champion in Howard McClay, "Howard McClay," *Los Angeles Herald and Express,* 9 June 1952: no pagination.
10. "Minimum of 40 in 12 Months in MGM $64,000,000 Budget," *Hollywood Reporter,* 16 August 1951: no pagination.
11. "Minimum of 40. . . ."

12. Gower Champion, letter to Marge Champion (Chicago: 12 March 1948), private collection of Marge Champion, Stockbridge, Massachusetts.
13. *"Everything I Have Is Yours,"* *Newsweek,* 2 November 1952: 106; Bosley Crowther, "The Screen in Review," *New York Times,* 30 October 1952: no pagination.
14. "Film Review—*Everything I Have Is Yours,"* *Variety,* 24 October 1952: no pagination.
15. "Film Review" no pagination; Ruth Waterbury, "Musical Plot Appeals," *Los Angeles Examiner,* 1 November 1952: no pagination; and Frank Quinn, "Champions' Film Shines at State," *New York Daily Mirror,* 30 October 1952: no pagination.
16. "Minimum of 40. . . ."
17. Jimmy Starr, "Dancing Champions in Lavish MGM Musical," *Los Angeles Herald-Express,* 9 June 1952: no pagination.
18. David Payne-Carter, *Gower Champion and the American Musical Theatre* (Ph.D. dissertation, New York University, 1987; Ann Arbor: UMI, 1988, #88-01561), 168.
19. Stephen M. Silverman, *Dancing on the Ceiling: Stanley Donen and His Movies* (New York: Alfred A. Knopf, 1996), 180.
20. Kevin Boyd Grubb, *Razzle Dazzle: The Life and Work of Bob Fosse* (New York: St. Martin's Press, 1989), 25.
21. Denny Martin Flinn, *Musical! A Grand Tour* (New York: Schirmer Books, 1997), 301.
22. Jess Gregg interviews.
23. Debbie Reynolds, personal interview, 29 July 2003.
24. Gregg interviews.
25. Gregg interviews.
26. "Song and Dance Pic Lacking in Sparkle," *Hollywood Reporter,* 1 December 1953: no pagination.
27. Philip Furia, *Ira Gershwin: The Art of the Lyricist* (New York: Oxford University Press, 1996), 212–213.
28. The account on pages 52–54 was confirmed by Debbie Reynolds on 1 June 2005.

Six: Performer and Choreographer
1. Marge Champion interviews; John A. Gilvey, *Gower Champion as Director: An Analysis of His Craft in Four Broadway Musicals, 1961–1968* (Ph.D. dissertation, New York University, 1995; Ann Arbor: UMI, 1996, #97-01496), 72–90.
2. Richard Dyer MacCann, "Husband and Wife Team Look Ahead," *Boston Christian Scientist Monitor,* 31 March 1953: 4; Harrison Carroll, "Burton's Huge Salary for *Robe* Will Go To Pay British Taxes," *Los Angeles Herald Express,* 26 February 1953: no pagination; David Payne-Carter, *Gower Champion and the American Musical Theatre* (Ph.D. dissertation, New York University 1987; Ann Arbor: UMI, 1988, #88-01561), 170–71.
3. "Marge and Gower Champion: Flamingo, Las Vegas," *Variety,* 4 May 1953: no pagination.
4. "Flamingo, Las Vegas," *Hollywood Reporter,* 4 May 1953: no pagination.
5. "The Marge and Gower Champion Story," narr. Ed Sullivan, prods. Marlo Lewis and Ed Sullivan, dir. John Wray, *Toast of the Town,* CBS, WCBS, New York, 14 June 1953—video recording of kinescope from private collection of Marge Champion. Prior to videotape, live programs were preserved via kinescope—a film of the performance as it appeared on the television screen.
6. "A Bouquet for Millie," *Variety,* 18 December 1953: no pagination.
7. Mason Wiley and Damien Bona, *Inside Oscar: The Unofficial History of the Academy Awards* (New York: Ballantine Books, 1996), 240.
8. Hazel Flynn, "Champions Spark *Jupiter's Darling* Spoof Spectacle," *Beverly Hills Daily News Life,* 14 March 1955: no pagination.
9. Gower Champion in "Champions Adapt to Elephants," *Syracuse Herald-Journal,* 25 January 1955: 20.
10. Champion in "Champions Adapt to Elephants."

11. Rex Reed, "A Champion—Almost Always," *New York Times,* 19 February 1967: D1, 3; "Mack and Mabel," *New York Sunday News,* 13 October 1974: D3.

12. Walter F. Kerr, "Belafonte and His Supersongs," *New York Herald-Tribune,* 17 April 1955: no pagination.

13. Kerr; Brooks Atkinson, *"3 for Tonight,"* *New York Times,* 17 April 1955: no pagination; Richard Watts Jr., "Bright Evening of Song and Dance," *New York Post,* 7 April 1955: no pagination.

14. Kerr.

15. George Oppenheimer, "On Stage: Song and Dance," *New York Newsday,* 15 April 1955: no pagination.

16. William Hawkins, *"3 for Tonight* More Like Party," *New York World-Telegram and Sun,* 7 April 1955: no pagination.

17. Thomas R. Dash, *"3 for Tonight* Plymouth Theatre," *Women's Wear Daily,* 7 April 1955: no pagination.

18. Atkinson.

19. *3 for Tonight,* narr. Hiram Sherman, prods. Paul Gregory and Charles Laughton, dir. Gower Champion, NBC, WNBC, New York, 22 June 1955. Video recording of kinescope from private collection of Marge Champion.

20. Jack Gould, *"3 for Tonight* Ideally Adapted to Medium," *New York Times,* 24 June 1955: no pagination.

21. Champion in Hedda Hopper, "How a Top Dancer Became a Director," *Boston Herald,* 15 November 1965: 16.

22. "Marge and Gower Champion Organize Own Corporation," *Hollywood Reporter,* 29 August 1955: no pagination; "It Happened In Hollywood: Champions Get 'Blues,' " *Film Daily,* 6 October 1955: no pagination; Louella Parsons, "The Champions and Their Lucky Number," *Los Angeles Times Pictorial TV Review,* 12 February 1956: no pagination.

23. Champion in Reed, D3.

24. Charles Chilton, "Broadway's Champ," *Detroit News (Pictorial Magazine),* 17 November 1963: 52.

25. Murry Frymer, "Gower Champion's Magic Hard to Define," *New York Newsday,* 4 January 1967: 3A.

26. Jess Gregg interview, 9 November 1998; Jess Gregg, "Scenes from a Memoir," *Dance Magazine,* September 1999: 57.

27. Gregg interview.

Seven: Director

1. Ed Oncken, "Night Club Review Digest: Marge and Gower Champs at Vegas," *Billboard,* 3 December 1955: no pagination.

2. Oncken.

3. Gus Lamp, Entertainment Director, Stein Hotels, telegram to Marge and Gower Champion, 3 January 1956.

4. Oncken.

5. "Nitery Review: New Frontier, Las Vegas, Nov. 16," *Variety,* 17 November 1955: no pagination.

6. *Carnival,* souvenir program, 7.

7. Gower Champion in Louis Jeriel Summers, Jr. *The Rise of the Director/Choreographer in the American Musical Theatre* (Ph.D. dissertation, University of Missouri-Columbia, 1976; Ann Arbor, UMI, 1978, #77-5661), 108.

8. "G.E. Dancers Go Straight in New Role," *Erie Times,* 4 November 1956: no pagination; " 'Rider on the Pale Horse': General Electric Theatre," *Variety,* 6 November 1956: no pagination.

9. Vernon Scott, press release, 16 May 1957: no pagination.

10. James Powers, *"Legend* Exotic Adventure; *Girl Most Likely,* Breezy," *Hollywood Reporter,* 2 December 1957: no pagination.

11. Paine Knickerbocker, *"The Girl Most Likely* Had a Skeleton in the Closet," *San Francisco Chronicle Magazine,* 16 February 1958: no pagination.

12. Marge Champion interviews.
13. Louella O. Parsons, "Gower Champion TV Actor Hurt in Crash," *Los Angeles Examiner,* 14 March 1957: II, 2.; "Gower Champion Hurt in Car Crash," *Los Angeles Herald Express,* 13 March 1957: no pagination; "Injury Knocks Gower Out of Dancing Role," *Los Angeles Times,* 31 March 1957: no pagination.
14. Gower Champion in Charles Mercer, "Happy Ending: Champions Glad Weekly Show Is Over," *Radio-Television Magazine of San Diego Union,* 28 July 1957: E 6.
15. Champion in Mercer, E 6.
16. Gower Champion in Dave Kaufman, "On All Channels," *Variety,* 23 December 1958: no pagination.
17. "Poor Marge Undone in Dance for the Queen," *Los Angeles Herald Express,* 19 October 1957: no pagination.
18. Ronald Singleton, " 'So Sorry' Philip Tells the Dancer and Sends Orchids," *Los Angeles Evening Herald Express,* 21 October 1957: no pagination.
19. "Champs Plan Dance School," *Beverly Hills Citizen,* 14 February 1958: 8.
20. Walter Whitworth, "What Gives in Avondale Fantasy?," *Indianapolis News,* 30 July 1958: no pagination.
21. "Accent on Love," *Variety,* 2 March 1959: no pagination.
22. Mason Wiley and Damien Bona, *Inside Oscar: The Unofficial History of the Academy Awards* (New York: Ballantine Books, 1996), 299.
23. Jess Gregg, "Scenes from a Memoir," *Dance Magazine,* September 1999: 57.
24. Elaine Shepard, "Russian Double Cross Gets Sullivan's Irish Up," *Boston Daily Globe,* 9 September 1959: no pagination; "Marge and Gower Champion Back From Russia," *New York Mirror,* 22 September 1959: no pagination; Sally Hammond, "How Marge and Gower Proved They Were Champions in Moscow," *New York Post,* 27 September 1959: 18.
25. John L. Scott, "Gower, Marge Breaking Up Dance Act," *Los Angeles Times,* 2 August 1959: no pagination.

Eight: A Revusical: Sardonic, Yet Stylish

1. "Let's Go Steady," *New York Journal American,* 17 August 1958: no pagination; Arthur Gelb, "Drama News," 10 July 1958: 5 (press release for *Let's Go Steady* found in *Bye Bye Birdie* clippings file, Billy Rose Theatre Collection, New York Public Library for the Performing Arts); "Stage News," press release for *Let's Go Steady (Bye Bye Birdie). Bye Bye Birdie* Clippings File, Billy Rose Theatre Collection, New York Public Library for the Performing Arts, 25 February 1958: 2; Nan Robertson, "Champion's Challenge," *New York Times,* 10 April 1960: no pagination; and John A. Gilvey, *Gower Champion as Director: An Analysis of His Craft in Four Broadway Musicals, 1961–1968,* Ph.D. dissertation, New York University, 1995; Ann Arbor, UMI, 1996, #97-01496), 91–120.
2. Charles Strouse in Al Kasha and Joel Hirschhorn, *Notes on Broadway: Conversations with the Great Songwriters* (Chicago: Contemporary Books, Inc., 1985), 275.
3. *Bye Bye Birdie,* souvenir program, 8.
4. "Stage News," 25 February 1958: 2 (press release for *Let's Go Steady* found in *Bye Bye Birdie* clippings file, Billy Rose Theatre Collection, New York Public Library for the Performing Arts).
5. Robertson.
6. Champion in Robertson.
7. Robertson.
8. Champion in Robertson.
9. Arthur Gelb, "Theatre Column," 7 August 1959: 1 (press release for *The Day They Took Birdie Away* found in *Bye Bye Birdie* clippings file, Billy Rose Theatre Collection, New York Public Library for the Performing Arts).
10. Robertson.
11. Marge Champion interviews.
12. Marge Champion interviews.

13. Jess Gregg interview.

14. Gregg interview.

15. *Bye Bye Birdie,* souvenir program: 7.

16. *Bye Bye Birdie,* souvenir program: 8.

17. Charles Stouse in Myrna Katz Frommer and Harvey Frommer, *It Happened on Broadway: An Oral History of the Great White Way* (Madison: University of Wisconsin Press, 2004), 141; Marge Champion interviews.

18. Gower Champion, Production Notes for *Bye Bye Birdie,* ms., Collection 346, Box 1, Department of Special Collections, Research Library of University of California, Los Angeles; Michael Stewart, *One of the Girls* typescript, Collection T-Mss 1990-018, Box 62–63, Billy Rose Theatre Collection, New York Public Library for the Performing Arts.

19. Champion, production notes for *Bye Bye Birdie.*

20. Champion, production notes for *Bye Bye Birdie.*

21. Gower Champion, production notes for *Bye Bye Birdie*; David Payne-Carter, *Gower Champion and the American Musical Theatre* (Ph.D. dissertation, New York University, 1987; Ann Arbor: UMI, 1988, #88-01561), 236.

22. Frommer and Frommer, 141.

23. Kenneth Tynan, "Sweet Birdie of Youth," *New Yorker,* 23 April 1960: 116.

24. Martin Gottfried, *Broadway Musicals* (New York: Harry N. Abrams, 1980), 141.

25. Ernie Schier, "*Bye Bye Birdie* Musical Bows Prior to New York," *Philadelphia Evening Bulletin,* 17 March 1960: 25.

26. Whitney Bolton, "*Bye Bye Birdie* Delightful Show," *New York Morning Telegraph,* 16 April 1960: no pagination.

27. Abe Laufe, *Broadway's Greatest Musicals* (New York: Funk and Wagnalls, 1977), 262.

28. Charles Strouse in Kasha and Hirschhorn, 277–78.

29. Strouse in Kasha and Hirschhorn, 277–78.

30. Champion in Robertson.

31. Walter Kerr, "*Birdie* Flies Above the Plot," *New York Herald Tribune,* 24 April 1960: no pagination.

32. Thomas R. Dash, "*Bye Bye Birdie* Rocks 'Em Rolls 'Em in the Aisles," *Women's Wear Daily,* 15 April 1960: no pagination; Jerry Gaghan, "*Birdie* Frolics at Shubert," *Philadelphia Daily News,* 17 March 1960: 44.

33. Tynan, 116; Schier, 25.

34. Schier, 25.

35. Watts, "Fresh and Humorous Musical Show," *New York Post,* 15 April 1960: 16.

36. Jess Gregg interviews.

37. Jess Gregg, "Scenes From a Memoir," *Dance Magazine,* September 1999: 58.

38. Cecil Smith, "Ghost of Gower Champion Still Haunts Broadway," *Los Angeles Times,* 10 January 1982: no pagination.

39. Gower Champion in Smith.

40. Susan Watson in Dennis McGovern and Deborah Grace Winer, *Sing Out, Louise! 150 Stars of the Musical Theatre Remember 50 Years on Broadway* (New York: Schirmer Books, 1993), 129.

41. Payne-Carter, 236.

42. Chita Rivera in McGovern and Winer, 128–29.

43. Gregg interviews.

44. John Chapman, *Bye Bye Birdie* a Funny, Fresh and Captivating Musical Show," *New York Daily News,* 15 April 1960: no pagination; Richard Watts Jr. "Fresh and Humorous Musical Show," *New York Post,* 15 April 1960: 16.; George Oppenheimer, "A Hit Hits Town," *New York Newsday,* 20 April 1960: no pagination.

45. *"Bye Bye Birdie,"* *Variety*, 23 March 1960: no pagination; John Beaufort, "Gower Champion Scores Hit as Musical Comedy Director," *Christian Science Monitor*, 23 April 1960: no pagination.

46. Tynan, 116.

47. Kerr.

48. Laufe, 281; Bolton.

49. Jerry Tallmer, *"Bye Bye Birdie,"* *Village Voice*, 20 April 1960: no pagination; Dash.

50. Gaghan, 44.

51. "A Challenge for a Champion," *New York World-Telegram and Sun Feature Section*, 20 February 1960: 14.

52. "A Challenge for a Champion," 14.

53. Cecil Smith and Glenn Litton, *Musical Comedy in America* (New York: Theatre Arts Books, 1981), 245; John Beaufort, "Gower Champion Scores Hit as Musical Comedy Director," *Christian Science Monitor*, 23 April 1960.

54. Richard Watts Jr., "Kind Words for the American Girl," *New York Post*, 24 April 1960: no pagination.

55. Richard Watts Jr., "Kind Words for the American Girl."

56. Gottfried, 140.

57. Lee Alan Morrow, *The Tony Award Book: Four Decades of Great American Theatre* (New York: Abbeville Press, 1987), 228.

58. Gottfried, 140.

59. Oliver Smith, personal interview, 24 October 1991; see Joshua Logan's notes for Richard Rodgers and Oscar Hammerstein II, *South Pacific* in *Six Plays by Rodgers and Hammerstein* (New York: The Modern Library, 1953), 281.

60. Jerome Robbins in Arthur Laurents and Stephen Sondheim, *West Side Story*, in *Ten Great Musicals of the American Theater*, ed. Stanley Richards (Radnor, Pennsylvania: Chilton, 1973), 362.

61. Gower Champion in Director's Script for *Bye Bye Birdie*, ms., 1–4–29.

62. Ken Mandelbaum, *"A Chorus Line" and the Musicals of Michael Bennett* (New York: St. Martin's Press, 1989), 17. Even by contemporary standards, the transition is impressive. In the 1992 revival of *Birdie* with Tommy Tune (Albert) and Ann Reinking (Rose), director Gene Saks staged it exactly as described above. At the performance this writer attended in Philadelphia during that summer, the audience was clearly spellbound by the effect as it unfolded. When it ended, they cheered and applauded heartily.

63. Gower Champion, "And How They Dance!" *Philadelphia Inquirer*, 27 August 1961: no pagination.

64. Howard Kissel, *David Merrick: The Abominable Showman* (New York: Applause Books, 1993), 286.

Nine: Gentle Blockbuster

1. Paul Gallico, "The Man Who Hated People," *Saturday Evening Post*, 28 October 1950: 22–128. A note that Deutsch appended to the original libretto for *Carnival* and which she later insisted be inserted as a preface to Stewart's final version (see Director's Script, UCLA Archives) names Gallico's *The Seven Souls of Clement O'Reilly* as inspiration for her 1951 screenplay, *Lili*. Neither periodical indexes nor Gallico's own short story anthologies bear the title of such a work. Both Lash (*Carnival* compact disc jacket notes) and Steven Suskin (*Opening Night on Broadway: A Critical Quotebook of the Golden Era of the Musical from "Oklahoma!" (1943) to "Fiddler on the Roof" (1964)* [New York: Schirmer Books, 1990], 137) cites "The Man Who Hated People" as the source of the 1953 film, *Lili*. Like Deutsch's screenplay, it develops the idea of a deeply wounded man who can only communicate his feelings for the woman he loves through his puppets. Also significant is the time of the story's publication, 1950, just a year before Deutsch's completion of the *Lili* script. Such facts strongly argue for viewing "The Man Who Hated People" as the film's source.

   In the same preface to *Carnival*, Deutsch further states that Gallico's novella *Love of Seven Dolls* (London: Michael Joseph Publishers) is frequently mistaken for *Lili*'s source. Larry L. Lash's notes to the 1989 compact disc release of *Carnival* are a recent case. As Deutsch correctly observes, *Love of*

Seven Dolls, an expansion and variation on "The Man Who Hated People" (with a dedication to Burr Tillstrom and Fran Allison), was published in 1954—a year after the film's release.

2. Howard Kissel, *David Merrick: The Abominable Showman* (New York: Applause Books, 1993), 208; "Projects," *New York Herald-Tribune*, 22 November 1959: no pagination.

3. Champion in E. B. Radcliffe, "Dancer Sets New Deal in Direction," *Cincinnati Enquirer*, 28 January 1962: no pagination.

4. Champion in Radcliffe.

5. For further discussion of the term, see both editions of Richard Kislan's *The Musical: A Look at the American Musical* (Englewood Cliffs, New Jersey: Prentice-Hall, 1980), 79; and rev. ed. (New York: Applause Books, 1995), 158.

6. "Gower Champion to NY," *Hollywood Reporter*, 10 August 1960: no pagination.

7. Gower Champion in "Gentle Blockbuster," *Newsweek*, 24 April 1960: no pagination. Because the libretto published by Tams-Witmark and the original cast album (including the recent compact disc release) use no exclamation point, none is used here.

8. Marge Champion interview, 5 November 1992; Samuel (Biff) Liff interview, 28 February 1994; John Kander interview, 17 April 1991 and Fred Ebb interview, 23 June 1992.

9. Bob Merrill in Kissel, 211.

10. Merrill in Kissel, 210.

11. Marge Champion in Kissel, 210.

12. Kissel, 34–78; *Carnival*, souvenir program, 12.

13. Kissel, 95–96.

14. Liff interview.

15. Marge Champion interview.

16. Helen Deutsch, *Carnival!*, typescript, Michael Stewart Papers, Billy Rose Theatre Collection, New York Public Library for the Performing Arts, 15 September 1960, F.

17. Deutsch, *Carnival!* typescript, F.

18. Deutsch, I, Prologue, 1.

19. Champion in Douglas Watt, "That Gower Is a Real Champion," *New York Sunday News*, 5 April 1964: 2:10.

20. Deutsch, II, 9, 45.

21. Tom Jones, personal interview, 17 July 1992; Harvey Schmidt, personal interview, 19 June 1992.

22. David Payne-Carter, *Gower Champion and the American Musical Theatre* (Ph.D. dissertation, New York University 1987; Ann Arbor: UMI, 1988; 88-01561), 243.

23. Deutsch, I, 8, 56; Kissel, 208.

24. Deutsch, *Carnival!*

25. Freddy Wittop, telephone interview, 13 July 1992.

26. Wittop interview.

27. Champion in Radcliffe.

28. Champion in Tom Tichenor, "A Case of Puppet Love," *Theatre Arts*, July 1961: 22.

29. Tichenor, 22.

30. Tichenor, 22.

31. Tichenor, 24, 77.

32. Tichenor, 77.

33. Tichenor, 22; *Carnival*, souvenir program, 14.

34. "Gower Champion's Still Seeking . . .", *New York Daily News*, 1 October 1960: no pagination.

35. Sidney Skolsky, "Inside Story on Anna Maria," *Los Angeles Citizen News*, 26 April 1961: no pagination.

36. Champion in Barbara L. Wilson, "The Theatre Scene: Champion Returns," *Philadelphia Inquirer*, 12 March 1961: 3.

37. Champion in Wilson, 4.

38. Jerry Orbach, telephone interview, 11 June 1992.
39. Orbach in Frances Herridge, "Across the Footlights," *New York Post,* 24 April 1961: no pagination.
40. Marge Champion interview.
41. James Mitchell interview, 25 June 1992.
42. Champion, Cast List/Rehearsal Schedule for *Carnival; Carnival,* souvenir program, 6.
43. *Carnival,* souvenir program, 13.
44. Pierre Olaf in William Peper, "How M. Olaf Got His Song," *New York World-Telegram and Sun,* 26 May 1961: no pagination.
45. Gower Champion, "And How They Dance!" *Philadelphia Inquirer,* 27 August 1961: no pagination.
46. Champion in Robert Wahls, "Don't Call Me a Chorus Girl," *New York Sunday News,* 21 May 1961: 2:8.
47. Champion in Murry Frymer, "Gower Champion's Magic Hard to Define," *New York Newsday,* 4 January 1967: 3A.
48. Champion in "Brr . . . But Burro's B'way Bound," *New York World-Telegram,* 28 December 1960: no pagination; Sheilah Graham, *Hollywood Reporter,* 8 April 1961: no pagination.
49. Marge Champion interview.
50. Wittop interview.
51. Peter Howard interview.
52. Gower Champion, Director's Script for *Carnival,* typescript, Collection 346, Box 1, Department of Special Collections, Research Library of Univ. of California, Los Angeles: I, ii, 29.
53. Champion in Margaret McCutcheon, "Dancing Should Aid Story," *Denver Rocky Mountain News,* 2 August 1962: no pagination.
54. Champion, Director's Script for *Carnival,* I, vi, 52–53.
55. Leo Lerman, "At the Theatre: *Carnival! Dance Magazine,* June 1961: 15.
56. Bob Merrill, lyrics for *Carnival.*
57. Ethan Mordden, *Broadway Babies: The People Who Made the Broadway Musical* (New York: Oxford University Press, 1983), 170.
58. Jess Gregg interview, 5 June 1992.
59. Gregg interview.
60. Mitchell interview.
61. Abe Laufe, *Broadway's Greatest Musicals* (New York: Funk and Wagnalls, 1977), 280; Lerman, 15.
62. *Dance Observer,* June 1961: no pagination.
63. Mordden, 169, 180.
64. Champion in Radcliffe.
65. Victor interview with Payne-Carter.
66. Anna Maria Alberghetti in Dennis McGovern and Deborah Grace Winer, *Sing Out, Louise! 150 Stars of the Musical Theatre Remember 50 Years on Broadway* (New York: Schirmer Books, 1993), 128.
67. Mitchell interview.
68. Champion in Walter Terry, "Dance: Broadway Choreographer," *New York Herald Tribune Magazine,* 1 March 1964: 29.
69. Orbach interview.
70. Champion in Gary Paul Gates, "The Antic Arts: Broadway's Champion," *Holiday,* February 1964: 92–93.
71. Mitchell interview.
72. Alberghetti in McGovern and Winer, 128.
73. Herridge.
74. Orbach interview.
75. Mitchell interview.
76. Mitchell interview.

77. Orbach interview.
78. Orbach interview.
79. Michael Stewart in Kissel, 211.
80. Howard interview.
81. Anita Gillette in McGovern and Winer, 28.
82. Gillette in McGovern and Winer, 28
83. Les Carpenter, "Shows Out of Town: *Carnival!*" *Variety,* 15 March 1961: no pagination.
84. Jay Carmody, "*Carnival* Restores Wonder to the Theatre," *Washington Evening Star,* 10 March 1961: A 14.
85. Tom Donnelly, "*Carnival* Rings the Bell," *Washington Daily News,* 10 March 1961: 27.
86. Jess Gregg, "Scenes from a Memoir," *Dance Magazine,* September 1999: 58.
87. Gregg, 58.
88. Les Carpenter, "Hopes for Perfect Musical," *Variety,* 29 March 1961: no pagination.
89. Champion in Carpenter.
90. *Carnival,* program, Forrest Theatre, Philadelphia, March 1961: 4; Donnelly, 27.
91. Orbach interviews, 11 June 1992 and 4 February 1994; Peter Howard, letter to author, 2 March 1994. Though the details of Kissel's account of this incident (p. 211) are colorful (with Merrick backing Champion up against the wall of the theatre, lifting "the short man" off the ground so that the two were eye-to-eye, then screaming at him to restore the show to the way it was in Washington), they are inaccurate. According to witnesses Orbach and Howard, the confrontation was verbal, not physical. Moreover, Champion, nearly six feet tall, was taller than Merrick. He was also in top physical condition and could easily have overpowered the producer. Finally, Biff Liff, Merrick's associate producer for many years, though not on *Carnival,* recalls no instance in which the producer settled differences with others through physical force (Liff interview, 28 February 1994).
92. Wilson, 3.
93. Howard Taubman, "It's a Carnival!" *New York Times,* 14 April 1961: 22.
94. John McClain, "Simplicity and Taste Make It Simply Great," *New York Journal-American,* 24 April 1961: 22.
95. Richard Watts Jr., "A Triumphant New Musical Play," *New York Post,* 14 April 1961: 68.
96. Melvin Maddocks, "With Happy Spells and Troubled Awakenings," *Christian Science Monitor,* 15 April 1961: no pagination; Howard Taubman, "Flashy Musical," *New York Times,* 23 April 1961: 2:1.
97. Michael Smith, "Still Lili," *Village Voice,* 22 June 1961: no pagination.
98. Whitney Bolton, "*Carnival* Called 'Perfect Musical,'" *New York Morning Telegraph,* 17 April 1961: 2; "*Carnival* A True Delight Should Endure for Years," *New York Morning Telegraph,* 15 April 1961: no pagination; Hobe Morrison, "*Carnival,*" *Variety,* 19 April 1961: no pagination.
99. John Chapman, "*Carnival* Magical New Musical," *New York Daily News,* 14 April 1961: no pagination.
100. Robert Coleman, "*Carnival* Is a Musical Triumph," *New York Mirror,* 14 April 1961: no pagination; Taubman, "Flashy Musical," 2: 1.
101. "Gentle Blockbuster"; Bolton.
102. Maddocks, Morrison; Oppenheimer.
103. Cooke; Dash.
104. Walter Kerr, "*Carnival,*" *New York Herald Tribune,* 14 April 1961: no pagination; Kerr, "Champion Enchantments," *New York Herald Tribune,* 23 April 1961: no pagination; "New Musical on Broadway," *Time,* 21 April 1961: 60.
105. Gregg, 58
106. Blake Gower Champion, later a promising dancer, died in an automobile accident in 1987 at the age of 25.
107. Lewis Funke, "News of the Rialto," *New York Times,* 7 May 1961: no pagination.

Ten: Down the Stairs, 'Round the Orchestra, Affirming Life

1. David Payne-Carter, *Gower Champion and the American Musical Theatre* (Ph.D. dissertation, New York University, 1987; Ann Arbor: 1988, #88-01561), 268.

2. Martin Gottfried, *Broadway Musicals* (New York: Harry B. Abrams, 1980), 22.

3. John Oxenford, "A Day Well Spent in Three Adventures," *Plays Submitted to the Lord Chamberlain*, Vol. 61, Feb.–Apr. 1836, ms., British Library, London, 480–496b.

4. Johann Nestroy, "*Einen Jux Will Er Sich Machen,*" *Johann Nestroy Komodien*, Vol. 2, ed. Franz H. Mautner (Frankfurt: Insel Verlag, 1970), 435–519.

5. As Stanley Green has noted, *Hello, Dolly!* shares certain plot and character similarities with the 1891 musical farce *A Trip to Chinatown* by Charles H. Hoyt (cf. Stanley Green, *Broadway Musicals Show By Show* [New York: Hal Leonard Books, 1996], 5, 204). In Hoyt's work, a coy young widow persuades a rich old man to allow her to chaperone his niece and nephew on an evening excursion through San Francisco's Chinatown. Unaware that she is using this as a pretext for taking them to a masked ball he has forbidden them to attend, he grants permission because he believes the widow is in love with him. Complications arise when all parties arrive at the same restaurant prior to the ball, where the uncle, whom the youngsters manage to avoid, misplaces his wallet and is forced to borrow money from a friend. See Charles H. Hoyt, *Five Plays by Charles H. Hoyt*, ed. Douglas L. Hunt (Princeton: Princeton University Press, 1941), 105–148.

  Like *Dolly!*, *A Trip to Chinatown* was the longest-running musical of its day, with a record of 657 performances (Gerald Bordman, *American Musical Theatre: A Chronicle* [New York: Oxford University Press, 1986], 115). Its score included three songs still heard today, "Reuben and Cynthia" and "The Bowery" by Hoyt, and "After the Ball" by Charles K. Harris.

6. Abe Laufe, *Broadway's Greatest Musicals* (New York: Funk and Wagnalls, 1977), 342.

7. The characters of the Oxenford, Nestroy, and Wilder plays, including that of Dolly herself, can be traced to "types" popularized by the Italian *commedia dell'arte* troupes of the sixteenth century. According to Oscar Brockett's *History of the Theatre*, these included the "innamorato," often opposed in his love affairs by an older man (as Cornelius is by Vandergelder), the "innamorata," a sophisticated young lady courted by both young and old (as Irene Molloy is by Corneluis and Vandergelder), and Pantalone, "a middle-aged or elderly merchant" (Vandergelder) with a fondness for proverbs who tried to appear younger than his years to win a younger woman. His extremely credulous nature made him easily deceived by others. At the center of every intrigue was Harlequin, a clever but foolish servant, who kept the plot moving by machinations that aided or hindered his master's agenda. In this respect, Dolly Levi's antics have much in common with Harlequin's (Oscar Brockett, *History of the Theatre* [Boston: Allyn and Bacon, 1974], 131).

8. Hobe Morrison, "Another *Dolly* Due Next Year," *Herald-News of Passaic, New Jersey*, 17 July 1977: no pagination; John Chapman, "An Adaptation Was Adapted for Dolly the Matchmaker," *New York Daily News*, 4 Feb. 1964: no pagination; Thornton Wilder, *The Merchant of Yonkers* (New York: Harper and Brothers, 1939), ii.

9. Morrison.

10. Thornton Wilder, *The Matchmaker*, in *Three Plays by Thornton Wilder* (New York: Harper and Brothers, 1957), 252. In 1981, Nestroy's play received yet another treatment as *On the Razzle* by Tom Stoppard. As the British playwright states in the "Introduction," he retained the characters, plot, and Viennese setting of *Einen Jux*, but composed his own dialogue, making his work an adaptation rather than a translation (cf. Tom Stoppard, *On the Razzle* [London: Faber and Faber, 1982], 7). Thus, with Stoppard's version, the story has come full circle—a British farce adapted from an Austrian farce adapted from a British farce.

11. Morrison, Wilder, *Three Plays*, 252.

12. Wilder, *Three Plays*, 252; Morrison, Chapman, Laufe, 342.

13. Wilder, *Three Plays*, 252.

14. Morrison. A film version featuring Shirley Booth (Dolly), Paul Ford (Vandergelder), Anthony Perkins (Cornelius), Robert Morse (Barnaby), and Shirley MacLaine (Irene Molloy) was released in 1958 by Paramount Studios.

15. Howard Kissel, *David Merrick: The Abominable Showman* (New York Applause Books, 1993), 285.

16. It has been incorrectly reported that Merrill provided two songs in Detroit: the nonsensical "Mother-hood March" a march sung by Dolly, Irene, and Minnie to deter Vandergelder from discovering Cornelius and Barnaby in the hat shop; and "Elegance," a parody on the social etiquette of the day that Cornelius, Barnaby, Irene, and Minnie sing en route to the Harmonia Gardens (see Steven Suskin, *Opening Night on Broadway* [New York: Schirmer Books, 1990], 300; Stanley Green, *Encyclopedia of the Musical Theater* [New York: Da Capo, 1976], 183). Both songs were written by Herman in collaboration with Merrill. They wrote "Motherhood March" early in the preproduction period, as is evidenced in the first draft of the musical (*Dolly! A Damned Exasperating Woman*) and in Champion's Pre-production Schedule of October 28. This was three weeks prior to the musical's disastrous Detroit debut and Merrill's arrival to provide new songs at Merrick's insistence. At that time, the two wrote "Elegance" (Jerry Herman, personal interview, 13 March 1991).

17. Marge Champion interview, 5 November 1992.

18. Harold Prince, *Contradictions* (New York: Dodd, Mead, 1974), 98; Avery Corman, "Curtain Call for the 'Ice Cream' Team," *New York Times,* 3 October 1993: H 5.

19. Stanley Green, *The World of Musical Comedy* (New York: Da Capo, 1980), 324.

20. Al Kasha and Joel Hirschhorn, *Notes on Broadway* (Chicago: Contemporary Books, 1985), 177.

21. Jerry Herman interview, 13 March 1991; John Molleson, "Bringing *Dolly* to Disks," *New York Herald Tribune,* 29 March 1964: 29.

22. Kasha and Hirschhorn, 177.

23. Kasha and Hirschhorn, 177.

24. Herman interview. Two songs, "Love, Look in My Window" and "World, Take Me Back," written for Merman and later dropped when Carol Channing won the role, were later restored to the score when Merman became Broadway's eighth and last Dolly on March 28, 1970. Originally released as a 45 RPM recording, *Ethel Merman Sings the New Songs from "Hello, Dolly!"* (Bar-Mike Records), they can now be heard on RCA Victor's Broadway Deluxe Collector's Edition of the original cast album on compact disk, 82876-51431-2.

25. McCandlish Phillips, "Dolly Replacing Liza as Fairest Lady," *New York Times,* 8 September 1970: 44; Herman interview. During the course of the show's historic Broadway run, Merrick made six additional appeals before Merman finally relented and agreed to become Broadway's final Dolly (Phillips, 44).

26. Morrison; Prince, 98; Frances Herridge, "A Wilting *Daisy* Gave Champion Blooming *Dolly,*" *New York Post,* 2 March 1964: no pagination; Payne-Carter, 283; Carol Ilson, *Harold Prince: From "Pajama Game" to "Phantom of the Opera"* (Ann Arbor: UMI Research Press, 1989), 82–83.

27. Prince, 99. Dolly's lines to Ambrose in I, iv prepare us for the joyous reception she receives from the waiters in II, iii: "Why every Saturday night, from the first day we were married, down those red stairs at the Harmonia Gardens we came and danced the night away! It's been ten years since I've been back but I can hear that music still!" At the time, either these lines were overlooked by Prince or were not yet part of Stewart's libretto.

28. Harry Haun, "Tony Legends: Role Models," *Playbill,* vol. 91, no. 5, May 1991: 32; Charles Nelson Reilly interview, to January 1995.

29. Carol Channing, personal interview, 21 June 1991; John S. Wilson, "Carol Channing as 'Dolly,'" *New York Times,* 12 January 1964: 2:3.

30. Gower Champion, "The Comeback of Sweetness and Light," *The Hollywood Reporter,* 20 November 1962: no pagination.

31. Rex Reed, "A Champion—Almost Always," *New York Times,* 19 February 1967: C1.

32. Champion in Reed, C3.

33. Champion in Herridge.

34. Hugh Fordin, *The Movies' Greatest Musicals; Produced in Hollywood USA by the Freed Unit* (New York: Frederick Ungar, 1984), 557.

35. Marge Champion interview, 5 November 1992.

36. Gene Lees, *Inventing Champagne: The Worlds of Lerner and Loewe* (New York: St. Martin's Press, 1990), 212. Because of Lerner's former partnership with Frederick Loewe and Rodgers's with Oscar Hammerstein, both were considered undisputed titans of the musical theatre, who, as the predominant creative forces of their productions, were accustomed to prescribing how directors ought to stage their works. In light of this, it is inconceivable that they would have given Champion the latitude he would have insisted upon. The director's altercation with Hellman may have given the lyricist (and composer) second thoughts. By insisting that Champion immediately go into production without a respite, Lerner may also have hoped to force him out of his commitment and thus obtain a more malleable replacement.

37. Lees, 212.

38. "Champion Signed," *New York Times*, 30 July 1963: no pagination.

39. Marge Champion interview, 5 November 1992.

40. Jess Gregg interview, 5 June 1992; Champion interview, 5 November 1992; Herman interview.

41. Herman interview.

42. Champion and Gregg interviews.

43. Charles Nelson Reilly, telephone interview, 11 January 1995; Gregg interview.

44. Wilson, 2:3; Channing interview.

45. Wilson, 2:3.

46. Channing interview. In *The Matchmaker*, the "Manure Speech" is Mrs. Levi's monologue at the end of Act IV containing the line, "Money, I've always felt, money—pardon my expression—is like manure; it's not worth a thing unless it's spread about encouraging young things to grow."

47. Channing interview.

48. Channing interview.

49. "Musical for Carol Channing," *New York Times*, 5 August 1963: no pagination.

50. Gordon Connell, personal interview, 5 March 1991.

51. Gower Champion, Pre-production Schedule for *Dolly! A Damned Exasperating Woman*, manuscript, Collection 346, Box 1, Department of Special Collections, Research Library of University of California, Los Angeles.

52. Gower Champion, Cast List for *Dolly! A Damned Exasperating Woman*, ms., Collection 346, Box 1, Department of Special Collections, Research Library of University of California, Los Angeles. The above-mentioned names were selected because they are each listed more than once. Although it is unclear whether each of the 40 actors actually auditioned, the list itself, in the director's own handwriting, is evidence that he gave serious consideration to each.

53. Lee Alan Morrow, *The Tony Award Book* (New York, Theatre Arts Books, 1981), 50.

54. Connell interview.

55. Gregg interview.

56. Herman interview.

57. Champion, Cast List for *Dolly! A Damned Exasperating Woman*. Carleton Carpenter was later selected by Champion to play Cornelius in the London production of *Hello, Dolly!*

58. Eileen Brennan, telephone interview, 14 January 1995.

59. *"Hello, Dolly!"* Playbill, St. James Theatre, New York, January 1964: 35.

60. *"Hello, Dolly!"* Playbill: 35.

61. Reilly interview; *"Hello, Dolly!"* Playbill: 34.

62. Reilly interview.

63. Hobe Morrison of *Variety*, as well as George Oppenheimer of *New York Newsday* and Howard Taubman of the *New York Times*, preferred a conventional treatment of these characters, to be discussed later.

64. *"Hello, Dolly!"* Playbill: 35, Sondra Lee, telephone interview, 9 May 1995.

65. Lee interview.

66. Connell interview.

67. Lucia Victor, interview with David Payne-Carter, typescript, David Payne-Carter Papers, New York University, Undergraduate Department of Theatre, New York, 4 April 1984; Suskin, 298.

68. Victor interview, 4 Apr. 1984.

69. Connell interview.

70. Gower Champion, Pre-production Schedule for *Dolly! A Damned Exasperating Woman*.

71. Morrow, 192.

72. Morrow, 192.

73. Oliver Smith, personal interview, 24 October 1991.

74. Smith interview.

75. Smith interview.

76. Smith interview.

77. Smith interview.

78. Smith interview.

79. Freddy Wittop, telephone interview, 13 June 1992.

80. Wittop interview.

81. Wittop interview.

82. Channing interview.

83. Wittop interview.

84. Wittop interview.

85. Wittop interview.

86. Wittop interview.

87. Lael Wertenbaker in Jean Rosenthal and Lael Wertenbaker, *The Magic of Light: The Craft and Career of Jean Rosenthal, Pioneer in Lighting for the Modern Stage* (Boston: Little, Brown, 1972), vii, 209–243. This book also contains Rosenthal's complete lighting plot and Oliver Smith's scenic drawings for *Hello, Dolly!* (pp. 178–201).

88. Rosenthal in Rosenthal and Wertenbaker, 76–77.

89. Rosenthal in Rosenthal and Wertenbaker, 76–77; Victor interview.

90. Victor interview, 4 Apr. 1984.

91. Victor interview, 4 Apr. 1984.

92. Victor interview, 4 Apr. 1984.

93. Victor interview, 4 Apr. 1984.

94. Gower Champion, Memorandum found in Director's Script for *Dolly! A Damned Exasperating Woman*, Collection 346, Box 1, Department of Special Collections, Research Library of University of California, Los Angeles.

95. Gottfried, 28.

96. Herman interview.

97. Champion in Reed, C 1.

98. Marge Champion interview, 5 November 1992.

99. Gregg interview.

100. Herman interview.

101. Connell interview.

102. Bordman, 633.

103. Marge Champion interview, 12 November 1992.

104. Peter Howard, personal interview, 2 July 1992.

105. Marge Champion interview, 12 November 1992.

106. Howard interview. On the original cast recording (Jerry Herman, *Hello, Dolly!*, RCA Victor compact disc 3814-2-RG, 1964), the leitmotif is heard in the final bars of "Dancing." Though the complete dance section was not recorded at the time, it can be heard on the 1994 cast recording (Jerry Herman, *Hello, Dolly!*, Varese Sarabande compact disc VSD-5557, 1994).

107. Victor interview, 11 April 1984; Doris Hering, "Broadway: Late Winter," *Dance magazine*, March 1964: no pagination.

108. Victor interview, 4 December 1983.

109. Victor interview, 11 April 1984.

110. Gower Champion, Rehearsal Schedule for *Dolly! A Damned Exasperating Woman*, Manuscript, Collection 346, Box 1, Department of Special Collections, Research Library of University of California, Los Angeles.

111. Glenn Litton, *Musical Comedy in America: From "The King and I" to "Sweeney Todd"* (New York: Theatre Arts Books, 1981), 272.

112. Michael Stewart and Jerry Herman, *Hello, Dolly!* (New York: Signet Books, 1968), 88–92.

113. Victor interview, 4 December 1984; Howard interview. Though the song, "Please Sir, Mrs. Levi Sent Me," was later dropped from the score in favor of "Elegance," its music remained as theme for "The Waiters' Gallop."

114. David Hartman, personal interview, 23 April 1991.

115. Champion, Rehearsal Schedule for *Dolly! A Damned Exasperating Woman*.

116. Channing interview.

117. Victor interview, 11 April 1984.

118. Herman interview.

119. Payne-Carter, 302.

120. Channing interview.

121. Hartman interview.

122. Champion, Rehearsal Schedule for *Dolly! A Damned Exasperating Woman*.

123. Litton, 272. Originally, Herman's melody to "Put on Your Sunday Clothes" was to be the title number of *The Spirit of the Chase*, a musical that was never produced (Reilly interview).

124. Champion, Pre-production Notes.

125. Champion, Pre-production Notes.

126. Victor interview, 11 April 1984. Conversely, Stanley Green (*The World of Musical Comedy* [p. 325]), Thomas S. Hischak (*Word Crazy: Broadway Lyricists from Cohan to Sondheim* [New York: Praeger, 1991; p. 163]) and Glenn Litton hold that "Sunday Clothes," as well as the title number, were purely gratuitous amusements designed solely to impress the audience. Litton, for example writes, "Neither 'Hello, Dolly!' nor 'Put on Your Sunday Clothes' was essential to the book; they were grand diversions, thrills" (p. 272). As we have seen, "Sunday Clothes" was a necessary lyrical and visual statement of the book's theme that the characters literally expressed as they took hold of the train bound for adventure in New York City. Furthermore, it prepared the audience for the fulfillment of the quest for adventure the young couples later enjoyed in "Dancing." Neglecting to show the response of these characters to the message of "Sunday Clothes" would have rendered the topper, "Dancing," meaningless. As for "Hello, Dolly!," it is the fulfillment of the adventure the heroine wishes for herself in "Before the Parade Passes By," the first act finale. There is nothing gratuitous about it.

127. Channing interview.

128. Howard Taubman, "*Hello, Dolly!* Has Premiere," *New York Times*, 17 January 1964: 22.

129. Gower Champion in Walter Terry, "Dance: Broadway Choreographer," *New York Herald Tribune Sunday Magazine*, 1 March 1964: 29.

130. Robert Berkson, *Musical Theatre Choreography* (New York: Back Stage Books, 1990), 62.

131. Entitled "I Still Love the Love I Loved When First in Love I Fell"—one of four songs Herman originally auditioned for Merrick.

132. Herman interview.

133. Champion, Pre-production Notes.

134. Brennan interview.

135. Gates, 88.

136. Channing interview.

137. Stewart and Herman, 77.

138. Mary Jo Catlett, telephone interview, 7 March 1991.

139. Catlett interview.

140. Champion in Terry, 29.

141. Marge Champion in Gillbert Millstein, "Good-bye, Lorelei—Hello, Dolly!," *Saturday Evening Post,* 22 February 1964: 79.

142. Marge Champion in Millstein, 79.

143. Champion in Terry, 29.

144. Payne-Carter, 292–293.

145. Janice Graham Glann, *An Assessment of the Functions of Dance in the Broadway Musical: 1940/41–1968/69,* (Ph.D. dissertation, Bowling Green State University, 1976; Ann Arbor UMI, 1978; 77–2691), 40.

146. Graham Glann, 40.

147. Herman interview.

148. Joe Cohen, "*Hello, Dolly* Insipid but Cast Does Well," *Windsor Star,* 19 November 1963: no pagination.

149. Armand Gilbert, "*Dolly* Has Its Moments but They're Not All Good," *Detroit News,* 19 November 1963: no pagination.

150. "*Hello, Dolly!,*" *Variety,* 20 November 1963: no pagination.

151. Shirley Eder, "Hi There, Dolly," *Northwest News,* 19 November 1963: no pagination.

152. Champion in Reed, C1.

153. Herman interview.

154. Hartman interview.

155. Hartman interview.

156. Kissel, 291.

157. Herman interview.

158. Herman interview; Kissel, 292.

159. Herman interview.

160. Kissel, 292–293.

161. Herman interview; Kissel, 292–293.

162. Kissel, 291.

163. Kissel, 291.

164. Smith and Catlett interviews.

165. Catlett, Smith, and Channing interviews. Concerning this altercation, Howard Kissell adds, "It was a gesture of bravado, but after Merrick stomped out Champion went to the writers, to Channing and other members of the cast and asked if they would contribute to buy the show from Merrick. They all felt the show had great potential and were willing to contribute money to save it from Merrick's wrath. Faced with this revolt, Merrick backed down . . ." (Kissell, 292).

    Although billed as a Merrick production, the show was actually co-produced with Champion-Five, Inc., a firm formed by the director, which had a five percent interest ($35,000). Consequently, Champion received a handsome return on the venture sharing in profits as an investor and co-producer and also sharing in the gross on a royalty basis for his contribution as director-choreographer ("*Dolly* Season's First Tuner Smash," *Variety,* 22 January 1964: 33).

166. Champion interview, 5 November 1992; Kissel, 292; Don Pippin, telephone interview, 17 August 1994.

167. Hartman and Catlett interviews.

168. Herman interview.

169. Channing interview.

170. Victor interview, 11 April 1984; "*Hello, Dolly!,*" *Variety.*

171. "*Hello, Dolly!,*" *Variety*; Director's Script for *Dolly! A Damned Exasperating Woman.*

172. Stewart and Herman, *Hello, Dolly!*: I, ii, 19; Gregg interview; Victor interview, 4 April 1984.

173. Victor interview, 4 April 1984; Stewart and Herman, *Hello, Dolly!*: I, ii, 13; Champion, Pre-production notes.

174. Stewart and Herman, *Hello, Dolly!*: I, ii, 13.

175. Gregg interview.

176. Director's Script for *Dolly! A Damned Exasperating Woman,* II, ii, 19.

177. Reilly interview. The six "Goodbyes" later became the introduction to "So Long, Dearie."

178. Gilbert, no pagination.

179. Victor interview, 4 April 1984.

180. Richard L. Coe, "*Hello, Dolly!* You're a Doll," *Washington Post,* 19 December 1963: no pagination; Jack Gaver, "*Hello, Dolly!* Is Doll of a Show," *New York World-Telegram and Sun,* 21 January 1964: no pagination.

181. Director's Script for *Dolly! A Damned Exasperating Woman,* II, i, 1–3.

182. Victor interview, 4 April 1984.

183. Howard Taubman, "Easy Does It," *New York Times,* 26 January 1964: no pagination; Taubman, "Hello, Dolly!," 22.

184. Brennan interview.

185. Reilly interview.

186. Reilly interview.

187. Reilly interview.

188. Lucia Victor in Peter Michaelmore, "Gower Champion: One Last Time," unpublished manuscript, October 1980: no pagination.

189. Michaelmore.

190. Michaelmore.

191. Payne-Carter, 305–306.

192. Gower Champion in Douglas Watt, "That Gower Is a Real Champion," *New York Sunday News,* 5 April 1964: 2:10.

193. Watt, 2:10.

194. Herman interview; Victor interview, 4 December 1983. The term came about because of Champion's joke, "Just add water and—instant glee club."

195. Herman in Stewart and Herman, 25.

196. Stewart in Stewart and Herman, 55.

197. Channing, Reilly, and Brennan interviews; Richard P. Cooke, "Carol's Blockbuster," *Wall Street Journal,* 20 January 1964: no pagination.

198. Champion, Director's Script, Book Two, II-2-26.

199. Gregg interview.

200. Hollis Alpert, *Broadway: 125 Years of Musical Theatre* (New York: Arcade Publishing, 1991), 26–28. For a comparison of *A Trip to Chinatown* and *Hello, Dolly!* see Note 5.

201. Alpert, 26–28.

202. Herman in Book Two of Director's scripts, "Butterfly" Insert.

203. Walter Kerr, "*Hello, Dolly!*—A Musical About Matchmakers," *New York Herald Tribune,* 17 January 1964: no pagination; Taubman, "Easy Does It."

204. Victor interview, 4 December 1983. "Penny in My Pocket" can be heard on the compact disc album *Michael Feinstein Sings the Jerry Herman Songbook,* Electra Nonesuch 9 79315-2, 1993.

205. Champion, Rehearsal Schedule for *Dolly! A Damned Exasperating Woman*; Herman interview; Victor interview, 4 December 1983.

206. Wilder, *Three Plays: The Matchmaker* (the "Manure Speech"), 396.

207. Herman interview; Payne-Carter, 319.

208. Herman interview; Payne-Carter, 320.

209. Payne-Carter, 319–320.

210. Herman interview.

211. Peter Michaelmore, "Gower Champion: One More Time," unpublished manuscript in author's collection.

212. "Before the Parade Passes By," from *Hello, Dolly!* Music and lyric by Jerry Herman. © 1964 (Renewed) JERRY HERMAN. All rights controlled by EDWIN H. MORRIS & COMPANY, a Division of MPL Music Publishing Inc. All Rights Reserved. Used by permission. See also Jerry Herman and Ken Bloom, *Jerry Herman: The Lyrics; A Celebration* (New York: Routledge, 2003), 50.

213. Channing interview; Herman in Peter Hay, *Broadway Anecdotes* (New York: Oxford University Press, 1989), 118–119.

214. Herman in Hay, 118–119.

215. Channing interview.

216. Kasha and Hirschhorn, 178.

217. An extended note vibrated by the string section.

218. Herman and Stewart, 73.

219. Wittop interview.

220. Wittop interview.

221. "Before the Parade Passes By," from *Hello, Dolly!* Music and lyric by Jerry Herman. © 1964 (Renewed) JERRY HERMAN. All rights controlled by EDWIN H. MORRIS & COMPANY, a Division of MPL Music Publishing, Inc. All Rights Reserved. Used by permission. See also Jerry Herman and Ken Bloom, 50.

222. Richard L. Coe, "Preening of *Dolly* May Gild B. O. Hit," *Washington Post,* 5 January 1964: no pagination.

223. Champion in Hedda Hopper, "How a Top Dancer Became a Director," *Boston Herald,* 15 November 1965: 16.

224. Payne-Carter, 320.

225. Brennan interview.

226. Coe, "*Hello, Dolly!* You're a Doll"; Jay Carmody, "Carol Restores Joy to Musical Stage," *Evening Star,* 19 December 1963: B 12.

227. Champion in Hopper, 16.

228. Payne-Carter, 323.

229. Coe, "Preening of *Dolly* May Gild B. O. Hit."

230. David Hartman, letter to author, 7 June 1995.

231. David Ewen, *New Complete Book of the American Musical Theater* (New York: Holt, Rinehart and Winston, 1970), 216.

232. Ewen, 216.

233. Payne-Carter, 326; Jack Mitchell, "The American Way," *Dance magazine,* June 1964: 77.

234. Champion in Payne-Carter, 326.

235. Kerr.

236. Kerr.

237. Taubman, " 'Hello, Dolly!' Has Premiere."
238. Whitney Bolton, *Hello, Dolly!* Robust, Delightful Musical; Channing Enchanting," *New York Morning Telegraph,* 18 January 1964: no pagination.
239. Richard Watts Jr., "A Bouncing New Musical Comedy," *New York Post,* 17 January 1964: no pagination.
240. Norman Nadel, *"Hello, Dolly!* Is Jewel of a Musical," *New York World-Telegram and Sun,* 17 January 1964: no pagination; Hobe Morrison, *"Hello, Dolly!,"* *Variety,* 30 January 1964: no pagination.
241. John McClain, *"Hello, Dolly!* A Tuneful Colossal Hit," *New York Journal-American,* 17 January 1964: no pagination; Harold Clurman, *"Hello, Dolly!"* *The Nation,* 10 February 1964: no pagination.
242. Kerr; John Chapman, "Carol Channing and David Burns Delightful Team in *Hello, Dolly!" New York Daily News,* 17 January 1964: no pagination.
243. Clurman.
244. Bolton; Clurman.
245. Clurman.
246. Taubman, *"Hello, Dolly!* Has Premiere."
247. McClain; Suzanne Mary Ramczyk, *A Performance Demands Analysis of Six Major Female Roles of the American Musical Theatre* (Ph.D. dissertation, University of Oregon, 1986; Ann Arbor: UMI, 1987; 87-05888), 212.
248. Ramczyk, 212; Kerr.
249. Kerr.
250. Cooke; Taubman, *"Hello, Dolly!* Has Premiere."
251. Elliot Norton, "Carol Channing Afire in *Hello, Dolly!,"* *Boston Record-American,* 18 January 1964: no pagination.
252. Kerr; Watts; Henry Hewes, "Hello and Goodbye," *Saturday Review of Literature,* 8 February 1964: no pagination; Gottfried; Laufe, 347.
253. Nadel.
254. Nadel; Bolton; Watts; Kerr; Cooke.
255. Morrison; George Oppenheimer, *"Hello, Dolly!* Channing Bows in Musical," *New York Newsday,* 17 January 1964: no pagination; Taubman, *"Hello, Dolly!* Has Premiere."
256. Cooke; Bolton; Louis Chapin, "Carol Channing's Matchmaker," *Christian Science Monitor,* 22 January 1964: no pagination; Oppenheimer; Cooke.
257. Nadel; Morrison: Oppenheimer.
258. Kerr; Nadel; McClain; Watts; Gottfried.
259. Edward Sothern Hipp, ' "Hello, Dolly!' Hot Number," *Newark Evening News,* 17 January 1964: no pagination; Oppenheimer; Hawes; Taubman, "Easy Does it."
260. Albin Krebs, "A Hit Is Born on Broadway," *New York Herald Tribune,* 18 January 1964: no pagination.
261. Krebs.
262. Krebs.
263. Payne-Carter, 327.
264. Champion in Reed, C 1.
265. Morrow, 232–234, At the 2001 Tony Awards, *The Producers* received a total of 12 awards (for Best Musical, Score, Book, Actor, Supporting Actor, Supporting Actress, Scenery, Costumes, Lighting, Director, Choreographer, and Orchestrations).
266. Morrow, 232–234.
267. Laufe, 348.
268. Stanley Green, *Encyclopedia of the Musical Theatre,* 182–183.
269. Champion in Reed, C 1; Lester Abelman, "Finale: It's Goodbye, Dolly!," *New York Daily News,* 28 December 1970: 4.
270. Kissel, 297.

271. Christian Dean Mendenhall, *American Musical Comedy from 1943 to 1964: A Theoretical Investiga-tion of Its Ritual Function* (Ph.D. dissertation, Northwestern University 1989; Ann Arbor: UMI, 1989; #89-14001), 220.

272. Mendenhall, 220.

273. Mendenhall, 220–221.

274. "At the Closing Performance . . . ," *New York Post*, 30 December 1970: no pagination.

Eleven: Metaphorical Marriage Presentational Style

1. Jess Gregg, personal interview, 5 June 1992; Marge Champion, notes from the first draft of chapter 2 of John Gilvey, *Gower Champion as Director: An Analysis of His Craft in Four Broadway Musicals. 1961–1968* (Ph.D. dissertation, New York University, 1995; Ann Arbor: UMI, 1996; #97-01496), 17–142; Stanley Green, *Broadway Musicals Show by Show* (New York: Hal Leonard Books, 1987), 208; Steven Suskin, *Opening Night on Broadway* (New York: Schirmer Books, 1990), 309.

2. Gregg interview.

3. Dennis McGovern and Deborah Grace Winer, *Sing Out, Louise! 150 Stars of the Musical Theatre Re-member 50 Years on Broadway* (New York: Schirmer Books, 1993), 129.

4. Gregg interview; Peter Michaelmore, "Gower Champion: One Last Time," unpublished manuscript in author's collection. October 1980: no pagination.

5. Green, 208; Suskin, 309.

6. Ken Mandelbaum, *Not Since Carrie: 40 Years of Broadway Musical Flops* (New York: St. Martin's Press, 1991), 298.

7. Gower Champion in Rex Reed, "A Champion—Almost Always," *New York Times*, 19 February 1967: D 1; John Springer, *A Pictorial History of the Movie Musical* (Secaucus, N.J.: Castle Books, 1969), 235.

   Ultimately, William Wyler directed *Funny Girl* (1968) and Herbert Ross, *Goodbye, Mr. Chips* (1969), which starred Peter O'Toole and Petula Clark with a score by British composer Leslie Bricusse.

8. David Payne-Carter, *Gower Champion and the American Musical Theatre,* (Ph.D. dissertation, New York University, 1987; Ann Arbor: UMI, 1988; #88-01561), 337; Gregory Chris Dennhardt, *The Director-Choreographer in the American Musical Theatre* (Ph.D. dissertation, University of Illinois at Urbana-Champaign, 1978; Ann Arbor: UMI, 1978; #78-1228), 209.

9. Champion in Reed, D 3; Georges Feydeau (1862–1921), French dramatist regarded by scholars as an outstanding writer of classical farce as exemplified in plays like *A Flea in Her Ear* (1907), which Champion later directed in 1969 for the American Conservatory Theatre.

10. Payne-Carter, 337.

11. Harvey Schmidt, personal interview, 19 June 1992.

12. Schmidt interview; Tom Jones, personal interview, 17 July 1992; Jerry Orbach, personal interview, 11 June 1992; Marge Champion, personal interview, 5 November 1992.

    Like *The Fantasticks*, *Carnival* employed the idea of a troupe of traveling performers who assem-bled and dismantled the setting. The former used the concept in an intimate setting with nine play-ers, the latter, a large setting with a full chorus of singer-dancers.

13. Jones and Schmidt interviews.

14. Schmidt interview.

15. Jan de Hartog, *The Fourposter* (New York: Random House, 1952).

16. Hobe Morrison, "*I Do! I Do!* A Success," *Morning Call* (Patterson, N.J.), 6 December 1966: 22.

17. *I Do! I Do!,* souvenir program, Theatre of the Stars, Los Angeles, June 1970: 4.

18. *I Do! I Do!,* souvenir program, Theatre of the Stars, 4; Fred Fehl, *On Broadway* (Austin: University of Texas Press, 1978), 195–199.

    After a year, the Cronyns left the Broadway production to initiate an extensive tour of the play, and were succeeded by Sylvia Sidney and Romney Brent, who started a second touring company after Betty Field and Burgess Meredith replaced them.

A film version with Lilli Palmer and Rex Harrison made in 1952 was less successful because it relied upon de Hartog's original play "rather than the much-doctored and tinkered-with version Cronyn had devised with the help of audience reactions on that summer theatre tour" (*I Do! I Do!*, souvenir program, Theatre of the Stars, 4).

19. Frances Herridge, "Stager Champion Does the Preposterous," *New York Post,* 30 April 1967: no pagination.

At first, Champion told Merrick, "Come on. You can't mean it," then, a few days later, he said, "It could be done if we can get Mary Martin and Robert Preston" (Champion in Herridge).

20. Schmidt interview.

21. Jones and Schmidt interviews.

22. Jones interview.

23. Morrison, 22; David Ewen, *New Complete Book of the American Musical Theater* (New York: Holt, Rinehart and Winston, 1970), 248.

24. "Inside Stuff—Legit," *Variety,* 14 December 1966: no pagination; Morrison, 22; Ewen, 248.

25. *Variety* further reported that following its eight-week tour in the summer of 1963, *No Bed of Roses* was auditioned for Gordon and Shelia MacRae (Gordon MacRae would later perform the matinees of *I Do! I Do!* with Carol Lawrence, and eventually replace Robert Preston). Though a Broadway installment was to have been produced by Bonnard Productions (Helen Bonfils and Haila Stoddard), with Dania Krupska as director-choreographer, Gerry Alters as orchestrator, and Biff McGuire and Jeannie Carson as the stars, it was later dropped. After the project was abandoned, Kalmanoff played a tape of the first two numbers (as performed by Cassel and Manners) for David Merrick ("Inside Stuff—Legit?").

Variety also stated that de Hartog had submitted an outline to Merrick on how his play might be adapted into a musical, to which librettist Jones replied: "Although it may be quite possible that de Hartog wrote some form of outline . . . , I would just like to make it clear that I never read or saw such an outline, and that in fact I never heard of it at all until I read your article in *Variety*" (Tom Jones in "Tom Jones Never Saw De Hartog *Do* Outline," *Variety,* 8 February 1967: no pagination).

26. Jones interview.

27. Samuel Hirsch, "Hirsch on Theatre," *Boston Herald,* 30 September 1966: no pagination.

28. Hirsch.

29. Jones and Schmidt interviews.

30. Schmidt interview.

31. Martin Gottfried, *Opening Nights: Theater Criticism of the Sixties* (New York: G. P. Putnam's Sons, 1969), 127; Jones and Schmidt interviews.

32. Schmidt interview.

33. Mary Martin, *My Heart Belongs* (New York: Quill Books, 1984), 282; Jones and Schmidt interviews. Ultimately, Louise Troy played Maggie in *Walking Happy* and Angela Lansbury, the title role in *Mame*.

34. Schmidt and Jones interviews.

35. Schmidt interview.

36. Jones interview.

37. Schmidt and Jones interviews.

38. Schmidt interview.

39. "Mitzi Gaynor Is In . . . ," *New York Journal-American,* 30 June 1965: no pagination. In the 1958 film version of *South Pacific,* Gaynor played Nellie Forbush, the role that Martin had originated on Broadway.

40. Schmidt and Jones interviews.

41. Hirsch.

42. "Mary Martin Is Set . . . ," *New York Daily News*, 3 August 1965: no pagination.

43. Herridge, 27 September 1966.

44. Betty Winsett, personal interview, 19 February 1991.

45. Winsett interview.

46. "Row Bursts over *Hello, Dolly!*," *London Daily Telegraph*, 6 December 1965: no pagination.

47. Stanley Green, *Encyclopedia of the Musical Theatre* (New York: DaCapo Press, 1976), 182.

48. Marge Champion, interview.

49. Goulet and Lawrence were probably contacted by Merrick around March 1966 when Champion was considering younger performers. Lawrence later recalled that "the show was offered to my ex-husband, Robert Goulet, and myself at the very beginning, and I didn't know about it. That's a little bit criminal. But I'd seen the show in the first week, and I was in love with it. Everyone was. Then I found myself on a plane, sitting next to David Merrick, and I congratulated him and told him I couldn't wait to do it in summer stock. He said to me, 'Well, then, why didn't you play it originally?' And I said, 'I beg your pardon?' Then he told me that it had been offered to me. I wanted to put on a parachute then and there and kill that person—who shall remain nameless—who hadn't told me about it" (McGovern and Winer, 182–183). Lawrence did not lose out completely. She played the matinee performances with Gordon MacRae, and eventually the evenings as well so Martin could do the national tour with Preston.

50. Schmidt interview.

51. Jones interview.

52. Jones and Schmidt interviews.

53. Martin, 284.

54. "*I Do! I Do!*—The Conception and Writing of a Musical Play," Press and Information (*RCA Victor Records*, n.d.), *I Do! I Do! Clippings File*, Billy Rose Theatre Collection, New York Public Library for the Performing Arts.

55. "Robert Preston Says, 'I Do! I Do!,' " *New York Daily News*, 20 June 1966: no pagination.

56. Champion in Reed, D 3.

57. Robert Salmaggi, "The Spell of Success," *New York World Journal Tribune*, 8 December 1966: no pagination.

58. Marge Champion interview, 12 November 1992.

59. Schmidt interview.

60. Schmidt interview.

61. Jones interview.

62. Schmidt interview.

63. Gower Champion in Lucia Victor, interview with David Payne-Carter, typescript, David Payne-Carter Papers, New York University Undergraduate Department of Theatre, New York, 4 December 1983.

64. Gower Champion in Oliver Smith, personal interview, 24 October 1991.

65. Smith interview.

66. Smith interview.

67. Smith interview.

68. Victor interview.

69. Freddy Wittop, telephone interview, 13 July 1992.

70. Wittop interview.

71. Wittop interview; Lee Silver, "Rare Bird Plumage Is Sought by Freddy," *New York Daily News*, 18 June 1966: no pagination.

72. Martin Gottfried, "*I Do! I Do!*," *Women's Wear Daily*, 6 December 1966: no pagination.

73. Schmidt interview.

74. Robert Preston in Reed, D 1.

75. Martin, 286.

76. Gower Champion in Samuel Hirsch, "Hirsch on Theatre," *Boston Herald,* 27 September 1966: no pagination.

77. Preston in Hirsch, 27 September 1966.

78. Martin, 283.

79. Philip D. Morehead, *The New American Dictionary of Music* (New York: Dutton Publishers, 1991), 545.

80. Gottfried, "*I Do! I Do!*"

81. Gottfried, *Opening Nights,* 127–128.

82. Gower Champion, Director's Script for *I Do! I Do!,* typescript, Collection 346, Box 2, Department of Special Collections, Research Library of University of California, Los Angeles, 1, P, 1.

83. Champion, Director's Script, I, P, 1.

84. Champion. Director's Script, I, P, 3.

85. Champion, Director's Script, I, P, 4.

86. Martin, 286.

87. Champion, Director's Notes, I, i, 5.

88. "*I Do! I Do!,*" *Saturday Review of Literature,* 24 December 1966: 61.

89. Preston in Hirsch, 27 September 1966.

90. Martin, 289–290.

91. Champion, Director's Script, I, i, 11.

92. Champion, Director's Script, I, i, 11.

93. Champion, Director's Script, I, i, 11.

94. Champion, Director's Script, I, i, 11.

95. Tom Jones in Tom Jones and Harvey Schmidt, Gower Champion Director's Script for *I Do! I Do!,* typescript, Collection 346, Box 2, Department of Special Collections, Research Library of University of California, Los Angeles, I-i-12.

96. Champion, Director's Script, I, i, 12.

97. Jones, I, i, 12.

98. Hirsch, 30 September 1966.

99. Schmidt interview.

100. Champion, Director's Script, I, i, 14–15.

101. Champion, Director's Script, I, i, 15.

102. Schmidt interview.

103. Hirsch, 25 September 1966.

104. Hirsch, 25 September 1966.

105. Hirsch, 25 September 1966.

106. Hirsch, 25 September 1966.

107. Schmidt interview.

108. Gregg interview.

109. Champion, Director's Script, I, i, 16.

110. Schmidt interview.

111. Schmidt interview.

112. Schmidt interview.

113. Champion, Director's Script, I, ii, 25.

114. Champion, Director's Script, I, ii, 25.

115. Champion, Director's Script, I, ii, 25.

116. Champion, Director's Script, I, ii, 25.

117. Champion, Director's Script, I, ii, 25.

118. Champion, Director's Script, I, ii, 25.

119. Champion, Director's Script, I, ii, 26.

120. Jones, I, ii, 26.
121. Jones, I, ii, 28.
122. Champion, Director's Script, I, ii, 25–28.
123. Martin, 289.
124. Martin, 289.
125. Martin, 289.
126. Payne-Carter, 345–346.
127. Norman Nadel, "*I Do! I Do!* a Hit," *New York World Journal Tribune*, 6 December 1966: 36.
128. Martin, 289.
129. Martin, 285.
130. Champion, Director's Script, I, ii, 30.
131. Hirsch, 30 September 1966.
132. Martin, 285.
133. Jones, I, iii, 41.
134. Walter Kerr, "Musical *I Do! I Do!* Arrives," *New York Times*, 6 December 1966: 58; *Saturday Review of Literature*, 68.
135. Richard P. Cooke, "The Martin-Preston Duet," *Wall Street Journal*, 7 December 1966: no pagination.
136. Martin, 285.
137. Nadel, 36; Kevin Kelly, "Enchanted Team in Sentimental Romp," *Boston Globe*, 27 September 1966: 55.
138. Champion, Director's Script, I, iii, 48–49.
139. Steven Suskin, jacket notes, *Lost in Boston II*, Varèse Sarabande compact disc, VSD-5485, 1994.
140. Chapman, 68.
141. Payne-Carter, 347.
142. Schmidt interview.
143. Kelly, 55.
144. Champion in Reed, D 3.
145. Jones interview.
146. Jones interview.
147. Champion, Director's Script, II, ii, 29.
148. Jones interview.
149. Gregg, Champion (3 February 1993), and Jones interviews; Michaelmore.
150. Richard Watts Jr., "An Evening of Domestic Bliss," *New York Post*, 6 December 1966: 68.
151. Nadel, 36.
152. Whitney Bolton, "*I Do! I Do!* Funny, Tuneful, Provocative," *New York Morning Telegraph*, 7 December 1966: no pagination.
153. Kerr, 58.
154. Kerr, 58.
155. Bolton.
156. Morrison, 22.
157. Morrison, 22.
158. Gottfried, "*I Do! I Do!*"
159. Watts, 68; Nadel, 36.
160. Gottfried, "*I Do! I Do!*"
161. Kerr, 58; Cooke.
162. Kerr, 58.
163. Morrison, 22.
164. Watts, 68.
165. Bolton; *Saturday Review of Literature*, 61; Morrison, 22.

166. Bolton; Morrison, 22; Watts, 68.

167. Bolton; Morrison, 22; Cooke; Morrison, 22.

168. Lee Alan Morrow, *The Tony Award Book* (New York: Abbeville Press, 1987), 237–238.

169. Jones, Tom, and Schmidt, Harvey. *I Do! I Do!* Original cast recording with Mary Martin and Robert Preston. Cond. John Lesko. Jacket notes Bill Rosenfield. RCA Victor Compact Disc, 1128-2-RC, 1966, 1992. Based on *The Fourposter* by Jan de Hartog.

Twelve: Memories, IMAX, and a Million Bucks

1. Champion in Rex Reed, "A Champion—Almost Always," *New York Times,* 19 February 1967: D3.

2. Champion in Reed, D 3.

3. Champion in Reed, D 3; Jess Gregg, personal interview, 5 June 1992.

4. Cecil Smith, "Young Mike Rupert Will Put on a Happy Face," *Los Angeles Times Calendar,* 22 October 1967: 22.

5. Samuel A. Taylor, *The Happy Time* (New York: Random House, 1950).

6. Bill Rosenfield, jacket notes, *The Happy Time,* RCA Victor Original cast recording, compact disc 09026-61016-2, 1992: 6; Taylor, vi.

7. David Merrick in William Goldman, *The Season: A Candid Look at Broadway* (New York, Limelight Editions, 1984), 291.

8. David Payne-Carter, *Gower Champion and the American Musical Theatre* (Ph.D. dissertation, New York University, 1987; Ann Arbor: UMI, 1988; 88-01561), 355.

9. N. Richard Nash in Goldman, 291.

10. Nash in Goldman, 291.

11. Merrick in Goldman, 291.

12. "Champion Musical at Ahmanson, Nov.," *Hollywood Reporter,* 9 June 1967: 1; Robert Fontaine, *The Happy Time* (New York: Simon and Schuster, Inc., 1945), *My Uncle Louis* (New York: McGraw-Hill Book Co., 1953), and *Hello to Springtime* (New York: Thomas Y. Crowell Co., 1955); *The Happy Time,* souvenir program, Ahmanson Theatre, Los Angeles, November 1967: 25; *The Happy Time,* souvenir program, Broadway Theatre, New York, January 1968.

13. John Kander, personal interview, 17 April 1991; Fred Ebb, personal interview, 23 June 1992.

14. Ebb interview.

15. Kander interview.

16. Kander and Ebb interviews; Smith, "Young Mike Rupert . . . ," 22.

17. Champion in Cecil Smith, " 'The Happy Time' for Theatre Group," *Los Angeles Times,* 9 June 1967: IV, 17.

18. Marge Champion, personal interview, 3 February 1993.

19. Smith, "Young Mike Rupert . . . ," 22.

20. Champion in Smith, " 'The Happy Time' for Theatre Group," 17. In Goldman, this quote reads, "The gimmick of the show is the projections, and they must not overpower the show." At no time did Champion ever refer to the IMAX system as a gimmick. He saw it as a visual metaphor of the memory play concept of the show, just as he saw the tent unit set as a visual metaphor for *Carnival.*

21. Kander and Ebb interviews; Goldman describes the initial draft of the musical as a chamber musical, 291.

22. Kander and Ebb interviews.

23. Merrick in Goldman, 293.

24. Kander interview.

25. Ebb interview.

26. William Brady, "Gower Champion's Aim: Anything But A Musical," *Staten Island Sunday Advance,* 3 March 1968: no pagination.

27. Goldman, 293. Goldman bases his view solely upon a comment made at the time by an unidentified "observer of the Broadway scene" who accused the director of trying to "prove I'm God" by making "Goulet a star"—which the performer already was at the time.

28. Ebb interview.

29. Ebb interview.

30. Robert Goulet, personal interview, 10 October 1992.

31. Goldman, 294.

32. Gower Champion, Rehearsal Schedule for *The Happy Time*, ms., Collection 346, Box 2, Department of Special Collections, Research Library of University of California, Los Angeles.

33. Kander and Ebb interviews.

34. "The Happy Time," *Playbill*, Broadway Theatre, New York, January 1968: 36.

35. Champion in Smith, "Young Mike Rupert . . . ," 22.

36. Champion in Smith, "Young Mike Rupert . . . ," 22.

37. Michael Rupert, personal interview, 20 November 1990.

38. Michael Rupert in Smith, "Young Mike Rupert . . . ," 22.

39. Cecil Smith, "*Happy Time* Getting the Kinks Out at the Ahmanson," *Los Angeles Times*, 23 November 1967: 22.

40. "The Happy Time," *Playbill*, 36.

41. "The Happy Time," *Playbill*, 36.

42. "The Happy Time," *Playbill*, 27.

43. Whitney Bolton, "A New Musical: *The Happy Time*," *New York Morning Telegraph*, 20 January 1968: no pagination.

44. Julius Novick, "*The Happy Time*," *Village Voice*, 8 February 1968: no pagination.

45. Champion, Rehearsal Schedule.

46. Gower Champion in N. Richard Nash and Fred Ebb, *The Happy Time* (Chicago: Dramatic Publishing Co., 1969), 7.

47. Rupert interview.

48. Nash in Nash and Ebb, 8.

49. Champion in Nash and Ebb, 10.

50. Champion in Nash and Ebb, 10.

51. Champion in Nash and Ebb, 10.

52. Cecil Smith, "*The Happy Time* Opens at the Ahmanson," *Los Angeles Times*, 20 November 1967: no pagination.

53. Champion in Nash and Ebb, 78.

54. Champion in Nash and Ebb, 78.

55. Champion in Nash and Ebb, 59.

56. Champion in Nash and Ebb, 59.

57. "*The Happy Time*," *Variety*, 21 November 1967: no pagination.

58. Brian Shyer, personal interview, 25 June 1992; Champion, Director's Script for *The Happy Time*, I, 41; Champion in Nash and Ebb, 62.

59. Shyer interview.

60. Rupert interview.

61. Gower Champion in Rupert interview.

62. Dennis McGovern and Deborah Grace Winer, *Sing Out, Louise! 150 Stars of the Musical Theatre Remember 50 Years on Broadway* (New York: Schirmer Books, 1993), 129.

63. Shyer interview.

64. "*The Happy Time*," *Dance Magazine*, April 1968: 27.

65. Marvin Laird, personal interview, 30 June 1992.

66. Laird interview.
67. Laird interview.
68. "Frère Jacques," *Newsweek,* 27 January 1968: no pagination.
69. Kander and Ebb interviews.
70. Ebb interview.
71. Shyer interview.
72. Ebb interview. For the musical's 1980 revival at the Goodspeed Opera House, East Haddam, Connecticut, the authors not only reinstated "I'm Sorry," but also "Jeanne-Marie" and "In His Own Good Time," likewise dropped by the director prior to the New York opening.
73. Though during the Log Angeles run singer Kate Smith recorded "If You Leave Me Now" for RCA Victor, it never achieved popularity. A more recent recording performed by Michael Rupert can be heard on the album *Lost in Boston,* Varèse Sarabande compact disc, VSD-5475, 1994.
74. Champion, Director's Script for *The Happy Time,* II, 43; Rupert interview.
75. Champion interview, 12 November 1992; Rupert interview.
76. Champion interviews, 3 February 1993 and 6 December 1998; Goulet interview.
77. Champion interview, 3 February 1993.
78. Champion interviews, 3 February 1993 and 6 December 1998.
79. Goulet interview.
80. Champion interview, 12 November 1992.
81. Kander interview.
82. James Powers, "The Happy Time," *Hollywood Reporter,* 21 November 1967: no pagination.
83. Champion interview, 12 November 1992.
84. Champion interview, 12 November 1992.
85. Ebb interview.
86. Goldman, 294.
87. Smith, "Young Mike Rupert . . . ," 22.
88. Goldman, 294–295.
89. Smith, "*The Happy Time* Opens At Ahmanson."
90. Smith, "*Happy Time* Getting the Kinks Out at the Ahmanson," V, 1.
91. Kander and Ebb interviews.
92. Goldman, 294.
93. Kander and Ebb interviews.
94. Ebb interview.
95. Gregg interview.
96. "Frère Jacques."
97. Champion in Smith, "*Happy Time* Getting the Kinks . . . ," V, 1.
98. Cecil Smith, "Happy Time in Store for 'Happy,' " *Los Angeles Times,* 26 December 1967: V, 6.
99. Gregg interview.
100. Gregg interview.
101. Gregg interview.
102. Gregg interview.
103. "The Happy Time," *Dance Magazine,* April 1968: 27.
104. John Chapman, " 'The Happy Time,' Too Complex," *New York Daily News,* 19 January 1968: no pagination.
105. Rupert interview.
106. Clive Barnes, " 'Happy Time' Has Its Premiere," *New York Times,* 19 January 1968: no pagination.
107. Rosenfield, 7.
108. Barnes.
109. Shyer interview.

110. Bolton.
111. Novick.
112. George Oppenheimer, " 'The Happy Time' Isn't Happy Most of the Time," *New York Newsday*, 19 January 1968: no pagination.
113. Chapman.
114. Barnes.
115. Barnes.
116. Barnes; Champion interview, 3 February 1993; Ebb interview.
117. Hobe Morrison, "The Happy Time," *Variety*, 19 January 1968: no pagination; Harold Clurman, "Theatre: 'The Happy Time,' " *The Nation*, 5 February 1968: no pagination.
118. Kerr.
119. Barnes; Bolton.
120. Barnes; Kerr.
121. Barnes; Oppenheimer.
122. Clurman; Morrison; Bolton.
123. Bolton; Clurman.
124. Oppenheimer; Louis Chapin, *"The Happy Time,"* *Christian Science Monitor*, 22 January 1968: no pagination.
125. Watts.
126. Clurman; Oppenheimer.
127. Champion in Brady.
128. Clive Barnes, telegram to Gower Champion, 22 April 1968, 12:50 P.M., *The Happy Time Scrapbook*, private collection of Marge Champion, Stockbridge, MA.
129. Gerald Bordman, *American Musical Theatre: A Chronicle* (New York: Oxford University Press, 1982), 656; Shyer interview; Rosenfield, 8.

Thirteen: A Most Peculiar Lady

1. Marge Champion interview, 3 February 1993.
2. Gregg Champion at Gower Champion Memorial Service, Winter Garden Theatre, 27 August 1980, audio recording courtesy of Will Mead.
3. Eric Shorter, "Marriage Charade Is Charming Musical," *London Daily Telegraph*, 17 May 1968: 21; Philip Hope Wallace, "*I Do! I Do!* at the Lyric Theatre," *The Guardian*, 17 May 1968: 10; B. A. Young, "*I Do! I Do!,*" *The Financial Times*, 17 May 1968: no pagination; "Theatre," *London Sunday Express*, 19 May 1968: no pagination.
4. Champion interview.
5. Champion interview.
6. Champion interview.
7. Champion interview.
8. Jess Gregg interview, 9 November 1998.
9. Champion interview.
10. David Payne-Carter, *Gower Champion and the American Musical Theatre* (Ph. D. dissertation, New York University, 1987; Ann Arbor: UMI, 1988; #88-01561), 372–73.
11. Howard Taubman, "Theatre with Pluck: American Conservatory Handles Full Load on Coast As It Seeks Fiscal Aid," *New York Times*, 18 February 1969: no pagination.
12. "10 Winners as Emcees," *Variety*, 5 March 1969: no pagination.
13. "Gower Champion Signed Harry Belafonte . . ." *New York Post*, 18 March 1969: no pagination.
14. Joyce Haber, "Champion Proves a Champ," *New York Post*, 16 April 1969: no pagination.
15. Mason Wiley and Damien Bona, *Inside Oscar* (New York: Ballantine Books, 1996), 422.
16. Champion in "10 Winners as Emcees."

17. Wiley and Bona, 422.
18. Wiley and Bona, 422.
19. Wiley and Bona, 422.
20. Joseph Morella, " 'Oscar' Handsomer with Champion Facelift but Hope Touch Is Missed," *Variety*, 16 April 1969: no pagination.
21. Morella.
22. Wiley and Bona, 424.
23. Wiley and Bona, 425.
24. Wiley and Bona, 427.
25. Haber.
26. Army Archerd, "Champion's Oncer; Wouldn't Repeat; Bar for Drinks Big Oscar Change," *Variety*, 16 April 1969: 15.
27. Tom Jones, personal interview 17 July 1992; "Champion to Film *Do* for United Artists," *Variety*, 20 November 1968: no pagination.
28. Payne-Carter, 364.
29. Clive Barnes, "Theatre: Feydeau Farce: ACT Presents *Flea in Her Ear* Here," *New York Times*, 4 October 1969: no pagination.
30. Barnes.
31. Richard Watts Jr., "Repertory at ANTA Puts *A Flea in Her Ear* on Stage," *New York Post*, 4 October 1969: 23.
32. Watts.
33. Jess Gregg, "Scenes from a Memoir," *Dance Magazine*, September 1999: 58–59.
34. Debbie Reynolds interview, 29 July 2003.
35. Payne-Carter, 382–383.
36. Jerry Herman, *Showtune: A Memoir* (New York: Donald I. Fine, 1996), 178.
37. Bob Merrill in Peter Filichia, "In Memoriam: *Prettybelle*, January 29, 1971–March 6, 1971," *Theater Week*, 18 March 1991: 13.
38. Gower Champion in Lewis Funke, "News on the Rialto," *New York Times*, 22 November 1970: no pagination.
39. Champion in Funke; Bob Merrill and Jule Styne, *Prettybelle* (First Draft, November 1970), author's collection.
40. Champion in Funke; Bert Michaels, personal interview, 30 January 2003.
41. Martin Gottfried, *Balancing Act: The Authorized Biography of Angela Lansbury* (Boston: Little, Brown, 1999), 202–204.
42. Merrill in Filichia, 13.
43. Louis Calta, "*Prettybelle* Gets Ready for Date on Broadway," *New York Times*, 2 January 1971: no pagination.
44. Merrill in Filichia, 13.
45. Merrill in Filichia, 13.
46. Merrill in Filichia, 13.
47. Jess Gregg, personal interview, 5 June 1992.
48. Michaels interview.
49. Oliver Smith, personal interview, 24 October 1991.
50. Gower Champion, "The Comeback of Sweetness and Light," *The Hollywood Reporter*, 20 November 1962: no pagination.
51. Gower Champion in Calta.
52. Calta.
53. Bert Michaels interview.
54. Jule Styne and Bob Merrill in Theodore Taylor, *Jule: The Story of Composer Jule Styne* (New York: Random House, 1979), 264.

55. Peter Howard, personal interview, 2 July 1992.

56. Robert Karl, personal interview, 13 February 2003.

57. Karl interview.

58. Bert Michaels interview.

59. Bert Michaels interview.

60. Merrill in Filichia, 13.

61. Smith interview.

62. Angela Lansbury in Rob Edelman and Audrey Kupferberg, *Angela Lansbury: A Life on Stage and Screen* (New York: Birch Lane Press, 1989), 151–152.

63. Kevin Kelly, "*Prettybelle* Opens at Shubert," *Boston Globe*, 2 February 1971: no pagination; "*Prettybelle*," *Variety*, 3 February 1971: no pagination; Roderick Nordell, "Champion Directs at Shubert . . . Miss Lansbury as Prettybelle," *Christian Science Monitor*, 3 February 1971: 7.

64. Samuel Hirsch, "*Prettybelle* Opens at the Shubert," *Boston Herald Traveler*, 1 February 1971: no pagination.

65. Kelly.

66. Elliot Norton, "*Prettybelle* Opens; Angela Magnificent," *Boston Record-American*, 2 February 1971: no pagination.

67. Merrill in Filichia, 13.

68. Norton.

69. Norton; Hirsch.

70. Hirsch.

71. Hirsch.

72. Hirsch.

73. Gregg interview, 5 June 1992.

74. Gregg interview, 5 June 1992.

75. Gregg interview, 5 June 1992.

76. Pat Michaels interview, 8 October 2004; Will Mead interview, 7 October 2004.

77. Bert Michaels interview.

78. Filichia, 13.

79. Bert Michaels and Karl interviews.

80. Bert Michaels interview.

81. Bert Michaels interview.

82. Filichia, 13.

83. Bert Michaels interview.

84. Angela Lansbury in Martin Gottfried, 202–204.

85. Will Mead, telephone interview, 23 November 2002.

86. Champion interview.

87. "*Prettybelle* Not Pretty Enough," *New York Morning Telegraph*, 2 March 1971: 3.

88. Bert Michaels interview.

89. Cohen in Gottfried, 203–204.

90. Filichia, 13–15.

91. Gottfried, 204.

92. "Last March in Boston . . . ," *Look*, 24 August 1971: no pagination.

93. Edelman and Audrey Kupferberg, 151–152.

94. Champion interview.

95. Bert Michaels and Karl interviews.

96. Bert Michaels interview.

97. Filichia, 13.

98. Gottfried, 204.

99. Lansbury in Gottfried, 204.
100. Champion in "*Prettybelle* Flop Setting a Record," *New York Post,* 28 January 1982: 33.
101. Gregg interview, 9 November 1998.

Fourteen: Confections New and Old

1. Robert Thören and Manfred Logan, *Fanfares of Love* (screenplay translation), 1951, Series 22: *One of the Girls* (c. 1970), Box 62–63, Michael Stewart Papers, Billy Rose Theatre Collection, New York Public Library for the Performing Arts.
2. Michael Stewart and Jerry Herman, *One of the Girls* (c. 1970), Box 62–63, Michael Stewart Papers, Billy Rose Theatre Collection, New York Public Library for the Performing Arts.; Jerry Herman, personal interview, 30 July 2003.
3. Letter from Jerry Herman to Michael Stewart, Series 22: *One of the Girls* (c. 1970), Box 62–63, Michael Stewart Papers, Billy Rose Theatre Collection, New York Public Library for the Performing Arts.
4. Steven Suskin, *More Opening Nights on Broadway* (New York: Schirmer Books, 1997), 879; Cameron Dewar, "*Sugar* Coming on March 7," *Boston Herald Traveler,* 17 February 1972: 45; Sheila Smith, personal interview, 23 November 2004.
5. Jerry Herman, personal interview, 30 June 2003, and Herman letter to Stewart.
6. Smith interview; David Payne-Carter, *Gower Champion and the American Musical Theatre* (Ph.D. dissertation, New York University, 1987; Ann Arbor: UMI, 1988; #88-01561), 372.
7. Bert Michaels, personal interview, 30 January 2002; Jule Styne in Theodore Taylor, *Jule: The Story of Composer Jule Styne* (New York: Random House, 1979), 264–265.
8. Suskin, 879–882.
9. Richard L. Coe, "We Can't Disappoint," *Washington Post,* 15 December 1971: B 14.
10. Peter Stone in Marty Bell, *Broadway Stories: A Backstage Journey Through Musical Theatre* (New York: Limelight Editions, 1993), 151.
11. Coe, B 14; Stone in Bell, 151.
12. "*Sugar,*" *Playbill Magazine,* Vol. 10, Issue 5, May 1973: 32.
13. Smith interview.
14. Coe, B 14.
15. Coe, B 14.
16. Coe, B 14.
17. Taylor, 265.
18. Michaels interview.
19. Taylor, 266.
20. Samuel (Biff) Liff, telephone interview, 28 February 1994.
21. Smith interview.
22. "Biography for Ina Ray Hutton," www.imdb.com/name/nm0404627/bio.
23. Payne-Carter, 375; and Mary C. Henderson, *Mielziner: Master of Modern Stage Design* (New York: Back Stage Books, 2001), 287.
24. Stone in Bell, 151.
25. Howard Kissel, *David Merrick: The Abominable Showman* (New York: Applause Books, 1993), 420.
26. Kissel, 420.
27. Stone in Bell, 151.
28. Smith interview.
29. Richard L. Coe, "*Sugar:* Well on Its Way," *Washington Post,* 18 January 1972: B 1; Frank Getlein, "*Sugar* Needs Sweetening," *Washington Evening Star,* 18 January 1972: no pagination.
30. Michaels interview.
31. Michaels interview.

32. American Tap Dance Foundation, New York City Tap Dance Hall of Fame Inductee 2002: Steve Condos (1918–1990), http://www.tapdancing.org.

33. Michaels interview.

34. Michaels interview.

35. Stone in Bell, 151–152.

36. Kissel, 418–419.

37. Peter Stone in Kenneth Jones, "Peter Stone Talks About the Creation of *Sugar,* Now Touring as *Some Like It Hot,*" www.playbill.com/news/article/71771: 2.

38. Kissel, 419; Taylor, 264–267; Liff interview.

39. Liff interview.

40. Liff interview.

41. Liff interview.

42. Michaels interview.

43. Liff interview.

44. Frank Getlein, "Re-viewing *Sugar:* A Faster, Sweeter Show Emerges," *Washington Sunday Star,* 30 January 1972: E 6.

45. Harvey Sabinson, Press Release "*Sugar* Is Title for New David Merrick Musical Production," 1 December 1972.

46. "May Extend Road Tour for *Sugar,*" *Variety,* 16 February 1972: 67.

47. Smith interview.

48. Michaels interview.

49. Michaels and Smith interviews.

50. Smith interview.

51. Smith interview; Taylor, 267–268; Payne-Carter, 379; Kissel, 418–420.

52. Styne in Taylor, 267–268.

53. Suskin, 879–882; Payne–Carter, 379; Smith interview; and Donald Saddler, personal interview, 13 July 2005.

54. Payne-Carter, 377.

55. Smith interview.

56. "Producer Merrick Asks Other Producers Shun *Sugar* Preem; 'Spoilers'?" *Variety,* 12 April 1972: 1.

57. Martin Gottfried, "*Sugar,*" *Women's Wear Daily,* 11 April 1972: 22.

58. Michaels and Smith interviews.

59. Clive Barnes, "Stage: Morse, Roberts Star in *Sugar,*" *New York Times,* 10 April 1972: no pagination.

60. Douglas Watt, "*Sugar,* A Musical Version of *Some Like It Hot,* Bows," *New York Daily News,* 10 April 1972: 50.

61. John Simon, "Lump It and Like It," *New York,* 24 April 1972: 58.

62. Harold Clurman, "Theatre," *The Nation,* 8 May 1972: 63.

63. Richard Watts, "The Boys in a Girls' Band," *New York Post,* 10 April 1972: 24; Hobe Morrison, "Shows on Broadway: *Sugar,*" *Variety,* 12 April 1972: 98; "*Sugar,*" *Saturday Review,* 6 April 1972: no pagination.

64. Marge Champion, personal interviews, 3 February 1993 and 6 December 1998.

65. Robert Emmet Long, *Broadway, the Golden Years* (New York: Continuum, 2001), 207.

66. "Marge and Gower Champion," *New York Times,* 22 December 1973: no pagination.

67. Tom Jones, personal interview, 17 July 1992.

68. Debbie Reynolds, personal interview, 29 July 2003.

69. Reynolds interview.

70. Stanley Green, *Encyclopedia of the Musical Theatre* (New York: Da Capo Press, 1976), 217.

71. Don Dunn, *The Making of "No, No, Nanette"* (New York: Dell Publishing Co, 1979), 8.

72. Harry Rigby in Wally Harper, personal interview, 1 July 1999.

73. Sheridan Morley, *John Gielgud: The Authorized Biography* (New York: Applause 2002), 394; Chris Chase, "No, No, Irene," *New York,* 12 March 1973: 64.

74. Tom McMorrow, "*Irene* The Hottest Warm-Up in Show Biz," *New York Sunday News,* 4 February 1973: Leisure 5.

75. Chase, 63; Reynolds interview; Debbie Reynolds with Patrick Columbia, *Debbie: My Life* (New York: Pocket Books, 1989), 367.

76. Guy Flatly, "Forget Your Troubles, Come On, Get Debbie!" *New York Times,* 25 February 1973: D1; McMorrow, Leisure 5; Reynolds with Columbia, 369; Harper interview.

77. Flatly, D8; Reynolds with Columbia, 369.

78. Reynolds interview; Reynolds with Columbia, 369.

79. Jones interview; Leo Seligsohn, "Gower: A Champion at Performing Musical Miracles," *Newsday,* 22 April 1973: II, 28.

80. Flatly, D1; McMorrow, Leisure 5.

81. Morley, 394.

82. Seligsohn, II, 28.

83. Seligsohn, II, 28.

84. Seligsohn, II, 28.

85. Harper, Reynolds, Smith interviews; Ethan Mordden, *Broadway Babies: The People Who Made the American Musical* (New York: Oxford University Press, 1983), 175.

86. Reynolds interview.

87. Harper interview.

88. Harper interview.

89. Gower Champion in Harper interview.

90. Jack F. Lee, personal interview, 10 September 2004.

91. Richard M. Nixon, "Theatre: Old Musical Draws Raves from New Critic," *Washington Post,* 23 February 1973: 5.

92. Reynolds with Columbia, 373.

93. Seligsohn, II 28.

94. Reynolds interview.

95. Reynolds interview.

96. Reynolds interview.

97. Lee interview.

98. Lee interview.

99. Gower Champion in Lee interview.

100. Stanley Green, *Broadway Musicals Show By Show* (Milwaukee: Hal Leonard Books, 1996), 238.

101. Ken Mandelbaum, liner notes for compact disc of Original Broadway Cast Recording of *Irene* (Sony Broadway, SK 32266: 10).

102. Earl Wilson, "Jane Speaks Out. . . ." *New York Post,* 11 February 1974: 41.

103. Jones interview.

Fifteen: Bathing Beauties, the Bard, and Bitterness

1. Karla Champion, personal interview, 28 July 2003; Karin Winner, "Arts and Pleasures: Gower Champion 'Smells' a Hit in *Mack and Mabel*," *Women's Wear Daily,* 28 August 1974: 17; Ellen Stock, "*Mack and Mabel*: Getting the Show Off the Road," *New York,* 7 October 1974: 49–52.

2. Karla Champion interview.

3. Jess Gregg, personal interview, 9 November 1998.

4. Gregg interview.

5. "Women in American History: 'Mabel Ethelreid Normand,'" *Encyclopedia Britannica* (http://search.eb.com/women/articles/Normand_Mabel_Ethelreid.html), 1999: 2–3; "Mabel Normand,"

Wikipedia (http://en.wikipedia.org/wiki/Mabel_Normand), December 2004: 1; and "Excerpts of Interview with Minta Duffee Arbuckle by Don Schneider and Stephen Normand," Angelfire.com (http://www.angelfire.com/mm/hp/minta1.html), 21 July 1974, Reel 3A: 2.

6. Note from Gower Champion to Michael Stewart found in the Michael Stewart Papers (1947–1987) in the Billy Rose Theatre Collection of the New York Public Library for the Performing Arts, Series 20: "Mack and Mabel," (first rough draft, "Hundreds of Girls"), Box 55, Folder 1.

7. Jerry Herman, personal interview, 30 June 2003.

8. Gower Champion in Winner, 17.

9. Winner, 17; "Merrick Film Delay; Wants Maximized Legit Run on *Mack and Mabel*," *Variety*, 3 July 1974: 23.

10. Winner, 17.

11. Herman interview; "Spigelgass Gets Credit For 'Idea' On *Mack and Mabel*," *Variety*, 20 March 1974: 73; David Payne-Carter, *Gower Champion and the American Musical Theatre* (Ph.D. dissertation, New York University 1987; Ann Arbor: UMI, 1988; 88-01561), 392; Howard Kissel, *David Merrick: The Abominable Showman*, (New York: Applause Books, 1993), 414–16; Steven Suskin, *More Opening Nights on Broadway* (New York: Schirmer Books, 1997), 564.

12. Karla Champion interview; Paine Knickerbocker, "There's *Good News* Even If *Mack and Mabel* Won't Open," *San Francisco Examiner and Chronicle Datebook*, 24 March 1974: 9.

13. Jerry Orbach, telephone interview, 11 June 1992.

14. Sidney Fields, "Only Human: The Music Man Is Back," *New York Daily News*, 15 October 1974: 55.

15. Marcia Rodd in Stock, 49–52.

16. Don Pippin, personal interview, 17 July 2002.

17. Gower Champion in Stock, 49–52.

18. Gower Champion in Stock, 49–52.

19. Earl Wilson, "It Happened Last Night: Who's 'Mabel' Now?" *New York Post*, 14 May 1974: 52; Stock, 49–52.

20. Bernadette Peters in Stock, 49–52.

21. Bernadette Peters in Bert Michaels, personal interview, 13 February 2003.

22. Gower Champion in Winner, 17.

23. Douglas Watt, "*Mack and Mabel* Giddy Look at Silent-Film Era," *New York Daily News*, 7 October 1974: 46.

24. Jerry Herman, personal interview, 30 June 2003.

25. Pippin interview.

26. Michael Stewart and Jerry Herman, *Mack and Mabel*, Original Production Script, private collection of Bert Michaels, New York: 1-1–4, 5.

27. Herman interview.

28. Henry Goodman, "Bathing Beauties and Custard Pie," *Wall Street Journal*, 10 July 1974: 14; Walter Kerr, "*Mack and Mabel* Makes Gloomy Stage Music," *New York Times*, 13 October 1974: 2:1.

29. Gower Champion in Stock, 49–52.

30. John Simon, "Champion of Fast Breaks," *New York*, 21 October 1974: 88; Goodman, 14; Rex Reed, "*Mack and Mabel*," *New York Sunday News*, 13 October 1974: L:5.

31. Clive Barnes, "*Mack and Mabel* and the Silent Film Era," *New York Times*, 7 October 1974: 54; Kerr, 2:1.

32. Simon, 88.

33. Simon, 88.

34. Watt, 46; Martin Gottfried, "Theater: Season's First New Musical," *New York Post*, 7 October 1974: 22.

35. Winner, 17

36. Bert Michaels interview.

37. Herman interview.

38. Winner, 17.

39. Herman interview.

40. Pippin interview.
41. Pippin interview.
42. Paul Hunter, "From Mack Sennett to Shakespeare on America," *Christian Science Monitor,* 3 July 1974: 12; *"Mack and Mabel," Variety,* 3 July 1974: 60; Kerr, 2:1.
43. Stock, 49–52.
44. Herman interview.
45. Karla Champion interview.
46. Stanley Eichelbaum, "*Mack and Mabel* May Go Hitless," *San Francisco Examiner and Chronicle Sunday Scene,* 11 August 1974: 10; Hunter, 12; *"Mack and Mabel," Variety,* 3 July 1974: 60.
47. Herman interview.
48. Wilson, 52; John Beaufort, "Excitement Reigns as *Mack and Mabel* Arrives," *Christian Science Monitor,* 9 October 1974: 14.
49. Pippin interview.
50. Patricia Michaels, personal interview, 13 February 2003.
51. Pippin interview.
52. Herman interview.
53. David Merrick in Stock, 49–52.
54. Richard L. Coe, " 'Helplessly Adrift' with *Mack and Mabel," Washington Post,* 5 September 1974: no pagination.
55. Herman interview.
56. Herman interview.
57. Stephen Citron, *Jerry Herman: Poet of the Showtune* (New Haven: Yale University Press, 2004), 202; "Mack and Mabel," Wikipedia (http://www.answers.com/topic/mack-mabel).
58. Coe, C3.
59. Gower Champion in Stock, 49–52.
60. Michael Stewart in Stock, 49–52.
61. Earl Wilson, "It Happened Last Night," *New York Post,* 7 October 1974: 38.
62. Gottfried, 22.
63. Watt, 46; George Oppenheimer, *"Mack and Mabel," Newsday,* 13 October 1974: 9.
64. Clive Barnes, *"Mack and Mabel* and the Silent Film Era," *New York Times,* 7 October 1974: 54.
65. Fields, "Only Human: The Music Man is Back," 55.
66. Barnes, 54.
67. David Merrick in Stock, 49–52.
68. Herman interview.
69. "Mack and Mabel Show Uses TV to Boost B.O.," *Variety,* 6 November 1974: 1; Patricia and Bert Michaels interviews.
70. Patricia and Bert Michaels interviews.
71. Bert Michaels interview.
72. Gower Champion in Jack Lee, personal interview, 10 September 2004.
73. Karla Champion interview.
74. Karla Champion interview.
75. *"Rockabye Hamlet," Playbill,* Minskoff Theatre: January 1976: no pagination; Sidney Fields, "Only Human: *Hamlet* Without Dialogue," *New York Daily News,* 17 February 1976: 30; Alan Weeks, telephone interview, 15 March 2005.
76. *"Kronborg: 1582," Variety,* 17 July 1974: 104; Betty Lee Hunt Associates, "*Rockabye Hamlet*" Press Release #1, *Lester Osterman Productions,* Billy Rose Theatre Collection, New York Public Library for the Performing Arts: no date.
77. Karla Champion interview.
78. Gower Champion in Marilyn Stasio, ". . . And Still Champion," *Cue,* 30 September 1974: 10.

79. Gower Champion in Stasio, 10.

80. Gower Champion in Stasio, 10.

81. Gower Champion in Stasio, 10.

82. *"Rockabye Hamlet"* Press Release #1.

83. Gregg interviews; Alan Weeks, telephone interview, 15 March 2005.

84. "Good Grief, Sweet Prince," *New York,* 26 January 1976: 59.

85. Weeks interview.

86. Fields, "Only Human: *Hamlet* without Dialogue," 30; *"Rockabye Hamlet," Playbill.*

87. Fields, "Only Human: *Hamlet* without Dialogue," 30.

88. Gordon Lowry Harrell in David Payne-Carter, personal interview, 5 December 1983.

89. Gower Champion in Bob Weiner, "Out Damn Spot," *Soho Weekly News,* 29 January 1976: 33.

90. Edwin Wilson, "Alas, Poor Yorick—and Hamlet, Too," *Wall Street Journal,* 19 February 1976: no pagination; Alan Rich, "Bad Night, Sweet Prince," *New York,* 1 March 1976: 59; Robert Emmet Long, *Broadway, the Golden Years: Jerome Robbins and the Great Choreographer-Directors* (New York: Continuum, 2001), 212.

91. Gregg interview.

92. Wilson; Rich, 60.

93. Weeks interview.

94. Karla Champion interview.

95. Gregg interview.

96. Gregg interview.

97. Payne-Carter, 410.

98. Howard Kissel, *"Rockabye Hamlet* . . . or Something's Rotten in New York," *Women's Wear Daily,* 18 February 1976: 47.

99. Douglas Watt, "Rock *Hamlet* Gaudy, Lifeless," *New York Daily News,* 18 February 1976: no pagination.

100. Martin Gottfried, "To Rock or Not to Rock," *New York Post,* 21 February 1976: 40.

101. Payne-Carter, 410.

102. Richard Watts, *"Rockabye* Unfair to Bard and Champion," *New York Post,* 23 February 1976: 20.

103. Rich, 59.

104. Clive Barnes, "Play: *Rockabye Hamlet," New York Times,* 18 February 1976: no pagination.

105. Rich, 59; Weeks interview.

106. Bert Fink, *Shakespeare on Broadway,* Various Artists. Varèse Sarabande, CD Recording VSD-5622, 1996: contains two songs from the score—"If My Morning Begins" and "The Last Blues." The musical was subsequently revised by Jones as *Somethin' Rockin' in Denmark* and produced successfully in 1981 at the Odyssey Theatre in Los Angeles.

107. Gower Champion in Leo Revi, personal interview, 9 November 1998; and in Jess Gregg, personal interview, 9 November 1998.

108. Karla Champion interview.

Sixteen: Reworking, Doctoring, Capitulating

1. Gower Champion in Karla Champion, personal interview, 28 July 2003

2. Karla Champion interview.

3. Karla Champion interview.

4. Will Mead, personal interview, 7 August 2002.

5. Gower Champion in Mead interview.

6. Mead interview.

7. Will Mead, personal interview and archival material, 7 August 2002.

8. Mead interview.

9. Jack F. Lee, personal interview, 10 September 2004.

10. Lee interview.
11. Lee interview.
12. Mead interview.
13. Debbie Reynolds, personal interview, 29 July 2003.
14. Reynolds interview.
15. John Kander and Fred Ebb as told to Greg Lawrence, *Colored Lights: Forty Years of Words and Music, Show Biz, Collaboration, and All That Jazz* (New York: Faber and Faber, 2003), 146; Maureen Orth with Peter S. Greenberg, "The Liza and Marty Show," *Newsweek,* 5 September 1977: 49.
16. Cy Feuer with Ken Gross, *I Got the Show Right Here* (New York: Simon and Schuster, 2003), 264.
17. Feuer with Gross, 264; Ebb in Kander, Ebb, and Lawrence, 145.
18. Fred Ebb, personal interview, 23 June 1992.
19. Ebb interview; Ebb in Al Kasha and Joel Hirschhorn, *Notes on Broadway: Conversations with the Great Songwriters* (Chicago: Contemporary Books, 1985), 198.
20. Dan Sullivan, "Liza's *The Act* Doesn't Shine in L.A.," *San Francisco Chronicle,* 5 September 1977: 39.
21. Cliff Jahr, "In *The Act,* The Drama Backstage Is Not an Act," *New York Times,* 23 October 1977: D 1.
22. Jahr, D 10.
23. Kasha and Hirschhorn, 106.
24. Jahr, D 10; Fred Ebb in Kander, Ebb, and Lawrence, 148.
25. Feuer with Gross, 276.
26. Ebb interview; Ebb in Kander, Ebb, and Lawrence, 151.
27. Kander and Ebb in Kander, Ebb, and Lawrence, 151.
28. Martin Gottfried, *Broadway Musicals* (New York: Harry N. Abrams, 1980), 144.
29. Kander in Kander, Ebb, and Lawrence, 151.
30. Jahr, D 10.
31. Kasha and Hirschhorn, 198.
32. Kasha and Hirschhorn, 198.
33. John Kander, personal interview, 17 April 1991.
34. Kander interview.
35. Kander in Kander, Ebb, and Lawrence, 150.
36. Feuer with Gross, 267.
37. Gower Champion in John Corry, "Broadway: If You're Just Wild About Eubie, This Is for You," *New York Times,* 12 May 1978: no pagination.
38. Gower Champion in Jahr, D 10.
39. Martin Gottfried, "Liza Gets Her Act Together," *New York Post,* 31 October 1977: 32.
40. Ebb interview.
41. George Furth and Fred Ebb, *The Act* (New York: Samuel French, 1987), 7.
42. Michael Stewart and Mark Bramble, *Pal Joey* (1977–1978), Box 64: Series 23, Michael Stewart Papers, Billy Rose Theatre Collection, New York Public Library for the Performing Arts; David Payne-Carter, *Gower Champion and the American Musical Theatre* (Ph.D. dissertation, New York University, 1987; Ann Arbor: UMI, 1988; 88-01561), 415; Ahmanson Theatre, Production History, *Pal Joey '78,* April 21–July 8, 1978.
43. Karla Champion interview.
44. Clive Barnes, "Champion Acting Director," *New York Post,* 5 May 1978: 33.
45. Barnes, 33; Douglas Watt, "Gower Champion a Good *Act,*" *New York Daily News,* 4 May 1978: no pagination.
46. Letter from Alvin Deutsch to Michael Stewart, 5 September 1978, Michael Stewart Papers, Billy Rose Theatre Collection, New York Public Library for the Performing Arts.
47. "A Broadway Musical," *Playbill,* 21 Dec. 1978: no pagination.
48. Steven Suskin, *More Opening Nights on Broadway* (New York: Schirmer Books, 1997), 114.
49. Ken Mandelbaum, *Not Since Carrie: Forty Years of Broadway Musical Flops* (New York: St. Martin's

Press, 1991), 138; Suskin, 114; Michael Kantor and Lawrence Maslon, *Broadway: The American Musical* (New York: Bulfinch Press, 2004), 434.

50. Don Pippin, personal interview, 17 July 2002.

51. Karla Champion interview.

52. Karla Champion interview.

53. Alan Weeks, telephone interview, 15 March 2005.

54. Jake Weisbarth, telephone interview, 21 August 2004.

55. Gower Champion in Weisbarth interview.

56. Weisbarth interview.

57. Mel Gussow, "Stage: Musical About a Musical," *New York Times*, 22 December 1978: C 3; Weisbarth interview.

58. Anne Francine in Dennis McGovern and Deborah Grace Winer, *Sing Out, Louise! 150 Stars of the Musical Theatre Remember 50 Years on Broadway* (New York: Schmirer Books, 1993), 101.

59. Patti Karr in McGovern and Winer, 101.

60. Anne Francine in McGovern and Winer, 101; Weisbarth interview.

61. "Macroglobulinemia of Waldenstrom," *Health Central: General Health Encyclopedia*, adam.com[itm] (http://www.healthcentral.com/mhc/top/000588.cfm); "What Is Waldenstrom's Macroglobulinemia?" International Waldenstrom's Macroglobulinemia Foundation (http://www.inmf.com/WhatIs WM.htm).

62. "Macroglobulinemia of Waldenstrom," *Health Central: General Health Encyclopedia*, adam.com[itm] (http://www.healthcentral.com/mhc/top/000588.cfm); "What Is Waldenstrom's Macroglobulinemia?" International Waldenstrom's Macroglobulinemia Foundation (http://www.inmf.com/WhatIsWM.htm); "Waldenstrom's Macroglobulinemia," The GAPS INDEX: Genetic Information and Patient Service, Inc. (GAPS), (http://www.icomm.ca/geneinfo/waldenst.html); Payne-Carter, 418.

63. Karla Champion interview.

64. Karla Champion interview.

65. Letter from Gower Champion to Michael Stewart, 7 June 1979, Michael Stewart Papers, Box 32, Folder 7, Billy Rose Theatre Collection, New York Public Library for the Performing Arts.

66. Letter from Gower Champion to Michael Stewart, 7 June 1979, Michael Stewart Papers, Box 32, Folder 7, Billy Rose Theatre Collection, New York Public Library for the Performing Arts.

Seventeen: Going into His Dance Once More

1. David Payne-Carter, *Gower Champion and the American Musical Theatre* (Ph.D. dissertation, New York University, 1987; Ann Arbor: UMI, 1988; 88-01561), 432.

2. Gower Champion in Peter Michelmore, "Gower Champion: One Last Time," unpublished manuscript in the author's collection, October 1980: no pagination.

3. Robin Wagner in Michelmore.

4. Robin Wagner in Michelmore.

5. Gower Champion in Carol Lawson, "Broadway: Gower Champion Returns to Broadway with a Vengeance," *New York Times*, 30 May 1980: no pagination.

6. Karla Champion, personal interview, 28 July 2003.

7. Karla Champion interview.

8. Karla Champion interview.

9. Debbie Reynolds, personal interview, 29 July 2003.

10. Reynolds interview

11. Payne-Carter, 434.

12. Payne-Carter, 443–434.

13. Michelmore.

14. Michelmore; note from Michael Stewart found in the Michael Stewart Papers (1947–1987) in the Billy

Rose Theatre Collection of the New York Public Library for the Performing Arts, Series 11: *42nd Street,* Box 33.

15. Gower Champion in Michelmore.
16. Gower Champion in Michelmore.
17. Payne-Carter, 441.
18. Cliff Jahr, "*42nd Street* Log—The Making of a Hit," *New York Times,* 7 September 1980: Sec 2:1; Hobe Morrison, "*42nd Street,*" *Variety,* 27 August 1980: 2:1.
19. Champion in Lawson, "Broadway—Gower Champion Returns."
20. Leo Herbert in Michelmore, "Broadway—Gower Champion Returns."
21. Patricia MacKay, "*42nd Street:* The Season's First Blockbuster Musical," *Theatre Crafts,* November–December 1980: no pagination.
22. Edwin Wilson, "*42nd Street* Opening: Art Intersects Life," *Wall Street Journal,* 29 August 1980: 13; Jahr, Sec 2:1.
23. David Merrick in Richard L. Coe, "David Merrick on the Street of Big Dreams," *Washington Post,* 6 July 1980: H1.
24. Jerry Orbach in Carol Lawson, "Broadway—Jerry Orbach," *New York Times,* 26 September 1980: no pagination.
25. Jerry Orbach, telephone interview, 11 June 1992.
26. Jahr, Sec. 2:1.
27. Lee Roy Reams in Myrna Katz Frommer and Harvey Frommer, *It Happened on Broadway: An Oral History of the Great White Way* (New York: Harcourt Brace and Company, 1998): 145.
28. Reams in Frommer and Frommer, 145–146.
29. Wanda Richert, personal interview, 25 April 2003.
30. Richert interview.
31. Richert interview; Will Mead, personal interview, 7 August 2002.
32. Jon Engstrom, personal interview, July 2003.
33. Gower Champion, "Rehearsal Schedule for *42nd Street,*" private collection of Karla Champion, Los Angeles, CA.
34. Gower Champion in "*42nd Street,*" *After Dark,* September 1980: 56.
35. Engstrom interview.
36. Lee Roy Reams in Dennis McGovern and Deborah Grace Winer, *Sing Out, Louise! 150 Stars of the Musical Theatre Remember 50 Years on Broadway,* (New York: Schirmer, 1993): 130.
37. Richert interview.
38. Engstom interview.
39. Engstom interview.
40. Engstom interview.
41. Engstom interview.
42. Engstom interview.
43. Engstom interview.
44. MacKay, 30.
45. Engstrom interview.
46. Gower Champion in Jack Lee, personal interview, 10 September 2004.
47. Champion in Lawson.
48. Lee Roy Reams in Frommer and Frommer, 146.
49. Danny Carroll in "*42nd Street,*" *After Dark,* September 1980: 56.
50. Carole Cook in "*42nd Street,*" *After Dark,* September 1980: 56.
51. Reams in Frommer and Frommer, 146.
52. Wanda Richert in "*42nd Street,*" *After Dark,* September 1980: 56
53. Engstrom interview.

54. Orbach interview.
55. Payne-Carter, 455.
56. Richert interview.
57. Lee Roy Reams in McGovern and Winer, 130.
58. Richert interview.
59. Gower Champion in Richert interview; Wanda Richert to David Payne-Carter, personal interview, 13 December 1984.
60. Gower Champion in Richert interview; Wanda Richert to David Payne-Carter, personal interview, 13 December 1984.
61. Richert in Jahr, Sec. 2:1.
62. Richert interview.
63. Richert, Engstrom interviews; Payne-Carter, 457–458.
64. Payne-Carter, 458.
65. Engstrom interview.
66. Jahr, Sec. 2:1.
67. David Merrick in Jahr, Sec. 2:1.
68. Jahr, Sec. 2:1.
69. Jahr, Sec. 2:1.
70. Gower Champion, Director's script for *42nd Street*, typescript, private collection of Karla Champion, Los Angeles, CA.
71. Jahr, 2:1.
72. Jahr, 2:1.
73. Reams in McGovern and Winer, 130.
74. Joseph Bova in McGovern and Winer, 130.
75. Bova in McGovern and Winer, 130.
76. Orbach interview.
77. Engstrom interview.
78. Gower Champion in Richert interview.
79. David Merrick in Carol Lawson, "Postponed *42nd Street* to Play Special Preview," *New York Times*, 9 August 1980: 10.
80. Richert interview.
81. Payne–Carter 461.
82. Jahr, Sec. 2:1.
83. Richert interview.
84. Mead interview. George Abbott (1887–1995) producer, playwright, and one of the great directors of the American musical stage.
85. Richert interview.
86. Jahr, Sec. 2:1.
87. Michael Stewart's transcript of conversation with David Merrick found in the Michael Stewart Papers (1947–1987) in the Billy Rose Theatre Collection of the New York Public Library for the Performing Arts, Series 11: *42nd Street*, Box 28, Folder 11. The conversation appears here exactly as it does in Stewart's notes, which clearly identify the "he" of Merrick's "and he's next" as Gower Champion. "He's referring to GC," wrote Stewart.
88. Jahr, Sec. 2:1.
89. Payne-Carter, 463–464.
90. Frommer and Frommer, 146.
91. Engstrom interview.
92. Gower Champion, Notes for *42nd Street*, Collection of Karla Champion, Los Angeles; Karla Champion interview.

93. Richert interview; Payne-Carter, 464.

94. Karla Champion interview.

95. Richert and Karla Champion interviews.

96. Marge Champion in Robert Emmet Long, *Broadway, The Golden Years* (New York: Continuum, 2001), 217.

97. Payne-Carter, 465.

98. Richert interview.

99. Karla Champion interview; Payne-Carter, 465; Earl Wilson, "The Greatest Exit," *New York Post,* 27 August 1980: no pagination.

100. Karla Champion interview.

101. Earl Wilson and Martin Burden, "Champion Dies As Curtain Rises on His Final Triumph," *New York Post,* 26 August 1980: 3.

102. John Corry, "Gower Champion Dies Hours Before Show Opens," *New York Times,* 26 August 1980: A1.

103. Engstrom interview.

104. Engstom and Richert interviews.

105. Corry, C7; Karla Champion interview.

106. Lee Roy Reams in McGovern and Winer, 130–131.

107. Bob Fosse to Lee Roy Reams in Frommer and Frommer, 146.

108. Frank Rich, "Theater: Musical *42nd Street,*" *New York Times,* 26 August 1980: C7.

109. Howard Kissel, "Theater: *42nd Street,*" *Women's Wear Daily,* 27 August 1980: 26.

110. John Simon, "And Still Champion," *New York,* 8 September 1980: 75.

111. Douglas Watt, "Champion's *42nd Street* Makes 'White Way' Great," *New York Daily News,* 26 August 1980: 17; Clive Barnes, "*42nd Street:* Gower's Legacy," *New York Post,* 26 August 1980: 29; Edwin Wilson, "*42nd Street* Opening: Art Intersects Life," *Wall Street Journal,* 29 August 1980: 13.

112. Rich, C7; Barnes, 29; "*42nd Street,*" *Variety,* 27 August 1980: 82

113. Audio recording of "Gower Champion Memorial Service," Winter Garden Theatre, 27 August 1980, courtesy of Will Mead.

114. Howard Kissel, *David Merrick: The Abominable Showman* (New York: Applause Books, 1993), 455–456.

Epilogue

1. Karla Champion, personal interview, 28 July 2003; Howard Kissel, *David Merrick: The Abominable Showman* (New York: Applause Books, 1993), 459.

2. Marge Champion, interviews, 3 February 1993 and 6 December 1998; and Kissel, 459.

3. Lee Alan Morrow, *The Tony Award Book: Four Decades of Great American Theater* (New York: Abbeville Press, 1987), 254–255.

4. Kissel, 540.

5. Karla Champion interview.

Afterword

1. Note from Michael Stewart found in the Michael Stewart Papers (1947–1987) in the Billy Rose Theatre Collection of the New York Public Library for the Performing Arts, Series 11: *42nd Street,* Box 33.

2. James Winston Challender, *The Function of the Choreographer in the Development of the Conceptual Musical: An Examination of the Work of Jerome Robbins, Bob Fosse, and Michael Bennett on Broadway Between 1944 and 1981* (Ph.D. dissertion, Florida State University, 1986; Ann Arbor, UMI, 1986; 86-26788), 5.

3. Ken Mandelbaum, *A Chorus Line and the Musicals of Michael Bennett* (New York: St. Martin's Press, 1989) 17.

4. Frank Rich, "Gower Champion Was a Broadway True Believer," *New York Times,* 31 August 1980: C 19.

5. Marge Champion, telephone interview, 30 May 2005.

Selected Bibliography

Books

Alpert, Hollis. *Broadway: 125 Years of Musical Theatre*. New York: Arcade Publishing, 1991.

Baral, Robert. *Revue: A Nostalgic Reprise of the Great Broadway Period*. New York: Fleet Press, 1970.

Bell, Marty. *Broadway Stories: A Backstage Journey Through Musical Theatre*. New York: Limelight Editions, 1993.

Berkson, Robert. *Musical Theater Choreography*. New York: Back Stage Books, 1990.

Black, Shirley Temple. *Child Star*. New York: Warner Books, 1989.

Bordman, Gerald. *American Musical Theatre: A Chronicle*. New York: Oxford University Press, 1982.

———. *The Oxford Companion to American Theatre*. New York: Oxford University Press, 1984.

Brockett, Oscar G. *History of the Theatre*. 2nd ed. Boston: Allyn and Bacon, 1974.

———. *The Theatre: An Introduction*. New York: Holt, Rinehart, and Winston, 1974.

Citron, Stephen. *Jerry Herman: Poet of the Showtune*. New Haven: Yale University Press, 2004.

Dunn, Don. *The Making of "No, No, Nanette."* New York: Dell Publishing, 1979.

Edelman, Rob, and Audrey Kupferberg. *Angela Lansbury: A Life on Stage and Screen*. New York: Birch Lane Press, 1989.

Ewen, David. *New Complete Book of the American Musical Theater*. New York: Holt, Rinehart, and Winston, 1970.

Eyman, Scott. *Lion of Hollywood: The Life and Legend of Louis B. Mayer*. New York: Simon and Schuster, 2005.

Feuer, Cy, with Ken Gross. *I Got the Show Right Here*. New York: Simon and Schuster, 2003.

Flinn, Denny Martin. *Musical! A Grand Tour*. New York: Schirmer Books, 1997.

Fontaine, Robert. *The Happy Time*. New York: Simon and Schuster, 1945.

———. *My Uncle Louis*. New York: McGraw-Hill, 1953.

———. *Hello to Springtime*. New York: Thomas Y. Crowell, 1955.

Fordin, Hugh. *The Movies' Greatest Musicals: Produced in Hollywood USA by the Freed Unit*. New York: Frederick Ungar, 1984.

Frommer, Myrna Katz, and Harvey Frommer. *It Happened on Broadway: An Oral History of the Great White Way*. Madison: University of Wisconsin Press, 2004.

Furia, Philip. *Ira Gershwin: The Art of the Lyricist*. New York: Oxford University Press, 1996.

Goldman, William. *The Season: A Candid Look at Broadway*. New York: Limelight Editions, 2000. First published in 1969 by Harcourt, Brace and World.

Gottfried, Martin. *Balancing Act: The Authorized Biography of Angela Lansbury*. Boston: Little, Brown, 1999.

———. *Broadway Musicals*. New York: Harry B. Abrams, 1980.

———. *More Broadway Musicals Since 1980*. New York: Harry B. Abrams, 1991.

———. *Opening Nights: Theater Criticism of the Sixties*. New York: G. P. Putnam's Sons, 1969.

Green, Stanley. *Broadway Musicals Show By Show*. Milwaukee: Hal Leonard Books, 1996.

———. *Encyclopedia of the Musical Theatre*. New York: Da Capo Press, 1976.

———. *The World of Musical Comedy*. New York: Prentice-Hall, 1986.

————. *Ring Bells! Sing Songs! Broadway Musicals of the Thirties.* New Rochelle, N.Y.: Arlington House, 1971.

Grubb, Kevin Boyd. *Razzle Dazzle: The Life and Work of Bob Fosse.* New York: St. Martin's Press, 1989.

Hay, Peter. *Broadway Anecdotes.* New York: Oxford University Press, 1989.

Henderson, Mary C. *Mielziner: Master of Modern Stage Design.* New York: Back Stage Books, 2001.

Herman, Jerry, and Ken Bloom. *Jerry Herman: The Lyrics; A Celebration.* New York: Routledge, 2003.

Herman, Jerry, with Marilyn Stasio. *Showtune: A Memoir.* New York: Donald I. Fine, 1996.

Hirschhorn, Clive. *The Hollywood Musical.* New York: Crown, 1981.

Hischak, Thomas S. *Word Crazy: Broadway Lyricists from Cohan to Sondheim.* New York: Praeger, 1991.

Ilson, Carol. *Harold Prince: From "Pajama Game" to "Phantom of the Opera."* Ann Arbor, Mich.: UMI Research Press, 1989.

Jackson, Arthur. *The Best Musicals from "Show Boat" to "A Chorus Line."* New York: Crown, 1977.

Kander, John, and Fred Ebb, as told to Greg Lawrence. *Colored Lights: Forty Years of Words and Music, Show Biz, Collaboration, and All That Jazz.* New York: Faber and Faber, 2003.

Kantor, Michael, and Lawrence Maslon. *Broadway: The American Musical.* New York: Bulfinch Press, 2004.

Kasha, Al, and Joel Hirschhorn. *Notes on Broadway: Conversations with the Great Songwriters.* Chicago: Contemporary Books, 1985.

Katz, Ephraim. *The Film Encyclopedia.* New York: Perigee Books, 1982.

Kislan, Richard. *The Musical: A Look at the American Musical Theater.* rev. ed. New York: Applause Books, 1995. First published in 1980 by Prentice-Hall.

Kissel, Howard. *David Merrick: The Abominable Showman.* New York: Applause Books, 1993.

Laufe, Abe. *Broadway's Greatest Musicals.* rev. ed. New York: Funk and Wagnalls, 1977.

Lees, Gene. *Inventing Champagne: The Worlds of Lerner and Loewe.* New York: St. Martin's Press, 1990.

Long, Robert Emmet. *Broadway, the Golden Years: Jerome Robbins and the Great Choreographer-Directors; 1940 to the Present.* New York: Continuum, 2001.

Mandelbaum, Ken. *"A Chorus Line" and the Musicals of Michael Bennett.* New York: St. Martin's Press, 1989.

————. *Not Since "Carrie": 40 Years of Broadway Musical Flops.* New York: St. Martin's Press, 1991.

Martin, Mary. *My Heart Belongs.* New York: Quill Press, 1984.

McGovern, Dennis, and Deborah Grace Winer. *Sing Out, Louise! 150 Stars of the Musical Theatre Remember 50 Years on Broadway.* New York: Schirmer Books, 1993.

McNamara, Brooks. *The Shuberts of Broadway.* New York: Oxford University Press, 1990.

Mordden, Ethan. *Broadway Babies: The People Who Made the American Musical.* New York: Oxford University Press, 1983.

Morehead, Philip D. *The New American Dictionary of Music.* New York: Dutton , 1991.

Morley, Sheridan. *John Gielgud: The Authorized Biography.* New York: Applause Books, 2002.

Morrow, Lee Alan. *The Tony Award Book: Four Decades of Great American Theater.* New York: Abbeville Press, 1987.

Prince, Hal. *Contradictions: Notes on 26 Years in the Theatre.* New York: Dodd, Mead, 1974.

Reynolds, Debbie, with David Patrick Columbia. *Debbie—My Life.* New York: Pocket Books, 1989.

Rosenthal, Jean, and Lael Wertenbaker. *The Magic of Light: The Craft and Career of Jean Rosenthal, Pioneer in Lighting for the Modern Stage.* Boston: Little, Brown, 1972.

Silverman, Stephen M. *Dancing on the Ceiling: Stanley Donen and His Movies.* New York: Knopf, 1996.

Smith, Cecil, and Glenn Litton. *Musical Comedy in America.* New York: Theatre Art Books, 1981.

Springer, John. *A Pictorial History of the Movie Musical.* Secaucus, N.J.: Castle Books, 1969.

Suskin, Steven. *Opening Night on Broadway: A Critical Quotebook of the Golden Era of the Musical from "Oklahoma!" (1943) to "Fiddler on the Roof" (1964).* New York: Schirmer Books, 1990.

————. *More Opening Nights on Broadway.* New York: Schirmer Books, 1997.

Taylor, Theodore. *Jule: The Story of Composer Jule Styne.* New York: Random House, 1979.

Tillstrom, Burr, and David Small. *The Kuklapolitan Players Present "The Dragon Who Lived Downstairs."* New York: William Morrow, 1984.

Wiley, Mason, and Damien Bona. *Inside Oscar: The Unofficial History of the Academy Awards.* New York: Ballantine Books, 1996.

Woll, Allen. *Black Musical Theatre: From "Coontown" to "Dreamgirls."* New York: Da Capo Press, 1991. First published in 1989 by Louisiana State University Press.

Interviews

Brennan, Eileen. Telephone interview. 14 Jan. 1995.

Catlett, Mary Jo. Telephone interview. 7 Mar. 1991.

Champion, Karla. Personal interview. 28 Jul. 2003.

Champion, Marge. Personal interviews. 5 Nov. 1992, 12 Nov. 1992, 3 Feb. 1993, 6 Dec. 1998, 22 June 2005, and 9 July 2005.

Channing, Carol. Personal interview. 21 Jun. 1991.

Connell, Gordon. Personal interview. 5 Mar. 1991

Ebb, Fred. Personal interview. 23 Jun. 1992.

Engstrom, Jon. Personal interview. 30 Jul. 2003.

Goulet, Robert. Telephone interview. 10 Oct. 1992.

Gregg, Jess. Personal interviews. 5 Jun. 1992 and 9 Nov. 1998.

Harper, Wally. Personal interview. 1 Jul. 1999.

Harrell, Gordon Lowry. Typescript of personal interview with David Payne-Carter. 5 Dec. 1983, David Payne-Carter Papers, New York University, Undergraduate Department of Theatre.

Hartman, David. Personal interview. 23 Apr. 1991.

Herman, Jerry. Personal interview. 13 Mar. 1991 and 30 Jun. 2003.

Howard, Peter. Personal interview. 2 Jul. 1992.

Hoyt, Jeanne Tyler. Telephone interview. 1 Mar. 1992.

Innes, Vera Fern. Personal interview. 14 Jul. 1999.

Jones, Tom. Personal interview. 17 Jul. 1992.

Kander, John. Personal interview. 18 Apr. 1991.

Karl, Robert. Personal interview. 13 Feb. 2003.

Laird, Marvin. Personal interview. 30 Jun. 1992.

Lee, Jack. Personal interview. 10 Sep. 2004.

Lee, Sondra. Telephone interview. 9 May. 1995.

Liff, Samuel (Biff). Telephone interview. 28 Feb. 1994.

Mead, Will. Personal interview. 7 Aug. 2002.

Michaels, Bert. Personal interviews. 30 Jan. 2003 and 13 Feb. 2003.

Michaels, Patricia. Personal interview. 13 Feb. 2003.

Mitchell, James. Personal interview. 25 Jun. 1992.

Orbach, Jerry. Telephone interviews. 11 Jun. 1992 and 4 Feb. 1994.

Pippin, Don. Telephone interview. 17 Aug. 1994. Personal interview. 17 Jul. 2002.

Reilly, Charles Nelson. Telephone interview. 10 Jan. 1995.

Revi, Leo. Personal interview. 9 Nov. 1998.

Reynolds, Debbie. Personal interview. 29 Jul. 2003.

Richert, Wanda. Personal interview. 25 Apr. 2003.

Rupert, Michael. Personal interview. 20 Nov. 1990.

Saddler, Donald. Personal interview. 13 July 2005.

Schmidt, Harvey. Personal interview. 19 Jun. 1992.

Shyer, Brian. Telephone interview. 25 Jun. 1992.

Smith, Oliver. Personal interview. 24 Oct. 1991.

Smith, Shelia. Personal interview. 23 Nov. 2004.

Steinman, Roger. Personal interview. 6 Aug. 2002.

Victor, Lucia. Typescripts of personal interviews with David Payne-Carter. 4 Dec. 1983, 4 Apr. 1984, and 11 Apr. 1984, David Payne-Carter Papers, New York University, Undergraduate Department of Theatre.

Weeks, Alan. Telephone interview. 15 Mar. 2005.

Weisbarth, Jake. Telephone interview. 21 Aug. 2004.

Winsett, Betty. Personal interview. 19 Feb. 1991.

Wittop, Freddy. Telephone interview. 13 Jul. 1992.

Plays, Libretti, and Screenplays

De Hartog, Jan. *The Fourposter*. New York: Random House, 1952.

Deutsch, Helen. *Carnival!* typescript. 15 Sep. 1960. Michael Stewart Papers, Series 8, Box 20, Billy Rose Theatre Collection, New York Public Library for the Performing Arts.

Furth, George, and Fred Ebb. *The Act*. New York: Samuel French, 1987.

Hoyt, Charles H. *A Trip to Chinatown*. In *Five Plays by Charles H. Hoyt*, ed. Douglas L. Hunt, 105–148. Princeton: Princeton University Press, 1941.

Jones, Tom. *I Do! I Do!* typescript. 1966. Gower Champion Collection 346, Box 2. Department of Special Collections, Research Library of University of California–Los Angeles.

Laurents, Arthur, and Stephen Sondheim. *West Side Story*. In *Ten Great Musicals of the American Theatre*, ed. Stanley Richards. Radnor, Penn.: Chilton, 1973.

Merrill, Bob, and Jule Styne. *Prettybelle* (first draft). Nov. 1970. Author's collection.

Nash, N. Richard, and Fred Ebb. *The Happy Time* (typescript). Gower Champion Collection 346, Box 2. Department of Special Collections, Research Library of University of California–Los Angeles.

Nestroy, Johann. *Einen Jux Will Er Sich Machen*. In *Johann Nestroy Komodien*, vol 2, ed. Franz H. Mautner, 435–519. Frankfurt: Insel Verlag, 1970.

Oxenford, John. *A Day Well Spent in Three Adventures* (manuscript). Feb.–Apr.1836. In *Plays Submitted to the Lord Chamberlain*. Vol. 61, 480–496b. British Library, London.

Rodgers, Richard, and Oscar Hammerstein II. *South Pacific*. In *Six Plays by Rodgers and Hammerstein*. New York: Modern Library, 1953.

Stewart, Michael, Lee Adams, and Charles Strouse. *Bye Bye Birdie*. New York: Tams-Whitmark Music Library, 1960.

Stewart, Michael, and Bob Merrill. *Carnival*. New York: Tams-Whitmark Music Library, 1961.

Stewart, Michael, and Jerry Herman. *Hello, Dolly!* New York: Signet Books, 1968.

———. *Mack and Mabel* original production script. 1974. Private collection of Bert Michaels, New York.

Stoppard, Tom. *On the Razzle*. London: Faber and Faber, 1982.

Taylor, Samuel A. *The Happy Time*. New York: Random House, 1950.

Thören, Robert, and Manfred Logan. *Fanfares of Love* (screenplay translation). 1951. Michael Stewart Papers, Series 22: *One of the Girls* (C. 1970), Box 62–63. Billy Rose Theatre Collection, New York Public Library for the Performing Arts.

Wilder, Thornton. *The Merchant of Yonkers*. New York: Harper and Brothers, 1939.

———. *The Matchmaker*. In *Three Plays by Thornton Wilder*. New York: Harper and Brothers, 1957.

Director's Scripts, Schedules, Lists, Notes, and Other Archival Materials

Champion, Gower. Production notes for *Bye Bye Birdie* (manuscript). Collection 346, Box 1. Department of Special Collections, Research Library of University of California–Los Angeles.

———. Director's script for *Bye Bye Birdie* (typescript). Collection, 346, Box 1. Department of Special Collections, Research Library of University of California–Los Angeles.

———. Scrapbook on *Bye Bye Birdie*. Private collection of Marge Champion, Stockbridge, Massachusetts.

———. Production schedule for *Carnival* (manuscript). Collection 346, Box 1. Department of Special Collections, Research Library of University of California–Los Angeles.

———. Cast list for *Carnival* (manuscript). Collection 346, Box 1. Department of Special Collections, Research Library of University of California–Los Angeles.

———. Rehearsal schedule for *Carnival* (manuscript). Collection 346, Box 1. Department of Special Collections, Research Library of University of California–Los Angeles.

———. Director's script for *Carnival* (typescript). Collection, 346, Box 1. Department of Special Collections, Research Library of University of California–Los Angeles.

———. Scrapbook on *Carnival*. Private collection of Marge Champion, Stockbridge, Massachusetts.

———. Preproduction schedule for *Dolly! A Damned Exasperating Woman* (original title of *Hello, Dolly!*) (manuscript). Collection 346, Box 2. Department of Special Collections, Research Library of University of California Los Angeles.

———. Cast list for *Dolly! A Damned Exasperating Woman* (manuscript). Collection 346, Box 2. Department of Special Collections, Research Library of University of California–Los Angeles.

———. Rehearsal schedule for *Dolly! A Damned Exasperating Woman* (manuscript). Collection 346, Box 2. Department of Special Collections, Research Library of University of California–Los Angeles.

———. Memorandum found attached to director's script of *Dolly! A Damned Exasperating Woman*. Collection 346, Box 2. Department of Special Collections, Research Library of University of California–Los Angeles.

———. Director's scripts for *Dolly! A Damned Exasperating Woman* (Book I), *Hello, Dolly!* (Book II), and *Hello, Dolly!* (Book III) (typescript). Collection 346, Box 2. Department of Special Collections, Research Library of University of California–Los Angeles.

———. Scrapbook on *Hello, Dolly!* (original cast). Private collection of Marge Champion, Stockbridge, Massachusetts.

———. Director's script for *I Do! I Do!* transcript. Collection 346, Box 2. Department of Special Collections, Research Library of University of California–Los Angeles.

———. Scrapbook on *I Do! I Do!* Private collection of Marge Champion, Stockbridge, Massachusetts.

———. Character sketches for *The Happy Time* (transcript). Collection 346, Box 2. Department of Special Collections, Research Library of University of California–Los Angeles.

———. Rehearsal schedule for *The Happy Time* (manuscript). Collection 346, Box 2. Department of Special Collections, Research Library of University of California–Los Angeles.

———. Director's script for *The Happy Time* (typescript). Collection 346, Box 2. Department of Special Collections, Research Library of University of California–Los Angeles.

———. Scrapbook on *The Happy Time*. Private collection of Marge Champion, Stockbridge, Massachusetts.

———. Director's script for *42nd Street* (transcript). Private collection of Karla Champion, Los Angeles.

———. Notes for *42nd Street*. Private collection of Karla Champion, Los Angeles.

———. Rehearsal schedule for *42nd Street*. Private collection of Karla Champion, Los Angeles.

Hoyt, Jeanne Tyler. Gower and Jeanne scrapbook. Private collection of Jeanne Tyler Hoyt, Redlands, California.

Payne-Carter, David. "Gower Champion and the American Musical Theatre." Ph.D. dissertation, New York University, 1987. Ann Arbor: University Microfilm International, 1988; #88-01561.

Stewart, Michael. Note on the occasion of the death of Gower Champion. 25 Aug. 1980. Michael Stewart Papers, 1948–1987, Series 11: *42nd Street* (1978–1987), Box 33. Billy Rose Theatre Collection, New York Public Library for the Performing Arts.

———. Manuscript in Stewart's hand of telephone conversation with David Merrick found in the Michael Stewart Papers (1947–1987), Series 11: *42nd Street*, Box 28, Folder 11. Billy Rose Theatre Collection, New York Public Library for the Performing Arts.

———. and Mark Bramble. *Pal Joey* (1977–1978). Michael Stewart Papers, Series 23, Box 64. Billy Rose Theatre Collection, New York Public Library for the Performing Arts.

———. and Jerry Herman. *One of the Girls* (C. 1970). Michael Stewart Papers, Series 22, Box 62–63. Billy Rose Theatre Collection, New York Public Library for the Performing Arts.

Films

The Bank Shot. Dir. Gower Champion. With George C. Scott, Joanna Cassidy, Sorrell Booke, and Bibi Osterwald. MGM, 1974.

Everything I Have Is Yours. Dir. Robert Z. Leonard. With Marge and Gower Champion, Monica Lewis, and Dennis O'Keefe. MGM, 1953.

The Girl Most Likely. Dir. Mitchell Leisen. Chor. Gower Champion. With Jane Powell, Cliff Robertson, Keith Andes, and Kaye Ballard. RKO, 1957.

Give a Girl a Break. Dir. Stanley Donen. With Marge and Gower Champion, Debbie Reynolds, and Bob Fosse. MGM, 1953.

Jupiter's Darling. Dir. George Sidney. With Esther Williams, Howard Keel, Marge and Gower Champion, and George Sanders. MGM, 1955.

Lovely to Look At. Dir. Mervyn LeRoy. With Kathryn Grayson, Howard Keel, Red Skelton, Marge and Gower Champion, and Ann Miller. MGM, 1952.

Mr. Music. Dir. Richard Haydn. With Bing Crosby, Nancy Olson, Charles Coburn, and Marge and Gower Champion. Paramount, 1950.

My Six Loves. Dir. Gower Champion. With Debbie Reynolds, Cliff Robertson, Eileen Heckart, and David Janssen. Paramount, 1963.

Show Boat. Dir. George Sidney. With Kathryn Grayson, Howard Keel, Ava Gardner, Joe E. Brown, Marge and Gower Champion, and William Warfield. MGM, 1951.

Three for the Show. Dir. H. C. Potter. With Betty Grable, Marge and Gower Champion, and Jack Lemmon. Columbia, 1955.

Till the Clouds Roll By. Dir. Richard Whorf. With Robert Walker, Van Heflin, Lucille Bremmer, and many guest stars, including Judy Garland, Lena Horne, Frank Sinatra, Angela Lansbury, and Tony Martin. Featured dancers were Cyd Charisse and Gower Champion (film debut). MGM, 1946.

Television and Radio Broadcasts, Video Recordings, and Archival Film Footage

"A Certain Girl" and title song from *The Happy Time*. With Robert Goulet, David Wayne, and Mike Rupert. Narr. Robert Goulet. Dir. and chor. Gower Champion. Prod. David Merrick. *22nd Annual Tony Awards*. NBC, WNBC, Shubert Theatre, New York, 21 Apr. 1968.

"Before the Parade Passes By" from *Hello, Dolly!* With Ginger Rogers and the Original Broadway Cast. Dir. and chor. Gower Champion. Prod. David Merrick. *The Ed Sullivan Show*, CBS, WCBS, New York, 22 Jan. 1967.

———. With Pearl Bailey and the African-American Broadway Cast. Dir. Gower Champion. Prod. David Merrick. *The Ed Sullivan Show*, CBS, WCBS, New York, 10 Dec. 1967.

42nd Street. With Jerry Orbach, Tammy Grimes, Wanda Richert, Lee Roy Reams, and the Original Broadway Cast. Dir. and chor. Gower Champion. Prod. David Merrick. Video recording of matinee performance, Winter Garden Theatre, New York, 17 Sep. 1980, Billy Rose Theatre Collection, New York Public Library for the Performing Arts.

———. "Lullaby of Broadway" from *42nd Street*. With Jerry Orbach, Wanda Richert, and the Original Broadway Cast. Dir. and chor. Gower Champion. Prod. David Merrick. Performed at the *35th Annual Tony Awards*, Mark Hellinger Theatre, 7 Jun. 1981 on *Broadway's Lost Treasures*, DVDAMP-2003, Acorn Media, Christopher A. Cohen Productions, 2003.

"Gower Champion Memorial Service," Audio recording. Winter Garden Theatre 27 Aug. 1980. Private collection of Will Mead, Los Angeles, California.

"Her Face" and "Yes, My Heart" from *Carnival*. With Anna Maria Alberghetti, Jerry Orbach and the Original Broadway Cast. Dir. and chor. Gower Champion. Prod. David Merrick. *The Ed Sullivan Show*, CBS, WCBS, New York, 16 Apr. 1961.

"Hymn for a Sunday Evening" from *Bye Bye Birdie*. With Paul Lynde, Marijane Maricle, Susan Watson, Johnny Borden and the Original Broadway Cast. Narr. Dick Van Dyke. Dir. and chor. Gower Champion. Prod. Edward Padula. *The Ed Sullivan Show*, CBS, WCBS, New York, 12 Jun. 1960.

Marge Champion. *Fresh Air*. Hosted by Terry Gross, National Public Radio, 23 Aug. 2001.

"The Marge and Gower Champion Story." With Marge and Gower Champion. Narr. Ed Sullivan. Prods. Marlo Lewis and Ed Sullivan. Dir. John Wray, *Toast of the Town*, CBS, WCBS, New York, 7 Jun. 1953. Video recording of kinescope from personal library of Marge Champion.

"Nobody's Perfect" from *I Do! I Do!* With Mary Martin and Robert Preston. Dir. and chor. Gower Champion. Prod. David Merrick. 22nd Annual Tony Awards, ABC, WABC, Shubert Theatre, New York, 26 Mar. 1967.

"Put on a Happy Face" from *Bye Bye Birdie*. With Dick Van Dyke, Sharon Lerit, and Original Broadway Cast. Dir. and chor. Gower Champion. Prod. Edward Padula. *The Ed Sullivan Show*, CBS, WCBS, New York, 13 Nov. 1960.

Sharon: Portrait of a Mistress. Dir. Robert Greenwald. With Trish Van Devere, Patrick O'Neal, Mel Ferrer, Gloria DeHaven, Gower Champion (cameo appearance). Television film, 1977.

"The Shriners' Ballet" from *Bye Bye Birdie* (reconstruction of original dance from Gower Champion Labanotation Notes). With Chita Rivera and the American Dance Machine. Dir. Rob Iscove. Found on *That's Singing*. Videocassette. A Woodcliff Production, 1991. 117 min.

Silent film footage in color from original Broadway performances of *Bye Bye Birdie, Carnival, Hello, Dolly!*, and *I Do! I Do!* Dir. and chor. Gower Champion. Archives of the Institute of the American Musical, 121 North Detroit Street, Los Angeles, CA 90036. Miles Kreuger, Founder and President. About 3–4 min. of each production.

3 for Tonight. Narr. Hiram Sherman, Prods. Paul Gregory and Charles Laughton. Dir. Gower Champion. NBC, WNBC, New York, 22 Jun. 1955. Video recording of kinescope from personal library of Marge Champion.

Audio Recordings and Jacket Notes

Herman, Jerry. *Hello, Dolly!* Original Broadway cast recording with Carol Channing, David Burns, Charles Nelson Reilly, Eileen Brennan, and Sondra Lee. Cond. Shepard Coleman. Jacket notes Daniel Guss. RCA Victor compact disc, LSOD-1087: 1964, 2003. Based on Thornton Wilder's *The Matchmaker*.

———. *Hello, Dolly!* 1994 cast recording with Carol Channing, Jay Garner, Michael DeVries, and Florence Lacey. Cond. Tim Stella. Varèse Sarabande compact disc, VSD-5557, 1994.

———. *Mack and Mabel*. Original Broadway cast recording with Robert Preston and Bernadette Peters. Cond. Donald Pippin. Jacket notes Max O. Preeo. MCA Classics Compact Disc, MCAD-10523, 1974, 1992.

———. "Penny in My Pocket" cut from *Hello, Dolly!*; heard on *Michael Feinstein Sings the Jerry Herman Songbook*. Electra Nonesuch compact disc 9 79315-2, 1993.

Jones, Cliff. "If My Morning Begins" and "The Last Blues" from *Rockabye Hamlet* found on *Shakespeare on Broadway*. Various Artists. Jacket notes Bert Fink. Varèse Sarabande compact disc recording VSD-5622 1996.

Kander, John, and Fred Ebb. *The Act*. Original Broadway cast recording with Liza Minnelli. Cond. Stanley Lebowsky. DRG Records compact disc, 1977.

———. "The Only Game in Town" cut from *The Act*; heard on *Lost in Boston II* with Liz Larsen, Sal Viviano, and various artists. Cond. James Stenborg. Jacket notes Steven Suskin. Varèse Sarabande compact disc, VSD-5485, 1994.

———. *The Happy Time*. Original Broadway cast recording with Robert Goulet, David Wayne, Julie Gregg, and Mike Rupert. Cond. Oscar Kosarin. Jacket notes Bill Rosenfield. RCA Victor compact disc, LSO-1144, 1968, 1992. Suggested by the characters in the stories by Robert Fontaine.

———. "If You Leave Me Now" cut from *The Happy Time*; heard on *Lost in Boston* with Michael Rupert, Liz Calloway, and various artists. Cond. James Stenborg. Jacket notes Steven Suskin. Varèse Sarabande compact disc, VSD-5564, 1995.

Kern, Jerome. *Lovely to Look At*. Original film soundtrack with Kathryn Grayson, Howard Keel, Red Skelton,

Marge and Gower Champion, and Ann Miller. Jacket notes Bruce Eder. Sony Music Entertainment compact disc, 1952, 1991.

———. *Show Boat.* Original film soundtrack with Kathryn Grayson, Howard Keel, Ava Gardner, Marge and Gower Champion, and William Warfield. Jacket notes Bruce Eder. Sony Music Entertainment compact disc, 1951, 1990.

———. *Till the Clouds Roll By.* Original film soundtrack with Judy Garland, Robert Walker, and cast. Jacket notes Bruce Eder. Sony Music Entertainment compact disc, 1946, 1992.

Lane, Burton, Johnny Green, Johnny Mercer, et al. *Everything I Have Is Yours.* Original film soundtrack with Marge and Gower Champion. Appears with *Summer Stock* and *I Love Melvin* on MCA Classics Soundtracks compact disc, MCAD-5948.

Merrill, Bob. *Carnival.* Original Broadway cast recording with Anna Maria Alberghetti, James Mitchell, Kaye Ballard, and Jerry Orbach. Cond. Saul Schechtman. Jacket notes Larry L. Lash. Polydor compact disc, 837195-2, 1961, 1989.

Schmidt, Harvey, and Tom Jones. *I Do! I Do!* Original Broadway cast recording with Mary Martin and Robert Preston. Cond. John Lesko. Jacket notes Bill Rosenfield. RCA Victor compact disc, 1128-2-RC, 1966, 1992. Based on *The Fourposter* by Jan de Hartog.

———. "Man and Wife," "We May as Well Stay Maried Now," "Thousands of Flowers," "Throw It Away" cut from *I Do! I Do!* heard on *Lost in Boston II* with Liz Larsen, Sal Viviano, and various artists. Cond. James Stenborg. Jacket notes Steven Suskin. Varèse Sarabande compact disc, VSD-5485, 1994.

Strouse, Charles, and Lee Adams. *Bye Bye Birdie.* Original Broadway cast recording with Chita Rivera, Dick Van Dyke, and Kay Medford. Cond. Elliot Lawrence. Jacket notes Didier C. Deutsch. Columbia compact disc, CK 2025, 1960, 1988.

———. "Lawyers" and "Smashing New York Times" from *A Broadway Musical* found on *Unsung Musicals.* Various Artists. Cond. Lanny Meyers. Jacket notes Ken Mandelbaum. Varèse Sarabande, compact disc, VSD-5622, 1996.

Styne, Jule, and Bob Merrill. *Prettybelle.* Members of the original cast recording with Angela Lansbury, Mark Dawson, and Peter Lombard. Cond. Milton Rosenstock. Jacket notes Peter Filichia and Barry Kleinbort. Varèse Sarabande compact disc, VSD-5439, 1982, 1993.

———. *Sugar.* Original Broadway cast recording with Robert Morse, Tony Roberts, Cyril Ritchard, and Elaine Joyce. Cond. Elliot Lawrence. United Artist compact disc, UA 0698, 1972.

Tierney, Harry, Joseph McCarthy, Charles Gaynor, and Otis Clements. *Irene.* Broadway cast recording with Debbie Reynolds, Monte Markham, George S. Irving, Ruth Warrick, and Patsy Kelly. Cond. Jack Lee. Jacket notes Ken Mandelbaum. Sony Broadway compact disc, SK 32266: 10. 1973, 1992.

Warren, Harry, and Al Dubin. *42nd Street.* Original Broadway cast recording with Tammy Grimes, Jerry Orbach, Wanda Richert, and Lee Roy Reams. Jacket notes Mort Goode. RCA Victor compact disc RCD1-3891, 1980.

Correspondence

Barnes, Clive. Telegram to Gower Champion. 22 Apr. 1968, 12:50 P.M. Gower Champion's scrapbook on *The Happy Time.* Private collection of Marge Champion, Stockbridge, Massachusetts.

Champion, Gower. Letter to Marge Champion. 12 Mar. 1948. Private collection of Marge Champion, Stockbridge, Massachusetts.

———. Note to Michael Stewart. Michael Stewart Papers (1947–1987), Series 20: "Mack and Mabel" (first rough draft "Hundreds of Girls"), Box 55, Folder 1. Billy Rose Theatre Collection, New York Public Library for the Performing Arts.

———. Letter to Michael Stewart. 7 Jun. 1979. Michael Stewart Papers, Box 32, Folder 7. Billy Rose Theatre Collection, New York Public Library for the Performing Arts.

Champion, Marge. Notes from first draft of this biography. Feb. 1994 and Apr. 1995.

Deutsch, Alvin. Letter to Michael Stewart. 5 Sep, 1978. Michael Stewart Papers. Billy Rose Theatre Collection, New York Public Library for the Performing Arts.

Hartman, David. Letters to the author. 7 Jun. 1995 and 30 May 2005.

Herman, Jerry. Letter to Michael Stewart. Michael Stewart Papers, Series 22: *One of the Girls* (C. 1970), Box 62–63. Billy Rose Theatre Collection, New York Public Library for the Performing Arts.

Howard, Peter. Letter to the author. 2 Mar. 1994.

Lamp, Gus (entertainment director, Stein Hotels). Telegram to Marge and Gower Champion, 3 Jan. 1956. Marge and Gower Champion scrapbooks. Private collection of Marge Champion, Stockbridge, Massachusetts.

Stewart, Michael. Note on Gower Champion. Michael Stewart Papers (1947–1987), Series 11: *42nd Street,* Box 33. Billy Rose Theatre Collection, New York Public Library for the Performing Arts.

Wittop, Freddy. Letter to the author. 14 Feb. 1994.

Index